Lives of the noble Grecians and Romans. Englished by Sir Thomas North anno 1579, with an introd. by George Wyndham

Plutarch Plutarch, Thomas North

THE TUDOR
TRANSLATIONS

EDITED BY

W. E. HENLEY

XI

PLUTARCH'S

LIVES OF THE NOBLE

GRECIANS AND ROMANS

ENGLISHED BY

SIR THOMAS NORTH

ANNO 1579

With an Introduction by

GEORGE WYNDHAM

FIFTH VOLUME

LONDON

Published by DAVID NUTT

IN THE STRAND

1896

DE
7
OC[?]
189[?]
1 5

Edinburgh   T and A Constable, Printers to Her Majesty

THE TABLE OF THE NOBLE GRECIANS AND ROMANES

compared by PLUTARKE of CHÆRONEA

VOLUME V

THE LIFE OF IULIUS CÆSAR

AT what time Sylla was made Lord of all, he would have had Cæsar put away his wife Cornelia, the daughter of Cinna Dictator: but when he saw, he could neither with any promise nor threate bring him to it, he tooke her joynter away from him. The cause of Cæsars ill will unto Sylla, was by meanes of mariage: for Marius thelder, maried his fathers own sister, by whom he had Marius the younger, whereby Cæsar and he were cosin germaines. Sylla being troubled in waightie matters, putting to death so many of his enemies, when he came to be conqueror, he made no reckoning of Cæsar: but he was not contented to be hidden in safety, but came and made sute unto the people for the Priesthoodshippe that was voyde, when he had scant any heare on his face. Howbeit he was repulsed by Syllaes meanes, that secretly was against him. Who, when he was determined to have killed him, some of his frendes told him, that it was to no purpose to put so young a boy as he to death. But Sylla told them againe, that they did not consider that there were many Marians in that young boy. Cæsar understanding that, stale out of Rome, and hidde him selfe a long time in the contrie of the Sabines, wandring still from place to place. But one day being caried from house to house, he fell into the handes of Syllaes souldiers, who searched all those places, and tooke them whom they found hidden. Cæsar bribed the Captaine, whose name was Cornelius, with two talentes which he gave him. After he had escaped them thus, he went unto the sea side, and tooke shippe, and sailed into

Cæsar tooke sea, and went unto Nicomedes, king of Bithynia.

5 : A

1

IULIUS
CÆSAR
Cæsar taken
of pirats.

Bithynia to goe unto king Nicomedes.   When he had bene
with him a while, he tooke sea againe, and was taken by
pyrates about the Ile of Pharmacusa : for those pyrates kept
all uppon that sea coast, with a great fleete of shippes and
botes.   They asking him at the first twentie talentes for his
ransome, Cæsar laughed them to scorne, as though they
knew not what a man they had taken, and of him selfe
promised them fiftie talents.   Then he sent his men up and
downe to get him this money, so that he was left in maner
alone among these theeves of the Cilicians, (which are the
cruellest butchers in the world) with one of his frends, and
two of his slaves only ∙ and yet he made so litle reckoning
of them, that when he was desirous to sleepe, he sent unto
them to commaunde them to make no noyse.   Thus was he
eight and thirtie dayes among them, not kept as prisoner,
but rather waited uppon by them as a Prince.   All this time
he woulde boldly exercise him selfe in any sporte or pastime
they would goe to.   And other while also he woulde wryte
verses, and make orations, and call them together to say
them before them ∙ and if any of them seemed as though
they had not understoode him, or passed not for them, he
called them blockeheades, and brute beastes, and laughing,
threatned them that he would hang them up.   But they
were as merie with the matter as could be, and tooke all in
good parte, thinking that this his bold speach came, through
the simplicity of his youth.   So when his raunsome was
come from the citie of Miletum, they being payed their
money, and he againe set at libertie . he then presently
armed, and manned out certaine ships out of the haven of
Miletum, to follow those theeves, whom he found yet riding
at ancker in the same Iland.   So he tooke the most of them,
and had the spoile of their goods, but for their bodies, he
brought them into the city of Pergamum, and there committed them to prison, whilest he him selfe went to speake

Iunius Prætor
of Asia.

with Iunius, who had the government of Asia, as unto whom
the execution of these pirats did belong, for that he was
Prætor of that contrie.   But this Prætor having a great
fancie to be fingering of the money, bicause there was good
store of it . answered, that he would consider of these

2

GRECIANS AND ROMANES

prisoners at better leasure. Cæsar leaving Iunius there, returned againe unto Pergamum, and there hung up all these theeves openly upon a crosse, as he had oftentimes promised them in the Ile he would doe, when they thought he did but jeast. Afterwardes when Syllaes power beganne to decay, Cæsars frendes wrote unto him, to pray him to come home againe. But he sailed first unto Rhodes, to studie there a time under Apollonius the sonne of Molon, whose scholler also Cicero was, for he was a very honest man, and an excellent good Rethoritian. It is reported that Cæsar had an excellent naturall gift to speake well before the people, and besides that rare gift, he was excellently well studied, so that doutlesse he was counted the second man for eloquence in his time, and gave place to the first, bicause he would be the first and chiefest man of warre and authoritie, being not yet comen to the degree of perfection to speake well, which his nature coulde have performed in him, bicause he was geven rather to followe warres and to mannage great matters, which in thende brought him to be Lord of all Rome. And therefore in a booke he wrote against that which Cicero made in the praise of Cato, he prayeth the readers not to compare the stile of a souldier, with the eloquence of an excellent Orator, that had followed it the most parte of his life. When he was returned againe unto Rome, he accused Dolabella for his ill behavior in the government of his province, and he had divers cities of Græce that gave in evidence against him. Notwithstanding, Dolabella at the length was dismissed. Cæsar, to requite the good will of the Græcians, which they had shewed him in his accusation of Dolabella, tooke their cause in hand, when they did accuse Publius Antonius before Marcus Lucullus, Prætor of Macedon: and followed it so hard against him in their behalfe, that Antonius was driven to appeale before the Tribunes at Rome, alleaging, to colour his appeale withall, that he coulde have no justice in Græce against the Græcians. Now Cæsar immediatly wan many mens good willes at Rome, through his eloquence, in pleading of their causes: and the people loved him marvelously also, bicause of the curteous manner he had to speake to every man, and to

3

IULIUS
CÆSAR
Cæsar loved
hospitalitie.

Cæsar a fol-
lower of the
people.

use them gently, being more ceremonious therein, then was
looked for in one of his yeres. Furthermore, he ever kept a
good bouide, and fared well at his table, and was very liberall
besides: the which in deede did advaunce him forward, and
brought him in estimacion with the people. His enemies
judging that this favor of the common people would soone
quaile, when he could no longer hold out that charge and
expence: suffered him to runne on, till by litle and litle he
was growen to be of great strength and power. But in fine,
when they had thus geven him the bridell to grow to this
greatnes, and that they could not then pull him backe,
though in dede in sight it would turne one day to the
destruction of the whole state and common wealth of Rome:
too late they found, that there is not so litle a beginning
of any thing, but continuaunce of time will soone make it
strong, when through contempt there is no impediment to
hinder the greatnes. Thereuppon, Cicero like a wise ship-
master that feareth the calmnes of the sea, was the first man
that mistrusting his manner of dealing in the common
wealth, found out his craft and malice, which he cunningly
cloked under the habit of outward curtesie and familliaritie.

Ciceroes
judgement
of Cæsar.

And yet, sayd he, when I consider howe finely he combeth
his faire bush of heare, and how smooth it lyeth, and that I
see him scrat his head with one finger only: my minde gives
me then, that such a kinde of man should not have so wicked
a thought in his head, as to overthrow the state of the
common wealth. But this was long time after that The

The love of
the people in
Rome unto
Cæsar.

first shewe and proofe of the love and good will which the
people did beare unto Cæsar, was: when he sued to be
Tribune of the souldiers (to wit, Colonell of a thowsand
footemen) standing against Caius Pompilius, at what time

Cæsar chosen
Tribunus
militum.

he was preferred and chosen before him. But the second
and more manifest proofe then the first, was at the death of
his aunt Iulia, the wife of Marius the elder. For being her

Cæsar made
the funerall
oration, at the
death of his
aunt Iulia.

nephew, he made a solemne oration in the market place in
commendacion of her, and at her buriall did boldly venter to
shew foorth the images of Marius: the which was the first
time that they were seene after Syllaes victorie, bicause that
Marius and all his confederates had bene proclaimed traitors

4

and enemies to the common wealth. For when there were
some that cried out apon Cæsar for doing of it : the people
on thother side kept a sturre, and rejoyced at it, clapping of
their handes, and thanked him, for that he had brought as
it were out of hell, the remembraunce of Marius honor againe
into Rome, which had so long time bene obscured and
buried. And where it had bene an auncient custom of long
time, that the Romanes used to make funerall orations in
praise of olde Ladies and matrons when they dyed, but not
of young women. Cæsar was the first that praised his owne
wife with funerall oration when she was deade, the which
also did increase the peoples good willes the more, seeing him
of so kinde and gentle nature. After the buriall of his wife,
he was made Treasorer, under Antistius Vetus Prætor, whom
he honored ever after : so that when him selfe came to be
Prætor, he made his sonne to be chosen Treasorer. Afterwardes, when he was come out of that office, he maried his
thirde wife Pompeia, having a daughter by his first wife
Cornelia, which was maried unto Pompey the great. Now
for that he was very liberal in expences, bying (as some
thought) but a vaine and short glorie of the favor of the
people. (where in deede he bought good cheape the greatest
thinges that coulde be.) Some say, that before he bare any
office in the common wealth, he was growen in debt, to the
summe of thirteene hundred talentes. Furthermore, bicause
he was made overseer of the worke, for the high way going
unto Appius, he disbursed a great summe of his owne money
towardes the charges of the same. And on the other side,
when he was made Ædilis, for that he did show the people
the pastime of three hundred and twentie cople of sword
players, and did besides exceede all other in sumptuousnes in
the sportes and common feastes which he made to delight
them withall: (and did as it were drowne all the stately
shewes of others in the like, that had gone before him) he so
pleased the people, and wan their love therwith, that they
devised daily to give him new offices for to requite him. At
that time there were two factions in Rome, to wit, the faction
of Sylla, which was very strong and of great power, and the
other of Marius, which then was under foote and durst not

IULIUS
CÆSAR

Cæsar the first
that praised
his wife in
funerall ora-
tion.

Cæsar made
Quæstor

Pompeia,
Cæsars third
wife.

Cæsars pro-
digality.

shew it selfe. But Cæsar, bicause he would renue it again, even at that time when he being Ædilis, all the feasts and common sports were in their greatest ruffe: he secretly caused images of Marius to be made, and of victories that caried triumphes, and those he set up one night within the Capitol. The next morning when every man saw the glistering of these golden images excellently well wrought, shewing by the inscriptions, that they were the victories which Marius had wonne apon the Cimbres: every one marveled much at the boldnes of him that durst set them up there, knowing well enough who it was. Hereuppon, it ranne straight through all the citie, and everie man came thither to see

them. Then some cried out apon Cæsar, and sayd it was a tyranny which he ment to set up, by renuing of such honors as before had bene troden under foote, and forgotten, by common decree and open proclamation: and that it was no more but a baite to gage the peoples good wils, which he had set out in the stately shewes of his common playes, to see if he had brought them to his lure, that they would abide such partes to be played, and a new alteracion of things to be made. They of Marius faction on thother side, incoraging one an other, shewed them selves straight a great number gathered together, and made the mount of the Capitoll ring againe with their cries and clapping of handes: insomuch as the teares ranne downe many of their cheekes for very joy, when they sawe the images of Marius, and they extolled Cæsar to the skies, judging him the worthiest man of all the kinred of Marius. The Senate being assembled thereuppon, Catulus Luctatius one of the greatest authoritie at that time in Rome, rose, and vehemently inveyed against Cæsar, and spake that then which ever since hath bene noted much · that Cæsar did not now covertly go to worke, but by plaine force sought to alter the state of the common wealth. Neverthelesse, Cæsar at that time aunswered him so that the Senate was satisfied. Thereupon they that had him in estimacion did grow in better hope then before, and perswaded him, that hardily he shoulde geve place to no man, and that through the good will of the people, he should be better than all they, and come to be the chiefest man of the citie.

GRECIANS AND ROMANES

At that time, the chiefe Bishoppe Metellus dyed, and two of the notablest men of the citie, and of greatest authoritie (Isauricus, and Catulus) contended for his roome: Cæsar notwithstanding their contention, would geve neither of them both place, but presented him selfe to the people, and made sute for it as they did. The sute being equall betwext either of them, Catulus, bicause he was a man of greater calling and dignitie than the other, doubting the uncertaintie of the election: sent unto Cæsar a good summe of money, to make him leave of his sute. But Cæsar sent him word againe, that he would lend a greater summe then that, to maintaine the sute against him. When the day of thelection came, his mother bringing him to the dore of his house, Cæsar weeping, kissed her, and sayd: Mother, this day thou shalt see thy sonne chiefe Bishoppe of Rome, or banished from Rome. In fine, when the voyces of the people were gathered together, and the strife well debated. Cæsar wanne the victorie, and made the Senate and noble men all affrayed of him, for that they thought that thenceforth he would make the people do what he thought good. Then Catulus and Piso fell flatly out with Cicero, and condemned him, for that he did not bewray Cæsar, when he knew that he was of conspiracie with Catiline, and had oportunitie to have done it. For when Catiline was bent and determined, not onely to overthrow the state of the common wealth, but utterly to destroy the Empire of Rome, he scaped out of the handes of justice for lacke of sufficient proofe, before his full treason and determination was knowen. Notwithstanding he left Lentulus and Cethegus in the citie, companions of his conspiracie · unto whom, whether Cæsar did geve any secret helpe or comfort, it is not well knowen. Yet this is manifest, that when they were convinced in open Senate, Cicero being at that time Consul, asking every mans opinion in the Senate, what punishment they should have, and every one of them till it came to Cæsar, gave sentence they should dye: Cæsar then rising up to speake, made an oration (penned and premeditated before) and sayd, that it was neither lawefull, nor yet their custome did beare it, to put men of such nobilitie to death (but in an extremitie)

The death of Metellus chiefe Bishop of Rome.

Cæsar made chiefe Bishop of Rome.

Cæsar suspected to be confederate with Catiline in his conspiracy

Cæsar went about to deliver the conspirators

7

without lawefull inditement and condemnation. And therefore, that if they were put in prison in some citie of Italie, where Cicero thought best, untill that Catiline were overthrowen: the Senate then might at their pleasure quietly take such order therein, as might best appeare unto their wisedoms. This opinion was thought more gentle, and withall was uttered with such a passing good grace and eloquence, that not only they which were to speake after him did approve it· but such also as had spoken to the contrarie before, revoked their opinion and stucke to his, until it came to Cato and Catulus to speake. They both

did sharpely invey against him, but Cato chiefly: who in his oration made Cæsar suspected to be of the conspiracie, and stowtly spake against him, insomuch that the offenders were put into the hands of the officers to be put to death. Cæsar comming out of the Senate, a company of young men which garded Cicero for the safetie of his person, did sette apon him with their swordes drawen. But some say, that Curio covered Cæsar with his gowne, and tooke him out of their handes. And Cicero selfe, when the young men looked apon him, beckened with his head that they should not kil him, either fearing the fury of the people, or els that he thought it too shamefull and wicked a parte. But if that were true, I marvell why Cicero did not put it into his booke he wrote of his Consulshippe. But certainly they blamed him afterwards, for that he tooke not the oportunitie offered him against Cæsar, onely for overmuch feare of the people, that loved him verie dearely. For shortly after, when Cæsar went into the Senate, to cleere him selfe of certaine presumptions and false accusations objected against him, and being bitterly taunted among them, the Senate keeping him lenger then they were wont: the people came about the counsell house, and called out alowde for him, bidding them let him out. Cato then fearing the insurrection of the poore needie persons, which were they that put all their hope in Cæsar, and did also move the people to sturre: did perswade the Senate to make a franke distribucion of corne unto them, for a moneth. This distribucion did put the common wealth to a new charge of five hundred

8

and fiftie Myriades. This counsell quenched a present great feare, and did in happie time scatter and disperse abroade the best parte of Cæsars force and power, at such time as he was made Prætor, and that for respect of his office he was most to be feared. Yet all the time he was officer, he never sought any alteracion in the common wealth, but contrarily he him selfe had a great misfortune fell in his owne house, which was this. There was a young noble man of the order of the Patricians, called Publius Clodius, who lacked neither wealth nor eloquence, but otherwise as insolent and impudent a person, as any was else in Rome. He became in love with Pompeia Cæsars wife, who misliked not withall: notwithstanding she was so straightly looked to, and that Aurelia (Cæsars mother) an honest gentlewoman had such an eye of her, that these two lovers could not meete as they would, without great perill and difficultie. The Romanes doe use to honor a goddesse which they call the good goddesse, as the Græcians have her whom they call Gynæcia, to wit, the goddesse of women. Her, the Phrygians doe claime to be peculiar unto them, saying that she is king Midas mother. Howbeit the Romanes hold opinion, that it is a nimphe of wodde, maried unto god Faunus. The Græcians, they say also, that she was one of the mothers of the god Bacchus, whom they dare not name. And for proofe hereof, on her feast day, the women make certaine tabernacles of vine twigges, and leaves of vine braunches, and also they make as the tale goeth, a holie dragon for this goddesse, and doe set it by her: besides, it is not lawful for any man to be present at their sacrifices, no not within the house it selfe where they are made. Furthermore, they say that the women in these sacrifices do many things amongest them selves, much like unto the ceremonies of Orpheus. Now when the time of this feast came, the husband, (whether he were Prætor or Consul) and all his men and the boyes in the house, doe come out of it, and leave it wholly to his wife, to order the house at her pleasure, and there the sacrifices and ceremonies are done the most parte of the night, and they doe besides passe the night away, in songes and musicke. Pompeia, Cæsars wife, being that yeare to celebrate this feast, Clodius

The love of P. Clodius unto Pompeia, Cæsars wife.

The good goddesse what she was, and her sacrifices.

who had yet no heare on his face, and therby thought he should not be bewrayed: disguised him selfe in a singing wenches apparell, bicause his face was verie like unto a young wenche. He finding the gates open, being secretly brought in by her chamber maide that was made privie unto it: she left him, and ranne to Pompeia her mistres, to tell her that he was come. The chamber maide taried long before she came againe, insomuch as Clodius being wearie waiting for her where she left him, he tooke his pleasure, and went from one place to an other in the house, which had very large roomes in it, still shunning the light, and was by chaunce met withall by one of Aureliaes maides, who taking him for a woman, prayed her to play. Clodius refusing to play, the maide pulled him forward, and asked him what he was: Clodius then answered her, that he taried for Abra one of Pompeiaes women. So, Aureliaes maide knowing him by his voyce, ranne straight where the lightes and Ladies were, and cried out, that there was a man disguised in womans apparell. The women therewith were so amazed, that Aurelia caused them presently to leave of the ceremonies of the sacrifice, and to hide their secret thinges, and having seene the gates fast locked, went immediatly up and downe the house with torche light to seeke out this man: who at

Clodius taken
in the sacri-
fices of the
good god-
desse.

the last was found out in the chamber of Pompeiaes maide, with whom he hidde him selfe. Thus Clodius being found out, and knowen of the women: they thrust him out of the dores by the shoulders. The same night the women tolde their husbandes of this chaunce as soone as they came home. The next morning, there ranne a great rumor through the citie, how Clodius had attempted a great villany, and that he deserved, not only to be punished of them whom he had slaundred, but also of the common wealth and the goddes. There was one of the Tribunes of the people that did indite him, and accuse him of high treason to the gods. Further-more, there were also of the chiefest of the nobilitie and Senate, that came to depose against him, and burdened him with many horrible and detestable facts, and specially with incest committed with his owne sister, which was maried unto Lucullus. Notwithstanding, the people stowtly defended

Clodius
accused for
prophaning
the sacrifices
of the good
goddesse.

GRECIANS AND ROMANES

Clodius against their accusations: and this did helpe him much against the Iudges, which were amazed, and affraid to stirre the people. This notwithstanding, Cæsar presently put his wife away, and thereupon being brought by Clodius accuser to be a witnes against him, he aunswered, he knew nothing of that they objected against Clodius. This aunswere being cleane contrarie to their expectacion that heard it, the accuser asked Cæsar, why then he had put away his wife · Bicause I will not, sayd he, that my wife be so much as suspected. And some say, that Cæsar spake truely as he thought. But others thinke, that he did it to please the common people, who were very desirous to save Clodius. So Clodius was discharged of this accusation, bicause the most parte of the Iudges gave a confused judgement, for the feare they stoode one way of the daunger of the common people if they condemned him: and for the ill opinion of thother side of the nobilitie, if they did quit him. The government of the province of Spayne being fallen unto Cæsar for that he was Prætor: his creditors came and cried out apon him, and were importunate of him to be payed. Cæsar being unable to satisfie them, was compelled to goe unto Crassus, who was the richest man of all Rome, and that stoode in neede of Cæsars boldnes and corage to withstand Pompeys greatnes in the common wealth. Crassus became his suretie unto his greediest creditors for the summe of eight hundred and thirtie talentes: whereuppon they suffered Cæsar to departe to the government of his province. In his jorney it is reported, that passing over the mountaines of the Alpes, they came through a litle poore village that had not many householdes, and yet poore cotages. There, his frendes that did accompanie him, asked him merily, if there were any contending for offices in that towne, and whether there were any strife there amongest the noble men for honor. Cæsar speaking in good earnest, aunswered: I can not tell that said he, but for my parte, I had rather be the chiefest man here, then the second person in Rome. An other time also when he was in Spayne, reading the history of Alexanders actes, when he had red it, he was sorowfull a good while after, and then burst out in weeping. His frends seeing

IULIUS
CÆSAR
Cæsar putteth away his wife Pompeia.

Clodius quit by the Iudges for prophaning the sacrifices of the good goddesse.

Cæsar Prætor of Spaine

Crassus surety for Cæsar to his creditors.

11

that, marveled what should be the cause of his sorow. He aunswered them, Doe ye not thinke sayd he, that I have good cause to be heavie, when king Alexander being no older than my selfe is now, had in old time wonne so many nations and contries: and that I hitherunto have done

nothing worthy of my selfe? Therefore when he was come into Spayne, he was very carefull of his busines, and had in few dayes joyned ten new ensignes more of footemen, unto the other twenty which he had before. Then marching forward against the Callæcians and Lusitanians, he conquered all, and went as farre as the great sea Oceanum, subduing all the people which before knew not the Romanes for their Lordes. There he tooke order for pacifying of the warre, and did as wisely take order for the establishing of peace. For he did reconcile the cities together, and made them frendes one with an other, but specially he pacified all sutes of law, and strife, betwext the detters and creditors,

which grewe by reason of userie. For he ordained that the creditors shoulde take yearely two partes of the revenue of their detters, untill such time as they had payed them selves: and that the detters should have the third parte to them selves to live withall. He having wonne great estimacion by this good order taken, returned from his government very riche, and his souldiers also full of rich spoyles, who called him Imperator, to say soveraine Captaine. Now the Romanes

having a custome, that such as demaunded honor of triumphe, should remaine a while without the city, and that they on thother side which sued for the Consulship, should of necessitie be there in person: Cæsar comming unhappely at that very time when the Consuls were chosen, he sent to pray the Senate to do him that favor, that being absent, he might by his frendes sue for the Consulshippe. Cato at the first did vehemently invey against it, vowching an expresse law forbidding the contrarie. But afterwards, perceiving that notwithstanding the reasons he alleaged, many of the Senators (being wonne by Cæsar) favored his request: yet he cunningly sought all he could to prevent them, prolonging time, dilating his oration untill night. Cæsar thereupon determined rather to geve over the sute of his triumphe, and to make sute for the Consulshippe: and so came into the citie, and had such a devise with him, as went beyond them all, but Cato only. His devise was this. Pompey and Crassus, two of the greatest personages of the city of Rome, being at jarre together, Cæsar made them frends, and by that meanes got unto him selfe the power of them both · for, by colour of that gentle acte and frendshippe of his, he subtilly (unwares to them all) did greatly alter and chaunge the state of the common wealth. For it was not the private discord betwene Pompey and Cæsar, as many men thought, that caused the civill warre . but rather it was their agreement together, who joyned all their powers first to overthrowe the state of the Senate and nobilitie, and afterwardes they fell at jarre one with an other. But Cato, that then foresaw and prophecied many times what woulde followe, was taken but for a vaine man but afterwardes they found him a wiser man, then happie in his counsell. Thus Cæsar being brought unto the assemblie of the election, in the middest of these two noble persons, whom he had before reconciled together · he was there chosen Consull, with Calphurnius Bibulus, without gaine saying or contradiction of any man. Now when he was entred into his office, he beganne to put foorth lawes meeter for a seditious Tribune of the people, than for a Consull . bicause by them he preferred the division of landes, and distributing of corne to everie citizen, Gratis, to please them withall. But when the noble men of the Senate were against his devise, he desiring no better occasion, beganne to crie out, and to protest, that by the overhardnesse and austeritie of the Senate, they drave him against his will to leane unto the people: and thereupon having Crassus on thone side of him, and Pompey on thother, he asked them openly in thassemblie, if they did geve their consent unto the lawes which he had put forth. They both aunswered, they did. Then he prayed them to stande by him against those that threatned him with force of sworde to let him. Crassus gave him his worde, he would. Pompey also did the like, and added thereunto, that he would come with his sword and target both, against them that would withstand him with their swords. These wordes offended much the Senate, being

Sidenotes:

IULIUS CÆSAR

Cæsar reconcileth Pompey and Crassus together.

Catoes foresight and prophecy.

Cæsars first Consulship with Calphurnius Bibulus.

Cæsars lawes. *Lex agraria*

farre unmeete for his gravetie, and undecent for the majestie and honor he caried, and most of all uncomely for the presence of the Senate whome he should have reverenced : and were speaches fitter for a rash light headed youth, than for his person. Howbeit the common people on thother side, they rejoyced. Then Cæsar bicause he would be more assured of Pompeis power and frendshippe, he gave him his daughter Iulia in mariage, which was made sure before unto Servilius Cæpio, and promised him in exchaunge Pompeis wife, the which was sure also unto Faustus the sonne of Sylla. And shortly after also, Cæsar selfe did marie Calphurnia the daughter of Piso, whom he caused to be made Consul, to succeede him the next yeare following. Cato then cried out with open mouth, and called the gods to witnes, that it was a shamefull matter, and not to be suffered, that they should in that sorte make havoke of the Empire of Rome, by such horrible bawdie matches, distributing among them selves through those wicked mariages, the governments of the provinces, and of great armies. Calphurnius Bibulus, fellow Consul with Cæsar, perceiving that he did contend in vaine, making all the resistaunce he could to withstand this lawe, and that oftentimes he was in daunger to be slaine with Cato, in the market place and assemblie : he kept close in his house all the rest of his Consulshippe. When Pompey had maried Iulia, he filled all the market place with souldiers, and by open force authorised the lawes which Cæsar made in the behalfe of the people. Furthermore, he procured that Cæsar had Gaule on his side, and beyond the Alpes, and all Illyria, with foure legions graunted him for five yeares. Then Cato standing up to speake against it : Cæsar bad his officers lay holde of him, and carie him to prison, thinking he would have appealed unto the Tribunes. But Cato sayd never a worde, when he went his way. Cæsar perceiving them, that not onely the Senators and nobilitie were offended, but that the common people also for the reverence they bare unto Catoes vertues, were ashamed, and went away with silence : he him selfe secretly did pray one of the Tribunes that he would take Cato from the officers. But after he had played this parte,

GRECIANS AND ROMANES

there were few Senators that would be President of the
Senate under him, but left the citie, bicause they could not
away with his doinges. And of them, there was an old
man called Considius, that on a time boldly told him, the
rest durst not come to counsel, bicause they were afrayed of
his souldiers. Cæsar aunswered him againe: And why then,
doest not thou kepe thee at home, for the same feare?
Considius replied, Bicause my age taketh away feare from
me: for having so short a time to live, I have no care
to prolonge it further. The shamefullest parte that Cæsar
played while he was Consul, seemeth to be this: when he
chose P. Clodius Tribune of the people, that had offred his
wife such dishonor, and profaned the holy auncient misteries
of the women, which were celebrated in his owne house.
Clodius sued to be Tribune to no other end, but to destroy
Cicero · and Cæsar selfe also departed not from Rome to his
army, before he had set them together by the eares, and
driven Cicero out of Italy. All these things they say he
did, before the warres with the Gaules But the time of the
great armies and conquests he made afterwards, and of the
warre in the which he subdued al the Gaules. (entring into
an other course of life farre contrarie unto the first) made
him to be knowen for as valliant a souldier and as excellent Cæsar, a valliant souldier,
and a skilfull
Captaine
a Captaine to lead men, as those that afore him had
bene counted the wisest and most valliantest Generalles that
ever were, and that by their valliant deedes had atchieved
great honor. For whosoever would compare the house of
the Fabians, of the Scipioes, of the Metellians, yea those
also of his owne time, or long before him, as Sylla, Marius,
the two Lucullians, and Pompey selfe,

Whose fame ascendeth up unto the heavens:

it will appeare that Cæsars prowes and deedes of armes,
did excell them all together. The one, in the hard contries
where he made warres: an other, in enlarging the realmes
and contries which he joyned unto the Empire of Rome: an
other, in the multitude and power of his enemies whome he
overcame: an other, in the rudenesse and austere nature of

15

men with whom he had to doe, whose maners afterwardes he softned and made civill: an other, in curtesie and clemencie which he used unto them whome he had conquered: an other in great bountie and liberality bestowed upon them that served under him in those warres: and in fine, he excelled them all in the number of battells he had fought, and in the multitude of his enemies he had slaine in battell. For in lesse then tenne yeares warre in Gaule he

tooke by force and assault above eight hundred townes: he conquered three hundred severall nations: and having before him in battell thirty hundred thowsand souldiers, at sundrie times he slue tenne hundred thowsand of them, and tooke

as many more prisoners. Furthermore, he was so entirely beloved of his souldiers, that to doe him service (where otherwise they were no more then other men in any private quarrell) if Cæsars honor were touched, they were invincible, and would so desperatly venter them selves, and with such furie, that no man was able to abide them. And

this appeareth plainly by the example of Acilius: who in a battell by sea before the city of Marselles, bording one of his enemies shippes, one cut of his right hand with a sword, but yet he forsooke not his target which he had in his left hand, but thrust it in his enemies faces, and made them flie, so that he wanne their shippe from them. And Cassius Scæva also, in a conflict before the city of Dyrrachium, having one of his eyes put out with an arrow, his shoulder striken through with a dart, and his thigh with an other, and having received thirty arrowes upon his shield: he called to his enemies, and made as though he would yeelde unto them. But when two of them came running to him, he clave one of their shoulders from his bodie with his sword, and hurt the other in the face: so that he made him turne his backe, and at the length saved him selfe, by meanes of his companions that came to helpe him. And in Britayne also, when the Captaines of the bandes were driven into a marrisse or bogge full of mire and durt, and that the enemies did fiercelie assaile them there: Cæsar then standinge to viewe the battell, he sawe a private souldier of his thrust in among the Captaines, and fought so valliantlie in

16

GRECIANS AND ROMANES

their defence, that at the length he drave the barbarous
people to flye, and by his meanes saved the Captaines, which
otherwise were in great daunger to have bene cast away.
Then this souldier being the hindemost man of all the Captaines, marching with great paine through the myre and
durt, halfe swimming, and halfe a foote: in the end got
to the other side, but left his shield behinde him. Cæsar
wondring at his noble corage, ranne to him with joy to imbrace him. But the poore souldier hanging downe his head,
the water standing in his eyes, fell downe at Cæsars feete,
and besought him to pardon him, for that he had left his
targette behinde him. And in Africke also, Scipio having
taken one of Cæsars shippes, and Granius Petronius abourde Granius
on her amongest other, not long before chosen Treasorer: he Petronius.
put all the rest to the sword but him, and sayd he would
geve him his life. But Petronius aunswered him againe:
that Cæsars souldiers did not use to have their lives geven
them, but to geve others their lives: and with those wordes
he drewe his sworde, and thrust him selfe through. Nowe
Cæsars selfe did breede this noble corage and life in them.
First, for that he gave them bountifully, and did honor them
also, shewing thereby, that he did not heape up riches in
the warres to maintaine his life afterwards in wantonnesse
and pleasure, but that he did keepe it in store, honorably
to reward their valliant service: and that by so much he
thought him selfe riche, by howe much he was liberall in
rewarding of them that had deserved it. Furthermore, they
did not wonder so much at his valliantnesse in putting him
selfe at every instant in such manifest daunger, and in taking
so extreame paines as he did, knowing that it was his greedie
desire of honor that set him a fire, and pricked him forward
to doe it: but that he alwayes continued all labour and
hardnesse, more then his bodie could beare, that filled them
all with admiration. For, concerning the constitucion of his
bodie, he was leane, white, and soft skinned, and often subject to headache, and otherwhile to the falling sickenes: (the Cæsar had the
which tooke him the first time, as it is reported, in Corduba, falling sicke-
a citie of Spayne) but yet therefore yeelded not to the disease nes.
of his bodie, to make it a cloke to cherishe him withall, but

contrarilie, tooke the paines of warre, as a medicine to cure his sicke bodie fighting alwayes with his disease, travelling continually, living soberly, and commonly lying abroade in the field.   For the most nights he slept in his coch or litter, and thereby bestowed his rest, to make him alwayes able to do some thing : and in the day time, he would travell up and downe the contrie to see townes, castels, and strong places. He had alwayes a secretarie with him in his coche, who did still wryte as he went by the way, and a souldier behinde him that caried his sword.   He made such speede the first time he came from Rome, when he had his office : that in eight dayes, he came to the river of Rhone.   He was so excellent a rider of horse from his youth, that holding his handes behinde him, he would galloppe his horse upon the spurre.   In his warres in Gaule, he did further exercise him selfe to indite letters as he rode by the way, and did occupie two secretaries at once with as much as they could wryte : and as Oppius wryteth, more then two at a time.   And it is reported, that Cæsar was the first that devised frendes might talke together by wryting ciphers in letters, when he had no leasure to speake with them for his urgent busines, and for the great distaunce besides from Rome.   How litle accompt

The temper-
ance of Cæsar
in his dyet.

Cæsar made of his dyet, this example doth prove it.   Cæsar supping one night in Milane with his frende Valerius Leo, there was served sparrage to his bourde, and oyle of perfume

put into it in stead of sallet oyle.   He simplie eate it, and found no fault, blaming his frendes that were offended : and told them, that it had bene enough for them to have absteyned to eate of that they misliked, and not to shame their frend, and how that he lacked good manner that found fault with his frend.   An other time as he travelled through the contrie, he was driven by fowle weather on the sodaine to take a poore mans cottage, that had but one litle cabin in it, and that was so narrowe, that one man could but scarce lye in it.   Then he sayd to his frendes that were about him : Greatest roomes are meetest for greatest men, and the most necessarie roomes, for the sickest persons.   And thereuppon he caused Oppius that was sicke to lye there all night : and he him selfe, with the rest of his frendes, lay

18

GRECIANS AND ROMANES

with out dores, under the easing of the house. The first
warre that Cæsar made with the Gaules, was with the Helvetians and Tigurinians, who having sette fire of all their good
cities, to the number of twelve, and foure hundred villages
besides, came to invade that parte of Gaule which was subject to the Romanes, as the Cimbri and Teutons had done
before: unto whome for valliantnesse they gave no place,
and they were also a great number of them (for they were
three hundred thowsand soules in all) whereof there were a
hundred, foure score, and tenne thowsande fighting men. Of
those, it was not Cæsar him selfe that overcame the Tigurinians, but Labienus his Lieutenaunt, that overthrewe them
by the river of Arax. But the Helvetians them selves came
sodainly with their armie to set apon him, as he was going
towardes a citie of his confederates. Cæsar perceiving that,
made hast to get him some place of strength, and there did
sette his men in battell raye. When one brought him his
horse to gette up on which he used in battell, he sayd unto
them: When I have overcome mine enemies, I will then get
up on him to followe the chase, but nowe lette us geve them
charge. Therewith he marched forward a foote, and gave
charge: and there fought it out a long time, before he
coulde make them flie that were in battell. But the greatest
trouble he had, was to distresse their campe, and to breake
their strength which they had made with their cartes. For
there, they that before had fledde from the battell, did not
onely put them selves in force, and valliantly fought it out:
but their wives and children also fighting for their lives to
the death, were all slaine, and the battell was scant ended
at midnight. Nowe if the act of this victorie was famous,
unto that he also added an other as notable, or exceeding
it. For of all the barbarous people that had escaped from
this battell, he gathered together againe above a hundred
thowsande of them, and compelled them to returne home
into their contrie which they had forsaken, and unto their
townes also which they had burnt: bicause he feared the
Germaines would come over the river of Rheyne, and occupie
that contrie lying voyde. The second warre he made, was
in defence of the Gaules against the Germaines: although

IULIUS
CÆSAR

The Tigurin-
ians slaine
by Labienus.
Arax fl.

Cæsar refused
his horse,
when he
fought a
battell.

The Helve-
tians slaine
by Cæsar.

Rheynus fl.

19

Cæsar made
warre with
king Ario-
vistus.

before, he him selfe had caused Ariovistus their king, to be received for a confederate of the Romanes. Notwithstanding, they were growen very unquiet neighbours, and it appeared plainely, that having any occasion offered them to enlarge their territories, they woulde not content them with their owne, but ment to invade and possesse the rest of Gaule. Cæsar perceiving that some of his Captaines trembled for feare, but specially the young gentlemen of noble houses of Rome, who thought to have gone to the warres with him, as onely for their pleasure and gaine: he called them to counsell, and commaunded them that were affrayed, that they should depart home, and not put them selves in daunger against their willes, sith they had such womanishe faint hartes to shrinke when he had neede of them. And for him selfe, he sayd, he would set apon the barbarous people, though he had left him but the tenth legion onely, saying, that the enemies were no vallianter than the Cimbri had bene, nor that he was a Captaine inferior unto Marius. This oration being made, the souldiers of the tenth legion sent their Lieutenauntes unto him, to thanke him for the good opinion he had of them: and the other legions also fell out with their Captaines, and all of them together followed him many dayes jorney with good will to serve him, untill they came within two hundred furlonges of the campe of the enemies. Ariovistus corage was well cooled, when he sawe Cæsar was come, and that the Romanes came to seeke out the Germaines, where they thought, and made accompt, that they durst not have abidden them: and therefore nothinge mistrustinge it woulde have come so to passe, he wondered much at Cæsars corage, and the more when he sawe his owne armie in a maze withall. But muche more did their corages fall, by reason of the foolishe women propheciers they had among them, which did foretell thinges to come: who, consideringe the waves and trouble of the rivers, and the terrible noyse they made runninge downe the streame, did forewarne them not to fight, untill the newe moone. Cæsar havinge intelligence thereof, and perceivinge that the barbarous people thereuppon sturred not: thought it best then to sette uppon them, being discoraged with this supersticious feare, rather

The wise
women of
Germany how
they did fore-
tell thinges
to come.

GRECIANS AND ROMANES

then losinge time, he shoulde tarie their leasure. So he did
skirmishe with them even to their fortes, and litle hilles
where they lay, and by this meanes provoked them so, that
with great furie they came downe to fight. There he overcame them in battell, and followed them in chase, with great
slaughter, three hundred furlonge, even unto the river of
Rheyn: and he filled all the fieldes thitherto with deade
bodies and spoyles. Howebeit Ariovistus flyinge with
speede, gotte over the river of Rheyn, and escaped with a
fewe of his men. It is sayd that there were slaine foure
score thowsande persons at this battel. After this exployte,
Cæsar left his armie amongest the Sequanes to winter there:
and he him selfe in the meane time, thinking of thaffayres
at Rome, went over the mountaines into Gaule about the
river of Po, being parte of his province which he had in
charge. For there, the river called Rubico, devideth the
rest of Italie from Gaule on this side the Alpes. Cæsar
lying there, did practise to make frendes in Rome, bicause
many came thither to see him: unto whom he graunted
their sutes they demaunded, and sent them home also,
partly with liberall rewards, and partly with large pro-
mises and hope. Now during all this conquest of the Gaules,
Pompey did not consider how Cæsar enterchaungeablie did
conquer the Gaules with the weapons of the Romanes, and
wanne the Romanes againe with the money of the Gaules.
Cæsar being advertised that the Belgæ (which were the warlikest men of all the Gaules, and that occupied the third
parte of Gaule) were all up in armes, and had raised a great
power of men together: he straight made towardes them
with all possible speede, and founde them spoyling and over-
runninge the contrie of the Gaules, their neighbours, and
confederates of the Romanes. So he gave them battell, and
they fighting cowardly, he overthrew the most parte of them
which were in a troupe together, and slue such a number of
them, that the Romanes passed over deepe rivers and lakes
a foote, upon their dead bodies, the rivers were so full of
them. After this overthrow, they that dwelt neerest unto
the sea side, and were next neighbours unto the Ocean, did
yeeld them selves without any compulsion or fight: where-

21

IULIUS
CÆSAR
Nervii the
stowtest war-
riers of all
the Belgæ.

upon, he led his army against the Nervians, the stowtest warriers of all the Belgæ. They dwelling in the wodde contrie, had conveyed their wives, children and goods, into a marvelous great forrest, as farre from their enemies as they could: and being about the number of sixe score thowsand fighting men and more, they came one day and set apon Cæsar, when his armie was out of order, and fortifying of his campe, litle looking to have fought that day. At the first charge, they brake the horsemen of the Romanes, and compassing in the twelfth and seventh legion, they slue all the Centurions and Captaines of the bands. And had not Cæsar selfe taken his shield on his arme, and flying in amongest the barbarous people, made a lane through them that fought before him: and the tenth legion also seeing him in daunger, ronne unto him from the toppe of the hill where they stoode in battell, and broken the ranckes of their enemies: there had not a Romane escaped a live that day. But taking example of Cæsars valliantnes, they fought desperatly beyond their power, and yet could not make the Nervians flie, but they fought it out to the death, till they were all in manner slaine in the field. It is wrytten that of three skore thowsand fighting men, there escaped only but five hundred: and of foure hundred gentlemen and counsellers of the Romanes, but three saved. The Senate understanding it at Rome, ordained that they shoulde doe sacrifice unto the goddes, and keepe feastes and solemne processions fifteene dayes together without intermission, having never made the like ordinaunce at Rome, for any victorie that ever was obteined. Bicause they saw the daunger had bene marvelous great, so many nations rising as they did in armes together against him: and further, the love of the people unto him made his victory much more famous. For when Cæsar had set his affaires at a stay in Gaule, on the other side of the Alpes: he alwayes used to lye about the river of Po in the winter time, to geve direction for the establishing of thinges at Rome, at his pleasure. For, not only they that made sute for offices at Rome were chosen Magistrats, by meanes of Cæsars money which he gave them, with the which, bribing the people, they bought their voyces, and

The Nervii
slaine by
Cæsar.

GRECIANS AND ROMANES

when they were in office, did al that they could to increase
Cæsars power and greatnes: but the greatest and chiefest
men also of the nobilitie, went unto Luke unto him. As
Pompey, Crassus, Appius, Prætor of Sardinia, and Nepos,
Proconsull in Spayne. Insomuch that there were at one
time, sixe score sergeaunts carying roddes and axes before
the Magistrats: and above two hundred Senators besides.
There they fell in consultacion, and determined that Pompey
and Crassus should againe be chosen Consuls the next yere
following. Furthermore, they did appoint, that Cæsar should
have money againe delivered him to pay his armie, and
besides, did proroge the time of his government, five yeares
further. This was thought a very straunge and an unreasonable matter unto wise men. For they them selves
that had taken so much money of Cæsar, perswaded the
Senate to let him have money of the common treasure, as
though he had had none before: yea to speake more plainly,
they compelled the Senate unto it, sighing and lamenting to
see the decrees they passed. Cato was not there then, for
they had purposely sent him before into Cyprus. Howbeit Faonius that followed Catoes steppes, when he sawe
that he could not prevaile, nor withstande them: he went
out of the Senate in choller, and cried out amongest the
people, that it was a horrible shame. But no man did
hearken to him: some for the reverence they bare unto
Pompey, and Crassus, and others favoring Cæsars proceed-
inges, did put all their hope and trust in him: and therefore
did quiet them selves, and sturred not. Then Cæsar returning into Gaule beyonde the Alpes unto his armie, founde
there a greate warre in the contrie. For two great nations
of Germanie had not long before passed over the river of
Rheyn, to conquer newe landes: and the one of these people
were called Ipes, and the other Tenterides. Now touching
the battell which Cæsar fought with them, he him selfe doth
describe it in his Commentaries, in this sorte. That the
barbarous people having sent Ambassadours unto him, to
require peace for a certaine time: they notwithstanding,
against lawe of armes, came and sette apon him as he
travelled by the way, insomuch as eight hundred of their

IULIUS
CÆSAR
The great
Lordes of
Rome, came
to Luca to
Cæsar.

Ipes, and
Tenterides,
people of
Germany.

23

Cæsars horse-
men put to
flight.

The Ipes and
Tenterides
slaine by
Cæsar.

Sicambri, a
people of the
Germaines.

Cæsar made a
bridge over
the river of
Rheyn.

men of armes overthrewe five thowsande of his horsemen, who nothinge at all mistrusted their comming. Againe, that they sent him other Ambassadours to mocke him once more: but that he kept them, and therewith caused his whole armie to marche against them, thinking it a follie, and madnesse, to keepe faith with such trayterous barbarous breakers of leagues. Canutius wryteth, that the Senate appointing againe to doe newe sacrifice, processions, and feastes, to geve thankes to the goddes for this victorie: Cato was of contrarie opinion, that Cæsar should be delivered into the handes of the barbarous people, for to pourge their city and common wealth of this breache of faith, and to turne the curse apon him, that was the author of it. Of these barbarous people, which came over the Rheyn (being about the number of foure hundred thowsand persons) they were all in maner slaine, saving a very fewe of them, that flying from the battell got over the river of Rheyn againe, who were received by the Sicambrians, an other people of the Germaines. Cæsar taking this occasion against them, lacking no good will of him selfe besides, to have the honor to be counted the first Romane that ever passed over the river of Rheyn with an armie: he built a bridge over it. This river is marvelous broade, and runneth with great furie. And in that place specially where he built his bridge, for there it is of a great bredth from one side to thother, and it hath so strong and swift a streame besides: that men casting downe great bodies of trees into the river (which the streame bringeth downe with it) did with the great blowes and force thereof marvelously shake the postes of the bridge he had set up. But to prevent the blowes of those trees, and also to breake the furie of the streame: he made a pile of great wodde above the bridge a good way, and did forciblie ramme them in to the bottome of the river, so that in ten dayes space, he had set up and finisht his bridge of the goodliest carpenters worke, and most excellent invention to see to, that could be possiblie thought or devised. Then passing over his army upon it, he found none that durst any more fight with him. For the Swevians, which were the warlikest people of all Germany, had gotten

GRECIANS AND ROMANES

them selves with their goodes into wonderfull great valleis
and bogges, full of woddes and forrestes. Nowe when he
had burnt all the contrie of his enemies, and confirmed the
league with the confederats of the Romanes: he returned
backe againe into Gaule after he had taried eighteene dayes
at the most in Germany, on thother side of the Rheyn. The
jorney he made also into England, was a noble enterprise,
and very commendable. For he was the first that sailed the
west Ocean with an army by sea, and that passed through
the sea Atlanticum with his army, to make warre in that
so great and famous Ilande: (which many auncient wryters
would not beleve that it was so in deede, and did make
them vary about it, saying that it was but a fable and a
lye) and was the first that enlarged the Romane Empire,
beyonde the earth inhabitable. For twise he passed over the
narrowe sea against the firme lande of Gaule, and fighting
many battells there, did hurt his enemies more, then enriche
his owne men: bicause, of men hardlie brought up, and poore,
there was nothing to be gotten. Whereuppon his warre had
not such successe as he looked for, and therefore takinge
pledges onely of the kinge, and imposing a yearely tribute
apon him, to be payed unto the people of Rome: he returned againe into Gaule. There he was no sooner landed,
but he founde letters ready to be sent over the sea unto him:
in the which he was advertised from Rome, of the death of
his Daughter, that she was dead with child by Pompey.
For the which, Pompey and Cæsar both, were marvelous
sorowfull: and their friends mourned also, thinking that
this alliance which mainteined the common wealth (that
otherwise was very tickle) in good peace and concord, was
now severed, and broken a sonder, and the rather likely,
bicause the childe lived not long after the mother. So the
common people at Rome tooke the corps of Julia, in dispite
of the Tribunes, and buried it in the fielde of Mars. Now
Cæsar being driven to devide his armie (that was very great)
into sundry garrisons for the winter time, and returning
againe into Italy as he was wont: all Gaule rebelled againe,
and had raysed great armies in every quarter to set apon
the Romanes, and to assay if they could distresse their forts

where they lay in garrison. The greatest number and most warlike men of these Gaules, that entred into action of rebellion, were led by one Ambiorix: and first did set upon the garrisons of Cotta, and Titurius, whom they slue, and all the souldiers they had about them. Then they went with three score thowsand fighting men to beseege the garrison which Quintus Cicero had in his charge, and had almost taken them by force, bicause all the souldiers were every man of them hurt: but they were so valiant and courageous, that they did more then men (as they say) in defending of them selves. These newes being come to Cæsar, who was farre from thence at that time, he returned with all possible speede, and levying seven thowsand souldiers, made haste to helpe Cicero that was in such distresse. The Gaules that did beseege Cicero, understanding of Cæsars comming, raysed their seege incontinently, to goe and meete him: making accompt that he was but a handfull in their handes, they were so fewe. Cæsar to deceive them, still drewe backe, and made as though he fled from them, lodging in places meete for a Captaine that had but a few, to fight with a great number of his enemies, and commaunded his men in no wise to sturre out to skirmish with them, but compelled them to rayse up the rampers of his campe, and to fortifie the gates, as men that were afraid, bicause the enemies should the lesse esteeme of them: untill that at length he tooke opportunitie, by their disorderly comming to assaile the trenches of his campe, (they were growen to such a pre-sumptuous boldnes and bravery) and then salying out apon them, he put them all to flight with slaughter of a great number of them. This did suppresse all the rebellions of the Gaules in those partes, and furthermore, he him selfe in person went in the middest of winter thether, where he heard they did rebell: for that there was come a newe supply out of Italy of three whole legions in their roome, which he had lost: of the which, two of them Pompey lent him, and the other legion, he him selfe had leavyed in Gaule about the river of Po. During these sturres, brake forth the beginning of the greatest and most daungerous warre that he had in all Gaule, the which had bene secretly practised

Cæsar slue the
Gaules led by
Ambiorix.

GRECIANS AND ROMANES

of long time by the chiefest and most warlike people of that
contry, who had leavied a wonderfull great power. For
every where they leavied multitudes of men, and great riches
besides, to fortefie their stronge holdes. Furthermore the
contry where they rose, was very ill to come unto, and specially at that time being winter, when the rivers were frosen,
the woodes and forrests covered with snowe, the meadowes
drowned with fluddes, and the fieldes so deepe of snow, that
no wayes were to be found, neither the marisses nor rivers to
be decerned, all was so overflowen and drowned with water :
all which troubles together were enough (as they thought)
to keepe Cæsar from setting upon the rebels. Many nations
of the Gaules were of this conspiracy, but two of the chiefest
were the Arvernians and Carnutes : who had chosen Vercingentorix for their Lieuetenant generall, whose father the
Gaules before had put to death, bicause they thought he
aspired to make him selfe king. This Vercingentorix dividing his armie into divers partes, and appointing divers
Captaines over them, had gotten to take his part, all the
people and contries thereabout, even as farre as they that
dwell towards the *sea Adriatick, having further determined
(understanding that Rome did conspire against Cæsar) to
make all Gaule rise in armes against him. So that if he
had but taried a litle lenger, untill Cæsar had entred into his
civill warres : he had put all Italy in as great feare and
daunger, as it was when the Cimbri did come and invade it.
But Cæsar, that was very valiant in all assaies and daungers
of warre, and that was very skilfull to take time and oportunitie : so soone as he understoode the newes of the rebellion,
he departed with speede, and returned backe the selfe same
way which he had gone, making the barbarous people know,
that they should deale with an armie unvincible, and which
they could not possibly withstand, considering the great
speede he had made with the same, in so sharpe and hard a
winter. For where they would not possibly have beleeved,
that a poste or currer could have come in so short a time
from the place where he was, unto them : they wondred
when they saw him burning and destroying the contry, the
townes and stronge forts where he came with his armie,

The second
rebellion of
the Gaules
against
Cæsar.

Vercingento-
rix Captaine
of the rebells
against Cæsar.

*Some say,
that in this
place is to
be redde in
the Greeke
πρὸς τὸν
Ἀραριν, which
is, the river
Saone.

27

IULIUS
CÆSAR
The Hedvi
rebell against
the Romanes.

taking all to mercy that yelded unto him: until such time as the Hedvi tooke armes against him, who before were wont to be called the brethren of the Romanes, and were greatly honored of them. Wherfore Cæsars men when they understoode that they had joyned with the rebells, they were marvelous sory, and halfe discouraged. Thereuppon, Cæsar departing from those partes, went through the contry of the Lingones, to enter the contry of the *Burgonians, who

*Sequani.

were confederats of the Romanes, and the nearest unto Italy on that side, in respect of all the rest of Gaule. Thither the enemies came to set apon him, and to environne him of all sides, with an infinit number of thowsands of fighting men. Cæsar on thother side taried their comming, and

Vercingen-
torix over-
throwen by
Cæsar.

fighting with them a long time, he made them so affraid of him, that at length he overcame the barbarous people. But at the first, it seemeth notwithstanding, that he had receyved some overthrowe: for the Arvernians shewed a sworde hanged uppe in one of their temples, which they sayde they had wonne from Cæsar. Insomuch as Cæsar selfe comming that way by occasion, sawe it, and fell a laughing at it. But some of his friendes going about to take it away, he would not suffer them, but bad them let it alone, and touch it not, for it was a holy thinge. Notwithstanding, such as at the first had saved them selves by fleeing, the most of them were

The seege
of Alexia.

gotten with their king into the citie of Alexia, the which Cæsar went and beseeged, although it seemed inexpugnable, both for the height of the wals, as also for the multitude of souldiers they had to defend it. But now during this seege,

Cæsars daun-
ger, and wise
policie.

he fell into a marvelous great daunger without, almost incredible. For an armie of three hundred thowsand fighting men of the best men that were among all the nations of the Gaules, came against him, being at the seege of Alexia, besides them that were within the citie, which amounted to the number of three score and tenne thowsand fighting men at the least: so that perceiving he was shut in betwixt two so great armies, he was driven to fortifie him selfe with two walls, the one against them of the citie, and the other against them without. For if those two armies had joyned together, Cæsar had bene utterly undone. And therefore, this seege of Alexia, and the battell he wanne before it, did deservedly winne him moe honor and fame, then any other. For there, in that instant and extreame daunger, he shewed more valiantnes and wisdom, then he did in any battell he fought before. But what a wonderfull thing was this? that they of the citie never heard any thing of them that came to ayde them, untill Cæsar had overcome them: and furthermore, that the Romanes them selves which kept watch upon the wall that was built against the citie, knew also no more of it, then they, but when it was done, and that they heard the cryes and lamentacions of men and women in Alexia, when they perceved on thother side of the citie such a number of glistering shields of gold and silver, such store of bloody corselets and armors, such a deale of plate and moveables, and such a numbe of tents and pavilyons after the facion of the Gaules, which the Romanes had gotten of their spoyles in their campe. Thus sodainely was this great armie vanished, as a dreame or vision: where the most part of them were slaine that day in battell. Furthermore, after that they within the citie of Alexia had done great hurt to Cæsar, and them selves also. in the ende, they all yelded them selves. And Vercingentorix (he that was their king and Capteine in all this warie) went out of the gates excellently well armed, and his horse furnished with riche capparison accordingly, and rode round about Cæsar, who sate in his chayer of estate. Then lighting from his horse, he tooke of his capparison and furniture, and unarmed him selfe, and layed all on the ground, and went and sate downe at Cæsars feete, and sayd never a word. So Cæsar at length committed him as a prisoner taken in the warres, to leade him afterwards in his triumphe at Rome. Nowe Cæsar had of long time determined to destroy Pompey, and Pompey him also. For Crassus being killed amongest the Parthians, who onely did see, that one of them two must needes fall: nothing kept Cæsar from being the greatest person, but bicause he destroied not Pompey, that was the greater · neither did any thing let Pompey to withstand that it should not come to passe, but bicause he did not first overcome Cæsar, whom onely he feared. For till then, Pompey had not long feared

Cæsars great victorie at Alexia.

Alexia yelded up to Cæsar.

29

The discord
betwixt Cæsar
and Pompey,
and the cause
of the civill
warres.

Cæsars
craftines.

The peoples
voices bought
at Rome for
money.

him, but alwayes before set light by him, thinking it an easie matter for him to put him downe when he would, sithe he had brought him to that greatnes he was come unto. But Cæsar contrarily, having had that drift in his head from the beginning, like a wrestler that studieth for trickes to overthrowe his adversary. he went farre from Rome, to exercise him selfe in the warres of Gaule, where he did trayne his armie, and presently by his valiant deedes did increase his fame and honor. By these meanes became Cæsar as famous as Pompey in his doings, and lacked no more to put his enterprise in execution, but some occasions of culler, which Pompey partly gave him, and partly also the tyme delivered him, but chiefly, the hard fortune and ill government at that tyme of the common wealth of Rome. For they that made sute for honor and offices, bought the voyces of the people with ready money, which they gave out openly to usury, without shame or feare. Thereupon, the common people that had sold their voyces for money, came to the market place at the day of election, to fight for him that had hyered them : not with their voices, but with their bowes, slings, and swordes. So that the assembly seldom tyme brake up, but that the pulpit for orations was defiled and sprinckled with the bloode of them that were slayne in the market place, the citie remayning all that tyme without government of Magistrate, like a shippe left without a Pilote. Insomuch, as men of deepe judgement and discression seing such furie and madnes of the people, thought them selves happy if the common wealth were no worse troubled, then with the absolut state of a Monarchy and soveraine Lord to governe them. Furthermore, there were many that were not affraid to speake it openly, that there was no other help to remedy the troubles of the common wealth, but by the authority of one man only, that should commaund them all . and that this medicine must be ministred by the hands of him, that was the gentlest Phisition, meaning covertly Pompey. Now Pompey used many fine speeches, making semblance as though he would none of it, and yet cunningly under hand did lay all the yrons in the fire he could, to bring it to passe, that he might be chosen

30

GRECIANS AND ROMANES

Dictator. Cato finding the mark he shot at, and fearing
least in the end the people should be compelled to make him
Dictator : he perswaded the Senat rather to make him sole
Consul, that contenting him self with that more just and
lawfull government, he should not covet the other unlawfull
The Senate following his counsel, did not only make him
Consul, but further did proroge his government of the provinces he had. For he had two provinces, all Spayne, and
Africk, the which he governed by his Lieuetenants : and
further, he received yearely of the common treasure to pay
his souldiers a thowsand talents. Hereuppon Cæsar tooke
occasion also to send his men to make sute in his name for
the Consulship, and also to have the government of his provinces proroged Pompey at the first held his peace. But
Marcellus and Lentulus (that otherwise hated Cæsar) with-
stood them, and to shame and dishonor him, had much
needeles speech in matters of weight. Furthermore, they
tooke away the fredom from the Colonyes which Cæsar had
lately brought unto the citie of Novum Comum in Gaule
towards Italy, where Cæsar not long before had lodged them.
And moreover, when Marcellus was Consul, he made one of
the Senators in that citie to be whipped with roddes, who
came to Rome about those matters : and said, he gave him
those markes, that he should know he was no Romane
Citizen, and bad him goe his way, and tel Cæsar of it.
After Marcellus Consulship, Cæsar setting open his cofers of
the treasure he had gotten among the Gaules, did franckely
give it out amongest the Magistrates at Rome, without
restrainte or spare. First, he set Curio, the Tribune cleare
out of debt and gave also unto Paule the Consul a thowsand five hundred talents, with which money he built that
notable pallace by the market place, called Paules Basilicke,
in the place of Fulvius Basilicke Then Pompey being affraid
of this practise, began openly to procure, both by him selfe
and his friends, that they should send Cæsar a successor ·
and moreover, he sent unto Cæsar for his two legions of men
of warre which he had lent him, for the conquest of Gaule.
Cæsar sent him them againe, and gave every private souldier,
two hundred and fiftie silver drachmas. Now, they that

Pom ey
governed
Spain and
Africk

Cæsar sueth
the second
time to be
Consul, and
to have his
government
proroged.

Cæsar bribeth
the Magis-
trates at
Rome.

31

Pompey
abused by
flatterers.

brought these two legions backe from Cæsar, gave out ill
and seditious wordes against him amonge the people, and
did also abuse Pompey with false perswasions and vaine
hopes, informing him that he was marvelously desired and
wished for in Cæsars campe : and that though in Rome, for
the malice and secret spite which the governours there did
beare him, he could hardly obteyne that he desired : yet in
Gaule he might assure him selfe, that all the armie was at
his commaundement. They added further also, that if the
souldiers there did once returne over the mountaines againe
into Italy, they would all straight come to him, they did so
hate Cæsar : bicause he wearied them with too much labor
and continuall fight, and withal, for that they suspected
he aspired to be king. These words breeding securitie in
Pompey, and a vaine conceit of him selfe, made him negligent in his doings, so that he made no preparation for warre,
as though he had no occasion to be affraid : but onely studied
to thwart Cæsar in speech, and to crosse the sutes he made.
Howbeit Cæsar passed not of all this. For the report went,
that one of Cæsars Captaines which was sent to Rome to
prosecute his sute, being at the Senate dore, and hearing
that they denied to proroge Cæsars time of government
which he sued for : clapping his hand upon his sword, he
said, Sith you wil not graunt it him, this shal give it him.

Cæsars re-
quests unto
the Senate.

Notwithstanding, the requests that Cæsar propownded, caried
great semblance of reason with them. For he said, that he
was contented to lay downe armes, so that Pompey did the
like : and that both of them as privat persons should come
and make sute of their Citizens to obtaine honorable recompence : declaring unto them, that taking armes from him,
and graunting them unto Pompey, they did wrongefully
accuse him in going about to make him selfe a tyranne, and
in the meane time to graunt the other meanes to be a tyranne.
Curio making these offers and perswasions openly before the
people, in the name of Cæsar : he was heard with great
rejoycing and clapping of hands, and there were some that
cast flowers and nosegayes upon him when he went his way,
as they commonly use to doe unto any man, when he hath
obteined victorye, and wonne any games. Then Antonius

one of the Tribunes, brought a letter sent from Cæsar, and made it openly to be read in despite of the Consuls. But Scipio in the Senate, Pompeys father in law, made this motion : that if Cæsar did not dismisse his armie by a certaine day appoynted him, the Romanes should proclayme him an enemie unto Rome. Then the Consuls openly asked in the presence of the Senators, if they thought it good that Pompey should dismisse his armie : but few agreed to that demaund. After that againe they asked, if they liked that Cæsar should dismisse his armie : thereto they all in manner aunswered, Yea, yea. But when Antonius requested agayne that bothe of them should lay downe armes : then they were all indifferently of his minde. Notwithstanding, bicause Scipio did insolently behave him selfe, and Marcellus also, who cryed that they must use force of armes, and not mens opinions against a theefe : the Senate rose straight upon it without further determination, and men chaunged apparel through the citie bicause of this dissention, as they use to do in a common calamity. After that, there came other letters from Cæsar, which semed much more reasonable : in the which he requested that they would graunt him Gaule, that lyeth betwene the Mountaines of the Alpes and Italy, and Illyria, with two legions only, and then that he would request nothing els, until he made sute for the second Consulship. Cicero the Orator, that was newly come from his government of Cilicia, travelled to reconcile them together, and pacified Pompey the best he could : who told him, he would yeld to any thing he would have him, so he did let him alone with his armie. So Cicero perswaded Cæsars friends to be contented, to take those two provinces, and six thowsand men onely, that they might be friends and at peace together. Pompey very willingly yelded unto it, and graunted them. But Lentulus the Consul would not agree to it, but shamefully drave Curio and Antonius out of the Senate : whereby they them selves gave Cæsar a happy occasion and culler, as could be, stirring up his souldiers the more against them, when he shewed them these two notable men and Tribunes of the people that were driven to flie, disguised like slaves, in a cariers cart. For, they were driven for feare to steale

Antonius
and Curio,
Tribunes of
the people, fly
from Rome
to Cæsar.

out of Rome, disguised in that manner. Nowe at that time, Cæsar had not in all about him, above five thowsand footemen, and three thowsand horsemen : for the rest of his armie, he left on thother side of the Mountaines to be brought after him by his Lieuetenants. So, considering that for thexecution of his enterprise, he should not neede so many men of warre at the first, but rather sodainly stealing upon them, to make them affraid with his valiantnes, taking benefit of the oportunitie of tyme, bicause he should more easily make his enemies affraid of him, comming so sodainly when they looked not for him, then he should otherwise distresse them, assailing them with his whole armie, in giving them leysure to provide further for him : he commaunded his Captaines and Lieuetenants to go before, without any other armor then their swords, to take the citie of Ariminum, (a great citie of Gaule, being the first citie men come to, when they come out of Gaule) with as litle bloodshed and tumult, as they could possible. Then committing that force and armie he had with him, unto Hortensius one of his friends : he remeyned a whole day together, openly in the sight of every man, to see the sworde players handle their weapons before him. At night he went into his lodging, and bathing his body a litle, came afterwards into the hall amongest them, and made mery with them a while, whome he had bidden to supper. Then when it was well forwarde night, and very darke, he rose from the table, and prayed his company to be mery, and no man to sturre, for he would straight come to them againe : howebeit he had secretly before commaunded a fewe of his trustiest frendes to followe him, not altogether, but some one way, and some an other way. He him selfe in the meane tyme tooke a coche he had hyered, and made as though he woulde have gonne some other waye at the first, but sodainely he turned backe againe towardes the citie of Ariminum. When he was come unto the litle ryver of

Cæsars doubtfull thoughts
at the river of
Rubicon.

Rubicon, which devideth Gaule on this side the Alpes from Italy : he stayed uppon a sodaine. For, the nearer he came to execute his purpose, the more remorse he had in his conscience, to thinke what an enterprise he tooke in hand : and

34

his thoughts also fell out more doubtfull, when he entred
into consideration of the desperatnes of his attempt.   So he
fell into many thoughts with him selfe, and spake never a
word, waving sometime one way, sometime an other way, and
often times chaunged his determination, contrary to him selfe.
So did he talke much also with his friends he had with him,
amongest whom was Asinius Pollio, telling them what mischieves the beginning of this passage over that river would
breede in the world, and how much their posteritie and them
that lived after them, would speake of it in time to come.
But at length, casting from him with a noble courage, all
those perillous thoughts to come, and speaking these words
which valiant men commonly say, that attempt daungerous
and desperat enterprises, 'A desperat man feareth no daunger,
come on': he passed over the river, and when he was come
over, he ranne with his coche and never staied, so that before
day light he was within the citie of Ariminum, and tooke it.
It is said, that the night before he passed over this river,
he dreamed a damnable dreame, that he carnally knew his
mother.   The citie of Ariminum being taken, and the rumor
thereof dispersed through all Italy, even as if it had bene
open warre both by sea and land, and as if all the lawes
of Rome, together with thextreme bounds and confines of
the same had bene broken up : a man would have sayd, that
not onely the men and women for feare, as experience proved
at other times, but whole cities them selves leaving their
habitations, fled from one place to another through all Italy.
And Rome it selfe also was immediatly filled with the flowing
repaire of all the people their neighbours thereabouts, which
came thither from all partes like droves of cattell, that there
was neither officer nor Magistrate that could any more commaund them by authoritie, neither by any perswasion of
reason bridle such a confused and disorderly multitude : so
that Rome had in maner destroyed it selfe for lacke of rule
and order.   For in all places, men were of contrary opinions,
and there were daungerous sturres and tumults every where :
bicause they that were glad of this trouble, could keepe in
no certaine place, but running up and downe the citie, when
they met with others in divers places, that seemed either to

IULIUS
CÆSAR

The Greeke
useth this
phrase of
speech, cast
the dye.

Cæsar tooke
the citie of
Ariminum.

Cæsars damn-
able dreame.

Rome in
uprore with
Cæsars
comming.

35

be affraid or angry with this tumult (as otherwise it is impossible in so great a citie) they flatly fell out with them, and boldly threatned them with that that was to come. Pompey him selfe, who at that time was not a litle amazed, was yet much more troubled with the ill wordes some gave him on the one side, and some on the other. For some of them reproved him, and sayd that he had done wisely, and had paid for his folly, because he had made Cæsar so great and stronge against him and the common wealth. And other againe did blame him, bicause he had refused the honest offers and reasonable condicions of peace, which Cæsar had offered him, suffering Lentulus the Consul to abuse him too much. On thother side, Phaonius spake unto him, and bad him stampe on the ground with his foote: For Pompey beeing one day in a braverie in the Senate, sayd openly: Let no man take thought for preparation of warre, for when he lysted, with one stampe of his foote on the ground, he would fill all Italy with souldiers. This notwithstanding, Pompey at that tyme had greater number of souldiers then Cæsar: but they would never let him follow his owne determination. For they brought him so many lyes, and put so many examples of feare before him, as if Cæsar had bene already at their heeles, and had wonne all: so that in the ende he yelded unto them, and gave place to their furie and madnes, determining (seeing all thinges in such tumult and garboyle) that there was no way but to forsake the citie, and thereuppon commaunded the Senate to follow him, and not a man to tary there, unles he loved tyrannie, more then his owne libertie and the common wealth. Thus the Consuls them selves, before they had done their common sacrifices accustomed at their going out of the citie, fled every man of them. So did likewise the moste parte of the Senators, taking their owne thinges in haste, such as came first to hande, as if by stealth they had taken them from another. And there were some of them also that alwayes loved Cæsar, whose witts were then so troubled and besides them selves, with the feare they had conceyved: that they also fled, and followed the streame of this tumult, without manifest cause or necessitie. But above all thinges, it

36

GRECIANS AND ROMANES

was a lamentable sight to see the citie it selfe, that in this
feare and trouble was left at all adventure, as a shippe tossed
in storme of sea, forsaken of her Pilots, and dispairing of her
safetie. This their departure being thus miserable, yet men
esteemed their banishment (for the love they bare unto
Pompey) to bee their naturall contry, and reckoned Rome
no better then Cæsars campe. At that tyme also Labienus,
who was one of Cæsars greatest friendes, and had bene
alwayes used as his Lieuetenant in the warres of Gaule, and
had valiantly fought in his cause : he likewise forsooke him
then, and fled unto Pompey. But Cæsar sent his money
and cariage after him, and then went and encamped before
the citie of Corfinium, the which Domitius kept, with thirty
cohorts or ensignes. When Domitius sawe he was beseeged,
he straight thought him selfe but undone, and dispayring
of his successe, he bad a Phisition, a slave of his, give him
poyson. The Phisition gave him a drinke which he dranke,
thinking to have dyed. But shortly after, Domitius hearing
them reporte what clemencie and wonderfull curtesie Cæsar
used unto them he tooke : repented him then that he had
dronke this drinke, and beganne to lament and bewayle his
desperate resolucion taken to dye. The Phisition did comfort him againe, and tolde him, that he had taken a drinke,
onely to make him sleepe, but not to destroy him. Then
Domitius rejoyced, and went straight and yelded him selfe
unto Cæsar : who gave him his life, but he notwithstanding
stale away immediatly, and fled unto Pompey. When these
newes were brought to Rome, they did marvelously rejoyce
and comfort them that still remayned there : and moreover
there were of them that had forsaken Rome, which returned
thither againe. In the meane time, Cæsar did put all
Domitius men in paye, and he did the like through all the
cities, where he had taken any Captaines, that leavied men
for Pompey. Now Cæsar having assembled a great and
dreadfull power together, went straight where he thought
to finde Pompey him selfe. But Pompey taried not his
comming, but fled into the citie of Brundusium, from whence
he had sent the two Consuls before with that armie he had,
unto Dyrrachium : and he him selfe also went thither after-

wards, when he understoode that Cæsar was come, as you shall heare more amply hereafter in his life. Cæsar lacked no good will to follow him, but wanting shippes to take the seas, he returned forthwith to Rome: So that in lesse then three skore dayes, he was Lord of all Italy, without any blood shed. Who when he was come to Rome, and found it much quietter then he looked for, and many Senatours there also: he curteously intreated them, and prayed them to send unto Pompey, to pacifie all matters betweene them, apon reasonable conditions. But no man did attempt it, eyther bicause they feared Pompey for that they had forsaken him, or els for that they thought Cæsar ment not as he spake, but that they were wordes of course, to culler his purpose withall. And when Metellus also, one of the Tribunes, would not suffer him to take any of the common treasure out of the temple of Saturne, but tolde him that it was against the

Silent leges inter arma.

lawe: Tushe, sayd he, tyme of warre and lawe are two thinges. If this that I doe, quoth he, doe offende thee, then get thee hence for this tyme: for warre can not abyde this francke and bolde speeche. But when warres are done, and that we are all quiet agayne, then thou shalt speake in the pulpit what thou wilt: and yet I doe tell thee this of favor, impayring so much my right, for thou art myne, both thou, and all them that have risen against me, and whom I have

Cæsar taketh money out of the temple of Saturne.

in my hands. When he had spoken thus unto Metellus, he went to the temple dore where the treasure laye: and finding no keyes there, he caused Smythes to be sent for, and made them breake open the lockes. Metellus thereuppon beganne agayne to withstande him, and certen men that stoode by praysed him in his doing: but Cæsar at length speaking biggely to him, threatned him he would kill him presently, if he troubled him any more: and told him furthermore, Younge man, quoth he, thow knowest it is harder for me to tell it thee, than to doe it. That word made Metellus quake for feare, that he gotte him away

Cæsars jorney into Spayne, against Pompeys Lieuetenants.

rowndly: and ever after that, Cæsar had all at his commaundement for the warres. From thence he went into Spayne, to make warre with Petreius and Varro, Pompeys Lieuetenants: first to gette their armies and provinces into

GRECIANS AND ROMANES

his hands which they governed, that afterwardes he might
follow Pompey the better, leaving never an enemie behinde
him. In this jorney he was oftentymes him selfe in daunger,
through the ambushes that were layde for him in divers
straunge sortes and places, and likely also to have lost all his
armie for lacke of vittells. All this notwithstanding, he
never left following of Pompeys Lieuetenants, provoking
them to battell, and intrenching them in: untill he had
gotten their campe and armies into his handes, albeit that
the Lieuetenants them selves fled unto Pompey. When
Cæsar returned agayne to Rome, Piso his father in lawe gave
him counsell to sende Ambassadors unto Pompey, to treate
of peace. But Isauricus, to flatter Cæsar, was against it.
Cæsar beeing then created Dictator by the Senate, called
home againe all the banished men, and restored their children
to honor, whose fathers before had beene slayne in Syllaes
tyme: and did somewhat cutte of the usuries that did
oppresse them, and besides, did make some such other
ordinances as those, but very fewe. For he was Dictator Cæsar
but eleven dayes onely, and then did yeld it uppe of him Dictator.
selfe, and made him selfe Consul, with Servilius Isauricus, Cæsar and
and after that determined to followe the warres. All the Isauricus
rest of his armie he left comming on the way behind him, Consulls.
and went him selfe before with six hundred horse, and five
legions onely of footemen, in the winter quarter, about the
moneth of Ianuary, which after the Athenians, is called
Posideon. Then having past over the sea Ionium, and landed Cæsar goeth
his men, he wanne the cities of Oricum and Apollonia. Then into the
he sent his shippes backe againe unto Brundusium, to trans- kingdom of
port the rest of his souldiers that could not come with that Epirus.
speede he did. They as they came by the way, (like men
whose strength of body, and lusty youth, was decayed) being
wearied with so many sundry battells as they had fought
with their enemies: complayned of Cæsar in this sorte. To Complaints
what ende and purpose doth this man hale us after him, up of the olde
and downe the world, using us like slaves and drudges? It souldiers
is not our armor, but our bodies that beare the blowes away: against
and what, shall we never be without our harnes of our backes, Cæsar.
and our shieldes on our armes? should not Cæsar thinke, at

the least when he seeth our blood and woundes, that we are all mortall men, and that we feele the miserie and paynes that other men doe feele? And now even in the dead of winter, he putteth us unto the mercie of the sea and tempest, yea which the gods them selves can not withstand: as if he fled before his enemies, and pursued them not. Thus spending time with this talke, the souldiers still marching on, by small jorneys came at length unto the citie of Brundusium. But when they were come, and found that Cæsar had already passed over the sea, then they straight chaunged their complaints and mindes. For they blamed them selves, and tooke on also with their Captaines, bicause they had not made them make more haste in marching: and sitting upon the rockes and clyffes of the sea, they looked over the mayne sea, towards the Realme of Epirus, to see if they could discerne the shippes returning backe, to transport them over. Cæsar in the meane time being in the citie of Apollonia, having but a small armie to fight with Pompey, it greved him for that the rest of his armie was so long a comming,

not knowing what way to take. In the ende he followed a daungerous determinacion, to imbarke unknowen in a litle pynnase of twelve ores onely, to passe over the sea againe unto Brundusium: the which he could not doe without great daunger, considering that all that sea was full of Pompeys shippes and armies. So he tooke shippe in the night apparelled like a slave, and went aborde upon this litle pynnase, and said never a word, as if he had bene some poore man of meane condicion. The pynnase laye in the

mouth of the river of Anius, the which commonly was wont to be very calme and quiet, by reason of a litle wind that came from the shore, which every morning drave backe the waves farre into the maine sea. But that night, by il fortune, there came a great wind from the sea that overcame the land wind, insomuch as the force and strength of the river fighting against the violence of the rage and waves of the sea, the encownter was marvailous daungerous, the water of the river being driven backe, and rebounding upward, with great noyse and daunger in turning of the water. Thereuppon the Maister of the pynnase seeing he could not possibly get out of the mouth of this river, bad the Maryners to cast about againe, and to returne against the streame. Cæsar hearing that, straight discovered him selfe unto the Maister of the pynnase, who at the first was amazed when he saw him. but Cæsar then taking him by the hand sayd unto him, Good fellow, be of good cheere, and forwardes hardily, feare not, for thou hast Cæsar and his fortune with thee. Then the Maryners forgetting the daunger of the storme they were in, laid on lode with ores, and labored for life what they could against the winde, to get out of the mouth of this river. But at length, perceiving they labored in vaine, and that the pynnase tooke in aboundance of water, and was ready to sincke: Cæsar then to his great griefe was driven to returne backe again. Who when he was returned unto his campe, his souldiers came in great companies unto him, and were very sory, that he mistrusted he was not able with them alone to overcome his enemies, but would put his person in daunger, to goe fetch them that were absent, putting no trust in them that were present. In the meane time Antonius arrived, and brought with him the rest of his armie from Brundusium. Then Cæsar finding him selfe strong enough, went and offered Pompey battel, who was passingly wel lodged, for vittelling of his campe both by sea and land. Cæsar on thother side, who had no great plenty of vittels at the first, was in a very hard case insomuch as his men gathered rootes, and mingled them with milke, and eate them. Furthermore, they did make breade of it also, and sometime when they skirmished with the enemies, and came alongest by them that watched and warded, they cast of their bread into their trenches, and sayd. that as longe as the earth brought forth such frutes, they would never leave beseeging of Pompey. But Pompey straightly commaunded them, that they should neither cary those words nor bread into their campe, fearing least his mens hartes would faile them, and that they would be affraid, when they should thinke of their enemies hardnes, with whome they had to fight, sithe they were weary with no paynes, no more then brute beastes. Cæsars men did daily skirmishe hard to the trenches of Pompeys campe. in the which Cæsar had ever the

5 · F

Cæsars armie
fled from
Pompey.

better, saving once only, at what tyme his men fled with
such feare, that all his campe that daye was in greate
hazarde to have beene caste awaye. For Pompey came on
with his battell apon them, and they were not able to abyde
it, but were fought with, and dryven into their campe,
and their trenches were filled with deade bodyes, which were
slayne within the very gate and bullwarkes of their campe,
they were so valiantly pursued. Cæsar stoode before them
that fledde, to make them to turne heade agayne: but he
coulde not prevayle. For when he woulde have taken the
ensignes to have stayed them, the ensigne bearers threw
them downe on the grounde: so that the enemyes tooke two
and thirtye of them, and Cæsars selfe also scaped hardely with
lyfe. For stryking a greate bigge souldier that fledde by
him, commaunding him to staye, and turne his face to his
enemie: the souldier beeing affrayde, lift uppe his sworde to
stryke at Cæsar. But one of Cæsars Pages preventing him,
gave him suche a blowe with his sworde, that he strake of
his showlder. Cæsar that daye was brought unto so greate
extremitie, that (if Pompey had not eyther for feare, or
spytefull fortune, left of to followe his victorie, and retyred
into his campe, beeing contented to have dryven his enemyes
into their campe) returning to his campe with his friendes,
he sayde unto them: The victorie this daye had beene our
enemies, if they had had a Captayne, that coulde have tolde
howe to have overcome. So when he was come to his lodging,
he went to bedde, and that nyght troubled him more, then
any nyght that ever he had. For still his mynde ranne with
great sorowe of the fowle faulte he had committed in leading
of his armie, of selfe will to remaine there so longe by the
sea side, his enemies being the stronger by sea: considering
that he had before him a goodly contrie, riche and plentifull
of all thinges, and goodly cities of Macedon and Thessaly, and
had not the witte to bringe the warre from thence, but to
lose his tyme in a place, where he was rather beseeged of his
enemyes for lacke of vittells, then that he did beseege them by
force of armes. Thus, fretting and chafing to see him selfe
so strayghted with vittells, and to thinke of his yll lucke,
he raysed his campe, intending to goe sette uppon Scipio,

Cæsars
wordes of
Pompeys
victory.

Cæsar
troubled in
mind, after
his losse.

making accompt, that either he should drawe Pompey to battell against his will, when he had not the sea at his backe to furnish him with plentye of vittells: or els that he should easily overcome Scipio, finding him alone, unles he were ayded. This remove of Cæsars campe, did much encourage Pompeys armie and his captaines, who would needes in any case have followed after him, as though he had bene overcome, and had fled. But for Pompey him selfe, he would in no respect hazard battell, which was a matter of so great importance. For finding him selfe wel provided of all thinges necessary to tary tyme, he thought it better to drawe this warre out in length, by tract of time, the rather to consume this litle strength that remayned in Cæsars armie: of the which, the best men were marveilous well trayned and good souldiers, and for valiantnes, at one daies battell, were incomparable. But on thother side againe, to remove here and there so ofte, and to fortifie their campe where they came, and to beseege any wall, or to keepe watch all night in their armor: the most part of them could not doe it, by reason of their age, beeing then unable to away with that paynes, so that the weakenes of their bodies did also take away the life and courage of their hartes. Furthermore, there fell a pestilent disease amonge them that came by ill meates hunger drave them to eate: yet was not this the worst. For besides, he had no store of money, neither could tell how to come by vittells: so that it semed in all likelihood, that in very short tyme he would come to nothing. For these respectes, Pompey would in no case fight, and yet had he but Cato onely of his minde in that, who stucke in it the rather, bicause he would avoyde sheding of his contry mens bloode. For when Cato had viewed the deade bodies slayne in the campe of his enemies, at the last skirmish that was betweene them, the which were no lesse then a thowsand persons: he covered his face, and went away weeping. All other but he, contrarily fell out with him, and blamed him, bycause he so long refrayned from battell: and some prickt him forward, and called him Agamemnon, and king of kinges, saying, that he delayed this warre in this sort, bicause he would not leave his authoritie to commaund them

Pompey
called Agamemnon, and
king of kings.

all, and that he was glad alwaies to see so many Captaines round about him, which came to his lodging to honor him, and waite upon him. And Faonius also, a harebraynd fellowe, frantykly counterfeating the round and playne speeche of Cato, made as though he was marvailous angry, and sayd: Is it not great pitie, that we shall not eate this yeare of Tusculum figges, and all for Pompeys ambicious minde to raigne alone? and Afranius, who not long before was but lately come out of Spayne, (where, bicause he had but ill successe, he was accused of treason, that for money he had solde his armie unto Cæsar:) he went busily asking, why they fought not with that Marchant, unto whom they sayde he had solde the province of Spayne? So that Pompey with these kinde of speeches, against his will, was driven to followe Cæsar, to fight with him. Then was Cæsar at the first, marvailously perplexed, and troubled by the waye: bicause he founde none that would give him any vittells, beeing despised of every man, for the late losse and overthrowe he had receyved. But after that he had taken the citie of

Gomphes in Thessaly, he did not onely meete with plentie of vittells to relieve his armie with: but he straungely also did ridde them of their disease. For the souldiers meeting with plentie of wyne, drinking harde, and making mery: drave awaye the infection of the pestilence. For they disposed them selves unto dauncing, masking, and playing the Baccherians by the waye: insomuch that drinking droncke they overcame their disease, and made their bodies newe agayne. When they both came into the contry of Pharsalia, and both campes laye before thother: Pompey returned agayne to his former determination, and the rather, bicause he had

ill signes and tokens of misfortune in his sleepe. For he thought in his sleepe that when he entred into the Theater, all the Romanes receyved him with great clapping of handes.

Whereuppon, they that were about him grewe to suche boldnes and securitie, assuring them selves of victorie: that Domitius, Spinther, and Scipio, in a bravery contended betweene them selves, for the chiefe Bishoppricke which Cæsar had. Furthermore, there were divers that sent unto Rome to hyre the nearest houses unto the market place, as

beeing the fittest places for Prætors, and Consuls : making
their accompt already, that those offices could not scape
them, incontinently after the warres. But besides those,
the younge gentlemen, and Romane knightes were marvelous
desirous to fight, that were bravely mounted, and armed
with glistering gilt armors, their horses fat and very finely
kept, and them selves goodly young men, to the number
of seven thowsand, where the gentlemen of Cæsars side, were
but one thowsand onely. The number of his footemen also
were much after the same reckoning. For he had five and
forty thowsand against two and twenty thowsand. Wherefore Cæsar called his souldiers together, and told them how
Cornificius was at hande, who brought two whole legions,
and that he had fifteene ensignes led by Calenus, the which
he made to stay about Megara and Athens. Then he asked
them if they would tary for that ayde or not, or whether
they would rather them selves alone venter battell. The
souldiers cryed out to him, and prayed him not to deferre
battell, but rather to devise some fetche to make the enemy
fight assoone as he could. Then as he sacrificed unto the
gods, for the purifying of his armie : the first beast was no
sooner sacrificed, but his Soothsayer assured him that he
should fight within three dayes. Cæsar asked him againe,
if he saw in the sacrifices, any lucky signe, or token of good
lucke. The Soothsayer aunswered, For that, thou shalt
aunswer thy selfe, better then I can doe : for the gods doe
promise us a marvelous great chaunge, and alteracion of
thinges that are now, unto an other cleane contrary. For if
thou beest wel now, doest thou thinke to have worse fortune
hereafter ? and if thou be ill, assure thy self thou shalt have
better. The night before the battell, as he went about
midnight to visite the watch, men saw a great firebrand in
the element, all of a light fire, that came over Cæsars campe,
and fell downe in Pompeys. In the morning also when they
releeved the watche, they heard a false alarom in the enemies
campe, without any apparant cause : which they commonly
call, a sodaine feare, that makes men besides them selves.
This notwithstanding, Cæsar thought not to fight that day,
but was determined to have raised his camp from thence, and

to have gone towards the citie of Scotusa: and his tents in his campe were already overthrowen when his skowtes came in with great speede, to bringe him newes that his enemies were preparing them selves to fight. Then he was very glad, and after he had made his prayers unto the gods to helpe him that day, he set his men in battell ray, and devided

Cæsars armie
and his order
of battell, in
the fieldes of
Pharsalia.

them into three squadrons: giving the middle battell unto Domitius Calvinus, and the left winge unto Antonius, and placed him selfe in the right winge, choosing his place to fight in the tenth legion. But seeing that against that, his enemies had set all their horsemen: he was halfe affraid when he saw the great number of them, and so brave besides. Wherefore he closely made six ensignes to come from the rerewarde of his battell, whom he had layd as an ambushe behind his right winge, having first appointed his souldiers what they should do, when the horsemen of the enemies came to give them charge. On thother side, Pompey placed

him self in the right winge of his battell, gave the left winge unto Domitius, and the middle battell unto Scipio his father in law. Now all the Romane knightes (as we have told you before) were placed in the left winge, of purpose to envyrone Cæsars right wing behinde, and to give their hottest charge there, where the generall of their enemies was: making their accompt, that there was no squadron of footemen how thicke soever they were, that could receive the charge of so great a trowpe of horsemen, and that at the first onset, they should overthrow them all, and marche upon their bellies. When the trompets on either side did sound the alarom to the

battell, Pompey commaunded his footemen that they should stande still without sturring, to receyve the charge of their enemies, untill they came to throwing of their darts. Wherefore Cæsar afterwardes sayde, that Pompey had committed a fowle faulte, not to consider that the charge which is given ronning with furie, besides that it giveth the more strength also unto their blowes, doth sette mens hartes also a fire: for the common hurling of all the souldiers that ronne together, is unto them as a boxe of the eare that settes men a fire. Then Cæsar making his battell marche forwarde to give the onsette, sawe one of his Captaines (a valiant man, and very

46

skillfull in warre, in whome he had also greate confidence) speaking to his souldiers that he had under his charge, encouraging them to fight lyke men that daye. So he called him alowde by his name, and sayde unto him: Well, Caius Crassinius, what hope shall we have to day? how are we determined, to fight it out manfully? Then Crassinius casting up his hand, aunswered him alowd: This day, O Cæsar, we shall have a noble victory, and I promise thee ere night thou shalt prayse me alyve or dead. When he had told him so, he was him selfe the foremost man that gave charge upon his enemies, with his band following of him, beeing about six score men, and making a lane through the foremost ranckes, with great slaughter he entred farre into the battell of his enemies: untill that valiantly fighting in this sort, he was thrust in at length in the mouth with a sworde, that the poynt of it came out agayne at his necke. Nowe the footemen of both battells being come to the sworde, the horsemen of the left winge of Pompey, did marche as fiercely also, spreading out their trowpes, to compasse in the right winge of Cæsars battell. But before they beganne to give charge, the six ensignes of footemen which Cæsar had layed in ambushe behinde him, they beganne to runne full apon them, not throwing away their dartes farre of as they were wont to doe, neyther striking their enemies on the thighes nor on the legges, but to seeke to hit them full in the eyes, and to hurt them in the face, as Cæsar had taught them. For he hoped that these lusty younge gentlemen that had not bene often in the warres, nor were used to see them selves hurt, and the which, beeing in the pryme of their youth and beautie, would be affrayd of those hurtes, aswell for the feare of the present daunger to be slayne, as also for that their faces should not for ever be deformed. As in deede it came to passe, for they coulde never abyde that they shoulde come so neare their faces, with the poyntes of their dartes, but honge downe their heades for feare to be hitte with them in their eyes, and turned their backes, covering their face, bicause they shoulde not be hurt. Then, breaking of them selves, they beganne at length cowardly to flye, and were occasion also of the losse of all the rest of

The battell in the fieldes of Pharsalia.

Cæsars stratageme.

47

Pompeys armie. For they that had broken them, ranne immediatly to sette upon the squadron of the footemen behind, and slue them. Then Pompey seeing his horsemen from the other winge of his battell, so scattered and dispersed, flying away: forgate that he was any more Pompey the great which he had bene before, but rather was like a man whose wittes the goddes had taken from him, being affrayde and amazed with the slaughter sent from above, and so retyred into his tent speaking never a worde, and sate there to see the ende of this battell. Untill at length all his army beeing overthrowen, and put to flight, the enemies came, and gotte up upon the rampers and defence of his campe, and fought hande to hande with them that stoode to defende the same. Then as a man come to him selfe agayne, he spake but this onely worde: What, even into our campe? So in

haste, casting of his coate armor and apparell of a generall, he shifted him, and put on such, as became his miserable fortune, and so stale out of his campe. Furthermore, what he did after this overthrowe, and howe he had put him selfe into the handes of the Ægyptians, by whome he was miserably slayne: we have sette it forthe at large in his life. Then Cæsar entring into Pompeys campe, and seeing the bodies layed on the grounde that were slayne, and others also that were a killing, sayde, fetching a great sighe: It was their owne doing, and against my will. For Caius Cæsar, after he had wonne so many famous conquests, and overcome so many great battells, had beene utterly condemned notwithstanding, if he had departed from his armie. Asinius Pollio writeth, that he spake these wordes then in Latyn, which he after-wards wrote in Greeke, and sayeth furthermore, that the moste parte of them which were put to the sworde in the campe, were slaves and bondmen, and that there were not slayne in all at this battell, above six thowsand souldiers. As for them that were taken prisoners, Cæsar did put many of them amongest his legions, and did pardon also many men of

estimation, amonge whome Brutus was one, that afterwardes slue Cæsar him selfe: and it is reported, that Cæsar was very sory for him, when he could not immediatly be founde after the battell, and that he rejoyced againe, when he knewe he was alyve, and that he came to yeelde him selfe unto him. Cæsar had many signes and tokens of victorie before this battell: but the notablest of all other that hapned to him, was in the citie of Tralles. For in the temple of victorie, within the same citie, there was an image of Cæsar, and the earth all about it very hard of it selfe, and was paved besides with hard stone: and yet some say that there sprange uppe a palme hard by the base of the same image. In the citie of Padua, Caius Cornelius an excellent Soothsayer, (a contry man and friende of Titus Livius the Historiographer) was by chaunce at that time set to beholde the flying of birdes. He (as Livie reporteth) knewe the very tyme when the battell beganne, and tolde them that were present, Even now they gave the onset on both sides, and both armies do meete at this instant. Then sitting downe againe to consider of the birdes, after he had bethought him of the signes: he sodainely rose up on his feete, and cryed out as a man possessed with some spirit, Oh, Cæsar, the victory is thine. Every man wondring to see him, he tooke the crowne he had on his heade, and made an othe that he would never put it on againe, till the event of his prediction had proved his arte true. Livie testifieth, that it so came to passe. Cæsar afterwards giving freedom unto the Thessalians, in respect of the victory which he wanne in their contry, he followed after Pompey. When he came into Asia, he gave freedom also unto the Guidians for Theopompus sake, who had gathered the fables together. He did release Asia also, the thirde part of the tribute which the inhabitants payd unto the Romanes. Then he came into Alexandria, after Pompey was slaine: and detested Theodotus, that presented him Pompeys heade, and turned his head at toe side bicause he would not see it. Notwithstanding, he tooke his seale, and beholding it, wept. Furthermore, he curteously used all Pompeys friendes and familiers, who wandring up and downe the contry, were taken of the king of Ægypt, and wanne them all to be at his commaundement. Continuing these curtesies, he wrote unto his friendes at Rome, that the greatest pleasure he tooke of his victorie, was, that he dayly saved the lives of some of his contry men that bare armes

5 . G   49

against him. And for the warre he made in Alexandria, some say, he needed not have done it, but that he willingly did it for the love of Cleopatra: wherein he wanne litle honor, and besides did put his person in great daunger. Others doe lay the fault upon the king of Ægypts Ministers, but specially on Pothinus the Euenuke, who bearing the greatest swaye of all the kinges servaunts, after he had caused Pompey to be slaine, and driven Cleopatra from the Court, secretly layd waite all the wayes he could, how he might likewise kill Cæsar. Wherefore Cæsar hearing an inckling of it, beganne thenceforth to spend all the night long in feasting and bancketing, that his person might be in the better safetie. But besides all this, Pothinus the Euenuke spake many thinges openly not to be borne, onely to shame Cæsar, and to stirre up the people to envie him. For he made his souldiers have the worst and oldest wheate that could be gotten: then if they did complayne of it, he told them, they must be contented, seeing they eate at anothers mans coste. And he would serve them also at the table in treene and earthen dishes, saying, that Cæsar had away all their gold and silver, for a debt that the kings father (that then raigned) did owe unto him: which was, a thowsand seven hundred and fiftie Miriades, whereof Cæsar had before forgiven seven hundred and fiftie thowsand unto his children. Howbeit then he asked a Myllion to paye his souldiours withall. Thereto Pothinus aunswered him, that at that tyme he should doe better to follow his other causes of greater importance, and afterwardes that he should at more leysure recover his dette, with the kinges good will and favor. Cæsar replyed unto him, and sayd, that he would not aske counsell of the Ægyptians for his affayres, but would be payd: and thereupon secretly sent for Cleopatra which was in the contry to come unto him. She onely taking Apollodorus Sicilian of all her friendes, tooke a litle bote, and went away with him in it in the night, and came and landed hard by the foote of the castell. Then having no other meane to come in to the court, without being knowen, she laid her selfe downe upon a mattresse or flockbed, which Apollodorus her frend tied and bound up together like a bundel with a

50

great leather thong, and so tooke her up on his backe, and brought her thus hamperd in this fardell unto Cæsar, in at the castell gate. This was the first occasion, (as it is reported) that made Cæsar to love her: but afterwards, when he sawe her sweete conversation and pleasaunt entertainment, he fell then in further liking with her, and did reconcile her again unto her brother the king, with condition, that they two joyntly should raigne together. Apon this newe reconciliation, a great feast being prepared, a slave of Cæsars that was his barber, the fearefullest wretch that lived, stil busily prying and listening abroad in every corner, being mistrustfull by nature: found that Pothinus and Achillas did lie in waite to kill his Maister Cæsar. This beeing proved unto Cæsar, he did sette such sure watch about the hall, where the feaste was made, that in fine, he slue the Euenuke Pothinus him selfe. Achillas on thother side, saved him selfe, and fled unto the kinges campe, where he raysed a marvelous daungerous and difficult warre for Cæsar: bicause he having then but a few men about him as he had, he was to fight against a great and strong city. The first daunger he fell into, was for the lacke of water he had: for that his enemies had stopped the mouth of the pipes, the which conveyed the water unto the castell. The seconde daunger he had, was, that seeing his enemies came to take his shippes from him, he was driven to repulse that daunger with fire, the which burnt the arsenall where the shippes lay, and that notable librarie of Alexandria withall. The third The great library of Alexandria burnt. daunger was in the battell by sea, that was fought by the tower of Phar: where meaning to helpe his men that fought by sea, he lept from the peere, into a boate. Then the Ægyptians made towardes him with their owers, on everie side: but he leaping into the sea, with great hazard saved him selfe by swimming. It is sayd, that then holding divers Cæsars swimming with bookes in his hand. bookes in his hand, he did never let them go, but kept them alwayes upon his head above water, and swamme with the other hand, notwithstanding that they shot marvelously at him, and was driven somtime to ducke into the water: howbeit the boate was drowned presently. In fine, the king comming to his men that made warre with Cæsar, he went

IULIUS
CÆSAR
Cæsar made
Cleopatra
Queene of
Ægypt.
Cæsarion,
Cæsars sonne,
begotten of
Cleopatra.

against him, and gave him battell, and wanne it with great slaughter, and effusion of blood. But for the king, no man could ever tell what became of him after. Thereuppon Cæsar made Cleopatra his sister, Queene of Ægypt, who being great with childe by him, was shortly brought to bedde of a sonne, whom the Alexandrians named Cæsarion. From thence he went into Syria, and so going into Asia, there it was told him that Domitius was overthrowen in battell, by Pharnaces, the sonne of king Mithridates, and was fled out of the realme of Ponte, with a few men with him: and that this king Pharnaces greedily following his victorie, was not contented with the winning of Bithynia, and Cappadocia, but further would needes attempt to winne Armenia the lesse, procuring all those kinges, Princes, and Governors of the provinces thereabouts, to rebell against the Romanes. Thereupon Cæsar went thither straight with three legions, and fought a great battell with king Pharnaces, by the citie of Zela, where he slue his armie, and drave him out of all the realme of Ponte. And bicause he would advertise one of his frendes of the sodainnes of this victorie, he onely wrote three words unto Anitius at Rome: *Veni, Vidi, Vici*: to wit, I came, I saw, I overcame. These three wordes ending all with like sound and letters in the Latin, have a certaine short grace, more pleasaunt to the eare, then can be well expressed in any other tongue. After this, he returned againe into Italie, and came to Rome, ending his yeare for the which he was made Dictator the seconde time, which office before was never graunted for one whole yeare, but unto him. Then he was chosen Consul for the yeare following. Afterwardes he was very ill spoken of, for that his souldiers in a mutine having slaine two Prætors, Cosconius, and Galba, he gave them no other punishment for it, but in steade of calling them souldiers, he named them citizens, and gave unto every one of them a thowsand Drachmas a man, and great possessions in Italie. He was much misliked also for the desperate parts and madnes of Dolabella, for the covetousnes of Anitius, for the dronkennes of Antonius and Cornificius, which made Pompeys house be pulled downe and builded up againe, as a thing not bigge

Cæsars victorie of king Pharnaces.

Cæsar wryteth three wordes to certifie his victory.

52

enough for him, wherewith the Romanes were maruelously offended. Cæsar knew all this well enough, and would have bene contented to have redressed them: but to bring his matters to passe he pretended, he was driven to serve his turne by such instrumentes. After the battell of Pharsalia, Cato and Scipio being fled into Africke, king Iuba joyned with them, and leauied a great puisant army. Wherefore Cæsar determined to make warre with them, and in the middest of winter, he tooke his jorney into Sicile. There, bicause he would take all hope from his Captaines and souldiers to make any long abode there, he went and lodged upon the very sandes by the sea side, and with the next gale of winde that came, he tooke the sea with three thowsand footemen, and a few horsemen. Then having put them a land, unwares to them, he hoysed sayle againe, to goe fetche the rest of his armie, being afrayed least they should meete with some daunger in passing over, and meeting them midde way, he brought them all into his campe. Where, when it was tolde him that his enemies trusted in an auncient Oracle, which sayd, that it was predestined unto the family of the Scipioes to be conquerors in Africke either of purpose to mocke Scipio the Generall of his enemies, or otherwise in good earnest to take the benefit of this name (geven by the Oracle) unto him selfe, in all the skirmishes and battells he fought, he gave the charge of his army, unto a man of meane quality and accompt, called Scipio Sallutius, who came of the race of Scipio African, and made him always his Generall when he fought. For he was eftsoones compelled to weary and harrie his enemies: for that neither his men in his campe had corne enough, nor his beastes forrage, but the souldiers were driven to take sea weedes, called Alga: and (washing away the brackishnes thereof with fresh water, putting to it a litle erbe called dogges tooth) to cast it so to their horse to eate. For the Numidians (which are light horsemen, and very ready of service) being a great number together, would be on a sodaine in every place, and spred all the fieldes over thereabout, so that no man durst peepe out of the campe to goe for forrage. And one day as the men of armes were staying to

IULIUS CÆSAR

Cæsars jorney into Africke, against Cato and Scipio.

Cæsars troubles in Africke

Alga, and dogges tooth, geven to the horse to eate

Cæsars daungers in Africke

53

beholde an African doing notable thinges in dauncing, and playing with the flute: they being set downe quietly to take their pleasure of the viewe thereof, having in the meane time geven their slaves their horses to hold, the enemies stealing sodainly upon them, compassed them in round about, and slue a number of them in the field, and chasing the other also that fled, followed them pell mell into their campe. Furthermore had not Cæsar him selfe in person, and Asinius Pollio with him gone out of the campe to the rescue, and stayed them that fled: the warre that day had bene ended. There was also an other skirmish where his enemies had the upper hande, in the which it is reported, that Cæsar taking the ensigne bearer by the coller that caried the Eagle in his hande, stayed him by force, and turning his face, tolde him: See, there be thy enemies. These advantages did lift up Scipioes hart aloft, and gave him corage to hazard battell: and leaving Afranius on the one hand of him, and king Iuba on the other hande, both their campes lying neere to other, he did fortifie him selfe by the citie of Thapsacus, above the lake, to be a safe refuge for them all in this battell. But whilest he was busie intrenching of him selfe, Cæsar having marvelous speedily passed through a great contrie full of wod, by bypathes which men would never have mistrusted: he stale upon some behinde, and sodainly assailed the other before, so that he overthrewe them all, and made them flie. Then following this first good happe he had, he went forthwith to set apon the campe of Afranius, the which he tooke at the first onset, and the campe of the Numidians also, king

Iuba being fled. Thus in a litle peece of the day only, he tooke three campes, and slue fifty thowsand of his enemies, and lost but fifty of his souldiers. In this sorte is set downe theffect of this battell by some wryters. Yet others doe wryte also, that Cæsar selfe was not there in person at thexecution of this battell. For as he did set his men

in battell ray, the falling sickenesse tooke him, whereunto he was geven, and therefore feeling it comming, before he was overcome withall, he was caried into a castell not farre from thence, where the battell was fought, and there tooke his rest till thextremity of his disease had left him. Now, for the Prætors and Consulls that scaped from this battell, many of them being taken prisoners, did kill them selves, and others also Cæsar did put to death: but he being specially desirous of all men else to have Cato alive in his hands, he went with all possible speede unto the citie of Utica, whereof Cato was Governor, by meanes whereof he was not at the battell. Notwithstanding being certified by the way that Cato had slaine him selfe with his owne handes, he then made open shew that he was very sorry for it, but why or wherfore, no man could tell. But this is true, that Cæsar sayd at that present time: O Cato, I envy thy death, bicause thou diddest envy my glory, to save thy life. This notwithstanding, the booke that he wrote afterwardes against Cato being dead, did shew no very great affection nor pitiefull hart towardes him. For how could he have pardoned him, if living he had had him in his handes: that being dead did speake so vehemently against him? Notwithstanding, men suppose he would have pardoned him, if he had taken him alive, by the clemencie he shewed unto Cicero, Brutus, and divers others that had borne armes against him. Some reporte, that he wrote that booke, not so much for any private malice he had to his death, as for a civil ambition, apon this occasion. Cicero had written a booke in praise of Cato, which he intituled, *Cato.* This booke in likelyhoode was very well liked of, by reason of the eloquence of the Orator that made it, and of the excellent subject thereof. Cæsar therewith was marvelously offended, thinking that to praise him, of whose death he was author, was even as much as to accuse him self: and therfore he wrote a letter against him, and heaped up a number of accusations against Cato, and intituled the booke *Anticaton.* Both these bookes have favorers unto this day, some defending the one for the love they bare to Cæsar, and others allowing the other for Catoes sake. Cæsar being now returned out of Africke, first of all made an oration to the people, wherein he greatly praised and commended this his last victorie, declaring unto them, that he had conquered so many contries unto the Empire of Rome, that he coulde furnishe the common wealth yearely, with two hundred thowsande busshells of wheate, and twenty hundred thow-

Right margin notes:

IULIUS CÆSAR

Cæsar was sory for the death of Cato.

Cæsar wrote against Cato being dead.

Cicero wrote a booke in praise of Cato being dead.

55

sand pound weight of oyle.   Then he made three triumphes, the one for Ægypt, the other for the kingdom of Ponte, and the third for Africke: not bicause he had overcome Scipio there, but king Iuba.   Whose sonne being likewise called Iuba, being then a young boy, was led captive in the showe of this triumphe.   But this his imprisonment fel out happily for him: for where he was but a barbarous Numidian, by the study he fell unto when he was prisoner, he came afterwards to be reckoned one of the wisest historiographers of the Græcians.   After these three triumphes ended, he very liberally rewarded his souldiers, and to curry favor with the people, he made great feasts and common sportes.   For he feasted all the Romanes at one time, at two and twenty thowsand tables, and gave them the pleasure to see divers sword players to fight at the sharpe, and battells also by sea, for the remembraunce of his daughter Iulia, which was dead long afore.   Then after all these sportes, he made the people (as the manner was) to be mustered: and where there were at the last musters before, three hundred and twenty thowsande citizens, at this muster only there were but a hundred and fifty thowsand.   Such misery and destruction had this civill warre brought unto the common wealth of Rome, and had consumed such a number of Romanes, not speaking at all of the mischieves and calamities it had brought unto all the rest of Italie, and to the other provinces pertaining to Rome.   After all these thinges were ended, he was chosen Consul the fourth time, and went into Spayne to make warre with the sonnes of Pompey: who were yet but very young, but had notwithstanding raised a marvelous great army together, and shewed to have had manhoode and corage worthie to commaunde such an armie, insomuch as they put Cæsar him selfe in great daunger of his life.   The greatest battell that was fought betwene them in all this warre, was by the citie of Munda.   For then Cæsar seeing his men sorely distressed, and having their hands full of their enemies: he ranne into the prease among his men that fought, and cried out unto them: What, are ye not ashamed to be beaten and taken prisoners, yeelding your selves with your owne handes to these young boyes?

Iuba, the sonne of king Iuba, a famous historiographer.

Cæsars feasting of the Romanes.

The muster taken of the Romanes.

Cæsar Consull the fourth time.

Battell fought betwixt Cæsar and the young Pompeyes, by the city of Munda.

56

And so, with all the force he could make, having with much
a doe put his enemies to flight: he slue above thirty thowsand
of them in the fielde, and lost of his owne men a thowsand of
the best he had. After this battell he went into his tent,
and told his frends, that he had often before fought for
victory, but this last time now, that he had fought for the
safety of his owne life. He wanne this battell on the very
feast day of the Bacchanalians, in the which men say, that
Pompey the great went out of Rome, about foure yeares
before, to beginne this civill warre. For his sonnes, the
younger scaped from the battell: but within few dayes
after, Diddius brought the heade of the elder. This was
the last warre that Cæsar made. But the triumphe he made
into Rome for the same, did as much offend the Romanes,
and more, then any thing that ever he had done before:
bicause he had not overcome Captaines that were straungers,
nor barbarous kinges, but had destroyed the sonnes of the
noblest man in Rome, whom fortune had overthrowen. And
bicause he had plucked up his race by the rootes, men did
not thinke it meete for him to triumphe so, for the calamities
of his contrie, rejoycing at a thing for the which he had but
one excuse to alleage in his defence, unto the gods and men:
that he was compelled to doe that he did. And the rather
they thought it not meete, bicause he had never before sent
letters nor messengers unto the common wealth at Rome,
for any victorie that he had ever wonne in all the civill
warres: but did alwayes for shame refuse the glorie of it.
This notwithstanding, the Romanes inclining to Cæsars prosperity, and taking the bit in the mouth, supposing that to
be ruled by one man alone, it would be a good meane for
them to take breth a litle, after so many troubles and
miseries as they had abidden in these civill warres: they
chose him perpetuall Dictator. This was a plaine tyranny:
for to this absolute power of Dictator, they added this,
never to be affraied to be deposed. Cicero propounded
before the Senate, that they should geve him such honors,
as were meete for a man: howbeit others afterwardes added
to, honors beyonde all reason. For, men striving who shoulde
most honor him, they made him hatefull and troublesome

IULIUS
CÆSAR

Cæsars victory
of the sonnes
of Pompey.

Cæsars
triumphe
of Pompeis
sonnes.

Cæsar
Dictator
perpetuall.

to them selves that most favored him, by reason of the
unmeasurable greatnes and honors which they gave him.
Thereuppon, it is reported, that even they that most hated
him, were no lesse favorers and furtherers of his honors, then
they that most flattered him: bicause they might have greater
occasions to rise, and that it might appeare they had just
cause and colour to attempt that they did against him. And
now for him selfe, after he had ended his civill warres, he
did so honorably behave him selfe, that there was no fault
to be founde in him: and therefore me thinkes, amongest

The temple
of clemency,
dedicated
unto Cæsar,
for his
curtesie.

other honors they gave him, he rightly deserved this, that
they should builde him a temple of clemency, to thanke him
for his curtesie he had used unto them in his victorie. For
he pardoned many of them that had borne armes against
him, and furthermore, did preferre some of them to honor

Cassius and
Brutus
Prætors

and office in the common wealth: as amongest others, Cassius
and Brutus, both the which were made Prætors. And where
Pompeys images had bene throwen downe, he caused them
to be set up againe: whereupon Cicero sayd then, that Cæsar
setting up Pompeys images againe, he made his owne to
stand the surer. And when some of his frends did counsell
him to have a gard for the safety of his person, and some
also did offer them selves to serve him: he would never con-

Cæsars saying
of death.

sent to it, but sayd, it was better to dye once, then alwayes
to be affrayed of death. But to win him selfe the love and

Good will of
subjectes, the
best gard and
safety for
Princes.

good will of the people, as the honorablest gard and best
safety he could have: he made common feasts againe, and
generall distributions of corne. Furthermore, to gratifie the
souldiers also, he replenished many cities againe with inhabitantes, which before had bene destroyed, and placed them
there that had no place to repaire unto: of the which the
noblest and chiefest cities were these two, Carthage, and
Corinthe, and it chaunced so, that like as aforetime they
had bene both taken and destroyed together, even so were
they both set a foote againe, and replenished with people,
at one selfe time. And as for great personages, he wanne
them also, promising some of them, to make them Prætors
and Consulls in time to come, and unto others, honors and
preferrements, but to all men generally good hope, seeking

GRECIANS AND ROMANES

all the wayes he coulde to make everie man contented with
his raigne. Insomuch as one of the Consulls called Maximus,
chauncing to dye a day before his Consulshippe ended, he
declared Caninius Rebilius Consull onely for the day that
remained.   So, divers going to his house (as the manner was)
to salute him, and to congratulate with him of his calling and
preferrement, being newly chosen officer : Cicero pleasauntly
sayd, Come, let us make hast, and be gone thither, before
his Consulshippe come out.   Furthermore, Cæsar being borne
to attempt all great enterprises, and having an ambitious
desire besides to covet great honors : the prosperous good
successe he had of his former conquestes bred no desire in
him quietly to enjoy the frutes of his labours, but rather
gave him hope of thinges to come, still kindling more and
more in him, thoughts of greater enterprises, and desire of
new glory, as if that which he had present, were stale and
nothing worth. This humor of his was no other but an
emulation with him selfe as with an other man, and a
certaine contencion to overcome the thinges he prepared
to attempt.   For he was determined, and made preparacion
also, to make warre with the Persians.   Then when he had
overcome them, to passe through Hyrcania (compassing in
the sea Caspium, and mount Caucasus) into the realme of
Pontus, and so to invade Scythia : and overrunning all the
contries, and people adjoyning unto high Germany, and
Germany it selfe, at length to returne by Gaule into Italie,
and so to enlarge the Romane Empire round, that it might
be every way compassed in with the great sea Oceanum.
But whilest he was preparing for this voiage, he attempted
to cut the barre of the straight of Peloponnesus, in the
place where the city of Corinthe standeth.   Then he was
minded to bring the rivers of Anienes and Tiber, straight
from Rome, unto the citie of Circees, with a deepe channell
and high banckes cast up on either side, and so to fall into
the sea at Terracina, for the better safety and commodity of
the marchants that came to Rome to trafficke there. Furthermore, he determined to draine and seawe all the water of the
marisses betwext the cities of Nomentum and Setium, to make
it firme land, for the benefit of many thowsandes of people :

59

and on the sea coast next unto Rome, to cast great high bankes, and to clense all the haven about Ostia, of rockes and stones hidden under the water, and to take away all other impedimentes that made the harborough daungerous for shippes, and to make new havens and arsenalls meete to harbor such shippes, as did continually trafficke thither. All these thinges were purposed to be done, but tooke no effecte.

But, the ordinaunce of the kalender, and reformation of the yeare, to take away all confusion of time, being exactly calculated by the Mathematicians, and brought to perfection, was a great commoditie unto all men. For the Romanes using then the auncient computacion of the yeare, had not only such incertainty and alteracion of the moneth and times, that the sacrifices and yearely feasts came by litle and litle to seasons contrary for the purpose they were ordained: but also in the revolution of the sunne (which is called Annus Solaris) no other nation agreed with them in account: and of the Romanes them selves, only the priests understood it. And therefore when they listed, they sodainly (no man being able to controll them) did thrust in a moneth, above their ordinary number, which they called in old time, *Merce-

donius. Some say, that Numa Pompilius was the first, that devised this way, to put a moneth betwene: but it was a weake remedy, and did litle helpe the correction of the errors that were made in the account of the yeare, to frame them to perfection. But Cæsar committing this matter unto the Philosophers, and best expert Mathematicians at that time, did set foorth an excellent and perfect kalender, more exactly calculated, then any other that was before: the which the Romanes doe use untill this present day, and doe nothing erre as others, in the difference of time. But his enemies notwithstanding that envied his greatnes, did not sticke to finde fault withall. As Cicero the Orator, when one sayd, To morow the starre Lyra will rise: Yea, sayd he, at the commaundement of Cæsar, as if men were compelled so to say and thinke, by Cæsars edict. But the chiefest cause that

made him mortally hated, was the covetous desire he had to be called king: which first gave the people just cause, and next his secret enemies, honest colour to beare him ill will.

GRECIANS AND ROMANES

This notwithstanding, they that procured him this honor
and dignity, gave it out among the people, that it was
written in the Sybilline prophecies, how the Romanes might
overcome the Parthians, if they made warre with them, and
were led by a king, but otherwise that they were unconquer-
able. And furthermore they were so bold besides, that
Cæsar returning to Rome from the citie of Alba, when they
came to salute him, they called him king. But the people
being offended, and Cæsar also angry, he said he was not
called king, but Cæsar. Then every man keeping silence, he
went his way heavy and sorowfull. When they had decreed
divers honors for him in the Senate, the Consulls and Prætors
accompanied with the whole assembly of the Senate, went
unto him in the market place, where he was set by the pulpit
for orations, to tell him what honors they had decreed for
him in his absence. But he sitting still in his majesty, disdaining to rise up unto them when they came in, as if they
had bene private men, aunswered them : that his honors had
more neede to be cut of, then enlarged. This did not onely
offend the Senate, but the common people also, to see that
he should so lightly esteeme of the Magistrates of the common
wealth : insomuch as every man that might lawfully goe his
way, departed thence very sorrowfully. Thereupon also Cæsar
rising, departed home to his house, and tearing open his
doblet coller, making his necke bare, he cried out alowde to
his frendes, that his throte was readie to offer to any man
that would come and cut it. Notwithstanding, it is reported,
that afterwardes to excuse this folly, he imputed it to his
disease, saying, that their wittes are not perfit which have
his disease of the falling evil, when standing of their feete
they speake to the common people, but are soone troubled
with a trembling of their body, and a sodaine dimnes and
guidines. But that was not true. For he would have risen
up to the Senate, but Cornelius Balbus one of his frendes
(but rather a flatterer) would not let him, saying : What, doe
you not remember that you are Cæsar, and will you not let
them reverence you, and doe their dueties ? Besides these
occasions and offences, there followed also his shame and reproache, abusing the Tribunes of the people in this sorte.

61

IULIUS
CÆSAR
The feast
Lupercalia.

At that time, the feast Lupercalia was celebrated, the which in olde time men say was the feast of sheapheards or heard men, and is much like unto the feast of the Lycæians in Arcadia. But howesoever it is, that day there are divers noble mens sonnes, young men, (and some of them Magistrats them selves that governe then) which run naked through the city, striking in sport them they meete in their way, with leather thonges, heare and all on, to make them geve place. And many noble women, and gentle women also, goe of purpose to stand in their way, and doe put forth their handes to be striken, as schollers hold them out to their schoole-master, to be striken with the ferula: perswading them selves that being with childe, they shall have good deliverie, and also being barren, that it will make them to conceive with child. Cæsar sate to beholde that sport apon the pulpit for orations, in a chayer of gold, apparelled in triumphing

Antonius
being Consull,
was one of the
Lupercalians.

manner. Antonius, who was Consull at that time, was one of them that ranne this holy course. So when he came into the market place, the people made a lane for him to runne at libertie, and he came to Cæsar, and presented him a Diadeame

Antonius pre-
sented the
Diademe to
Cæsar.

wreathed about with laurell. Whereupon there rose a certaine crie of rejoycing, not very great, done onely by a few, appointed for the purpose. But when Cæsar refused the Diadeame, then all the people together made an outcrie of joy. Then Antonius offering it him againe, there was a second shoute of joy, but yet of a few. But when Cæsar refused it againe the second time, then all the whole people showted. Cæsar having made this proofe, found that the people did not like of it, and thereupon rose out of his chayer, and commaunded the crowne to be caried unto Iupiter in the Capitoll. After that, there were set up images of Cæsar in the city with Diadeames upon their heades, like kinges. Those, the two Tribunes, Flavius and Marullus, went and pulled downe: and furthermore, meeting with them that first saluted Cæsar as king, they committed them to prison. The people followed them rejoycing at it, and called them Brutes: bicause of Brutus, who had in old time driven the kings out of Rome, and that brought the kingdom of one person, unto the government of the Senate and people. Cæsar was so offended withall, that he deprived Marullus and Flavius of their Tribuneshippes, and accusing them, he spake also against the people, and called them Bruti, and Cumani, to witte, beastes, and fooles. Hereuppon the people went straight unto Marcus Brutus, who from his father came of the first Brutus, and by his mother, of the house of the Servilians, a noble house as any was in Rome, and was also nephew and sonne in law of Marcus Cato Notwithstanding, the great honors and favor Cæsar shewed unto him, kept him backe that of him selfe alone, he did not conspire nor consent to depose him of his kingdom. For Cæsar did not onely save his life, after the battell of Pharsalia when Pompey fled, and did at his request also save many more of his frendes besides: but furthermore, he put a marvelous confidence in him. For he had already preferred him to the Prætorshippe for that yeare, and furthermore was appointed to be Consul, the fourth yeare after that, having through Cæsars frendshippe, obtained it before Cassius, who likewise made sute for the same. and Cæsar also, as it is reported, sayd in this contention, In deede Cassius hath alleaged best reason, but yet shall he not be chosen before Brutus. Some one day accusing Brutus while he practised this conspiracy, Cæsar would not heare of it, but clapping his hande on his bodie, told them, Brutus will looke for this skinne· meaning thereby, that Brutus for his vertue, deserved to rule after him, but yet, that for ambitions sake, he woulde not shewe him selfe unthankefull nor dishonorable. Nowe they that desired chaunge, and wished Brutus only their Prince and Governour above all other. they durst not come to him them selves to tell him what they woulde have him to doe, but in the night did cast sundrie papers into the Prætors seate where he gave audience, and the most of them to this effect: Thou sleepest Brutus, and art not Brutus in deede Cassius finding Brutus ambition sturred up the more by these seditious billes, did pricke him forwarde, and egge him on the more, for a private quarrell he had conceived against Cæsar the circumstance whereof, we have sette downe more at large in Brutus life. Cæsar also had Cassius in great gelouzie, and suspected him much; whereuppon he sayd on

IULIUS CÆSAR

Cæsar saved Marcus Brutus life, after the battell of Pharsalia.

Brutus conspireth against Cæsar

Cassius stirreth up Brutus against Cæsar.

63

a time to his frendes, What will Cassius doe, thinke ye? I like not his pale lookes. An other time when Cæsars frendes complained unto him of Antonius, and Dolabella, that they pretended some mischiefe towardes him: he aunswered them againe, As for those fatte men and smooth comed heades, quoth he, I never reckon of them: but these pale visaged and carian leane people, I feare them most, meaning Brutus and Cassius. Certainly, destenie may easier be foreseene, then avoyded: considering the straunge and wonderfull signes that were sayd to be seene before Cæsars death. For, touching the fires in the element, and spirites running up and downe in the night, and also these solitarie birdes to be seene at noone dayes sittinge in the great market place: are not all these signes perhappes worth the noting, in such a wonderfull chaunce as happened? But Strabo the Philosopher wryteth, that divers men were seene going up and downe in fire: and furthermore, that there was a slave of the souldiers, that did cast a marvelous burning flame out of his hande, insomuch as they that saw it, thought he had bene burnt, but when the fire was out, it was found he had no hurt. Cæsar selfe also doing sacrifice unto the goddes, found that one of the beastes which was sacrificed had no hart: and that was a straunge thing in nature, how a beast could live without a hart. Furthermore, there was a certaine Sooth-sayer that had geven Cæsar warning long time affore, to take heede of the day of the Ides of Marche, (which is the fifteenth of the moneth) for on that day he shoulde be in great daunger. That day being come, Cæsar going unto the Senate house, and speaking merily to the Soothsayer, tolde him, The Ides of Marche be come: So be they, softly aunswered the Sooth-sayer, but yet are they not past. And the very day before, Cæsar supping with Marcus Lepidus, sealed certaine letters as he was wont to do at the bord: so talke falling out amongest them, reasoning what death was best: he prevent-ing their opinions, cried out alowde, Death unlooked for. Then going to bedde the same night as his manner was, and lying with his wife Calpurnia, all the windowes and dores of his chamber flying open, the noyse awooke him, and made him affrayed when he saw such light: but more, when he

Cæsars day
of his death
prognosti-
cated by a
Soothsayer.

64

heard his wife Calpurnia, being fast a sleepe, weepe and sigh, and put forth many fumbling lamentable speaches. For she dreamed that Cæsar was slaine, and that she had him in her armes. Others also doe denie that she had any suche dreame, as amongest other, Titus Livius wryteth, that it was in this sorte. The Senate having set upon the toppe of Cæsars house, for an ornament and setting foorth of the same, a certaine pinnacle: Calpurnia dreamed that she sawe it broken downe, and that she thought she lamented and wept for it. Insomuch that Cæsar rising in the morning, she prayed him if it were possible, not to goe out of the dores that day, but to adjorne the session of the Senate, untill an other day. And if that he made no reckoning of her dreame, yet that he woulde searche further of the Soothsayers by their sacrifices, to knowe what should happen him that day. Thereby it seemed that Cæsar likewise did feare and suspect somewhat, bicause his wife Calpurnia untill that time, was never geven to any feare or supersticion: and then, for that he saw her so troubled in minde with this dreame she had. But much more afterwardes, when the Soothsayers having sacrificed many beastes one after an other, tolde him that none did like them: then he determined to sende Antonius to adjorne the session of the Senate. But in the meane time came Decius Brutus, surnamed Albinus, in whom Cæsar put such confidence, that in his last will and testament he had appointed him to be his next heire, and yet was of the conspiracie with Cassius and Brutus: he fearing that if Cæsar did adjorne the session that day, the conspiracie woulde out, laughed the Soothsayers to scorne, and reproved Cæsar, saying: that he gave the Senate occasion to mislike with him, and that they might thinke he mocked them, considering that by his commaundement they were assembled, and that they were readie willingly to graunt him all thinges, and to proclaime him king of all the provinces of the Empire of Rome out of Italie, and that he should weare his Diadeame in all other places, both by sea and land. And furthermore, that if any man should tell them from him, they should departe for that present time, and returne againe when Calpurnia shoulde have better dreames: what would his

IULIUS
CÆSAR
The dreame of Calpurnia, Cæsars wife.

Decius Brutus Albinus perswasion to Cæsar.

IULIUS
CÆSAR

enemies and ill willers say, and how could they like of his frendes wordes? And who could perswade them otherwise, but that they would thinke his dominion a slaverie unto them, and tirannicall in him selfe? And yet if it be so, sayd he, that you utterly mislike of this day, it is better that you goe your selfe in person, and saluting the Senate, to dismisse them till an other time. Therewithall he tooke Cæsar by the hand, and brought him out of his house. Cæsar was not gone farre from his house, but a bondman, a straunger, did what he could to speake with him: and when he sawe he was put backe by the great prease and multitude of people that followed him, he went straight unto his house, and put him selfe into Calpurniaes handes to be kept, till Cæsar came backe againe, telling her that he had great matters to imparte unto him. And one Artemidorus also borne in the Ile of Gnidos, a Doctor of Rethoricke in the Greeke tongue, who by meanes of his profession was verie familliar with certaine of Brutus confederates, and therefore knew the most parte of all their practises against Cæsar: came and brought him a litle bill wrytten with his owne hand, of all that he ment to tell him. He marking howe Cæsar received all the supplications that were offered him, and that he gave them straight to his men that were about him, pressed neerer to him, and sayed: Cæsar, reade this memoriall to your selfe, and that quickely, for they be matters of great waight and touche you neerely. Cæsar tooke it of him, but coulde never reade it, though he many times attempted it, for the number of people that did salute him: but holding it still in his hande, keeping it to him selfe, went on withall into the Senate house. Howbeit other are of opinion, that it was some man else that gave him that memoriall, and not Artemidorus, who did what he could all the way as he went to geve it Cæsar, but he was alwayes repulsed by the people. For these things, they may seeme to come by chaunce: but the place where the murther was prepared, and where the Senate were assembled, and where also there stoode up an image of Pompey dedicated by him selfe amongest other ornamentes which he gave unto the Theater: all these were manifest proofes that it was the

Decius Brutus brought Cæsar into the Senate house.

The tokens of the conspiracy against Cæsar.

The place where Cæsar was slaine.

66

ordinaunce of some god, that made this treason to be executed, specially in that verie place. It is also reported, that
Cassius (though otherwise he did favour the doctrine of
Epicurus) beholding the image of Pompey, before they
entred into the action of their traiterous enterprise: he did
softely call upon it, to aide him. But the instant daunger
of the present time, taking away his former reason, did
sodainly put him into a furious passion, and made him like
a man halfe besides him selfe. Now Antonius, that was a
faithfull frende to Cæsar, and a valliant man besides of his
handes, him, Decius Brutus Albinus entertained out of the
Senate house, having begon a long tale of set purpose. So
Cæsar comming into the house, all the Senate stoode up on
their feete to doe him honor. Then parte of Brutus companie and confederates stoode rounde about Cæsars chayer,
and parte of them also came towardes him, as though they
made sute with Metellus Cimber, to call home his brother
againe from banishment: and thus prosecuting still their
sute, they followed Cæsar, till he was set in his chayer. Who,
denying their petitions, and being offended with them one
after an other, bicause the more they were denied, the more
they pressed upon him, and were the earnester with him:
Metellus at length, taking his gowne with both his handes,
pulled it over his necke, which was the signe geven the confederates to sette apon him. Then Casca behinde him strake
him in the necke with his sword, howbeit the wounde was
not great nor mortall, bicause it seemed, the feare of such a
develishe attempt did amaze him, and take his strength from
him, that he killed him not at the first blowe. But Cæsar
turning straight unto him, caught hold of his sword, and
held it hard: and they both cried out, Cæsar in Latin: O
vile traitor Casca, what doest thou? and Casca in Greeke
to his brother, Brother, helpe me. At the beginning of this
sturre, they that were present, not knowing of the conspiracie
were so amazed with the horrible sight they sawe: that they
had no power to flie, neither to helpe him, not so much, as
once to make any outcrie. They on thother side that had
conspired his death, compassed him in on everie side with
their swordes drawen in their handes, that Cæsar turned him

Antonius,
Cæsars faith-
full frend.

Casca, the
first that
strake at
Cæsar.

no where, but he was striken at by some, and still had naked swords in his face, and was hacked and mangeled amonge them, as a wilde beaste taken of hunters. For it was agreed among them, that every man should geve him a wound, bicause all their partes should be in this murther: and then Brutus him selfe gave him one wounde about his privities. Men reporte also, that Cæsar did still defende him selfe against the rest, running everie waye with his bodie: but when he sawe Brutus with his sworde drawen in his hande, then he pulled his gowne over his heade, and made no more resistaunce, and was driven either casually, or purposedly, by the counsell of the conspirators, against the base where-upon Pompeys image stoode, which ranne all of a goare bloude, till he was slaine. Thus it seemed, that the image tooke just revenge of Pompeys enemie, being throwen downe on the ground at his feete, and yelding up his ghost there, for the number of wounds he had upon him. For it is reported, that he had three and twenty wounds apon his body: and divers of the conspirators did hurt them selves, striking one body with so many blowes. When Cæsar was slaine, the Senate (though Brutus stood in the middest amongest them as though he would have sayd somewhat touching this fact) presently ran out of the house, and flying, filled all the city with marvelous feare and tumult. Insomuch as some did shut to their dores, others forsooke their shops and warehouses, and others ranne to the place to see what the matter was: and others also that had seene it, ran home to their houses againe. But Antonius and Lepidus, which were two of Cæsars chiefest frends, secretly conveying them selves away, fled into other mens houses, and forsooke their owne. Brutus and his confederats on thother side, being yet hotte with this murther they had committed, having their swordes drawen in their hands, came all in a troupe together out of the Senate, and went into the market place, not as men that made countenaunce to flie, but other-wise boldly holding up their heades like men of corage, and called to the people to defende their libertie, and stayed to speake with every great personage whome they met in their way. Of them, some followed this troupe, and went amongest

GRECIANS AND ROMANES

them, as if they had bene of the conspiracie, and falsely
chalenged parte of the honor with them: among them was
Caius Octavius, and Lentulus Spinther.   But both of them
were afterwards put to death, for their vaine covetousnes of
honor, by Antonius, and Octavius Cæsar the younger: and
yet had no parte of that honor for the which they were put
to death, neither did any man beleve that they were any of
the confederates, or of counsell with them.   For they that
did put them to death, tooke revenge rather of the will they
had to offend, then of any fact they had committed.   The
next morning, Brutus and his confederates came into the
market place to speake unto the people, who gave them such
audience, that it seemed they neither greatly reproved, nor
allowed the fact: for by their great silence they showed, that
they were sory for Cæsars death, and also that they did reverence Brutus.   Nowe the Senate graunted generall pardonne
for all that was paste, and to pacifie every man, ordained
besides, that Cæsars funeralls shoulde bee honored as a god,
and established all thinges that he had done: and gave certaine provinces also, and convenient honors unto Brutus and
his confederates, whereby every man thought all things were
brought to good peace and quietnes againe.   But when they
had opened Cæsars testament, and found a liberall legacie of
money, bequeathed unto every citizen of Rome, and that
they saw his body (which was brought into the market place)
al bemangled with gashes of swordes: then there was no
order to keepe the multitude and common people quiet, but
they plucked up formes, tables, and stooles, and layed them
all about the body, and setting them a fire, burnt the corse.
Then when the fire was well kindled, they tooke the fire-
brandes, and went unto their houses that had slaine Cæsar,
to set them a fire.   Other also ranne up and downe the citie
to see if they could meete with any of them, to cut them
in peeces: howbeit they could meete with never a man of
them, bicause they had locked them selves up safely in their
houses.   There was one of Cæsars frends called Cinna, that
had a marvelous straunge and terrible dreame the night
before.   He dreamed that Cæsar bad him to supper, and
that he refused, and would not goe: then that Cæsar tooke

IULIUS
CÆSAR

him by the hand, and led him against his will. Now Cinna hearing at that time, that they burnt Cæsars body in the market place, notwithstanding that he feared his dreame, and had an agew on him besides: he went into the market place to honor his funeralls. When he came thither, one of meane sorte asked what his name was? He was straight called by his name. The first man told it to an other, and that other unto an other, so that it ranne straight through them all, that he was one of them that murdered Cæsar: (for in deede one of the traitors to Cæsar, was also called

The murther of Cinna.

Cinna as him selfe) wherefore taking him for Cinna the murderer, they fell upon him with such furie, that they presently dispatched him in the market place. This sturre and furie made Brutus and Cassius more affrayed, then of all that was past, and therefore within fewe dayes after, they departed out of Rome: and touching their doings afterwards, and what calamity they suffered till their deathes, we have wrytten it at large, in the life of Brutus. Cæsar

Cæsar 56 yere olde at his death.

dyed at six and fifty yeres of age: and Pompey also lived not passing foure yeares more then he. So he reaped no other frute of all his raigne and dominion, which he had so vehemently desired all his life, and pursued with such extreame daunger: but a vaine name only, and a superficiall glory, that procured him the envy and hatred of his contrie.

The revenge of Cæsars death.

But his great prosperitie and good fortune that favored him all his life time, did continue afterwards in the revenge of his death, pursuing the murtherers both by sea and land, till they had not left a man more to be executed, of al them that were actors or counsellers in the conspiracy of his death.

Cassius being overthrowen at the battell of Philippes, slue himselfe with the selfe same sword wherewith he strake Cæsar.

Furthermore, of all the chaunces that happen unto men upon the earth, that which came to Cassius above all other, is most to be wondered at. For he being overcome in battell at the jorney of Philippes, slue him selfe with the same sworde, with the which he strake Cæsar. Againe, of signes in the element, the great comet which seven nightes together was seene very bright after Cæsars death, the eight night after was never seene more. Also the brightnes of

Wonders seene in the

the sunne was darkened, the which all that yeare through rose very pale, and shined not out, whereby it gave but

70

small heate : therefore the ayer being very clowdy and darke, by the weakenes of the heate that could not come foorth, did cause the earth to bring foorth but raw and unrype frute, which rotted before it could rype. But above all, the ghost that appeared unto Brutus shewed plainly, that the goddes were offended with the murther of Cæsar. The vision was thus : Brutus being ready to passe over his army from the citie of Abydos, to the other coast lying directly against it, slept every night (as his manner was) in his tent, and being yet awake, thinking of his affaires : (for by reporte he was as carefull a Captaine, and lived with as litle sleepe, as ever man did) he thought he heard a noyse at his tent dore, and looking towards the light of the lampe that waxed very dimme, he saw a horrible vision of a man, of a wonderfull greatnes, and dreadfull looke, which at the first made him marvelously afraid. But when he sawe that it did him no hurt, but stoode by his bedde side, and sayd nothing : at length he asked him what he was. The image aunswered him : I am thy ill angell, Brutus, and thou shalt see me by the citie of Philippes. Then Brutus replied againe, and sayd : Well, I shall see thee then. Therewithall, the spirit presently vanished from him. After that time Brutus being in battell neere unto the citie of Philippes, against Antonius and Octavius Cæsar, at the first battell he wan the victorie, and overthrowing all them that withstoode him, he drave them into young Cæsars campe, which he tooke. The second battell being at hand, this spirit appeared again unto him, but spake never a word. Thereuppon Brutus knowing he should dye, did put him selfe to all hazard in battell, but yet fighting could not be slaine. So seeing his men put to flight and overthrowen, he ranne unto a litle rocke not farre of, and there setting his swordes point to his brest, fell upon it, and slue him selfe, but yet as it is reported, with the helpe of his frend, that dispatched him.

element after Cæsars death.

A great Comet.

Brutus vision.

A spirit appeared unto Brutus.

The second appearing of the spirit, unto Brutus.

THE END OF CÆSARS LIFE

THE LIFE OF PHOCION

THE Orator Demades on a time florished in Athens, bicause in all his doings and sayings in the administration and government of the common wealth, he alwayes favored the Macedonians and Antipater: in respect whereof he was eftsoones compelled, both in his counsell and lawes, to preferre many things to the dishonor of his city, saying, that they must pardon him, bicause he governed the shippewrackes of his contrie. This was an arrogant speache: but yet referring it to the government of Phocion he said truely. For in deede Demades selfe was the shippewracke of the common weale, bicause he lived so insolently, and governed so lewdly. Insomuch as Antipater sayd of him, after he was very old: that there was nothing left of him, no more then of a beast sacrificed, but the tongue and belly. But the vertues of Phocion, which had to fight against the cruell and bitter enemy of the time, were so obscured by the calamities of Græce: that his fame was nothing so great as he deserved. For we must not credit Sophocles words, making vertue of it selfe but weake, in these verses:

When stormes of sore adversities (O king) do men assaile,
It dauntes their corage, cuts their combs, and makes their harts to
  quaile.

But we must onely give place to fortune, who when she frowneth uppon any good and vertuous men, her force is so great, that where they deserve honor and favor, she violently heapeth false and malicious accusations against them, which maketh their vertue lame, and not of that credit which in dede it deserveth. And yet it seemeth to many, that free cities are most cruel unto their good citizens in time of prosperity: bicause they flow in wealth and live at ease, which maketh them of hauty mindes. But it is cleane contrary.

Demades arrogant saying.

The power of vertue and fortune.

72

GRECIANS AND ROMANES

For adversity commonly maketh mens maners sower, chollericke, and very hasty: besides, slow to heare, churlish, and offended with every litle sharpe word. For he that correcteth them that offend, seemeth to cast their adversitie in their teeth: and he that telleth them plainly of their faultes, seemeth also to despise them. For like as honnie sweete by nature, applied unto woundes, doth bring both smart and paine: even so, sharpe wordes, though profitable, doe bite the unfortunate man, if they be not tempered with discretion and curtesie. And therefore Homer the Poet calleth swete and pleasaunt thinges μενοεικῆ, as yeelding and not striving with contrariety, against that parte of the minde, whereby we be angrie and froward. For even as sore eyes doe like to looke on blacke and darke colours, and can not abide the bright and glaring: so in a city, where for want of foresight and government, things goe not well, men be so divers and unwilling to heare of their owne fault and estate, that they had rather continue in their follie and daunger, then by sharpnes of words to be rebuked and restored. So that it being impossible to amend one fault with a greater, that common wealth must be in great daunger, that when it hath most nede of helpe, is lothest to receive any: and he also hazardeth him selfe, that plainly telleth them their faultes. Like as therefore the Mathematician sayth, that the sunne doth not altogether follow the motion of the highest heaven, nor yet is moved directly contrary, but fetching a compase a litle overthwart, maketh an oblique circle, and by variety of approching and departing preserveth all things, and kepeth the world in good temperature. Even so, too severe government, contrarying the peoples mindes in all things, is not good: as also it is marvelous daungerous, not to correct offendors when they offend, for feare of the peoples displeasure. But the meane, sometime to yeelde unto the people to make them the more willing to obey, and to graunt them things of pleasure, to demaund of them againe things profitable: that is a good way to governe men the better by. For, by gentle meanes they are brought to doe many profitable things, when they seeke it not of them, by rigor and authority. In deede this meane is very hard to be observed, bicause authority is hardly tempered with lenity. But when they meete together, there is no harmony more musicall, nor concordance more perfit than that: and therfore it is said, that thereby God doth governe the world, working rather a voluntary, then a forced obedience in men. But this fault of severenes was in Cato the younger, for he could not fashion him selfe to the peoples maners, neither did they like his: neither did he win his estimacion in the common wealth by flattering of

Ciceroes saying of Cato, and the common wealth at Rome.

them. And therefore Cicero sayd, that he was put by the Consulship, for that he behaved him selfe as though he lived in the common wealth devised by Plato, and not amongest the disordered and corrupt posterity of Romulus. Me thinketh I can liken him properly unto untimely frute: the which though men doe take pleasure to see and wonder at,

Catoes plaine maner, became not the corrupt and suttle time.

yet they eate them not. Even so, the auncient simplicity of Catoes maner (having so long time bene out of use, and comming then to shew it selfe in that corrupt time and ill maners of the city) was in deede much praiseworthy: but yet not the convenientest, nor the fittest for him, bicause it aunswered nor respected not the use and maners of his time. For he found not his contry (as Phocion did) utterly destroyed, but tossed in a daungerous tempest: and being not of authority like the pilot to take the stern in hand, and governe the shippe: he tooke him selfe to tricking the sailes, and preparing the tacle, so to assist men of greater power. And yet being in no greater place, he so thwarted fortune (which seemed to have sworne the overthrowe of the estate of Rome) that with much a doe, with great difficulty, and a long time after, she executed her malice. And yet the common wealth had almost gotten the victory of her, by meanes of Cato and his vertue: with whom I doe compare the vertue of Phocion, who yet in my opinion, were not in all thinges alike, neither in their honesty, nor policy of government. For there is difference betwext manhood and manhood, as there was betwext that of Alcibiades, and that of Epaminondas: betwext wisedom and wisedom, as betwext that of Aristides, and that of Themistocles: and betwext justice and justice, as betwext that of Numa, and that of

GRECIANS AND ROMANES

Agesilaus. But the vertues of these men (to him that shall superficially regard, and slightly consider them) seeme all one in quality, in maner, and use, both alike in temperance of curtesie with severity, and manhood with wisdom: a vigilant care for others, with presence of corage and security of mind for them selves, abhorring all filthines and corruption, and imbrasing constancy and love of justice: that for any man to discerne the difference betwene them, it requireth an excellent good wit and judgement. Now touching Cato, every man knoweth that he was of a noble house, as we wil shew you hereafter in his life: but for Phocion, I gesse he came of no base parentage. For if he had bene the sonne The parentage of a spoonemaker, as Idomeneus testifieth: Glaucippus the of Phocion. sonne of Hyperides, having in an invective he wrote against him, rehersed all the mischiefes he could of him, he would not have forgotten to have upbraid him with his base parentage, neither he him self also (if that had bene true) had bene so well brought up as he was. For when he was but a young man, he was Platoes scholler, and afterwards Xenocrates scholler, in the schoole of Academia: and so, even from his first beginning, he gave him selfe to followe them that were learned. For as Duris Phocion writeth, never Athenian saw him weepe nor laugh, nor never wept, washe him selfe in any common bathe, nor his hands out of nor laughed. his sleeves when he ware a long gowne. For when he went to the warres, he would alwaies goe afoote, and never wore gowne, unles it were extreame cold: and then the souldiers to mocke him withall, would say it was a signe of a sharpe winter, when they sawe Phocion in his gowne. Nowe, though Phocions in deede he was very curteous and gentle of nature, yet he maners. had such a grymme looke withall, that no man had any desire to talke with him, but such as were of his familliar acquaintance. And therefore when Chares the Orator one day mocked him for the bending of his browes, and that the Athenians fell in a laughter withall: My Maisters, quoth Phocion, the bending of my browes have done you no hurt, but the foolery and laughing of these flatterers, have made ye oftentymes to weepe. Furthermore, his maner of speech was very profitable, for the good sentences and counsells he

75

uttered: but it was mixed with an imperious, austere, and bitter shortnes. For as Zeno the Philosopher sayeth, that the wise man should temper his wordes with witte and reason, before he utter them: even so was Phocions speech, the which in few words comprehended much matter. And thereupon it seemeth that Polyeuctus Sphettian sayd, that Demosthenes was an excellent Orator, but in speech, Phocion was very wittie. For like as coynes of gold or silver, the lighter they waye, the finer they be of goodnes: even so the excellencie of speeche consisteth in signifying much, by fewe wordes.

And touching this matter, it is reported, that the Theater being full of people, Phocion walked all alone upon the scaffold where the players played, and was in a great muse with him selfe: whereuppon, one of his friendes seeing him so in his muses, said unto him, Surely Phocion, thy minde is occupied about somewhat. In deede so is it, sayd he: for I am thinking with my selfe, if I could abridge any thing of that I have to say to the people. For Demosthenes selfe litle esteming all other Orators, when Phocion rose up to speake, he would round his friendes in their eares, and told them: See, the cutter of my wordes riseth. Peradventure he ment it by his manners also: for when a good man speaketh, not a word onely, but a wincke of an eye, or a nod of his head, doth countervaile many artificiall words and speeches of Rethoritians. Furthermore, when he was a

young man, he went to the warres under Captaine Chabrias, and followed him: of whom he learned to be a perfit souldier, and in recompence thereof, he reformed many of his Captaines imperfections, and made him wiser then he was. For Chabrias otherwise beeing very dull and slothfull of him selfe, when he came to fight, he was so hotte and corageous, that he would thrust himselfe into danger with the desperatest persons: and therefore for his rashnes, it afterwards cost him his life, in the citie of Chio, where launching out with his gally before the rest, he pressed to land in despite of his enemies. But Phocion being wise to loke to him selfe, and very quicke to execute: on the one side quickned Chabrias slownes, and on the other side also, by wisedom cooled his heate and furie. Chabrias therefore, being a good man and

curteous, loved Phocion very well, and did preferre him in
matters of service, making him famous amongest the Græcians,
and employed him in his hardiest enterprises. For by his
meanes he atchieved great fame and honor in a battell by
sea, which he wanne by the Ile of Naxos, giving him the left
winge of his armie : on which side the fight was sharpest of
all the battell, and there he soonest put the enemies to flight.
This battel being the first which the citie of Athens wanne
with their owne men onely, after it had bene taken : gave
the people cause to love Chabrias, and made them also to
make accompt of Phocion, as of a noble souldier, and worthy
to have charge. This victory was gotten on the feast day of
the great misteries, in memory whereof, Chabrias did yearly,
on the sixtenth day of the moneth Boedromion (now called
August) make all the people of Athens drinke. After that
time, Chabrias sending Phocion to receive the tribute of the
Ilanders, their confederats, and the shippes which they should
send him he gave him twenty gallies to bringe him thither.
But Phocion then (as it is reported) said unto him : if he
sent him to fight with his enemies, he had neede to have
moe shippes : but if he sent him as an Ambassador unto his
friendes, then, that one shippe would serve his turne. So he
went with one gallie onely : and after he had spoken with
the cities, and curteously dealt with the governors of every
one of them, he returned backe, furnished of their confederats,
with a great fleete of shippes and money, to cary unto Athens.
So Phocion did not onely reverence Chabrias while he lived,
but after his death also he tooke great care of his friendes
and kinsmen, and sought to make his sonne Ctesippus, an
honest man. whom, though he sawe very wilde and unto-
ward, yet he never left to reforme him, and hide his fault.
It is sayde also, that when this young man did trouble him
much with vaine frivolous questions, serving then under him,
he being Captaine, and taking upon him to give him counsell,
to reprove him, and to teache him the dutie of a Captaine ·
he could not but say, O Chabrias, Chabrias . now doe I paye
for the love thou didest beare me when thou wert alive, in
bearing with the folly of thy sonne. But when he saw that
the heads of the citie of Athens had as it were by lot devided

amonge them selves the offices of warre and peace, and that some of them, as Eubulus, Aristophon, Demosthenes, Lycurgus, and Hyperides were common speakers and preferrers of matters in counsells and Senate : and that others, as Diopithes, Menestheus, Leosthenes, and Chares, became great men by the warres, and had charge of armies : he determined rather to follow the manner of government, of Pericles, Aristides, and Solon, as being mingled of both. For either of them, seemed (as the Poet Archilocus sayth) :

> To bee both Champions stowt, of Marsis warlyke band,
> And of the Muses eke, the artes to understand.

He knew also, that Pallas the goddesse and protector of Athens, was called Polemica, and Politica : to wit, skilfull to rule both in warre and peace. So, having thus disposed of him selfe in government, he alwaies perswaded peace and quietnes, and yet was often chosen Captaine, and had charge of armies, being the onely man that of all the Captaines afore him, and in his time, did never sue for charge, neither yet refused it at any time, when he was called to serve the common wealth. It is certen that he was chosen five and forty times Prætor, and was alwaies absent at the elections, but yet sent for. Whereuppon all the wise men wondred to see the manner of the people towards him, considering that Phocion had never done nor sayd any thing to flatter them withall, but commonly had bene against their desires : and how they used other governours notwithstanding, that were more pleasant and delightfull in their orations, like men to sport at, as it is sayd of kings, who after they have washed their handes to goe to their meate, doe use to have Iesters and flatterers to make them mery : but on thother side when they had occasion of warres in deede, how then like wise men they could bethinke them selves, and choose the wisest and stowtest man of the citie, and that most would withstand their mindes and desires. For on a time an oracle of Apollo Delphias, beeing openly red before them, which sayd, that all the other Athenians being agreed, yet there was one amonge them that was contrary to all the rest of the citie : Phocion stepping forth before them all, bad them never seeke further for the man, for it was he that liked none of all their doings. Another time he chaunced to say his opinion before all the people, the which they all praised and approved: but he saw they were so sodeinly become of his minde, he turned backe to his friendes, and asked them: Alas, hath not some evill thing slipped my mouth unawares? Another time a generall collection being gathered of the people at Athens, towardes the solemnizing of a sacrifice: other men of his estate having payd their part, he was often also called upon to pay his. But he aunswered them againe, Aske them that be rich, for it were a shame for me to give you any thing, being yet in this mans debt: pointing to Callicles the Userer, who had lent him money. But when they left him not for all this, to cry out apon him for the contribution, he began to tell them this tale: that on a time there was a coward preparing to goe to the warres, and as he was ready to depart, he heard the Ravens what a crying they made, and taking it for an ill signe, he put of his harnes, and kept him at home. After that he put on his harnes againe, and went on his way towards the campe: the Ravens beganne againe to make a goodlier cry behind him. But thereuppon he staied straight, and at length sayd: Ye shall crooke as lowd as ye list, before ye feede of my carkas. An other time the Athenians being in warre under his charge, would needes have him to leade them to give charge uppon their enemies, but he would not: thereuppon they called him coward, and sayd he durst not. Well, sayd he againe, it is not you can make me valiant, no more then my selfe can make you cowards: and yet one of us know an other. Another time in a marvelous daungerous time, the people handled him very churlishly, and would needes have him presently deliver accompt of his charge: but he aunswered them, O my friendes, first save your selves. Furthermore, the people beeing very lowly and humble, for feare, in time of warres: and presently in peace againe waxing brave in wordes against Phocion, charging him that he had taken the victorie out of their handes: he onely sayd this to them, You are happy that have a Captaine that knowes you, els you would singe a new songe. Another time there was a quarrell betwixt the

Bœotians, and them, about their bounds and fronters: the which they would not try by lawe, but by battel. But Phocion told them, they did they wist not what, and counselled them rather to fight it out in words, in which they were the stronger, and not with weapons, where they were the weaker. Another time they so much misliked his opinion in the assembly, that they woulde not abide to heare him, nor suffer him to speake. Wel, my Maisters, quoth he then, you may make me doe that which is not to be done: but you shall never compell me, against my minde, to say that which is not to be spoken. He would as gallantly also gird the Orators his adversaries, when they were busie with him. As on a time he aunswered Demosthenes, that sayd unto him: The people, Phocion, will kill thee one day, and if it take them in the heades. Yea thee, quoth he, if they be wise. Agayne, when Polyeuctus Sphettian, in a hotte day perswaded the people of Athens to make warre with king Philip, sweating, and with much a doe fetching his breath, being a fatte man, that he was driven oftentymes to drinke water, to ende his oration: Surely sayd Phocion, ye shall doe marvelous wisely, to make warre at such a mans motion. Why, what thinke ye will he do, when he hath his curats and his target upon him, and that the enemies be ready to fight: that now in making an oration onely before you, which he hath studied long before, is almost stifled? Another time also when Lycurgus in his oration had openly reproved him for many things before the people, and among the rest, for that Alexander demaunding tenne Citizens of Athens to do with them what he thought good, that he had counselled them to deliver them: Phocion aunswered him, I have oftentimes counselled them for the best, but they would never follow my councell. There was one Archibiades at that time in Athens, that counterfeated the Lacedæmonian, with a marvelous long beard, a beggerly cloke, and a sower looke. Phocion being checkt one day before the people, appealed unto Archibiades for a witnes, to confirme that he spake. But he rising up, counselled the people contrarily, to flatter them withall. Phocion perceiving it, tooke him by the beard, and sayd unto him: Alas Archibiades, why

80

diddest thou not then clippe thy beard, seeing thou wouldest needes flatter? There was another great pleader, one Aristogiton, that in all assemblies of the citie, did nothing but busse warres continually in their eares. Afterwardes when men were to be leavied and mustered, and their names entred that should goe to the warres: Aristogiton came halting into the market place with a staffe in his hand, and both his legges bound up, to make the people beleeve that he was sicke and disseased. Phocion spying Aristogiton farre of, cryed out to the Clearke that wrote the bills: Put in Aristogiton, lame, and impudent. So that oftentymes it makes me muse, howe, or wherefore so sharpe and severe a man (as by these examples it appeareth he was) could come to the surname of good. Notwithstanding, in the ende I find it a hard thing, but not impossible, that a man should be like wine, both sweete and sharpe together: as there are others to the contrary, that at the first sight, seeme very curteous and gentle of conversation, and apon better acquaintance, prove churlishe and dogged. It is reported also, that Hyperides the Orator one day should say to the Athenians: I pray you (my Lords) note me not for my sharpenes, but consider if my sharpenes be without profit. As who should say, men were not troublesom, but for covetousnes onely, and as if the people did not rather feare and hate them, that of insolencie and malice did abuse and contemne their authority. Phocion on thother side, he never did Citizen hurt, for any private malice he bare him: but was ever sharpe and cruell to them, which were against any matter he preferred for the benefit of the common wealth. For in all other things, he shewed him self marvelous lowly and curteous to every body, and would be familliar with his adversaries, and helpe them if they wanted, or were otherwise in daunger of displeasure with the state. Insomuch as his friendes therefore reproved him on a time, when he spake in the behalfe of a naughty man, an offender: O, sayd he, honest men neede no helpe. An other time, Aristogiton the Sycophant, beeing clapped up in prison, sent unto Phocion to pray him to come and speake with him, after he was condemned. Phocion went into the prison to him,

PHOCION
Aristogiton, a Sycophant, and coward.

Phocion called by surname, good.

5 : L

though his friendes perswaded him the contrary, and aunswered them: O, let me alone, sayd he, for where could I see Aristogiton more gladly then in prison? Furthermore, when there went any army to sea out of Athens, if there were any other chosen generall but Phocion: the townes and Ilandes all alongest the sea coast, (which were friendes and confederats of the Athenians) fortified their walls, filled up their havens, and brought their wives, slaves, and cattell, and all their goods into their townes and cities, as if they had bene enemies, and open warre proclaimed. Contrarily also, if Phocion had bene Capteine and generall: they would send out their shippes to the sea to meete him farre of, crowned with garlands in token of common joy, and so would bringe him to their cities. King Philip secretly seking to winne the Ile of Euboea, sent an armie thither out of Macedon, and intised the townes by tyrannes to rebell: whereuppon, Plutarke Eretrian praied in ayde of the Athenians, to take this Iland from the Macedonians, which they daily wanne more and more, if they came not presently

to ayde them. So Phocion was sent general thither, but with a fewe men onely, bicause they made account the men of that contry would straight joyne with him, for the good will they bare him. But when he came thither, he found them all traytors, and rebells, and brybed with king Philippes money, which he lavished out amonge them: so that he was brought into great daunger. Thereupon he retyred to a litle hill that is severed from the fieldes of Tamynes, with a great large valley, and there fortified him selfe with that litle armie he had. Then he perswaded his Captaines not to care for all those rebels, pratlers, and cowards which fled out of their tents, and forsooke their ensignes and Captaines, but that they should let them goe out of the campe where they would. For, sayd he, such disobedient souldiers here will doe us no service, and moreover will hinder them that have good will to serve well: and at home also, knowing them selves in faulte, for that they forsooke the campe without licence, they dare not complayne apon us. Afterwards when the enemies came to set apon him, he commaunded his men to arme, and put them selves in readines, and not

Phocion perswadeth his
Captaines, to
suffer the
mutinous
souldiers and
cowards to
depart the
campe.

GRECIANS AND ROMANES

to sturre, untill he had done sacrifice: but he stayed long before he came, either bicause he could have no lucky signes of the sacrifices, or els for that he would draw his enemies nearer. Thereuppon Plutarke Eretrian supposing he deferred to marche for feare, went him selfe first into the field, with certen light horsemen he had in pay. Then the men of armes seeing them give charge, could hold no lenger, but followed him also, stragling out of the campe one after an other disorderly, and so did set apon their enemies. The first being overthrowen, all the other dispersed them selves, and Plutarke him self fled. Then certen bandes of the enemies thinking all had bene theirs, followed them even into their campe, and came to throw downe their rampiers. In the meane time, Phocion having ended his sacrifice, the Athenians came out of their campe, and set apon them, and made part of them flie immediatly, and part of them also they slue hard by the trenches of their campe. Then Phocion commaunded that the battell should stand still, to receive their men that were scattered up and downe the fieldes: and in the meane space, he him selfe, with the choycest men of his armie, gave charge apon the enemies. The fight was cruell betwene them. For the Athenians fought very valiantly, ventring their persons: but of them all, two young men fighting by their generall, (Glaucus, the sonne of Polymedes, and Thallus, the sonne of Cineas) caried the praise away. And so did Cleophanes that daye also shewe him selfe very valiant. For he crying out still apon the horsemen that fled, and perswading them to come and helpe their generall that was in daunger: brought them backe againe, and thereby gotte the footemen the victorie. After this battell he drave Plutarke out of Eretria, and tooke the castell of Zaretra, standing in a very commodious place for this warre, where the Ile draweth to a straightnes, envyronned on either side with the sea: and would not suffer his men to take any Græcians prisoners, fearing least the Orators at Athens might move the people sodeinly in a rage, to put them to death. After all these thinges were done, Phocion returned backe to Athens. But then did the confederats of the Athenians straight wishe for his justice

83

and curtesie : and the Athenians them selves also knewe his skilfulnes and manhood. For his successor Molossus, that was generall for the rest of the warre, delt so undiscreetely : that he him selfe was taken prisoner there. Then king Philip beeing put in marvailous great hope, went with all his armie into Hellespont, perswading him selfe, that he should straight take all Cherronesus, the cities of Perinthe and Bizantium. The Athenians thereuppon determining to send ayde, to prevent king Philips comming : the Orators made great sute, that Chares might be chosen Captaine. But he being sent thither with a good number of shippes, did no service worthy commendacion, neither would the cities receive his navie into their havens : but being suspected of every man, and despised of his enemies, he was driven to sayle up and downe, and to get money of the allyes. The people being incensed by the Orators, were marvelously offended, and repented them selves that they had sent ayde unto the Bizantines. Then Phocion rising up, spake unto the people, and told them, that it was no reason that mistrusting their confederats they should be offended with them : but to be angry with their Captaines that deserved to be mistrusted. For they, said he, doe make your confederats affraide of you, who without you notwithstanding can not save themselves. The people chaunging their mindes by his oration, made Phocion againe their Captaine, and sent him with an armie into Hellespont to helpe their confederats there, which was of great importance to save the citie of Byzantium. Furthermore, Phocions fame was so great, that Cleon, the greatest man of vertue and authoritie in Bizantium, and had before bene Phocions companion and familiar in the Academy : he made sute for him unto the citie. Then the Byzantines would not suffer him (though he desired it) to campe without the walls of their citie, but opening their gates, received him in, and mingled the Athenians amongest them. Who, perceiving how much the Citizens trusted them, did so honestly behave them selves in their conversation amongest them, that they gave them no maner of cause to complaine of them : and shewed them selves so valiant besides in all battells and

Phocion
saved the
citie of
Byzantium.

84

conflicts, that Philip (which before was thought dreadfull
and invincible, every man beeing affraid to fight any battell
with him) returned out of Hellespont without any thing
done, and to his great discredit: where Phocion wanne some
of his shippes, and recovered againe the strong holdes, in
the which he had placed his garrisons. Furthermore, making
divers invasions into his contries, he destroyed his borders ·
till that at length he was sore hurt there, and so driven
to returne home againe, by meanes of a great armie that
came against him, to defend the contry. Shortly after, the
Megarians secretly sent unto him, to deliver their citie into
his hands. Phocion fearing if the Bœotians understood it,
that they would prevent him: he called a common assembly
earely in the morning, and told the people what message
the Magarians had sent unto him. The people apon his
motion being determined to ayde them: Phocion straight
sounding the trumpet at the breaking up of the assembly, gave
them no further leysure, but to take their weapons, and so
led them incontinently to Megara. The Megarians receiving him, Phocion shut up the haven of Nisæa, and brought
two long walls from the citie unto it, and so joyned it unto the
sea: whereby he stood not greatly in feare of his enemies
by land, and for the sea, the Athenians were Lordes of it.
Now when the Athenians had proclaimed open warre against
king Philip, and had chosen other Captaines in his absence,
and that he was returned from the Iles: above all thinges,
he perswaded the people (king Philip requiring peace, and
greatly fearing the daunger) to accept the condicions of
peace. Then one of these busy Orators that was still accusing one or other, said unto him: Why, Phocion, how darest
thou attempt to turne the Athenians from warre, having
now their swordes in their hands? Yes truely, said Phocion
though in warre I know I shal commaund thee, and in peace
thou wilt commaund me. But when the people would not
harken to him, and that Demosthenes caried them away
with his perswasions, who counselled them to fight with
king Philip, as farre from Attica as they could I pray thee
friend, quoth Phocion unto him, let us not dispute where we
shall fight, but consider how we shall overcome, the which if

we can so bring to passe, be sure we shall put the warre farre enough from us. For men that are overcome, be ever in feare and daunger, wheresoever they be. When the Athenians had lost a battell against Philip, the seditious Orators that hunted after innovacion, preferred Charidemus to be chosen generall of the Athenians: whereuppon, the Magistrates and Senatours being affraid, and taking with them all the Court and Senate of the Areopagits, they made such earnest sute to the people, with the teares in their eyes, that at last (but with much a doe) they obteyned, that the affaires of the citie might be put into Phocions handes and government. He thought good to accept the articles and gentle condicions of peace which Philip offered them. But after that the Orator Demades moved that the citie of Athens would enter into the common treatie of peace, and common assembly of the states of Græce, procured at king Philips request: Phocion would not agree to it, untill they might understand what demaunds Philip would make at the assembly of the Græcians. When his opinion through the perversnes of time could not be liked of them, and that he saw the Athenians soone after repented them that they did not followe his counsell, when they heard they should furnish king Philip with shippes and horsemen: then he told them, The feare whereof ye now complaine, made me to withstand that, which now ye have consented unto. But sithence it is so that you have nowe past your consents, you must be contented, and not be discoraged at it: remembring that your auncestors in times past have sometyme commaunded, and other while obeyed others, and yet have so wisely and discreetely governed them selves in both fortunes, that they have not onely saved their citie, but all Græce besides. When newes came of king Philips death, the people for joy would straight have made bonfires and sacrifices to the goddes for the good newes: but Phocion would not suffer them, and sayd, that it was a token of a base minde, to rejoyce at any mans death, and besides that, the armie which overthrew you at Chæronea, hath not yet lost but one man. And when Demosthenes also would commonly speake ill of Alexander, and specially when he was so neare

To rejoyce at any mans hurt, sheweth a base mind, and vile nature.

GRECIANS AND ROMANES

Thebes with his armie: Phocion rehearsed unto him these
verses of Homer:

> How great a folly is it for to stand
> Against a cruell king,
> Which beeing armd and having sword in hand,
> Seekes fame of every thing!

What, when there is such a great fire kindled, wilt thou
cast the citie into it? for my part therefore, though they
were willing, yet will I not suffer them to cast them selves
away: for to that ende have I taken upon me this charge
and government. And afterwards also, when Alexander
had rased the citie of Thebes, and had required the Athenians to deliver him Demosthenes, Lycurgus, Hyperides, and
Caridemus, and that the whole assembly and counsell not
knowing what aunswer to make, did all cast their eyes uppon
Phocion, and cryed unto him to say his opinion: he then
rose uppe, and taking one of his friendes unto him called
Nicocles, whome he loved and trusted above all men els,
he sayd thus openly unto them: These men whome Alexander requireth, have brought this citie to this extremitie,
that if he required Nicocles here, I would give my consent to
deliver him: for I would thinke my selfe happy to lose my
life, for all your safetie. Furthermore, though I am right
hartely sory (sayd he) for the poore afflicted Thebans, that
are come into the citie for succour: yet I assure ye, it is
better one citie mourne, then two. And therefore I thinke
it best to intreate the Conqueror for both, rather then to our
certeine destruction to fight with him that is the stronger.
It is sayd also that Alexander refused the first decree which
the people offered him uppon Phocions request, and sent
awaye the Ambassadors, and would not speake with them.
But the second, which Phocion him selfe brought, he tooke:
beeing tolde by his fathers olde servaunts, that king Philip
made great accompt of him. Whereuppon, Alexander did
not onely give him audience, and graunt his request, but
further followed his counsell. For Phocion perswaded him,
if he loved quietnes, to leave warre: if he desired fame,
then, that he should make warre with the barbarous people,

Alexander
pacified with
the Athen-
ians, by
Phocions
meanes.

87

but not with the Græcians. So Phocion feeding Alexanders humor with such talke and discourse as he thought would like him best: he so altered and softened Alexanders disposition, that when he went from him, he willed him that the Athenians should looke to their affayres, for if he should dye, he knewe no people fitter to commaund then they. Furthermore, bicause he would be better acquainted with Phocion, and make him his friend: he made so much of him, that he more honored him, then all the rest of his friends. To this effect, Duris the historiographer writeth, that when Alexander was growen very great, and had overcome king Darius: he left out of his letters this worde Chærin (to wit, joy, and health) which he used commonly in all the letters he wrote, and would no more honor any other with that maner of salutacion, but Phocion, and Antipater. Chares also writeth the same. And they all doe confesse, that Alexander sent Phocion a great gift out of Asia, of a hundred silver talents. This money being brought to Athens, Phocion asked them that brought it, why Alexander gave him such a great reward, above all the other Citizens of Athens. Bicause, sayd they, he onely esteemeth thee to be a good, and honest man. Phocion replied againe, Then let him give me leave to be what I seeme, and am, whilest I live. The Messengers would not so leave him, but followed him home to his house, where they saw his great husbandrie, and thriftines: For they found his wife her selfe baking, and he him selfe drewe water before them, out of the well, to wash his feete. But then they were more earnestly in hand with him than before, and prayed him to take the kings present, and were offended with him, saying it was a shame for Alexanders friend to live so miserably and beggerly as he did. Then Phocion seeing a poore old man goe by, in a threede bare gowne, asked them, whether they thought him worse then he? No, God forbid, aunswered they againe. Then replied he againe, He lives with lesse then I do, and yet is contented, and hath enough. To be short, said he, if I should take this summe of money and occupy it not, it is as much as I had it not: on thother side, if I occupy it, I shall make all the citie speake ill of the king

Phocions
vertue and
integrity,
refusing of
Alexanders
money.

88

and me both. So this great present was sent backe from
Athens, whereby he shewed the Græcians, that he was richer
that needed not such golde and silver, then he that gave it
him. But when Alexander wrote againe unto Phocion, that
he did not reckon them his friendes, that would take nothing
of him: Phocion notwithstanding would not take the money,
but onely requested him for his sake, that he would set these
men at libertie, which were kept prisoners in the citie of Sardis,
for certeine accusations layde against them: Echecratides
the Rhetorician, Athenodorus borne in the citie of Imbros,
and two Corinthians, Demaratus and Spartus. Alexander
presently set them at libertie, and sent Craterus into
Macedon, commaunding him to give Phocion the choyce of
one of these foure cities of Asia, which he liked best: Cios,
Gergitha, Mylassis, Elea: sending him worde, that he would
be much more angrier with him now, if he did refuse this
offer, then he was at the first. But Phocion would never
accept any one of them: and Alexander shortly after dyed.
Phocions house is seene yet at this day in the village of
Melita, set forth with plates of copper, but otherwise very
meane, and without curiositie. For his wives he maryed,
there is no mention made of the first, saving that Cephiso-
dotus the image graver was her brother. But for his second
wife, she was no lesse famous at Athens for her honestie, and
good housewiverie: then Phocion for his justice and equitie.
And for proofe thereof, it is reported, that the Athenians
beeing one daye assembled in the Theater, to see newe
tragedies played, one of the players when he shoulde have
comen apon the scaffolde, to have played his parte, asked
the setter forth of the playes, the apparell of a Queene, and
certeine Ladyes to wayte uppon her, bycause he was to playe
the parte of the Queene. The setter forth of the playes
denying him, the player went awaye in a rage, and left the
people staring one at another, and woulde not come out
upon the stage. But Melanthius the setter forth of the
playes, compelling him, brought him by force on the stage,
and cryed out unto him: Doost thou not see Phocions wife,
that goeth uppe and downe the citie, with one mayde onely
wayting on her? and wilt thou playe the foole, and marre the

modestie of the women of Athens? The people hearing his wordes, filled all the Theater with joye and clapping of handes. The same Ladye, when a certaine gentlewoman of Ionia came to Athens to see her, and shewed her all her riche jewells and precious stones she had: she aunswered her agayne, All my riches and jewells, is my husband Phocion, who these twenty yeares together, hath continually beene chosen generall for the Athenians. Phocions sonne telling his father on a tyme, that he was desirous to contend with other younge men for the victorie, who should cunningliest leape out, and gette uppe agayne into the charretts or coches, running their full course, at the feastes Panathenæa at Athens: his father was contented he shoulde, not that he was desirous his sonne shoulde have the honor of the victorie, but bicause by this honest exercise he should growe to better manner, for that he was a dissolute younge man, and much given to wine. Yet he wanne the victorie at that tyme, and there were divers of his fathers friendes, that prayed him to doe them that honour, that they might keepe the feast of this victorie in their houses. Phocion denyed them all, but one man, and him he suffered to shewe his good will unto his house, and went thither him selfe to supper to him. Where amongest many fine and superfluous thinges prepared, he found passing bathes of wine and sweete smelling spices to washe the feete of the bydden guestes as they came to the feast: whereuppon he called his sonne to him, and asked him, Howe canst thou abyde Phocus, that our friend should thus disgrace thy victorie with excesse? But bicause he would withdrawe his sonne from that licentious life, he brought him to Sparta, and placed him there amonge younge boyes brought uppe after the Laconian discipline. The Athenians were much offended at it, to see that Phocion did so much despise his owne contrie manner and facions. Also when Demades the Orator one daye sayde unto Phocion: Why doe we not perswade the Athenians to live after the Laconian manner? As for me (sayde he) if thou wilt make one to sette it forwarde: I am ready to be the first man to move the matter. In deede, quoth Phocion, thou art a meete man to perswade the Athenians to live Laconian like, in common together at their meales, and to prayse Lycurgus straight lawe: that art thy selfe commonly so perfumed, and fine in thy apparell. Another tyme when Alexander wrote letters unto Athens to sende him some shippes, and that the Orators perswaded them not to graunt him, the people called uppon Phocion chiefly to saye his opinion: then Phocion tolde them plainely, Me thinkes ye must eyther make your selves the strongest in warres, or beeing the weaker, procure to be friendes unto the stronger. Pythias, a newcome Orator, beeing full of tongue, and impudent, would still make one to speake in every matter: wherefore Phocion sayde unto him, Good goddes, will this noves never leave babling? And when Harpalus king Alexanders Lieue- tenant of the province of Babylon, fledde out of Asia, and came to Attica with a greate summe of golde and silver: straight these men that solde their tongues to the people for money, flocked about him like a sight of swallowes. And he stucke not to give every one of them a peece of money to baste them with: for it was a trifle to him, considering the great summes of money he brought. But to Phocion him selfe, he sent unto him seven hundred talents, and offered him selfe and all that he had into his handes of trust. But Phocion gave him a sharpe aunswer, and tolde him, that he woulde make him repent it, if he corrupted the citie of Athens in that manner. So Harpalus beeing amated there- with, left him at that tyme, and went unto them that had taken money of him. But shortly after, when the Athenians sate in counsell about him, he perceived that those which had taken his money, were shronke from him, and that they did accuse him, where they should have excused him, to bleere the world, that men should not suspecte them they had beene corrupted: and that Phocion on thother side which had refused his money, having respect to the common wealth, had also some regarde to save his life: he once more at- tempted all the wayes he could to wynne him. Howbeit he found him so constant, that no money could cary the man. Then Harpalus, falling in friendshippe with Charicles (Pho- cions sonne in lawe) he made him to be ill spoken of, and greatly suspected, bicause men sawe that he trusted him in all thinges, and employed him in all his affayres. As, in committing to his trust the making of a sumptuous tombe for Pythonicé, the famous Curtisan that was deade, whom he loved, and by whome he had a Daughter: the taking apon him whereof was no lesse shame unto Charicles, then the finishing thereof was disgrace unto him. This tombe is seene unto this daye in a place called Hermium, in the hie waye from Athens to Eleusin: the workemanshippe thereof being nothing like neare the charge of thirtie talents, which was reported to bee given by Harpalus unto Charicles, for the finishing of the same. Furthermore, after Harpalus death, Charicles and Phocion tooke his Daughter, and carefully brought her uppe. Afterwardes also, Charicles beeing accused for the money he had taken of Harpalus, he besought his father in lawe Phocion, to helpe to ease him in his judgement. But Phocion flatly denyed him, and sayde: Charicles, I tooke thee for my sonne in lawe, in all honest and just causes onely. Furthermore, when Asclepiades, the sonne of Hipparchus, brought the first newes of the deathe of Kinge Alexander, Demades the Orator woulde not beleeve him: For, sayde he, if it were true, all the earthe woulde smell of the savour of his corse. Phocion then perceyving the people beganne to bee highe minded, and sought innovacion: he went about to brydle and pacifie them. But when many of the Orators gotte uppe to the pulpitte for orations, and cryed out, that Asclepiades newes were true of Alexanders deathe: Well then, quoth Phocion, if it bee true to daye, it shall be true also to morrowe, and the next day after. And therefore my Maisters, bee not too hasty, but thinke of it at better leysure, and sette your affayres at a sure staye. When Leosthenes also by his practise had brought the citie of Athens into the warre called the Greekes warre, and in skorne asked Phocion, that was offended at it, what good he had done to the common wealth so many yeares together as he had beene Generall over the Athenians: Phocion aunswered him, No small good, sayde he, for all my contrye men have beene buryed at home in their owne graves. Another tyme Leosthenes speaking prowdely and insolently

GRECIANS AND ROMANES

to the people, Phocion one daye sayde unto him: Younge
man my friende, thy wordes are lyke to a Cypres tree, which
is highe and greate, but beareth no frute.   Then Hyperides
rising uppe, asked Phocion: When wilt thou then counsell
the Athenians to make warre? When I shall see younge men,
sayde he, not forsake their rancks, riche men liberall, and
Orators leave to robbe the common wealth.   When the
Athenians wondred to see suche a goodly greate armie as
Leosthenes had leavied: and that they asked Phocion howe
he lyked it: A goodly armie, quoth he, for a furlonge, but I
feare their returne, and the continuance of this warre: for I
doe not see the citie able to make any more money, nor moe
shippes, neyther yet any moe souldiers than these.   The
which proved true, as it fell out afterwardes.   For at the
first, Leosthenes did notable exployts.   He overcame the
Bœotians in battell, and drave Antipater into the citie of
Lamia: the which did put the Athenians in suche a hope
and jolitie, that they made continuall feastes and sacrifices
through the citie, to thanke the gods for these good newes.
And there were some amonge them, that to take Phocion in
a trippe, asked him if he did not wish that he had done all
those things? Yes in deede, aunswered he, I would I had
done them, but yet I would not have given the counsel to
have done them.   Another tyme also when letters came,
dayly, one after an other, bringing good newes, Good gods,
sayde he, when shall we leave to overcome? When Leosthenes was deade in this voyage, they that feared Phocion
shoulde bee appoynted Captayne in his place, and that he
woulde pacifie the warre: did thrust in a man of meane
havior, and unknowen, that sayde in the affemblie, he was
Phocions friende and schoolefellowe, and therefore besought
the people that they woulde spare Phocion, bicause they had
not suche another man as he, and that they woulde make
Antiphilus Generall of their armie.   The people were contented withall.   But then Phocion stoode uppe, and sayde,
that this man was never scholler with him, neyther did he
ever knowe him before that tyme: But nowe sayde he, from
henceforth I will take thee for my friende, for thou hast
given the people the best counsell for me.   The people not-

withstanding determining to make warre with the Bœotians, Phocion spake agaynst it all he coulde. Thereuppon, his friendes bidding him beware of suche speeches : howe he did offende the people, least they killed him : he aunswered them, They shall wrongefully put me to death, quoth he, speaking for the benefitte of my contrye, but otherwise they shall have reason to doe it, if I speake to the contrarye. But when he sawe nothing woulde pacifie them, and that they went on still with their intent : then he commaunded the Herawlde to proclayme by sownde of trompet, that all Citizens from fourteene yeares to three score, able to cary weapon, should presently uppon breaking up of thassembly, arme them selves, and followe him with five dayes provision for vittells. Then was there greate sturre amonge them in the citie, and the olde men came and complayned unto him for his over straight commaundement. He tolde them agayne, I doe you no wronge : for I am foure skore my selfe, and yet will goe with you. By this meanes he pacified them at that tyme, and quenched their fond desire of warre. But when all the sea coast was full of souldiers, both of the Macedonians, and other straungers which were ledde by Micion their Captaine, that landed in the territorie of the village Rhamnus, and spoyled the contry thereaboutes : then Phocion ledde the Athenians thither. But when he was there, divers taking upon them the office of a Lieuetenant, and going about to counsell him, some to lodge his campe upon such a hill, and others to send his horsemen to such a place, and others to campe here : O Hercules, quoth he, how many Captaines doe I see, and how fewe souldiers ! Afterwardes when he had set his footemen in battell raye, there was one amonge them that left his rancke, and stepped out before them all. Thereuppon one of his enemies also made towardes him, to fight with him : but the Athenians hart failed him, and he went backe againe to his place. Then sayd Phocion unto him : Art thou not ashamed young lowte to have forsaken thy rancke twise ? the one where thy Captaine had placed thee, and the other in the which thou haddest placed thy self ? So Phocion giving charge apon the enemies, he overthrew them, and slue Micion their

94

GRECIANS AND ROMANES

Captaine, with divers others. Furthermore, the armie of
the Græcians being at that time in Thessaly, wanne a battell
against Antipater, and Leonatus, that joyned with him with
the Macedonians which he had brought out of Asia : where
Leonatus was slaine in the field, Antiphilus beeing generall
of the footemen, and Menon Thessalian, Colonell of the
horsemen. Shortly after, Craterus comming out of Asia
into Europe with a great armie, they fought a battell by the
citie of Cranon, where the Græcians were overthrowen : yet
was not the overthrowe nor slaughter greate, although it
came through the disobedience of the souldiers to their
Captaines, which were but young men, and used them over
gently. Moreover, when Antipater practised to make their
cities revolt, they betrayed them, and shamefully forsooke
to defend their common libertie : whereuppon Antipater
marched forthwith with his armie, to the citie of Athens.
Demosthenes and Hyperides understanding that, forsooke
the citie. Then Demades, that was in disgrace and defamed
for lacke of payment of such fynes as were set upon his head
(being seven severall times condemned, bicause he had so
many tymes moved matters contrary to the law) and could
not therefore be suffered any more to speake in the assembly,
was then dispensed withall, and licensed to speake : whereuppon he moved the people to send Ambassadors unto
Antipater, with full commission and authoritie to treate
with him of peace. The people fearing to put to any mans
trust this absolute authoritie to treate of peace : they called
for Phocion, saying, that he onely was to be trusted with the
ambassade. Then Phocion aunswered them : If you had
beleeved my former counsells I alwaies gave you, such weighty
matters should not now have troubled you at all. So the
decree being confirmed by the people, Phocion was sent
Ambassador unto Antipater, that laye then in the castell of
Cadmea, being ready at that time to invade the contrye of
Attica. Phocion first requested him, that before he removed
from thence, he would make peace with the Athenians.
Craterus presently aunswered him : Phocion, thy request is
unreasonable, that lying here we should eate out our friendes,
and destroy their contry : when we may live of our enemies,

and enriche our selves with their spoyle. But Antipater taking Craterus by the hand, tolde him : We must needes doe Phocion this pleasure. And for the rest, touching the capitulacions of peace, he willed that the Athenians should send them a blancke, and referre the condicions of peace unto them : like as he him selfe being beseeged in the citie of Lamia, had referred all capitulacions and articles of peace, unto the discression of Leosthenes their generall. So when Phocion was come backe to Athens, the Athenians seeing there was no remedie, were compelled to be contented with such offer of peace, as the enemie made them. Then Phocion was sent back againe to Antipater at Thebes, with other Ambassadors joyned in commission with him : amongest whom also, was that famous Philosopher Xenocrates. The

estimation of his vertue was so great with all men, that it was thought there was no living man so prowd, cruel, disdainful, or hasty of nature, but that the onely looke of Xenocrates would soften and qualifie him, and make him to reverence him. But yet with Antipater it fell out contrary, by his perverse nature, which hated all vertue : for he im-

braced all the rest, and would not once salute Xenocrates. Whereuppon, some say, that Xenocrates said then : Antipater doth well to be ashamed, to see me a witnes of the discurtesie and evill he meaneth unto the Athenians. So when Xenocrates beganne to speake, Antipater would not abide to heare him, but interrupted him, and checked him, and in the ende commaunded him to holde his peace. When Phocion had spoken, Antipater aunswered them : that he would make peace with the Athenians, so they delivered him Demosthenes and Hyperides : that they should keepe their auncient lawes and government, that they should receive a garrison into the haven of Munychia, that they should defray the charges of this warre, and also paye a raunsome besides. All the other Ambassadors but Xenocrates, willingly accepted these condicions of peace, as very reasonable and favourable : but he sayde, that for slaves, Antipater did handle them favorably : but for free men, he delt too hardly with them. Then Phocion besought him that he would yet release them of their garrison. But Antipater (as it is sayde) aunswered him · Phocion, we would gladly graunt thee any thing, saving that which should undoe thee, and us both. Some other write notwithstanding, that Antipater sayd not so, but asked him, if he would become suertie for the Athenians, that they should attempt no alteracion, but faithfully keepe the articles and conditions of this peace, if he did release them of this garrison. Phocion then holding his peace, and delaying aunswer, there was one Callimedon surnamed Carabos, (a bolde man, and hated the libertie of the people) that brake forth in these words · If Phocion were so fond to give his word for the Athenians, wouldest thou, Antipater, beleve him therefore, and leave to doe that thou hast determined ? Thus were the Athenians driven to receive the garrison of the Macedonians, of the which Menyllus was captaine, an honest man, and Phocions friend. This commaundement to receive the garrison within the haven of Munichya, was found very stately, and done by Antipater, rather of a vaine glory to boast of his power : then for any profit could otherwise come of it. For not long after, on that day when he tooke possession of the castell, he further increased their griefe : bicause the garrison entred the twenty day of Bœdromion (to wit, the moneth of August) on the which the feast day of their misteries was celebrated, at what time they make their procession called Iacchus, from the citie of Athens, unto Eleusin. Therefore the solemnitie of this holy feast beeing thus confused, many beganne to consider, that in olde tyme when their Realme did flourishe, there were heard and scene voyces and images of the goddes on that day, which made the enemies both afraid, and amazed : and nowe in contrary manner, in the very selfe same solemnitie of the gods, they sawe the greatest calamitie that could have happened unto Græce. And the holiest feast which was kept all the yere through before, became then too prophaned with the title of the greatest misfortune and event, that ever happened unto the Græcians, which was, the losse of their libertie. For not many yeares before, there was brought an oracle from Dodone unto Athens : that they shoulde looke well to the rockes of Diana, that straungers shoulde not possesse them. And about that tyme also, the coverings with the which

Presages of the miseries of the Athenians.

they doe adorne the holy beddes of the mysteries, beeing wette with water, became from a purple culler which they had before, to looke yellowe and pale, as it had beene the covering of a deade bodie. Yea, and that which was moste to bee wondered at of all other, was this: that taking other coverings which were not holy, and putting them in the same water, they did without chaunging keepe their culler they had before. When one of the Ministers of the temple also did washe a litle pygge in the sea, in a cleane place by the wharfe: there sodainely came a greate fishe that bytte at it, and caryed the hinder partes of the pygge cleane awaye with it. Whereby men conjectured that the goddes did signifie unto them, that they should lose the lowest parte of their citie nearest to the sea, and should keepe the highest partes thereof. This notwithstanding, the garrison did not offend nor trouble the Athenians, bicause of the honestie of their Captaine Menyllus. Now there were above twelve thowsand Citizens, that for their povertie lost the benefit of their freedome: of the which, parte of them remayned at Athens, unto whome it seemed they offered great wronge and injurie: and parte of them also went into Thracia, where Antipater assigned them townes and landes to inhabite. They seemed to be men like unto them that had beene taken by assaulte, or by seege within a citie, which had beene compelled to forsake their contrie. Furthermore, the shamefull death of Demosthenes in the Ile of Calauria, and of Hyperides, by the citie of Cleones, (whereof we have written heretofore) were almost occasion given them to lament the tymes of the raigne of king Philip and Alexander. As it is reported, that when Antigonus was slayne, they that had overcomen him, were so cruell unto their subjectes: that a laborer in the contrie of Phrygia digging the earthe, beeing asked what he sought for, aunswered, sighing: I seeke for Antigonus. Then many men beganne to say as much, when they remembred the noble mindes of those two great Princes, howe mercifull they were to pardon in their anger, forgetting their displeasure: not like Antipater, who craftily cloked his tyrannicall power which he usurped, by beeing famillier, going simplely apparelled, and faring meanely: and yet showed

98

hım selfe notwithstanding a more cruell Lorde and tyrant unto them whome he had overcome. Nevertheles, Phocıon obtayned of hım the restoring agayne of divers men, whome he had banıshed : and those whome he coulde not gette to bee restored, yet he procured that they shoulde not be banished ınto so farre contries, as others whıch had beene sent beyonde the Mountaınes Acroceraunians, and the head of Tænarus out of Græce, but that they had libertie to remayne withın the contrie of Peloponnesus : amonge the which, was one Agnonıdes a Sycophant, and false accuser. Furthermore, he governed them that remayned ın Athens wıth gıeat justice and lenitie, and such as he knewe to be good men and quiet, them he alwayes preferred to some office . but such as he sawe were fantastyke people, and desırous of chaunge, he kept them from office, and tooke all occasion from them, so that they vanıshcd awayc of them selȷes, and learned in tyme to loʌe the contrye, and to followe tillage. When he sawe Xenocrates also paye a certeine pension or trıbute to the common wealth, ʌhich all straungers dwelling in Athens did use yearely to payc : he woulde have made him ɑ fıee man, and offered to put hıs name amongest the number of free Cıtızens. But Xenocrates refused ıt, saying, he woulde have no parte of that freedome, for the hinderance whereof, he had beene sent Ambassador. And when Menyllus had sent Phocion money, he made him aunswer : that Menyllus was no greater Lorde then Aleʌander had beene, neyther had he at that tyme any greater occasion to receyve hıs present, then when he had refused Kıng Alexanders gyfte. Menyllus ıeplyıng agayne, sayde that if he had no needc of it for hım selfe, yet he mıght let hıs sonne Phocus have it. But Phocion aunswered : If my sonne Phocus will leave his naughtye lyfe, and become an honest man, that whıch I wıll leave hım, shall serve hıs turne ʌery well : but if ıt bee so that he will still holde on the course he hath taken, there is no rıches then that can suffice him. Aıı other tyme also he aunswered Antipater more rowndely, when he ʌoulde have had hım done an unhonest thinge · Antıpater, sayde he, can not have me his friende, and flatterer both. Antıpater selfe was wont to saye, that he had two

99

friendes in Athens, Phocion and Demades: of the which, he coulde never make the one to take any thinge of him, and the other, he coulde never satisfie him. And truely Phocions

Phocion loved povertie.

povertye was a greate glorye of his vertue, sythe he was growen olde, continuing in the same, after he had beene so many tymes generall of the Athenians, and had receyved suche friendshippe and curtesie, of so many Kinges and Princes. Where Demades to the contrarye delighted to

The insolencie of Demades the Orator.

shewe his riches in thinges that were contrarye to the lawes of the citie. For, a decree beeing made at Athens, commaunding that no straunger, uppon forfeyture of a thowsand Drachmas to bee payed by the defrayer of the daunces to the citie, shoulde bee any of the Dauncers that daunced at any common playes or sportes: Demades one daye making certeyne games and sportes at his owne charges, brought a hundred Dauncers of straungers at one tyme, and withall, brought also a hundred thowsand Drachmas to paye the forfeyture thereof. Another tyme when he maryed his sonne Demas, he sayde unto him: Sonne, when I maryed thy mother, there was so small roste, that my next neyghbour knewe not of it: where nowe at thy maryage, Kinges and Princes are at the charge of the feaste. Furthermore, when the Athenians were importunate with Phocion to goe to Antipater, to intreate him to take his garrison out of their citie: he still refused the ambassade, eyther bycause he had no hope to obtayne it, or for that he sawe the people more obedient unto reason, for feare of the garrison. Howebeit he obtayned of Antipater, that he shoulde not bee too hastye in demaundinge of his money, but shoulde deferre it tyll a further tyme. So the Athenians perceiving they could doe no good with Phocion, they intreated Demades, who willingly tooke the matter upon him, and went with his sonne into Macedon, whether doubtles his destinie caried him to his utter destruction, even at that very time when Antipater

Cassander king Antipaters sonne.

was fallen sicke of a dissease whereof he dyed: whereby the affayres of the Realme went through the handes of Cassander his sonne, who had intercepted a letter of this Demades, which he had sent unto Antigonus in Asia, willing him to come in all possible speede to winne Græce and Macedon, which hong but of an old rotten threde, mocking Antipater in this maner. Wherfore Cassander being advertised of his arrival, he made him presently to be apprehended, and setting his sonne hard by him, slue him before his father, so neere him, that the blood of his sonne sprang upon him: so that the father was all bloodied with the murther of his sonne. Then Cassander casting in Demades teeth his ingratitude, and trecherous treason against his father, géving him all the reproachfull words he could devise: at the length he slue him with his owne hands. Now Antipater before his death, had established Polyperchon General of the armie of the Macedonians, and Cassander his sonne, only Colonell of a thowsand footemen. He notwithstanding, after his fathers decease, taking upon him the government of the realme: sent Nicanor with speede to succeede Menillus in the Captaineship of the garrison of Athens, before his death should be revealed, commaunding him first in any case, to take the castell of Munychia, which he did. Shortly after, the Athenians understanding of the death of Antipater, they accused Phocion, for that he had knowen of his death long before, and yet kept it secret to please Nicanor. But Phocion regarded not this accusation, but fell in acquaintance notwithstanding with Nicanor: whom he handled so wisely, that he made him not only frendly unto the Athenians, but furthermore perswaded him to be at some charge to geve the people the pastime of common playes, which he made to be done at his cost. In the meane time, Polyperchon, who had the government of the kings person, meaning to geve Cassander a slampant and blurt, he sent letters pattentes unto the people at Athens, declaring how the young king did restore unto them their popular state againe, and commaunded that all the Athenians should use their former auncient lawes of their citie. This was a wile and craftie fetche against Phocion. For Polyperchon devising this practise to get the city of Athens into his hands (as it fel out afterwards by proofe) had no hope to obtaine his purpose, unles he found meanes first to banish Phocion: and thought that he shoulde easily bring that to passe, when suche as had before bene put of their freedom, by his meanes,

PHOCION

The unfortunate end of Demades.

Polyperchon Generall of the armie of the Macedonians.

Polyperchons conspiracie against Phocion.

101

should come againe to have voyces in thassembly, and that the seditious Orators and accusers might be turned at liberty againe, to say what they would. The Athenians having heard the contentes of these letters pattentes, beganne to be somewhat quickened, and moved withall : whereupon Nicanor desiring to speake with the Athenians in their Senate, which was assembled in the haven of Piræa : he went and hazarded his person amongest them, apon Phocions faith and word. Dercyllus Captaine for the king, being secretly advertised thereof, and in the field, not farre from the citie, did what he could to take Nicanor : but Nicanor having warning of it in time, saved him selfe. Then it appeared, that Nicanor would presently be revenged of the citie, and they accused Phocion bicause he kept him not, but did let him goe. Whereunto he aunswered : that he trusted Nicanors word, and that he did not thinke he would offer the citie any hurt, but if it should fall out otherwise, he had

rather the world should know, that he had the wrong offred him, then that he should offer any. This truely appeared to be nobly spoken, in respect of him selfe. But considering that he being then Generall, did thereby hazard the safety of his contrie : I can not tell whether he did not breake a greater faith which he ought to have had, to the safetie of his contriemen. Neither coulde he also alleage for his excuse, that he did not laye handes on Nicanor, for feare to bring the city into manifest warre : but that for a colour he did preferre the faith which he had sworne and promised unto him, and the justice that he would observe in his behalfe : that for his sake, Nicanor should afterwards keepe him selfe in peace, and doe no hurte to the Athenians. Howbeit in troth it seemed, that nothing deceived Phocion : but by the over trust he had in this Nicanor. The which seemeth to be so, bicause when divers came to him to complaine of Nicanor, that he sought all the secret meanes he coulde to surprise the haven of Piræa, and that he dayly passed over souldiers in the Ile of Salamina, and practised to bribe certaine of the inhabitants within the precinct of the haven : he would never heare of it, and muche lesse beleve it. Furthermore, when Philomedes Lamprian made a motion, that the Athenians

102

should prepare to be in readines to waite apon their Captaine
Phocion, to do as he commaunded them: he made no account
of it, untill he saw Nicanor come out with his souldiers from
the fort of Munychia, and that he beganne to cast trenches
to compasse in the haven of Piræa. But then, when Phocion
thought to lead out the people to prevent him: he found
they mutined against him, and no man would obey his commaundement. In the meane time, Alexander the sonne of
Polyperchon came with an armie, pretending to aide them of
the citie against Nicanor, where in deede he ment (if he
could) to get the rest of the city into his hands, then
specially, when they were in greatest broile one against an
other, and the rather, bicause the banished men entred hand
over head with him, and divers straungers also, and other
defamed men: so that there was a confused counsel and
assembly of Omnigatherum kept within the citie, without
any order, in the which Phocion was deprived of his office of
Generall, and others were also chosen Captaines in his place.
And had they not seene this Alexander talking alone with
Nicanor, and returning many times hard to the walles of the
citie, which made the Athenians affrayed and mistrustfull:
they had never saved it from taking. At that time Phocion
was presently accused of treason by the Orator Agnonides:
the which Callimedon and Pericles fearing, got them out of
the citie betimes. And Phocion also with his frends that
were not fled, went unto Polyperchon: with whom also Solon
Plataeian, and Dinarchus Corinthian, went for company, who
thought to have found frendshippe and familiarity with
Polyperchon. Howbeit Dinarchus falling sicke by the way,
in the citie of Elatia, they stayed there many dayes, hoping
of his recoverie. But in the meane time, the people at the
perswasion of the Orator Agnonides, and at the request of
Archestratus, stablished a decree, to sende Ambassadors unto
Polyperchon, to accuse Phocion: insomuch as both parties
met at one selfe time, and found him in the field with the
king about a village of the contrie of Phocide, called Pharyges,
standing at the foote of the mountaine Acrorion, which they
surname also Galaten. There Polyperchon commaunded a
cloth of gold to be set up, and caused the king to be set

Alexander,
the sonne of
Polyperchon,
practiseth
treason
against the
Athenians.

under the same, and all his chiefest frendes about him. But to beginne withall, he made Dinarchus to be taken, and commaunded them to put him to death after they had racked him : then he willed the Athenians to tell what they had to say. Then they beganne to quarrell, and to be lowde one with an other, accusing one an other in the presence of the king and his counsell : untill Agnonides at length stepped forth, and sayd : My Lordes of Macedon, put us all in prison, and then send us bound handes and feete to Athens, to geve accompt of our doinges. The king laughed to heare him say so. But the noble men of Macedon that were present then, and divers straungers besides to heare their complaints : made signe to the Ambassadors to utter their accusations before the king, rather then to referre them to the hearing of the people at Athens. Howbeit both parties had not alike indifferent hearing : for Polyperchon checked up Phocion oftentimes, and did still cut of his tale, as he thought to purge him selfe : insomuch as in anger, he bet his staffe he had in his hand against the ground, and commaunded him at length to hold his peace, and to get him thence. And when Hegemon also told Polyperchon, that he him selfe could best witnesse, howe Phocion had alwayes faithfully served and loved the people : he angrily aunswered him, Come not hether to lye falsely upon me, in the presence of the king. Therewith the king rose out of his seate, and tooke a speare in his hand, thinking to have killed Hegemon : had not Polyperchon sodainly embraced him behinde, and stayed him. So the counsell rose, and brake up, but presently Phocion was apprehended, and they that stoode by him. Certaine of his frends seeing that, which stoode further of, muffeled their faces, and straight conveyed them selves away.

The rest were sent prisoners to Athens by Clitus, not so muche to have their causes heard there, as to have them executed for condemned men. Furthermore, the manner of the carying of them to Athens was shamefull. For they were caried upon cartes through the great streete Ceramicum, unto the Theater : where Clitus kept them, untill the Senate had assembled the people, excepting no bondman, no straunger, nor defamed person out of this assemblie, but left the

104

Theater wide open to all comers in whatsoever they were,
and the pulpit for Orations free for everie man that would
speake against them. So first of all, the kings letters were
read openly, by the which he did advertise the people, that
he had found these offendors convicted of treason : notwithstanding, that he referred the sentence of their condemnation unto them, for that they were free men.   Then Clitus
brought his prisoners before the people, where the noble men
when they saw Phocion, were ashamed, and hiding their
faces, wept to see him.   Howbeit, there was one that rose
up, and sayd : My Lordes, sith the king referreth the judgement of so great persons unto the people, it were great reason
all the bondmen and straungers which are no free citizens of
Athens, should be taken out of this assembly.   The people The furie of
would not agree to it, but cried out, that such traitors should the Athen-
be stoned to death, that favor the authoritie of a few, and ians against
are enemies of the people : whereupon silence was made, and Phocion.
no man durst speake any more for Phocion.   Neverthelesse
when Phocion with muche a doe had obteyned audience, he
asked them : My Lords, will ye justly, or wrongfully put us
to death ? Some aunswered him : Justly.   Howe then can
ye doe it, quoth he, that will not heare our justifications ?
Yet coulde they not be heard for all this.   Then Phocion
comming neerer, sayd unto them : For my selfe, my Lordes,
I confesse I have done you wrong, and have in government
committed faults deserving death : but for these prisoners
with me, what have they done, why you shoulde put them to
death ? The common people aunswered him : Bicause they
are thy frends.   With this aunswere Phocion departed, and
spake never a word more.   Then the Orator Agnonides holding a decree in his hand ready wrytten, red it openly to the
people, declaring how they should be judged by voyces,
whether the offendors had deserved death or not : and if it
were found they had, then that they should all be put to
death.   And there were that when this decree was red, cried The crueltie
out, that they should adde further unto the decree, that of the Athen-
before Phocion should be put to death, they should first ians unto
torment him : and therewithall commaundement was geven Phocion.
that the wheele should be sette up to breake his joints apon

5 : O   105

it, and also that the hangman should be sent for. But then Agnonides perceiving that Clitus was offended with it, and thinking besides it were too beastly and barbarous a parte to use him in that sorte, he sayd openly: My Lordes, when you shall have such a varlet in your handes as Callimedon, then you may cast him on the wheele: but against Phocion, I would not with such cruelty. Then rose up a noble man among them, and added to his words: Thou hast reason to say so, Agnonides: for if Phocion should be layed on the wheele, what should we then doe with thee? The decree being confirmed, according to the contents thereof, judgement was geven by voyces of the people, no man sitting but all standing up, and most of them with garlandes on their heades, for the joy they had to condemne these prisoners to death. With Phocion there were condemned, Nicocles, Thudippus, Hegemon, and Pythocles: but Demetrius Phalerian, Callimedon, and Charicles, were also in their absence condemned to dye. Now when the assembly was broken up, and that the persons condemned were caried backe to prison, from thence to be conveyed to execution: others imbracing their frends, and taking their last leave of them as they went, wept, and lamented their cursed fortune. But Phocion looking as cheerefully of it as he was wont to doe being Generall, when they honorably waited on him to his house, from the assembly: he made many of them pitie him in their harts, to consider his constancie, and noble corage. On thother side also, there were many of his enemies that came as neere unto him as they could, to revile him, amongst whom there was one that stepped before him, and did spit in his face. Then Phocion turning him unto the Magistrates, sayd: Will you not cause this impudent fellow to leave his rayling? When they were in prison, Thudippus seeing the hemlocke which they brayed in a morter to geve them to drinke: he beganne desperatly to curse and banne, saying, that they wrongfully put him to death with Phocion. Why, sayd Phocion againe: and doost thou not rather rejoyce to dye with me? When one that stoode by asked Phocion, if he would any thing to his sonne Phocus: Yes, quoth he, that I will: bid him never revenge the wrong the Athenians do

106

me. Then Nicocles one of Phocions dearest frendes, prayed him to let him drinke the poyson before him. Phocion aunswered him, Thy request is grievous to me, Nicocles: but bicause I never denyed thee any thing in my life, I wil also graunt thee this at my death. When al the rest had dronke, there was no more poyson left, and the hangman sayd he would make no more unlesse they gave him twelve Drachmas, for so much the pound did cost him. Phocion perceiving then that the hangman delayed time, he called one of his frends unto him, and prayed him to geve the hangman that litle money he demaunded, sith a man can not dye at Athens for nothing, without cost. It was the nineteenth day of the moneth of Munichion, (to wit, Marche) on which day the Knights were wont to make a solemne procession in the honor of Iupiter: howbeit some of them left of the garlandes of flowers which they shoulde have worne on their heades, and others also looking towards the prison dore as they went by, burst out a weeping. For, they whose harts were not altogether hardned with crueltie, and whose judgements were not wholly suppressed with envie, thought it a grievous sacriledge against the goddes, that they did not let that day passe, but that they did defile so solemne a feast, with the violent death of a man. His enemies notwithstanding, continuing still their anger against him, made the people passe a decree, that his bodie should be banished, and caried out of the bondes of the contry of Attica, forbidding the Athenians that no fire should be made for the solemnising of his funeralls. For this respect no frend of his durst touch his body. Howebeit a poore man called Conopion, that was wont to get his living that way, being hyered for money to burne mens bodies: he tooke his corse, and caried it beyond the city of Eleusin, and getting fire out of a womans house of Megara, he solemnised his funeralls. Furthermore, there was a gentlewoman of Megara, who comming by chaunce that way, with her gentlewomen, where his body was but newly burnt: she caused the earth to be cast up a litle where the body was burnt, and made it like to a hollow tombe, whereupon she did use such sprincklings and effusions, as are commonly done at the funeralls of the dead: and then

Phocion gave money to be put to death

Phocions funeralls

107

taking up his bones in her lappe in the night, she brought them home, and buried them in her harth, saying: O deare harth, to thee I bequeath the relikes of this noble and good man, and pray thee to keepe them faithfully, to bring them one day to the grave of his auncesters, when the Athenians shall come to confesse the fault and wrong they have done unto him. And truly it was not long after, that the Athenians found by the untowardnes of their affaires, that they had put him to death, who only maintained justice, and honesty at Athens. Whereupon they made his image to be set up in brasse, and gave honorable buriall to his bones, at the charges of the citie. And for his accusers, they condemned Agnonides of treason, and put him to death them selves. The other two, Epicurus and Demophilus being fled out of the citie, were afterwardes met with by his sonne Phocus, who was revenged of them. This Phocus as men reporte, was otherwise no great good man, who fancying a young maide which a bawde kept, comming by chaunce one day into the schoole of Lycæum, he heard Theodorus the Atheist (to wit, that beleved not there were any goddes) make this argument: If it be no shame, sayd he, to deliver a mans frend from bondage, no more shame is it to redeeme his leman which he loveth: even so it is all one to redeeme a mans leman, as his frende. This young man taking this argument to serve his turne, belevinge that he might lawefully doe it, got the young maide he loved from the bawde.
Furthermore, this death of Phocion did also revive the
lamentable death of Socrates unto the Græcians: for
men thought that it was a like hainous offence
and calamitie unto the citie of Athens.

THE END OF PHOCIONS LIFE

GRECIANS AND ROMANES

THE LIFE OF CATO UTICAN

THE family and house of Cato, tooke his first glorie and name of his great grand-father, Cato the Censor: who for his vertue (as we have declared in his life) was one of the famousest and worthiest men of Rome in his time. This Cato whom we nowe wryte of, was left an orphan by his father and mother, with his brother Cæpio, and Porcia his sister. Servilia was also Catoes halfe sister, by his mothers side. All these were brought up with their uncle Livius Drusus, at that time the greatest man of the citie: for he was passing eloquent, and verie honest, and of as great a corage besides, as any other Romane. Men report, that Cato from his childhood shewed him selfe both in word and countenaunce, and also in all his pastimes and recreacions, verie constant, and stable. For he would goe through with that he tooke apon him to doe, and would force him selfe above his strength: and as he could not away with flatterers, so was he rough with them that went about to threaten him. He would hardly laugh, and yet had ever a pleasaunt countenance. He was not chollerike, nor easie to be angerd: but when the blood was up, he was hardly pacified. When he was first put to schoole, he was very dull of understanding, and slow to learne: but when he had once learned it, he would never forget it, as all men else commonly doe. For such as are quicke of conceite, have commonly the worst memories: and contrarily, they that are hard to learne, doe keepe that better which they have learned. For every kinde of learning is a motion and quickening of the minde. He seemed besides not to be light of credit, and that may be some cause of his slownes in conceite. For truely he suffereth somewhat that learneth, and thereof it commeth, that they that have least reason to resist, are those which doe give lightest credit. For young men are easelyer perswaded then old men, and the sicke then the whole. And where a man hath least reason for his douts: there he is soonest brought to beleve any thing. This notwithstanding, it is reported that Cato was obedient unto his schoolemaister, and would doe what he commaunded him: howbeit he would aske him still the cause and reason of every thing. In deede his schoolemaister was very gentle, and readier to teach him, then to strike him with his fist.

His name was Sarpedo. Furthermore, when Cato was but a young boy, the people of Italie which were confederats of the Romanes, sued to be made free citizens of Rome. At that time it chaunced one Pompedius Silo, a valliant souldier, and of great estimacion among the confederats of the Romanes, and a great frend besides of Drusus: to be lodged many dayes at his house. He in this time falling acquainted with these young boyes, sayd one day unto them: Good boyes, intreate your uncle to speake for us, that we may be made free citizens of Rome. Cæpio smiling nodded with his head, that he would. But Cato making no aunswere, looked very wisely apon the straungers that lay in the house. Then Pompedius, taking him aside, asked him: And thou, my pretie boy, what sayest thou to it? Wilt thou not pray thine uncle, as well as thy brother, to

be good to his guestes? Cato still held his peace, and aunswered nothing, but shewed by his silence and looke, that he would not heare their request. Then Pompedius taking him up in his armes, did put him out of the window, as if he would have let him have gone: and speaking more sharply to him then he did before, he cast him many times out of his armes without the window, and sayd, Promise us

The mar-
velous con-
stancie of
Cato when he
was a child

then, or else I will let thee fall. But Cato abid it a long time, and never quinched for it, nor shewed countenaunce of feare. Thereupon Pompedius setting him downe againe, told his frends that stoode by him: O what good happe doth this child promise one day unto Italie, if he live? sure if he were a man, I beleve we should not have one voice of all the people of our side. An other time, there were some of Catoes neere kinsemen, that keeping the feast day of his birth, bad many young boyes to supper, and amongest others this Cato. The boyes to occupie them selves till supper was ready, gathered them selves together great and small, into some private place of the house. Their play was, counterfeating pleadinges before the judges, accusing one an other, and carying them that were condemned to prison. Amongest them, a goodly young boy was caried by a bigger boy into a litle chamber, bounde as a condemned person. The boy perceiving he was locked up, cried out to Cato: who mistrusting what it was, went straight to the chamber dore and putting them by by force that withstoode him to come unto it, he tooke out the young boy, and caried him very angrily with him to his owne house, and all the other young boyes followed him also. So Cato had such name among the young boyes, that when Sylla made the game of young boyes running a horsebacke, which the Romanes call Troia: to appoint them before that they might be ready at the day of the show, he having gotten all the young boyes of noble houses together, appointed them two Captaines. Of them, the boyes tooke the one, bicause of his mother Metella, which was the wife of Sylla: but they would none of the other called Sextus, who was nephewe to Pompey the great, neither would they be exercised under him, nor followe him. Wherefore Sylla asked them, which of them they would have: they all cried then Cato, and Sextus him selfe did willingly geve him the honor, as the worthier of both. Sylla was their fathers frend, and therefore did send for them many times to come unto him, and he would talke with them: the which kindnes he shewed to few men, for the majestie and great authority he had. Serpedo also (Catoes schoolemaister) thinking it a great preferrement and safetie for his schollers, did commonly bring Cato unto Syllaes house, to waite upon him: the which was rather like unto a jayle or prison, for the great number of prisoners which were dayly brought thither, and put to death. Cato being then but foureteene yeares of age, and perceiving that there were many heades brought which were sayed to be of great men, and that every bodie sighed and mourned to see them: he asked his schoolemaister, how it was possible the tyran scaped, that some one or other killed him not? Bicause,

Syllaes love
unto Cato,
being but
a boy.

Catoes hate
being a boy
against a
tyran.

111

quoth Serpedo, that all men feare him, more than they hate him. Why then, replyed Cato againe, diddest thou not geve me a sword that I might kill him, to deliver my contry of this slavery and bondage? Serpedo hearing the boy say so, and seeing his countenaunce and eyes on fire with choller, he marvelled muche at it, and afterwardes had a very good eye unto him, least rashly he should attempt some thing against Sylla.

When he was but a litle boy, some asked him whom he loved best? My brother, sayed he. Then the other continuing stil to aske him, And who next? he answered likewise, his brother. Then the third time againe, likewise his brother. Till at length he that asked him, was weary with asking him so oft. Yea and when he was comen of age also, he then confirmed the love he bare to his brother in his deedes. For twenty yeares together he never supped without his brother Cæpio, neither went he ever out of his house into the market place, nor into the fields without him: but when his brother did noynt him selfe with sweete oyles of perfume, he would none of that, and in all things else, he led a straight and hard life. So that his brother Cæpio being commended of every man for his temperaunce, honesty, and sober life: he graunted in deede that in respect of others, he led a sober and temperate life: but when I doe (sayd he) compare my life with my brother Catoes, me thinkes then there is no difference betwext me and Sippius. This Sippius was at that time noted and pointed at, for his fine and curious effeminate life. After that Cato was once chosen Apolloes Priest, he went from his brother and tooke his portion of the goods of his father, which amounted to the summe of a hundred and twentie talentes. Then he lived more hardly then he did before. For he fell

in acquaintaunce with Antipater Tyrian, a Stoicke Philosopher, and gave him selfe chiefly unto the studie of morall and civill Philosophie, imbracing all exercise of vertue with suche an earnest desire, that it seemed he was prickt forward by some god: but above all other vertues, he loved the severitie of justice, which he would not wrest for any gift nor favor. He studied also to be eloquent, that he might speake openly before the people, bicause he would there

should be certaine warlike forces entertained in civill Philosophie, as also in a great citie. Notwithstanding, he would
not exercise it before any bodie, neither would he ever have
any man to heare him speake when he did learne to speake.
For when one of his frends told him one day, that men did
mislike he spake so litle in company : It skilleth no matter,
quoth he, so they can not reprove my life, for I will beginne
to speake, when I can say some thing worthy to be spoken.
Hard by the market place there was the common pallace or
towne house of the citie, called Basilica Porcia, the which
Porcius Cato the elder had built, in the time of his Censor-
ship. There the Tribunes were wont to keepe their audience :
and bicause there was a piller that troubled their seates, they
would either have taken it away, or else have set it in some
other place. That was the first cause that made Cato
against his will to goe into the market place, and to get up
into the pulpit for orations, to speake against them : where
having geven this first proofe of his eloquence and noble
minde, he was marvelously esteemed of. For his oration was
not like a young man, counterfeating finenes of speache and
affectation, but stout, full of wit and vehemency : and yet
in the shortnes of his sentences, he had such an excellent
grace withall, that he marvelously delighted the hearers : and
furthermore, shewing in nature a certaine gravetie besides,
it did so please them, that he made them laugh. He had a
very full and audible voyce that might be heard of a marvelous number of people, and such a strong nature besides,
that he never fainted, nor brake his speache : for many times
he would speake a whole day together, and was never wearie.
So when he had obtained his cause against the Tribunes, he
returned againe to keepe his former great silence, and to
harden his bodie with painefull exercises, as to abide heate,
frost, and snow bare headed, and always to goe a foote in
the fielde, where his frendes that did accompany him rode
a horsebacke, and sometime he would come and talke with
one, somtime with an other, as he went a foote by them.
He had a wonderfull pacience also in his sickenes. For when
he had any agew, he would be alone all day long, and suffer
no man to come and see him, untill he perceived his fit

CATO
UTICAN

Catoes act
for Basilica
Porcia.

Catoes
exercises.

was of him, and that he founde he was better. When he supped with his frendes and familiars, they drewe lottes who should choose their partes. If he chaunced not to choose, his frendes notwithstanding gave him the preferrement to choose: but he refused it, saying it was no reason, sith the goddesse Venus was against him. At the first he did not use to sitte long at the table, but after he had dronke one draught only, he would straight rise. But when he came to be elder, he sate long at the table: so that oftentimes he would sit it out all night with his frends, till the next morning. But they seeking to excuse it, sayd, that his great busines and affaires in the common wealth was the cause of it. For following that all the day long, having no leasure nor time to studie when night came, he delighted to talke with learned men, and Philosophers, at the bord. Wherefore when Memmius on a time being in company, sayed, that Cato did nothing but drinke all night: Cicero taking his tale out of his mouth, aunswered him, Thou doest not adde this unto it, that all the day he doth nothing but play at dyse. To be short, Cato thinking that the maners and facions of mens lives in his time were so corrupt, and required such great chaunge and alteracion: that to goe uprightly, he was to take a contrarie course in all thinges. For he saw that purple, red, and the lightest colours were best esteemed of: he in contrarie maner desired to weare blacke. And many times also after dinner he would goe abroade bare footed without shooes, and without any gowne: not bicause he would be wondered at for any suche straungenes, but to acquaint him selfe to be ashamed only of shameles and dishonest things, and to despise those which were not reproved, but by mens opinions. Furthermore, land being left him to the value of an hundred talentes by the death of a cousin of his, that likewise was called Cato: he put it all into ready money, to lend to his frendes that lacked, and without usury. And there were some of his frends also that would morgage his land, or his slaves, to the chamber of the city, for their owne private busines: the which he him selfe would either give them to morgage, or else afterwards confirme the morgage of them. Further-

more, when he was comen of age to marry, having never
knowen woman before, he was made sure to Lepida. This
Lepida had bene precontracted unto Metellus Scipio: but
afterwardes the precontract being broken, he forsooke her,
so that she was free, when Cato was contracted to her.
Notwithstanding, before Cato maried her, Scipio repenting
him that he had refused her, made all the meanes he could
to have her againe: and so he had. Cato tooke it so
grievously, that he thought to goe to lawe for her: but
his frendes disswaded him from it. Then seeing no other
remedie, to satisfie his angrie minde, he wrote verses against
Scipio, in the which he reviled him all he coulde: using the
bitter tauntes of Archilocus verses, but not suche impudent,
lewde, and childishe reproaches as be there. After that, he
maried Attilia, Soranus daughter, being the first woman he
ever knewe: yet not the onely woman whome he did knowe,
as is reported of Lælius, Scipioes frende, who therein was
counted the happier, bicause all that long time wherein
he lived, he never knewe other woman but his first wife.
Furthermore, in the warre of the bondemen (otherwise called
Spartacus warre) one Gellius was chosen Prætor of the armie
under whom Cato served of his owne good will, for the love
he bare unto his brother Cæpio, who in that armie had
charge of a thowsand footemen. Now Cato could not as he
wished, shewe his valliantnesse and good service, bicause of
the insufficiencie of the Prætor that gave ill direction. This
notwithstanding, in the middest of al the riot and insolency
of them in the campe, he shewing him selfe a stayed man
in all his doinges, valliant where neede was, and very wise
also: all men esteemed him to be nothing inferior unto Cato
the elder. Whereuppon Gellius the Prætor gave him many
honors in token of his valliantnes, which are given in reward
of mens good service: howebeit Cato refused them, and
sayd, that he was nothing worthie of those honors. These
thinges made him to be thought a marvelous straunge man.
Furthermore, when there was a lawe made, forbidding all
men that sued for any office in the common wealth, that
they should have no prompters in any of the assemblies, to
blowe into their eares the names of private citizens: he alone

Catoes
mariages.

Attilia
Catoes wife.

Lelius
mariage.

Catoes first
souldierfare,
in the warre
of the bond-
men.

115

making sute to be Colonell of a thowsand footmen, was obedient to the law, and committed all the private citizens names to memory, to speake unto every one of them, and to call them by their names: so that he was envied even of them that did commend him. For, by how much they knew his deedes praiseworthie, by so muche more were they grieved, for that they could not followe them. So Cato being chosen Colonell of a thowsande footemen, he was sent into Macedon, unto Rubrius, Prætor there. Some say, that at his departure from thence, his wife lamenting, and weeping to see him go: one Munatius a frend of his sayd unto her, Take no thought Attilia, and leave weeping, for I promise thee I will kepe thy husband for thee. It is well sayd, aunswered Cato. Then when they were a dayes jorney from Rome, Cato after supper said unto this Munatius: Thou must looke well to thy promesse thou hast made Attilia, that thou wouldest keepe me for her, and therefore forsake me not night nor day. Thereupon he commaunded his men that from thence forth they should prepare two beds in his chamber, that Munatius also might lye there: who was rather pleasantly him selfe looked unto by Cato, then Cato by him. He had fiftene slaves with him, two free men, and foure of his frends, which rode, and he himselfe went a foote, somtime talking with one, otherwhile with an other as he went. When he came to the campe, where there were many legions of the Romanes, the Prætor immediatly gave him charge of one of them: who thinking it smal honor to him for himselfe only to be valliant, sith he was but one man, he practised to make all his souldiers under him, like unto himselfe. The which he did not by feare and terror, but by lenitie and gentle perswasion, training and instructing them in every point what they should doe: adding to his gentle instruction and perswasions, reward to those that did well, and punishement to them that offended. Whereby it was hard to judge, whether he had made them more quiet, then warlicke: more valliant, then just: so dreadfull they shewed them selves to their enemies, and curteous to their frendes: fearefull to doe evill, and readie to winne honor. Whereof followed that which Cato least accounted

116

of, that is, he wanne fame, and good will: for his souldiers did greatly honor and love him, bicause he him selfe would ever first set his hande to any thing he commaunded them, and bicause also both in his diet, in his apparrell, and in any jorney or paines, he was rather like unto the meanest souldier, then any of the other Captaines. In contrarie maner also, in good nature, noble corage, and eloquence, he farre exceded all the other Colonells and Captaines. For the true love of vertue, (to wit, the desire to followe it) taketh no roote in mens mindes, onlesse they have a singular love and reverence unto the person, whome they desire to followe. When Cato understoode that Athenodorus surnamed Cordylion, a Stoicke Philosopher, excellently well learned, dwelt at that time in the city of Pergamum, being a very old man, and one that stiffely refused the frendship of kings, Princes, and noble men, desirous to have him about them: to write to him, he thought it was but lost labor. Wherefore having two moneths liberty by the lawes of the Romanes, to followe his owne affaires: he tooke sea, and went into Asia to him, hoping he should not lose his jorney, for the great vertues he knew in him. So when he had spoken with him, and talked of divers matters together: at length he brought him from his first determination, and caried him to the campe with him, esteeming this victorie more, then all the conquestes of Lucullus or Pompey, who had conquered the most parte of all the provinces and realmes of the East partes of the world. In the meane time, whilest he lay at his charge in the campe, being Colonell of a thowsand footemen: his brother preparing to go into Asia, fell sicke in the citie of Ænus, in the contrie of Thracia. Cato having speedie intelligence thereof, tooke sea presently, when it was marvelous rough and boysterous, and imbarked in a litle crayer of a marchaunts of Thessalie, with two of his frends, and three bondmen only, and did scape drowning very narrowly: and yet by good fortune arrived safely, a litle after his brother Cæpioes death. He tooke his death more sorowfully, then became a Philosopher, not onely mourning and lamenting for him, imbracing the deade corse of his brother: but also for the exceding charge and sumptuous funerals, which he

The love of vertue from whence it proceedeth.

Athenodorus the stoicke, Catoes frend.

The death of Cæpio, Catoes brother.

117

CATO
UTICAN

Catoes
mourning for
his brother
Cæpioes
death.

bestowed upon him, in perfumes, sweete savors, and sumptuous silkes that were burnt with his bodie: and furthermore, in the stately tombe of Thracian marble which he made for him, and set up in the market place of the Ænians, that cost eight talents. Some did mislike this vaine charge that Cato bestowed, considering the modestie and temperance he used in all things else, not regarding with judgement his tender love and affection towards his kinsemen, which was mingled in him with his severity and hardnes, against all voluptuousnes, feare, and shamelesse requests. Divers cities, Princes and noble men sent him many sundrie presents, to honor the funeralls of his brother Cæpio: howbeit he tooke no money of all them, saving only spyces, and sweete savors, and such other ornamentes, as honored the obsequies of the dead, and yet payed for them, unto those that brought them, as much as they were worth. Furthermore, in the land that fell unto him, and a litle daughter of his, by the death of his brother: notwithstanding the charge he had bene at, in his funeralls, he did not reckon it in the particion of the land, betwext him and his brother Cæpioes daughter.

*It seemeth
to be ment of
Cæsar, which
wrote the
booke called
Anticaton.

All the which things when they were solemnised, some* write notwithstanding, that he did clense the imbers where his brothers body had bene burnt, through a sieve or riddell, where through they clense corne, and all to get out the gold and silver that was molten there. But suche thinke that their wrytinges should be as farre from controlement, as their doings. So when Catoes time of his charge was expired, they did accompany him at his departure, not only with ordinary praises, vowes, and prayers to the goddes for his health: but with imbracings, teares, and marvelous lamentations of the souldiers, which spred their garments on the ground as he went, and kissing of his hands, which honor the Romanes did but to verie fewe of their Generalls. Further-

Catoes jorney
into Asia.

more, Cato being determined before he returned to Rome to deale in the affaires there, to go and see Asia, partly to be an eye witnes of the maners, customes, and power of every province as he went: and partly also to satisfie king Deiotarus request, who having bene his fathers frend, had earnestly intreated him to come and see him: he went the jorney, and used it in this sorte. First, by peepe of day, he sent his baker and cooke before, where he ment to lye that night. They comming soberly into the city or village, inquiered if there were none of Catoes frends and acquaintance there, and if they found none, then they prepared his supper in an Inne, and troubled no man : but if there were no Inne, then they went to the Governors of the towne, and prayed them to helpe them to lodging, and did content them selves with the first that was offered them. Oftentimes the townes men did not beleve they were Catoes men, and made no accompt of them : bicause they tooke all things so quietly, and made no a do with the officers. Insomuch as Cato somtime came himselfe, and found nothing ready for him, and when he was come, they made as small account of him, seeing him set apon his cariages, and speake never a word : for they tooke him for some meane man, and a timerous person. Notwithstanding, sometime he called them unto him, and tolde them. O poore men, learne to be more curteous to receive travelling Romanes that passe by you, and looke not always to have Catoes to come unto you : and therefore see that you use them with such curtesie and entertainment, that they may bridle the authority they have over you : for you shall finde many that will desire no better colour nor occasion, by force to take from you that they would have : bicause you unwillingly also do graunt them the things they would, and nede. There is a report of a pretie jeast happened him in Syria. When he came to Antioche, he found a great number of people devided on either side of the streete, standing a row one by an other verie decently : the young men by them selves in fayer clokes, boyes by them selves in seemely aray, and priests and other officers of the city also, all in white garments, crowned with garlands. Cato thought straight they had made this solemne precession to honor him, and fell out with his men he had set before, bicause they did suffer them to make such preparacion for his comming. So he made his frends light from their horses, and go a foote to accompany him. But when they came neere to the gate of the city, the maister of these ceremonies that had assembled all that company (an

119

Demetrius a
slave, great
with Pompey.

old man, having a rodde in his hand, and a crowne on his head) came to Cato without saluting of him, and asked him only, where they had left Demetrius, and when he would come. This Demetrius had bene one of Pompeis slaves, and bicause Pompeis fame was great with all men, his servant Demetrius also was much honored and made of above his deserte, for that he was in great credit with Pompey. Catoes frendes hearing what question the olde man asked him, burst out a laughing as they went through this precession. Cato being ashamed of it, sayd no more then: but, O, unfortunate citie. Afterwards notwithstanding, when he told it to any body, he would laugh at it him selfe. So Pompey rebuked them, that through ignorance had failed to honor Cato. When Cato came to the citie of Ephesus, and was comming towardes Pompey to salute him, being the elder man, and of greater dignitie and estimacion then he, who at that time also was Generall of a great and puisant armie: Pompey seeing him comming towards him a farre of, would not tary till he came to him, sitting in his chaire of estate, but rising up went to meete him, as one of the greatest and noblest persons of Rome, and taking him by the hande, after he had imbraced and welcomed him, he presently fell in praise of his vertue before his face, and afterwards also commended him in his absence, when he was gone from him. Whereuppon, everie man after that had him in great veneracion for those things, which before they despised in him, when they considered better of his noble and curteous mind. For men that saw Pompeis entertainment towards him, knew well enough that Cato was a man which he rather reverenced, and for a kinde of duty observed, more then for any love he bare him: and they noted further, that he honored him greatly while he was with him, but yet that he was glad when Cato went from him. For he sought to kepe backe all the young gentlemen of Rome that went to see him, and desired them to remaine with him: but for Cato, he was nothing desirous of his company, for that in his presence he thought he could not commaund as he would, and therfore was willing to let him go, recommending his wife and his children to him, the which he never did before

Cato honored
of Pompey
in Asia.

Pompey
rather sus-
pected Cato
then loved
him.

120

unto any other Romane that returned to Rome: howbeit in
dede Cato was partly allied unto him. After that time, all
the cities whereby he passed, devised (in emulacion one of the
other) which of them should honor him most, and made him
great feasts and bankets: in the which he prayd his frends
to have an eye to him, least unwares he shold prove Curioes
words true. For Curio somtime being his frend, and a
familiar of his, misliking notwithstanding his severity: asked
Cato if he would go see Asia, when his charge were expired.
Cato answered againe, that it was his full determination.
Oh well sayd, quoth Curio, I hope then thou wilt returne
more pleasaunt and civill. And these were Curioes wordes.
Furthermore, Deiotarus king of Galatia, being a very old
man, sent for Cato to come into his contrie to recommend
his sonnes and house unto him: who, when he arrived there,
had great rich presents of all sortes offered him by the king,
intreating him all he could to take them. This so muche
misliked and angered Cato, that he comming thither in the
evening, (after he had taried there one whole day onely) the
next morning he went his waye from thence at the thirde
hower. Howbeit he had not gone one dayes jorney, but he
found greater giftes that taried him, with Deiotarus letters,
at the citie of Pessinunta: in the which he instantly requested
him to take them, or at the least if he would refuse them him
selfe, that then he would let them be devided amongest his
frendes, sith every way they did deserve it, but specially for
his sake, for that his goodes also were not so great, as could
content all his frends. But Cato would not suffer them to
take any jot of it more then before, although he saw well
enough that there were some of them so tender harted, that
they complayned of him, for that he woulde not suffer them
to take any of it. For he tolde them, that otherwise, corruption and briberie could lacke no honest colour to take:
and for his frends, they should alwayes have parte with him
of that which was his owne justly. So he returned king
Deiotarus presentes backe againe. Nowe when he was readie
to imbarke, to passe over the sea againe unto Brundusium:
some of his frendes perswaded him, that it was better to put
the ashes of his brother Cæpioes bones into an other shippe.

Catoes jorney
unto king
Deiotarus,
and his
abstinence
from gifts.

But he aunswered them, that he would rather lose his owne life, then to leave his brothers relikes. Thereuppon he presently hoysed sayle, and it is reported that he passed over in great daunger, where other shippes arrived very safely. When he was returned unto Rome, he was alwayes either talking Philosophie with Athenodorus the Philosopher, or else in the market place to pleasure his frendes. When his turne came that he was to make sute to be Quæstor, he would never sue for it, before he had first diligently perused all the ordinaunces touching the office of Quæstor, and that he had particularly made enquierie of men of greatest experience to knowe what the authoritie of the office was. So, he no sooner came to his office, but he presently made great alteraciou amongest the clearkes and officers of the treasurie: who having the lawes and recordes in their handes, and exercising the office commonly under young men which were chosen treasurers (who for their ignoraunce and lacke of experience, stoode rather in neede of maisters to teache them, then that they were able to correct others) they them selves were the officers, and controlled them. But Cato not contenting him selfe with the name and honor of the thing, did throughly understande what the clearkes and registers shoulde be, and therefore would have them to be as they ought to be, ministers under the Quæstors only, telling them of their briberie and corruption which they committed, and reformed them also, that fauted through ignoraunce. And when he sawe some insolent and impudent persons, that curried favour with other treasurers to be against him: he caused the chiefest of them to be condemned for falsehoode, in making division betwext two coheires, and consequently turned him cleare out of his office, for ever doing any thing there any more. He accused an other also for forging of a will, whome Catulus Luctatius defending, being then Censor, and a man of great honor for the dignity of his office, but chiefly for his vertue, being counted the justest man one of them in his time at Rome, and one of those also that highly commended Cato, and was conversant with him for his honest life: when he perceived that he could not defend his man by no reason, he prayed them at his request that they would pardon him.

GRECIANS AND ROMANES

But Cato would in no wise graunt it. But Catulus earnestly
intreating still for him : then Cato plainely sayd unto him,
It is a shame for thee (Catulus) thou that art Censor, and
shouldest reforme all our lives, thus to forget the duetie
of thine office, to please our ministers. Catulus looking at
Cato when he had spoken, as though he would aunswere him :
whether it were for shame, or anger, he went his way, and
sayd never a word more. Yet was not the partie condemned,
though there was one voyce more that did condemne then
cleere him, bicause of the absence of one of the Iudges. For
Marcus Lollius, one of Catoes colleagues in the Quæstorship,
being sicke at that time, and absent, Catulus sent unto him,
to pray him to come and helpe the poore man. Thereuppon
Lollius being brought thither in a litter after judgement
geven, gave his last voyce, which absolutely cleared him.
Cato, this notwithstanding, would never use him as a clearke,
nor pay him his wages, nor would count of Lollius voyce
among others. Thus having pulled downe the pride and
stomacke of these clearkes, and brought them unto reason :
in short time he had all the tables and records at his commaundement, and made the treasure chamber as honorable,
as the Senate it selfe : so that every man thought, and sayd, Cato made
that Cato had added unto the Quæstorshippe the dignity the Quæstor-
of the Consulship. For finding divers men indetted before shippe of
unto the common wealth, and the common wealth also unto great dignity.
divers men : he sette downe such an order, that neither the
common wealth should be deceived by any man, nor that
any man also should have wrong of it. For being rough
with them that were indetted to the chamber, he compelled
them to pay their det, and willingly and quickely also payed
them to whom the chamber ought any thing : so that the
people were ashamed to see some pay which never thought
to have payed any thing, and on the contrary side also
others payed, which never looked to have had any parte of
their dettes payed them. Furthermore, divers men did
before make false billes of their dets, and brought them
so to be put into the cofer of the Quæstors : and many
times also his predecessors were wont of favor and frendship
to receive false messages. For whilest he was Quæstor, he

never did passe away matters so lightly. For one day, he being doubtfull of a message that was sent unto him, to knowe whether it was true or no: albeit divers men did witnesse it was true, yet would he not beleve it, untill such time as the Consulls them selves came in their owne persons to justifie it was true, and to sweare, that it was so ordained. Now there were many unto whom Lucius Sylla being Dictator, had appointed in his second proscription twelve thowsand silver Drachmas for every citizen and outlaw which they had slaine with their owne handes. These men, though every man did hate them, and knew them to be wicked people and cruell murtherers: yet no man durst offer to be revenged of

them. Cato called these men in sute, as those that did wrongfully detaine the money of the common treasure, and compelled them to repay it backe againe: sharpely reproving (and justly) the wicked develish fact they had committed. So when they had repayed the money, they were straight accused by others for murder: and as if they had bene wrongfully condemned by one judgement, they were brought into an other, to the great joy of all the Romanes, who then thought they saw all the tyranny of that time rooted out, and Sylla him selfe punished. Besides all this, Catoes continuall paines and care of the treasure, was so well thought of, and liked of the people, as could be. For he was always the first that came to the coffer of the treasurers, and also the last that went from thence, and was never wearie of any paines. Furthermore, he never missed to be at any assembly of the people or Senate, fearing, and being alwayes carefull, least lightly by favor, any money due to the common wealth should be forgiven: or else that they should abate the rent of the farmers, or that they should geve no money but to them that had justly deserved it. Thus having ridde all accusers, and also filled the coffers with treasure: he made men see, that the common wealth might be riche, without oppressing of any man. In deede at his first comming in to the office, his colleagues and companions founde him marvelous troublesome and tedious, for that they thought him too rough and severe: howbeit they all loved him in the end, bicause he only withstoode the complaints and cries of

124

all men against them (which complained that they would not for any mans respect or favor let go the money of the common treasure) and was contented his companions should excuse them selves unto their frends that were importunate, and lay the fault apon him, saying, that it was unpossible for them to bring Cato unto it. The last day that he went out of his office, being very honorably brought home to his house by the people: it was told him that Marcellus, being in the treasure chamber, was attempted and environned with many of his frends, and men of great authoritie, that were earnestly in hande with him to record a certaine gift of money, as a thing that had bene due by the common wealth. This Marcellus had bene Catoes frend even from their childhood, and whilest Cato was in office, he did orderly execute his office with him: but when he was left alone, he was of so gentle a nature, that he would easily be intreated, and was as much ashamed to deny any man, as he was also overreadie to graunt everie man that he required. Cato straight returned backe uppon it, and finding that Marcellus had yeelded unto their importunacye, and recorded the gift: he caused the bookes to be brought unto him, and did rase it out before his face, Marcellus speaking never a word to the contrary. After that, Marcellus brought Cato home, and never once repyned against that he had done, neither then, nor at any time after, but continued still friendshippe with him, as he had done before. But now, though Cato was out of his office of Quæstor, he was not without spialls of his men in the treasure chamber: who marked alwayes, and wrote what was done and passed in the treasurie. And Cato him self having bought the bookes of accompt for the summe of five talents conteyning the revenue of the whole state of the common wealth, from Syllaes time untill the very yeare of his Quæstorshippe: he ever had them about him, and was the first man that came to the Senate and the last that went out of it. There many times the Senators tarying long before they came, he went and sate downe in a corner by him selfe, and red closely the booke he had under his gowne, clapping his gowne before it, and would never bee out of the citie on that day when he knew the Senate should assemble. After that, Pompey and his consorts perceiving that it was unpos-

125

sible to compell Cato, and much lesse to winne or corrupt him, to favor their unjust doings: they sought what meanes they could to keepe him from comming to the Senate, and defending certeine of his friends causes, and to occupy him some other wayes about matters of arbitrement. But Cato finding their wiles and craft, to encounter them, he tolde his friendes once for all, whom he would pleasure: that when the Senate did sit, no mans cause could make him be absent

Catoes minde
and determin-
ation to take
charge in the
common
wealth.

from thence. For he came not to serve the common wealth to enrich him selfe as many did, neither for any glorye or reputacion, nor yet at all adventure: but that he had advisedly chosen to serve the common wealth, like a just and honest man, and therefore thought him selfe bound to be as carefull of his dutie, as the bee working her waxe in the honny combe. For this respect therefore, to performe his dutie the better, by the meanes of his friendes which he had in every province belonging to the Empire of Rome: he gotte into his handes the copies of all the chiefest actes, edicts, decrees, sentences, and the notablest judgements of the governors that remayned in recorde. Once Cato perceiving that Publius Clodius a seditious Orator amongest the people, did make great sturre, and accused divers unto the assembly, as the Priestes and Vestall Nunnes: (amonge the which Fabia Terentia, Ciceroes wives sister was accused) he taking

their cause in hand, did so disgrace Clodius their accuser, that he was driven to flie the citie. Cicero therefore giving Cato thankes, Cato tolde him, that he must thanke the common wealth, not him, for whose sake onely he both sayd and did that he had done. Hereby Cato wanne him great fame. For when a certein Orator or common counseller

preferred one witnes unto the Iudges, the counseller on thother side tolde them, that one witnes was not to be credited, though it were Cato him selfe. Insomuch as the people tooke it up for a proverbe among them, that when any man spake any straunge and unlikely matter, they would say: Nay, though Cato him selfe said it, yet were it not to be beleved. When on a time a certaine prodigall man had made a long oration in the Senate, in praise and commendacion of sobrietie, temperance, and thriftines: one

GRECIANS AND ROMANES

Amnæus a Senator rising up, said unto him, Alas, frend, what thinkest thou? who can abide to heare thee any lenger with pacience: that farest at thy table like Crassus, buildest like Lucullus, and speakest to us like Cato? So men commonly (in sport) called them Catoes, which were grave and severe in their wordes, and dissolute in their deedes. When divers of his friends were in hand with him to sue to be Tribune of the people, he told them he thought it not meete at that time: for such an office (quoth he) of great authoritie as that, is not to be imployed, but like a stronge medicine in time of neede. So, the tearme and matters of lawe ceassing for that tyme, Cato went into the contry of Luke to take his pleasure there, where he had pleasant houses: and tooke with him both his bookes and Philosophers to keepe him company. Bicause, meeting as he went, with divers sumpters and great cariage, and a great traine of men besides, he asked them whose cariage it was: they told him it was Metellus Nepos that returned to Rome, to make sute to be Tribune. Thereuppon Cato stayed sodainely, and bethinking him selfe, commaunded his men to returne backe againe. His friends marvailing at it, he aunswered them: Doe not you know that Metellus is to be feared of him selfe, for his rashnes and folly? and now that he commeth instructed by Pompey, like a lightning he would set all the common wealth a fire? for this cause therefore, we must not now goe take our pleasure in the contry, but overcome his folly, or otherwise dye honorably in defence of our libertie. Yet at his friendes perswasions, he went first unto his house in the contry, but taried not long there, and returned straight againe to Rome. When he came thither overnight, the next morning betimes he went into the market place, and sued to be Tribune of the people, purposely to crosse Metellus enterprise, bicause the power and authoritie of the Tribune consisteth more in hindring, than in doing any thing: for if all men els were agreed of a matter, and that he onely were against it, the Tribune would cary it from them all. Cato at the first had not many of his friendes about him, but when they heard of his intent, why he made sute for the Tribuneship: all his friends and noble men straight tooke part with him, confirmed his determination, and incoraged him to go on withall, for that he did it rather to serve the common wealth, then his owne turne, considering, that where many times before he might (without resistance or deniall) have obteined the same, the state being toward no trouble, he then would never sue for it, but now that he saw it in daunger, where he was to fight for the common wealth, and the protection of her libertie. It is reported that there was such a number of people about him to favour his sute, that he was like to have ben stifled among them, and thought he should never have comen to the market place, for the preasse of people that swarmed about him. Thus when he was chosen Tribune with

Metellus and others, he perceived how they bought and sold the voyces of the people when the Consuls were chosen: whereupon he made an oration, and sharply tooke them up for this detestable marchandise, and after his oration ended, solemnly protested by othe, that he would accuse him, and bewray his name, which had given money to be chosen Consul. Howbeit he spake nothing of Syllanus, whose sister, Servilia, he had maried: but he flatly accused Lucius Muræna, that had obtained to be Consul with Syllanus, by meanes of his money. Now a law being provided, that the party accused might have a keeper or spiall to follow the accuser, to see what he would accuse the party with, that he might the better be able to defend him selfe, knowing what should be objected against him: Muræna having one for him to waite upon Cato, to consider throughly what course he tooke, when he saw that he went not maliciously to worke, but tooke a plaine common way of a just accuser: he had so great confidence in Catoes upright mind and integritie, that not regarding the narrow sifting of him otherwise, he did one day aske him him selfe in the market place, (or at home in his owne house) if that day he were determined to prosecute any matter against him touching

his accusation. If Cato aunswered him that he did not: then he went his way and simply beleved him. When the day came in deed that his cause was to be heard, and pleaded unto: Cicero being Consul that yere, defending Muræna,

played so pleasantly with the Stoicke Philosophers, and their
straunge opinions, that he made all the Iudges laughe : insomuch as Cato him selfe smiling at him, tolde them that were
by him : See, we have a pleasant Consul that makes men
laugh thus. So Muræna being discharged by this judgement, did never after malice Cato for that, but so long as
he remained Consul, he was alwaies ruled by his counsel in
all his affaires, and continued ever to honor him, following
his counsell in all thinges touching his office. Hereof Cato
him selfe was cause, who was never rough nor terrible, but
in matters of counsell, and in his orations before the people,
for the maintenance onely of equitie and justice : for otherwise, he was very civil and curteous to al men. But before
he entred into his Tribuneship, Cicero being yet Consul, he
did helpe him in many things touching his office, but specially, in bringing Catilins conspiracie to goode ende, which
was a noble act done of him. For Catilin did practise a
generall commotion and sturre in the common wealth, to
overthrowe the whole state of Rome, by civill discorde
within Rome, and open warres abroade : who beeing discovered and overcome by Cicero, he was driven in the ende
to flie Rome. But Lentulus, Cethegus, and many other of
the accomplices of this conspiracie, blamed Catiline for his
faynt and cowardly proceeding in it. For their partes, they
had determined to burne the whole citie of Rome, and to
put all the Empire thereof in uprore, by straunge warres,
and rebellions of forreine nations and provinces. Howbeit
this treason being discovered, as appeareth more largely in
the life of Cicero, the matter was referred unto the judgement of the Senate, to determine what was to bee done
therein. Syllanus beeing the first who was asked his opinion
therein, sayde, that he thought it good they should suffer
cruell paines : and after him also, all the rest said the like,
untill it came to Cæsar. Cæsar being an excellent spoken man,
and that rather desired to nourish then to quench any such
sturres or seditions in the common wealth, being fit for his
purpose long determined of : made an oration full of sweete
pleasant wordes, declaring unto them, that to put such men
as them to death without lawfull condemnation, he thought

*The con-
spiracie of
Catilin
against
Rome.*

it altogether unreasonable, and rather that they should doe better to keepe them in prison. This oration of Cæsar so altered all the rest of the Senators minds, for that they were affraid of the people: that Syllanus self mended his opinion againe, and said, that he ment not they should put them to death, but keepe them fast in prison, bicause that to be a prisoner, was the greatest paine a Romane Citizen could abide. Thus, the Senators minds being so sodainly chaunged, and bent to a more favorable sentence: Cato rising up to say his opinion, beganne very angrily with marvelous eloquence, grievously to reprove Syllanus for chaunging his mind, and sharply to take up Cæsar, that under a populer semblance, and maske of sweete sugred words, 'he sought 'under hand to destroy the common wealth, and also to 'terrifie and make the Senate affraid: where he him selfe 'should have bene affraid, and thinke him selfe happy, if he 'could scape from beeing suspected, giving such apparant 'cause of suspicion as he did, going about so openly to take 'the enemies and traytors of the common wealth out of the 'hands of justice, seming to have no pitie nor compassion of 'his naturall citie, of such nobilitie and fame, being even 'brought in maner to utter destruction, but rather to lament 'the fortune of these wicked men, that it was pity they 'were ever borne, and whose death preserved Rome from 'a thowsand murthers and mischiefs.' Of all the orations that ever Cato made, that only was kept: for Cicero the Consul, that day had dispersed divers penne men in sundry places of the Senate house, which had marvelous swift hands, and had further taught them how to make briefe notes and abridgements, which in fewe lines shewed many words. For untill that time, writers were not knowen that could by figures and ciphers expresse a whole sentence and word, as afterwards they could: being then the first time that ever they were found out. So Cato at that time prevailed against Cæsar, and made them all chaunge their mindes againe, that these men were put to death. But that we may not leave out a jot of his maners, as the very pattern and impression of his mind: it is reported, that when Cato that day was so whot, and vehement against Cæsar, that all the Senate

could but looke at them, to heare them both: a letter
was delivered Cæsar, sent him into the house. Cato began
presently to suspect it, and so earnestly misliked of it, that
many of the Senators being offended, commaunded his letter
should be seene and red openly. Cæsar thereupon reached
his letter unto Cato, that sate not farre from him. When
Cato had red it, and found that it was a love letter which
his sister Servilia had written unto Cæsar, whom she loved,
and had knowen: he cast it againe to Cæsar, and said, There,
dronkard. After that he went on againe with his matter,
which he had begon before. In fine, it seemeth that Cato
was very unfortunate in his wives: for this Servilia, as
we have sayd, had an ill name by Cæsar. And the other
Servilia also, which was his sister, was worse defamed. For
she being maried unto Lucullus, one of the greatest men of
Rome, by whom she had a sonne, was in the ende put away
from him, for her naughty life. But worst of all, his owne
wife Attilia also was not altogether cleare without suspicion:
for though he had two sonnes by her, yet he was driven
to be divorced from her, she was so naught and common.
After that, he maried Martia, the Daughter of Philip, which
by report seemed to be a very honest gentlewoman. It is
she that is so famous amonge the Romanes. For in the life
of Cato, this place (as a fable or comedy) is disputable, and
hard to be judged. For thus it was, as Thraseas writeth:
who referreth all to the report and credit of one Munatius,
Catoes very famillier friend. Amonge many that loved
Catoes vertues, and had them in admiration, some of them
did shew him more what he was, then other some did:
amongest the which, was Q. Hortensius, a man of great
honestie and authoritie. He, desiring not onely to be
Catoes friend and famillier, but also to joyne with him in
alliance, and by affinitie to make both their houses one: was
not abashed to move him, to let him have his Daughter
Porcia in mariage, (which was Bibulus wife, and had brought
him two children) that he might also cast abroade the seede
of goodly children, in that pleasant fertile ground. And
though to men this might seeme a straunge mind and desire,
yet that in respect of nature, it was both honest and profit-

able to the common wealth, not to suffer a young woman in the prime of her youth, to lose the frute of her wombe, being apt to beare children: nor also that he should impoverish his sonne in lawe with moe children, then one house needed. And further, that communicating women in this sort from one to another, specially beeing bestowed apon worthy and vertuous men: that vertue should thereby bee increased the more, being so dispersed in divers families, and the citie likewise should be the stronger, by making alliances in this sort together. And if it be so, quoth he, that Bibulus doe love his wife so dearly, that he wil not depart from her altogether, then that he would restore her to him again, when he had a child by her, that therby he might be the more bound in friendship to him, by meanes of this communication of children with Bibulus selfe, and with him. Cato aunswered him, that he loved Hortensius well, and liked of his alliance: howbeit that he marvelled he would speake to him to let him have his Daughter to get children of, sith he knew that she was maried to an other. Then Hortensius altering his tale, stucke not to tell him his mind plainly, and to desire his wife of him, the which was yet a young woman, and Cato had children enough. But a man can not tell whether Hortensius made this sute, bicause he saw Cato make no reckoning of Martia, for that she was then with child by him. In fine, Cato seeing the earnest desire of Hortensius, he did not deny him her, but told him, that he must also get Philips good wil, the father of Martia. He knowing that Cato had graunted his good wil, would not therfore let him have his daughter, before that Cato him selfe by his presence did confirme the contract and mariage with him. Though these thinges were done longe after, yet having occasion to talke of Catoes wives, I thought it not amisse to anticipate the time. Now Lentulus, and his consorts of Catilines conspiracie being put to death: Cæsar, to cloke the accusations wherewith Cato charged him in open Senate, did put him self into the peoples hands, and gathering the rakehells and seditious persons together, which sought to set al at six and seven, he did further encorage them in their mischievous intent and practises.

132

GRECIANS AND ROMANES

Whereuppon, Cato fearing least such rabble of people should put all the common wealth in uprore and daunger : he perswaded the Senat to winne the poore needy people that had nothing, by distributing of corne amongest them, the which was done : for the charge thereof amownted yearely unto twelve hundred and fifty talents. This liberalitie did manifestly drinke up and quench all those troubles which they stoode in feare of. But on thother side, Metellus entring into his Tribuneship, made certen seditious orations and assemblies, and preferred a law to the people, that Pompey the great should presently be called into Italy with his armie, that he should keepe the citie by his comming, from the present daunger of Catilins conspiracie. These were but words spoken for facions sake, but in deede the law had a secret meaning, to put the whole common wealth and Empire of Rome into Pompeys hands. Hereuppon the Senate assembled, wherein Cato at his first comming, spake somewhat gently, and not to vehemently against Metellus, as his maner was to be sharpe unto them that were against him : but modestly perswaded him, and fell to intreate him in the end, and highly to extoll his house, for that they had alwaies taken part with the Senate and nobilitie. But Metellus therewith tooke such pride and conceit of him selfe, that he began to despise Cato, thinking he had used that mildnes, as though he had beene affraide of him : insomuch as he gave out prowd speeches against him, and cruell threats, that in despite of the Senate he would do that which he had undertaken. Then Cato chaunging his countenaunce, his voice and speech, after he had spoken very sharply against him : in the ende he roughly protested, that while he lived, he would never suffer Pompey to come into Rome with his armie. The Senate hearing them both, thought neither of both well in their witts, but that Metellus doings was a furie, which proceeding of a cancred stomake and extreame malice, would put all in hazard : and that which Cato did, was a ravishment and extacy of his vertue, that made him beside him selfe, contending for justice and equitie. When the day came that this law should passe by voyces of the people, Metellus fayled not to be in the market place with a

133

worlde of straungers, slaves, and fensers, armed, and set in battell raye, besides a number of the common people that were desirous to see Pompeys returne, hoping after chaunge. Besides all those, Cæsar then being Prætor, gave ayde likewise with his men, in the behalf of Metellus. On the contrary part also, the noble men and Senators of the citie were as angry as Cato, and said it was a horrible shame: howbeit they were his friendes, rather in misliking the matter, then in defending the common wealth. Whereuppon, all his friendes at home, and his whole family, were marvailously perplexed and sorowfull, that they both refused their meate, and also could take no rest in the night for feare of Cato. But he, as one without feare, having a good hart with him, did comfort his people, and bad them not sorow for him: and after he had supped, as he commonly used to doe, he went to bed, and slept soundly all night, till the morning that Minutius Thermus, his colleague and fellow Tribune, came and called him. So they both went together into the market place, accompanied with a very few after them: whereuppon divers of their friends came and met them by the way, and bad them take heede unto them selves. When they were come into the market place, and that Cato saw the temple of Castor and Pollux full of armed men, and the degrees or steppes kept by sword players and fensers, and Metellus on the top of them set by Cæsar: turning to his friends he sayd, See I pray you the coward there, what a number of armed men he hath gotten together, against one man naked, and unarmed. Therewithall he straight went forward with his companion Thermus unto that place, and they that kept the degrees, opened of them selves to let him passe, but they would let no other goe up but him selfe: But Cato with much a doe, taking

Minutius by the hand, got him up with him, and when he was come up, he sate him downe betwixt Metellus and Cæsar, to keepe them a sonder, that they should not whisper one in anothers eare. Neither of them both could tell what to say to him. Whereuppon the noble men that considered Catoes countenaunce and boldnes, wondring to see it, drew neare, and by their cryes willed him not to be affrayd, but en-

GRECIANS AND ROMANES

coraged one another to sticke by him, that stoode for defence
of their libertie. So, there was a servaunt that tooke the
written law in his hand, and would have red it to the
people: but Cato woulde not let him. Then Metellus tooke
it him selfe in his handes to reade it: but Cato also snatched
it out of his handes. Metellus notwithstanding, having it
perfect without booke, would needes declare the effect of it
by harte. But Thermus clapped his hande before his mouthe
to keepe him that he shoulde not speake. Metellus seeing
these two men bent by all meanes to keepe this law from
passing, and that the people did leane on their side: he
beckned to his men to goe for the armed men which were
at home in his house, that they should come with terror and
cryes to make them affrayd, and so they did. The people
thereuppon were dispersed here and there for feare, that Cato
was left alone in the market place, and they threwe stones
at him from beneath. But then Muræna, who had before
[beene] accused [by] Cato for buying of the Consulshippe,
forsooke him not in that daunger, but holding his longe
gowne before him, cryed out unto them beneath, that threwe
at Cato, to leave. So shewing him the daunger he had
brought him selfe unto, holding him still by the armes, he
brought him into the temple of Castor and Pollux. Then
Metellus seing the pulpit for orations voyded, and his enemies
flying out of the market place, he thought he had wonne the
gole: Whereuppon commaunding his souldiers to depart,
then proceeding gently, he attempted to passe his lawe.
But his enemies that fled for feare, being gathered againe
together in the market place, beganne a freshe to cry out
against Metellus, with greater boldnes and corage then before.
Then Metellus and his adherents being affrayd and amazed,
doubting that their enemies had gotten weapons, and were
provided, and therefore were the bolder: they fled, and all
of them left the pulpit for orations. So, when Metellus and
his company were gonne, Cato came agayne to the pulpit for
orations, and greatly commended the people for the good
will they had shewed, and perswaded them to continue in
their well doing. Whereuppon the common people were
then against Metellus, and the Senate also being assembled

135

gave order, that Cato should have better ayde then he had before, and that by all meanes possible they should resist Metellus lawe, which onely tended to move sedition and civill warre in Rome. For Metellus selfe, he was yet vehemently bent to followe his attempt and enterprise : but perceiving that his friendes were marvelously affraide of Cato, as a man whom they thought invincible, he sodainely came into the market place, and assembling the people, told them many reasons in his oration, supposing to bringe Cato in disgrace with the people, and amongest other thinges he sayd, that he would withdraw him selfe out of this tyrannicall power of Catoes, and his conspiracie against Pompey, the which peradventure the citie before it were long, should repent, for that they had shamed and defaced so noble a man. After that, he presently departed Rome, and went into Asia to informe Pompey of all this matter. Cato on thother side was greatly estemed for his doings, for that he had freed the common wealth from the great trouble of such a foolish Tribune, and by overthrowing Metellus, he had also suppressed the power of Pompey. But he was yet much more commended, when he was against the Senate, who would have noted Metellus of infamie, and deprived him of his office, the which he would not suffer them to doe. The common people thought him of a curteous and gentle nature, bicause he would not treade his enemie under his foote, when he had the upper hand of him, nor be revenged of him when he had overcome him : but wise men judged it otherwise, that it was wisely done of him not to provoke Pompey. About this time returned Lucullus from the warre, of the which it semed that Pompey had taken the honor and glory from him for the ending of it, and was likely also to have bene put from his honor of triumph, for that Caius Memmius was his adversary, who layed many accusations against him before the people, rather to please Pompey, then for any malice els he had towards him. But Cato, both
for that Lucullus was his brother in law, and had maried his owne sister Servilia, as also for that he saw they did him wrong : resisted this Memmius, and defended many accusations against him. So that in the end, though Memmius

had labored that Cato should be deprived of his office, as
from a tyrannicall power: yet Cato compelled Memmius at
the last to leave of his accusations, and to prosecute law no
more against him. Thus Lucullus having obteined honor
of triumph, did embrace Catoes friendship more then before,
taking him for a sure bulwarcke and defense against the
power of Pompey the great. But Pompey shortly after returning home againe, with great honor from his conquests,
trusting that for respect of his welcome he should be denyed
nothing at the peoples hands when he came home: sent
before unto the Senate, to pray them for his sake to deferre
the election of the Consuls, untill he came to Rome, that
being present he might favor Pisoes sute, suing to be Consul.
Thereunto the most part of the Senate gave their consent, Cato resisteth
but Cato on thother side was against it, not that the defer- Pompey.
ring of the time was a matter of such importance, but to
cut all hope from Pompey to goe about to attempt any
newe devises, insomuch that he made the Senate chaunge
opinion againe, and Pompeys request was denied. Pompey
being marvelously troubled withall, and perceiving that Cato
would be against him in all things if he found not some
devise to winne him: he sent for his friend Munatius, by
his meanes to demaund Catoes two Neces of him which were
mariable: the eldest for him self, and the youngest for his
sonne. Others say also, that they were not his Neces, but
his own daughters. Munatius did Pompeys message, and
brake the matter unto him, his wife, and to his sisters, who
marvelously desired Pompeys alliance, for the greatnes and
dignitie of his person. But Cato making no farther delay,
without other deliberation, as not greatly pleased with the
motion, aunswered him presently: Munatius, goe thy way Cato refuseth
unto Pompey againe, and tell him that Cato is not to be allyance with
wonne by women, though otherwise I mislike not of his Pompey.
friendship: and withall, that so long as he shall deale uprightly in all causes, and none otherwise, that he shall find
him more assuredly his friend, then by any alliance of mariage:
and yet, that to satisfie Pompeys pleasure and will against
his contry, he wil never give him such pledges. The women
and his friends at that time were angry with his aunswer

and refusall, saying, it was too stately and uncurteous. But afterwardes it chaunced, that Pompey suing to have one of his friendes made Consul, he sent a great summe of money to brybe the voyces of the people, which liberalitie was noted, and spoken of, bicause the money was told in Pompeys owne garden. Then did Cato tell the women of his house, that if he had now bene bound by allyance of mariage unto Pompey, he should then have bene driven to have bene partaker of Pompeys shamefull acts. When they heard what he had told them, they all confessed then that he was wiser to refuse such alliance, then they were that wished and desired it. And yet, if men should judge of wisedom, by the successe and event of things: I must needes say, that Cato was in great fault for refusing of this allyance. For thereby he was the cause of Pompeys matching with Cæsar, who joyning both their powers together, was the whole destruction of the Empire of Rome: whereas peradventure it had not fallen out so, if Cato fearing Pompeys light faultes, had not caused him by increasing his power with another, to commit farre greater faultes. Howbeit those thinges were yet to come. Furthermore, Pompey being at jarre with Lucullus, touching certain ordinances which he had made in the Realme of Pontus, bicause both the one and the other would have their ordinances to take place: Cato favoured Lucullus, who had open wronge. Pompey therefore seeing that he was the weaker in the Senate, tooke

parte with the people, and put forthe the lawe for dividing of the landes amongest the souldiers. But Cato stowtly resisting that lawe agayne, he put it by, and made Pompey thereby in a rage to acquaynte him selfe with Publius Clodius, the moste seditious and boldest person of all the Tribunes, and besides that, made allyance even at that tyme with Cæsar, whereof Cato him selfe was the onely Author. Cæsar returning out of Spayne from his Prætorshippe, requyred the honour of tryumphe, and withall made sute to bee Consull. But beeing a lawe to the contrary, that they that sued to bee Consulls shoulde bee present them selves in the citie, and suche also as desired honour of triumphe, shoulde bee without the citie: he earnestly re-

138

GRECIANS AND ROMANES

quired the Senate, that he myght sue for the Consulshippe by his friendes. The moste parte of the Senate were willing unto it, but Cato was flatly agaynst it. He perceyving that the other Senatours were willing to gratifie Cæsar, when it came to him to deliver his opinion, he spent all the whole daye in his oration, and by this pollicie prevented the Senate, that they coulde not conclude any thinge. Then Cæsar letting fall his tryumphe, made sute to be Consull, and entring the citie, joyned friendshippe with Pompey. Here-uppon he was chosen Consull, and immediatly after maryed his Daughter Iulia unto Pompey: and so having made in manner a conspyracie agaynst the common wealth betweene them selves, Cæsar preferred the lawe Agraria, for distribut-ing the landes unto the Citizens, and Pompey was present to mainteyne the publicacion thereof. Lucullus and Cicero on thother side taking parte with Bibulus the other Consull, did what they coulde agaynst it, but specially Cato: who fearing muche this allyance of Cæsar and Pompey, that it was a pacte and conspiracie to overthrowe the common wealth, sayde, that he cared not so muche for this lawe Agraria, as he feared the rewarde they looked for, who by suche meanes dyd intise and please the common people. Therewithall, the Senate were wholly of his opinion, and so were many other honest men of the people besides, that were none of the Senate, and tooke his parte: marvailing muche, and also beeing offended with Cæsars greate unreasonablenes and im-portunitie, who by the authoritie of his Consulshippe did preferre suche thinges, as the moste seditiousest Tribunes of the people were wont commonly to doe, to currye favour with the people, and by suche vile meanes sought to make them at his commaundement. Wherefore, Cæsar and his friends fearing so greate enemies, fell to open force. For to beginne withall, as the Consul Bibulus was going to the market place, there was a basket of donge powred uppon his heade: and furthermore, the Officers roddes were broken in their handes, which they caryed before him. In fine, dartes were throwen at them out of every corner, and many of them beeing hurt, they all at length were driven to flye, and leave the market place. But Cato, he came laste of all, keeping his wonted pace, and often cast backe his heade, and cursed such Citizens. So, they did not onely passe this lawe Agraria by voyces of the people, but furthermore they added to it: that all the Senate shoulde bee sworne to stablishe that lawe, and bee bounde to defende the same, (if any attempted the alteracion thereof) uppon greate penalties and fines to bee sette on his heade, that shoulde refuse the othe. All the other Senators sware agaynst their wills, remembring the example of the mischiefe that chaunced unto the olde Metellus, who was banished out of Italy, bicause he would not sweare to suche a like lawe. Whereuppon, the women that were in Catoes house, besought him with the teares in their eyes, that he woulde yeelde and take the othe:

and so did also divers of his friendes besides. Howebeit, he that moste inforced and brought Cato to sweare, was Cicero the Orator: who perswaded him, that peradventure he woulde bee thought unreasonable, that beeing but one man, he shoulde seeme to mislike that, which all other had thought meete and reasonable: and that it were a fonde parte of him wilfully to put him selfe in so greate daunger, thinking to hynder a matter already past remedie. But yet that besides all this, a greater inconvenience woulde happen, if he forsooke his contrye (for whose sake he did all these thinges) and left it a praye unto them, which sought the utter subversion of the same, as if he were glad to bee ridde from the trouble of defending the common wealth. For, sayde he, though Cato have no neede of Rome, yet Rome hath neede of Cato, and so have all his friendes: of the which, Cicero sayde he was the chiefe, and was moste maliced of P. Clodius the Tribune, who sought to drive him out of the contrye. It is sayde that Cato beeing wonne by these like wordes and perswasions at home, and openly in the market place, they so softened him, that he came to take his othe laste of all men, but one Phaonius, a very friende of his. Cæsars harte beeing then lift uppe, for that he had brought his first purpose to passe: beganne nowe to preferre an other lawe, to divide all Campania, and the contrye called Terra Di Lavoro, (the lande of labour) unto the poore needy people of Rome, and no man stoode against

140

him but Cato. Whereuppon Cæsar made his officers to take
him from the pulpit for orations, to cary him to prison. All
this made not Cato stowpe, nor leave his franke speeche, but
as he went he still spake against this edicte, and perswaded
the people to beware of them that preferred suche lawes.
All the Senate, and the beste sorte of Citizens followed Cato
with heavy hartes, shewing by their silence, that they were
offended and angrye for the injurye they did unto him,
beeing so worthy a man. Insomuch as Cæsars selfe perceived that the people were offended with it, and yet of
ambition and stomacke, he looked alwayes when Cato would
have appealed unto the people. So when he saw that Cato
ment no such matter, at length overcomen with shame and
dishonor, he him selfe procured one of the Tribunes to
take Cato from the Sergeaunts. In fine, all Cæsars practise
tended to this ende, that when he had wonne the peoples
favor by such lawes: they should then graunt him the
government of all the Gaules, (aswell on this side, as beyond
the mountaines) and all Illyria, with an armie of foure legions,
for the space of five yeares, notwithstanding that Cato told
the people before, that they them selves with their own
voyces did set uppe a tyrant, that one day would cut their
throats. They did also chuse Publius Clodius Tribune of
the people, which was of a noble house: a thing directly
contrary to the law. But this Clodius had promised them,
so that they would helpe him to banish Cicero out of Rome,
to do all that he could for them. Furthermore, they made
Calphurnius Piso (Cæsars wifes father) and Gabinius Paulus,
(a man wholly at Pompeys commaundement, as they write
which knew his life and manners) Consuls the next yeare
following. Now, notwithstanding they had the rule of the
common wealth in their owne handes, and that they had
wonne parte of the citie with brybes, and the other parte
also with feare: yet they were both affraid of Cato, when
they considered what trouble they had to overcome him,
which they did very hardly notwithstanding, and to their
great shame, beeing driven to use force, and yet thought
they should never have done it. Furthermore, Clodius
utterly dispaired that he could possibly banish Cicero, so

Cato com-
mitted to
prison by
Cæsar.

P. Clodius,
Tribune of
the people.

The crafty
jugling be-
twixt Cæsar
and Pompey
with P.
Clodius.

141

longe as Cato was there. So devising wayes howe to doe it, when he had taken possession of his office, he sent for Cato, and beganne to tell him, that he thought him the honestest and justest man of Rome, and that he was ready to performe it to him by deede. For, where many made sute unto him to be sent into Cyprus, to make warre with king Ptolomy: he thought none so worthy as him selfe, and therefore for the goodwill he bare him, he was very willing to offer him that pleasure. Cato strayght cryed out with open mowth, that this was a devise to intrappe him, not to pleasure him. Then Clodius prowdly and fiercely aunswered him, Well, seeing thou wilt not goe with good will, thou shalt goe then against thy will: and so he did. For at the

first assemblye of the citie, he caused the people to graunt his commission for his jorney thither: but they neyther appoynted him shippes, nor souldiers, nor any other Ministers to goe with him, saving two Secretaries onely, of the which, the one of them was a very villayne and arrant theefe, and the other, one of Clodius followers. Besides all this, as if they had appoynted him but litle to doe in Cyprus agaynst Ptolomy, he made them commaunde him after that, to goe and restore the outlawes and banished men of the citie of Byzantium, unto their contrye and goodes agayne, of purpose onely to keepe Cato farre enoughe from Rome, whylest he continued Tribune. Cato beeing driven by necessitie to obeye, he counselled Cicero (whome Clodius pursued) to beware that he made no sturre agaynst him, for feare of bringing Rome into civill warre and murther for his sake: but rather, to absent him selfe, that he might an other tyme preserve his contrye. After that, he sent his friende Canidius before into Cyprus, unto Ptolomye, to perswade him to bee quiet without warre: declaring unto him, that he shoulde nether lacke honour nor riches, for the Romanes woulde graunt him the priesthoode of Venus in the citie of Paphos. Cato in the meane tyme remayned in the Ile of Rhodes, preparing him selfe there, and abyding his

aunswer. In the tyme of these sturres, Ptolomy king of Ægypt, for a certen offence and discorde with his subjectes, departing out of Alexandria, sayled towardes Rome, hoping

142

that Cæsar and Pompey with a greate armie woulde restore him to his crowne and kingdome agayne. He beeing desirous to see Cato, sent unto him, supposing he woulde come at his sending for. Cato by chaunce was occupyed at that tyme about some busines, and badde the Messenger will Ptolomy to come to him, if he woulde see him. So when Ptolomy came, he nether went to meete him, nor rose uppe unto him, but onely welcomed him, and badde him sitte downe. It amazed the king at the first, to see under so simple and meane a trayne, suche a statlines and majestie in Catoes behavior. But when he hearde him boldely talke with him of his affayres, and suche grave talke come from him, reproving his follye he had committed, to forsake suche princely pleasure and wealth, to goe and subject him selfe unto suche dishonour, suche extreame paynes, and suche passing greate giftes and presents, as he shoulde throwe awaye, to satisfie the covetousnes of the rulers at Rome, the which was so unsatiable, that if all the Realme of Egypt were converted into silver to give amonge them, it woulde scarce suffice them: in respect whereof, he counselled him to returne backe with his navye, and to reconcile him selfe agayne with his subjectes, offering him selfe also to goe with him, to helpe to make his peace. Then Ptolomy comming to him selfe, and repenting him of his follye, knowing that Cato tolde him truely, and wisely: he determined to followe his counsell, had not his friendes turned his mynde to the contrarye. So when Ptolomy came to Rome, and was driven to wayte at the gates of the Magistrates that were in authoritie: he sighed then, and repented his follye, for that he had not onely despised the counsell of a wise man, but rather the Oracle of a god. Furthermore, the other Ptolomy that was in Cyprus (a happye turne for Cato) poysoned him selfe. Cato beeing also informed that he lefte a wonderfull summe of money behynde him, he determyned to goe him selfe unto Byzantium, and sent his Nephewe Brutus into Cyprus, bicause he durst not truste Canidius so farre. Then having restored the banished men unto the peoples favour agayne, settinge agreement betwixt them, he returned into Cyprus. There he founde a marvailous greate treasure, and plate bothe of

143

Catoes dili-
gence about
money in
Cyprus.

golde and silver, tables, precious stones, hanginges, and
purple silkes, all the which he was to make readye money of.
There he tooke greate care and paynes to rayse all thinges
to the utmoste and dearest pryces that coulde bee, and he
him selfe was present at all, to keepe reckoning of the laste
penney. Wherefore, to bringe this to passe, he woulde not
stande to the common use of the sale of the cryer, but
suspected them all, bothe cryers, praysers, and his owne
friendes, and therefore talked him selfe with the praysers,
and made them sette highe pryses uppon every thinge that
was to bee solde. And thus were the moste parte of the
goodes solde and caryed awaye, at the dearest pryces. This
did marvelously offende the moste of his friendes, when they

The envy
betwixt
Cato and
Munatius.

sawe that he did mistruste them: but Munatius specially,
his dearest friende, tooke it so inwardely, that he thought
never to bee friendes with him agayne. Insomuche as in the
booke Cæsar wrote agaynst Cato, in this place he forceth
moste the accusation agaynst him. Munatius notwithstanding wryteth, that he was not angrye so muche with Cato for
that he mystrusted him, but for a certayne disdayne he had
him selfe of Cato, and for the emulacion betwixt him and
Canidius. For Munatius wrote a booke of Catoes deedes
and sayinges, whome Thraseas in his historye chiefly followed.
In this booke he sheweth that he came late into Cyprus, and
was very ill lodged. And furthermore also, that when he
woulde have comen into Catoes house, they kept him out of
the gates, for that Cato was busie, doing some thinge with
Canidius. He modestly complayning of it unto Cato, had

To much love
oftentymes
causeth hate.

this churlish aunswer: Overmuch love, sayth Theophrastus,
oftentimes causeth hate. So fareth it with thee, who over-
loving me, doest thinke that I esteeme thee not as thou
deservest, and therefore art angry with me. And for
Canidius, I must tell thee truely, I doe rather employe him
for his skill and faithfulnes in thinges, then any man els:
for that he hath beene with me from the beginning, and as
farre as I learne, was never brybed, but cleane handed still.
These wordes Cato tolde Munatius secretly betweene them
two: but afterwardes he knewe that he had also reported
them unto Canidius. When he sawe that, he would no more

144

go and suppe with Cato as he was wont, and when he was
also called to counsell, he would not come there nether.
Wherefore Cato threatned him, that he would sease upon all
his goods and cariage, as they use to handle them that are
disobedient unto justice. This notwithstanding, Munatius
cared not for it, but tooke sea, and returned againe to Rome,
bearing Cato grudge a long time. Then Martia, being at
that time Catoes wife, spake with him, and were both bidden
to supper together, unto a friend of theirs, called Barca.
Thereuppon Cato also arrived, and came thither, when they
were all sette at supper, and asked where he should sit : Barca
tolde him agayne, where it pleased him. Then casting his
eyes about, he sayd he would sitte by Munatius : and so
fetching a compasse about the borde, he went and sate by
him, but offered him no friendshippe and familiaritie all
supper tyme. Afterwardes notwithstanding, at the request
of Martia, that was earnestly in hande with Cato for him :
he wrote unto him, and willed him to come and speake with
him. Munatius went to Catoes house in the morning, where
Martia stayed him, and kept him companie, untill all the
rest that came to salute Cato, were departed. Then Cato
comming to him, embraced him in his armes, and made very
muche of him. We have the willinglier dilated this matter
at length, bicause mens natures and manners might be discerned even in these small matters of friendshippe privately,
as otherwise in the greatest publicke causes. Now touching
Catoes commission, he gotte together litle lesse then seven
thowsand silver talents. Furthermore, fearing the farrenesse
of the jorney he had to goe by sea, he made divers litle cofers,
and put into every one of them two talents, and five hundred
Drachmas, and tyed unto eache of them a longe rope, and
a greate peece of corcke : bicause that if the shippe should
fortune to miscarye, those corckes might shewe where the
chestes with money laye in the bottome of the sea. Thus
was all the money saved, saving a litle, and brought safely
to Rome. Cato having made two bookes wherin he had
noted all thinges done in his jorney, he could neither save
thone nor thother of them. For one of his bondmen made
free, called Philargyrus, tooke the one away : who taking

shippe at the haven of Cenchrees, was him selfe drowned, and the booke he had also, lost with him. The other booke which he him selfe had kept, untill he came unto Corfou: he lying in the market place of the citie in his tents, which he caused to be set uppe: the Mariners being very cold in the night, made so great a fire, that it burnt the tents, stuffe, booke and all. Notwithstanding, he brought certaine of the late king Ptolomyes slaves with him, who while he lived, had the charge and custodie of all his treasure and riches, the which he brought as witnesses, to stoppe the mouthes of his malicious enemies, that would have accused him in any thinge. But yet the losse of them did grieve him, not so much for the greate care and paynes he had taken in setting downe the accompt of his charge, for the justification and proofe of his fidelitie and good service: but also, for that they might have served for a good memoriall and example unto all others, to have bene a like carefull in their charge, as him self. But the goddes denyed him this good happe. Newes beeing brought that he was come to Rome by water, when they understood that he was at hand, by and by all the Magistrats, the Priestes, the Senate, and the most part of the people also went out to meete him by the rivers side: so that both sides of the river of Tyber were full of people,

and the receiving of him in, seemed not inferior to the entry of a triumphe. Notwithstanding, some thought him very presumptuous, that the Consuls and Prætors comming out to meete him, he did not stay his gally, but rowed still up the streame (beeing in a kinges galley of six owers to every bancke) and never stayed, untill all his fleete arryved in the haven. This notwithstanding, when the cofers with mony were caried thorough the market place into the treasure chamber, the people wondred to see so great a quantitie of it. And thereuppon the Senate being assembled, with great and honorable words they gave Cato an extraordinary Prætorship, and priviledge also, at any common sports to weare a purple gowne. Cato refused all these honours, and onely besought the Senate to make Nicias a free man, Steward of the late diseased king Ptolomy, being a witnes of his faith and great paynes he had taken in this service. Philip the

GRECIANS AND ROMANES

father of Martia, was that yeare Consul, so that after a sorte, the authoritie of the Consul was in Cato: bicause Lentulus, colleague and fellowe Consul with Philip, did no lesse reverence Cato for his vertues, then Philip did for his allyance with him. Furthermore, when Cicero was restored agayne from his banishment, the which Publius Clodius (beeing then Tribune of the people) had put apon him, and beeing agayne growen to great credit: he went one day into the Capitoll, in the absence of Clodius, by force to take awaye the tables which Clodius had consecrated there, in the which were comprised all his doings during the tyme he was Tribune. Thereuppon the Senate beeing assembled, Clodius did accuse Cicero of this violent facte. Cicero aunswered him agayne: that bicause Clodius was chosen Tribune, directly against the lawe, therefore all his doings were voyde, and of no validitie. Then stoode uppe Cato, and sayde: he knewe that all that which Clodius did when he was Tribune, was scantly good and allowable, but yet if generally any man shoulde undoe all that he had passed by that authoritie: then all that he him selfe had done likewise in Cyprus, must of necessitie bee revoked. For the commission that was graunted unto him (by vertue whereof he had done many thinges) shoulde be unlawfull: bicause the Tribune also that did graunt it him, was not lawfully chosen. And therefore, that Publius Clodius was not made Tribune agaynst the lawe, who by consent of the lawe was taken out from a noble house, and made a populer person: howebeit, if he had behaved him selfe unduetifully in his office, as other men that happely had offended: then he was to be accused to make him mend his faulte, and not to destroye the authoritie of the officer, which in it selfe was lawfull. After that, there fell misliking betwixt Cicero and Cato, for this counter buffe he had given him: and Cicero continued a long tyme after, before he did shewe him any countenaunce of friendshippe as he had at other tymes done. But afterwardes they were reconciled together agayne, by this occasion. Pompey and Crassus having bene with Cæsar to talke with him (who for that purpose came out of Gaule beyond the Alpes) made an agreement there betwixt them, to demaund

147

the second Consulship together, and when they had it, then to proroge Cæsars government for five yeares more, and also they woulde have the best provinces and greatest, for them selves, with great armies, and money enough to paye them with. This was in deede a playne conspiracie to devide the Empire of Rome betweene them, and utterly to overthrow the state of the common wealth. At that time there were many noble men, which came to make sute for the Consulship. But when they sawe Pompey and Crassus offer to make sute for it, all the reste gave over, but Lucius Domitius that had maryed Porcia, Catoes sister: through whose perswasion he woulde not relinquishe his sute, considering that it was not the office onely of the Consulship that was the chiefest matter of importance, but the libertie of the Senate and people. Straight there ranne a rumor through the most parte of the people, that they were not to suffer Pompeys power to be joyned with Crassus, by meanes of this office: for then his authoritie woulde bee too great and stronge, and therefore, that of necessitie one of these two were to bee denyed. For this cause therefore, the good men tooke Domitius parte, and did encourage him to goe on with his sute, assuring him of ayde under hande of divers, which durst not bee seene openly for feare of those two great men, who at the daye of the election would procure him voyces in his favour. Pompey and Crassus mistrusting this, made Domitius bee sette uppon, going with torche light before daye into the fielde of Mars, where the election was always made: and first striking the torche bearer that went before him, they hurt him so sore, that he fell downe deade at his feete. Then they layed at the rest in like case, who finding them selves cruelly hurt, ranne awaye every man of them, and left Domitius and Cato post alone. But Cato, notwithstanding he was hurt in one of his armes, still helde Domitius fast, and prayed him to tary, and not to leave to defende the libertie of their contrie, agaynst tyrants, which playnely shewed after what manner they woulde governe, sithe by suche wicked meanes they aspyred to tyrannicall government. All this notwithstanding, Domitius woulde tarye no lenger, but betooke him to his legges, and ranne home. Thus were

GRECIANS AND ROMANES

Crassus and Pompey without denyall proclaymed Consuls. Cato never yeelded therefore, but came and sued to bee Prætor, bicause that thereby he might yet make it some strength and countenaunce to him against their Consulshippe, that beeing no private person, he shoulde have some better authoritie to resist them that were the chiefest persons. But they fearing, that the Prætorshippe by the estimation of Cato, woulde come to equall their authoritie of the Consulshippe: first assembled the Senate (the most parte of the Senators not hearing of it) and in that assemblye caused the Senate to decree: that all suche as were chosen Prætors, shoulde presently goe to their charge, not attending the tyme and libertie appoynted by the lawe, during which tyme men might accuse those which had bought the voyces of the people with money. Then having by this culler and decree sette yll doers at libertie, without feare of punishment, they pretending to use corruption, did preferre some of their owne Ministers to make sute for the Prætorshippe, them selves giuing money to corrupt the people, and beeing present also at the election. But notwithstanding all these practises, the vertue and reputacion of Cato overcame him. For the people had him in so great reverence, that they thought it too shamefull a parte to sell Cato by voyces, who deserved rather to bee hyered to take the Prætorshippe apon him. Then the first Tribe beeing called to give their voyces, declared him Prætor. Pompey seeing that, straight brake of the assemblye, making a shamefull lye, telling that he heard it thunder: the which the Romanes doe marvelously detest, and will conclude nothing when it thundereth. Howebeit afterwardes they gave more money, then they had done before, and thereby drave awaye the chiefest men out of the fielde of Mars, and by practise obtayned, that Vatinius was chosen Prætor for Cato. And the reporte went, that they that had so wickedly given their voyces, feeling them selves pricked in conscience, fledde immediatly out of the fielde: and the honest men that remayned, were both very sory and angrie, for the injurie they had offered Cato. At that tyme one of the Tribunes keeping an assemblye of the citie, Cato stoode uppe, and tolde (as if he had prophecied) before them

CATO UTICAN
Why Cato sued to be Prætor.

Cato put from the Prætor-ship by Pompey

149

all, what woulde happen to the common wealth by these practises, and stirred uppe the people agaynst Pompey, and Cæsar, saying: that they were giltye of those thinges, and therefore procured them to bee done, bicause they were affrayde that if Cato had beene Prætor, he would too narrowly have sifted out their devises. In fine, Cato going home to his house, had more companye to wayte uppon him alone, then all the other Prætors that had beene chosen. When Caius Trebonius, Tribune of the people, had preferred a lawe for the deviding of the provinces unto the newe Consuls, Spayne and Africke unto the one, and Ægpyt and Syria unto the other, with full power to make warre as they thought good bothe by sea and lande: all other men having no hope to keepe it backe, did let it alone, and spake nothing to contrarye it. Then Cato getting uppe into the pulpit for orations, before the people beganne to give their voyces, coulde hardly have two howers space to speake: but at length, they perceyving that he delayed tyme by foretelling thinges to come, woulde suffer him to speake no longer, but sent a Sergeaunt to him, and plucked him by force out of the pulpit. But when he was beneath, and cryed out notwithstanding, and divers gave good eare unto him: the Sergeaunt went to him agayne, and tooke him, and caryed him out of the market place. Howebeit the Officer had no sooner left him, but he went strayght towardes the pulpit for orations, and there cryed out more vehemently then before, and willed the people to have an eye to ayde the libertie of their common wealth, which went to ruine. When he oftentymes together did this, Trebonius the Tribune being madde withal, commaunded his Sergeaunt to cary him to prison. The people followed him hard notwithstanding, to heare what he sayd unto them. Whereuppon Trebonius fearing some sturre, was forced to commaund his Sergeaunt to let Cato goe. So Cato drave of all that day without any matter concluded. The next morning notwithstanding, the contrary faction having partly put the Romanes in feare, and wonne the other parte also by fayre wordes and money, and by force of armes likewise kept Aquilius, one of the Tribunes, from comming out of the Senate: and after they

Cato was
against the
law for the
provinces of
Pompey and
Crassus.

150

had also violently driven Cato out of the market place, for
saying that it thundred, and having hurt many men, and
also slayne some out of hande in the market place: in the
ende they forcibly passed the decree by voyces of the people.
Many beeing offended therewith, went a company of them
together to plucke downe Pompeys images: but Cato would
not suffer them. And afterwardes also, when they preferred
an other law for the prorogacion of the provinces and armies
which Cæsar demaunded: Cato would speake no more to the
people to hinder it, but protested unto Pompey him selfe,
that he saw not how he plucked Cæsar apon him, and that he
should feele the weight of his force before he looked for
it: and then when he could neither suffer nor remedy it, he
would even cast his burden and him selfe apon the common
wealth, and too late would remember Catoes warnings, which
were privately as profitable for Pompey, as openly just and
reasonable for the common wealth. Cato used many of
these perswasions sundry times unto him, but Pompey never
made accompt of them: for he woulde not be perswaded
that Cæsar would ever chaunge in that sorte, and besides
he trusted too much to his owne power and prosperitie.
Furthermore, Cato was chosen Prætor for the next yeare
following, in the which it appeared (though he ministred
justice uprightly) that he rather defaced and impaired the
majestie and dignitie of his office, then that he gave it grace
and countenaunce by his doings: for he would oftentimes
go a foote barelegged, and without any coate, unto his
Prætors chaire, and there geve sentence of life and death,
otherwhiles of men of great account. And some report,
that he would geve audience when he had dyned, and dronke
wine: but that is untrue. Now Cato perceiving that the
citizens of Rome were marred by bribes and gifts of those,
which aspired unto offices, and that the people made it an
arte and facultie to gaine by: to roote this vice altogether
out of the common wealth, he perswaded the Senate to make
a law, that such as hereafter should be chosen Consulls or
Prætors, should (if there were no man to accuse them) come
and offer them selves before the judges, and taking their
othe, should truely declare what meanes they had used to

Cato fore-
shewed
Pompey the
things which
happened
unto him,
by Cæsar.

Cato chosen
Prætor.

Cato pre-
ferred a law
for unlawfull
bribing.

attaine to their office. This offended the suters for the
offices, but muche more the mercenarie multitude. Whereuppon, a great number of them went in a morning together
where he kept his audience, and all cried out upon him,
reviled him, and threw stones at him : insomuch as they
that were there, were forced to flie thence, and him selfe
also was driven out of the place by the prease of people, and
had much a doe to get to the pulpit for orations, where
standing on his feete, he presently pacified the tumult of the
people, by the boldnes and constancie of his countenaunce
only. Then when all was pacified by the present perswasions
he used, aptly spoken to purpose for the instant, they geving
attentive eare, without sturre or uprore. The Senate geving
him great commendacion therefore, he told them roundly
and plainly : But I have no cause to praise you, to leave
a Prætor in such daunger of his life, offering no aide to
helpe him. But the suters for the offices, they were in a
marvelous case : for one way, they were affrayed to geve
money to buy the peoples voyces, and on thother side, they
were affraied also if any other did it, that they should go
without their sute. So they were all agreed together, every
man to put downe twelve Myriades and a halfe a peece, and
then they should make their sute justly and uprightly : and
whosoever were taken fauty, and that had otherwise made
his way by corruption, that he should lose the money he
had layed downe. This agreement being concluded betwene
them, they chose Cato (as it is reported) for their arbitrator,
and keeper of all the same money. This match was made in
Catoes house, where they all did put in caution or sureties to
aunswere the money : the which he tooke, but would not
meddle with the money. The day being come, Cato assist-
ing the Tribune that governed the election, and carefully
marking howe they did geve their voyces : he spied one of
the suters for the office breake the accord agreed upon, and
condemned him to pay the forfeiture unto the rest. But
they greatly commending his justice and integritie, forgave
the forfeiture, thinking it punishment enough unto him that
had forfeited, to be condemned by Cato. But therby Cato
procured him selfe the displeasure of the other Senators, for

that he seemed therein to take apon him the power and
authoritie over the whole court, and election. For there is
no vertue, whereof the honor and credit doth procure more
envy, then justice doth : bicause the people doe commonly
respect and reverence that, more then any other. For they
doe not honor them as they doe valliant men, nor have them
in admiration, as they do wise men : but they love and trust
them better. As for the two first, the one they are affrayed
of, and the other they distrust : beside, they suppose that
valliancy and wisdom commeth rather by the benefite of
nature, then of our intent and choyce, esteeming wisedome,
as a readines of conceit, and fortitude, a presence and courage
of the minde. For every man may be just that will, and
therefore injustice is of all other vices most shamefull : for
it is a wilfull and malicious defaut, and therefore can not be
excused. Loe this was the cause why all the noble men in
manner were against Cato, as though he only had overcome
them. Pompey, he thought that the estimacion of Cato was
altogether the discountenaunce of his power and greatnesse,
and therefore did dayly raise up many railers against him.
Of them Publius Clodius that seditious Tribune, who was
againe fallen in frendship with Pompey : he accused Cato,
and cried out upon him, how he had robbed the common
wealth of a wonderfull treasure, by his commission in Cyprus :
and that he was enemy unto Pompey, bicause he did refuse
to marry his daughter. Cato thereto made aunswere, that
he had brought more golde and silver out of Cyprus, into
the treasure of Rome, without the allowance of either horse or
souldier : then Pompey had done with all his triumphes and
warres, with the which he had troubled all the world. And
moreover, that he did never seeke alliance with Pompey, not
that he thought him unworthie of it, but bicause he saw he
delt not as uprightly in the common wealth as he him selfe
did. I, sayd he, have refused a province offred me when
I came out of my Prætorshippe : but Pompey hath taken
some by force, and geven away unto others. And to conclude, he lent Cæsar not long since, an armie of six thowsand
men to serve him in the warres in Gaule : the which he
never required of us, nor Pompey graunted them him by

our consent. But we see, that so many armies, armors and weapon, so many men and horses, by common pleasures of our private citizens, geven and lent at our charge. And Pompey him selfe reserving onely the name of Emperour, and Lieutenaunt generall, assigneth over his armies and provinces to the government of others, whilest he him selfe besiegeth here the walls of the citie, with seditious and tumultuous election of officers, craftily underminding therby the state of the common wealth, to bring all to confusion, that he him selfe might be absolute Prince, and rule alone. Thus was he revenged of Pompey. Among Catoes frends,

he had one called Marcus Faonius, such a one as Apollodorus Phalerian was sayd to be in old time, unto Socrates, who did counterfeate to be an other him selfe, in doing all thinges as he did. This man would be farre out of reason, and passionate in his talke, storming like a dronkard. He one yere made sute to be Ædilis, but he was rejected. Howbeit Cato that furthered his sute, marked, that the tables wherein the voyces were wrytten, were all one hande. So, he finding out the falsehoode, appealed thereuppon unto the Tribunes, and made the election voyde for that time.

After that Faonius was created Ædilis, Cato did helpe him forth in all the other charges of his office, and specially in setting foorth playes in the Theater, which are customably done at the comming in of every such new officer, to geve the people pastime: and gave unto the common players and dauncers in those playes, no golden crownes, as other Ædiles did, but crownes of wilde olive twigges, as they commonly use in Græce at the Olympian games. And where others gave unto the poore rich gifts, he gave the Græcians leekes, lettises, radishes, and peares: and unto the Romanes, they had earthen pottes full of wine, porke, figges, cowcombres, and fagots of wodde of small value. Insomuch as some thought scorne of them they were so meane, others were verie glad of them, seeing that Cato which was severe and hard of nature, had a doing in them, and by litle and litle they turned this austeritie of his into pleasure. In fine, Faonius him selfe sitting downe amongest the people, which looked apon the players, clapped his hands for joy at Cato:

and cried out to him, that he should geve them good rewardes
that played well, alluring them also about him to doe the
like, and told them that he had made Cato the whole ruler
of those sportes. At the selfe same time, Curio, Faonius
colleague and companion in the office of Ædilis, had likewise
goodly playes in an other Theater: but all the people forsooke his, and went to see Faonius playes, who sate among
them like a private man, and Cato as the maister of the
playes. Cato did this in scorne and mockerie, of vaine
charge and expences, which men are wont to bestow in
such trifles, shewing thereby, that whosoever will make any
playes, he should make the charge but a sport also, furnish-
ing it only with a convenient grace, but with no vaine
expence or charge about such a trifle. Shortly after, when
Scipio, Hypseus and Milo, sued all three together to be
Consuls, not only by briberie of money (a common fault
then in suing for any of the offices in the common wealth)
but by plaine force of armes, slaying and killing as in a
civill warre, they were so desperat and insolent: some preferred a lawe, that they should make Pompey President in
these elections, bicause men should move their sute after
a lawfull sorte. But Cato straight was against it, saying,
that the law could have no safety by Pompey, but Pompey
might have safety by the lawe. Notwithstanding, when he
sawe this trouble continewe of a long time, without any
Consuls in Rome, and that dayly there were three campes in
the market place, that it was almost impossible to prevent
the mischiefe at hand, and to stay that it should goe no
further: then he thought it better, that the Senate of their
owne good willes, rather then by compulsion, should put the
government of the state into Pompeis hands alone, choosing
the lesser evill, to withstand the greater, and so to yeeld
to the absolute government, without constraint, which the
sedition would bring it unto. Therefore Bibulus, Catoes
frend and kinseman, made a motion to the Senate, that they
would choose Pompey sole Consul. For, sayd he, either the
common wealth shall be well governed by him, or else Rome
shall serve an ill Lord. Cato then rising up, beyonde all
mens expectacion confirmed Bibulus opinion, and sayd: that

155

the citie were better to have one soveraine Magistrate then none, and that he hoped Pompey could geve present order for the pacifying of this confusion, and that he would be carefull to preserve the citie, when he sawe that they trusted him with the government thereof. Thus was Pompey by Catoes meanes chosen sole Consull. Then he sent for Cato to come to his gardens to him, which were in the suburbes of the citie. Cato went thither, and was received with as great honor and curtesie of Pompey, as could be devised: and in thend, after he had geven him great thankes for the honors he had done him, he prayed him to afford him his advise and counsell in his government. Cato answered him thus, that he had not spoken any thing before that time in respect of any ill will he bare him, neither that he delivered this last opinion of his in respect of his frendshippe, but wholly for the common wealthes sake: howbeit otherwise, that for his owne private affaires, if he thought good to use his advise, whensoever it pleased him to aske his opinion, he would tell him the best he could. But for common causes, that he would alwayes tell what he thought, though he never asked him: and in fine, he performed all he sayd. For first of all, when Pompey did set grievous penalties and new fines apon their heades, which had bought the peoples voyces for money: Cato counselled him to provide for thinges to come, and to let that alone which was already past. For sayd he, it is a hard thing to determine any certaine time, in the which a man should seeke to reforme the faults that are past: and furthermore, if the punishments appointed were newer then the offences committed, then they shoulde doe wrong unto them that were already accused, to punish them by a new law which they had not offended. Afterwards also, certaine men of good calling (Pompeis frends) being accused, Cato perceiving that Pompey grew remisse, and yeelded in many things: he sharply reproved, and reformed him. Furthermore, where Pompey had by law taken away the praises which were wont to be spoken of the offenders that were accused: he him selfe notwithstanding having wrytten an oration in the praise of Munatius Plancus, sent it unto the Iudges, whilest his cause was a hearing. Cato being one

156

of the Iudges at that time, stopped his eares with both his
hands, and would not have it red. Wherefore Plancus
refused him for one of his Iudges, after his cause was
pleaded unto: howebeit he was condemned notwithstanding.
To conclude, Cato was such a griefe and trouble unto them
that were accused, that they coulde not tell well howe to
deale with him. For, once they durst not lette him be any
of their Iudges, neither could they well also refuse him. For
there were many that were condemned, which refusing Cato,
seemed unto others that they were giltie: and many also
were shamefully reproved, bicause they would not accept
Cato for their Iudge, when he was offered them. Thinges
proceeding in this sorte at Rome, Cæsar remained in Gaule
with his armie, where he made warres: neverthelesse he
wanne him frends still in Rome, by gifts and money, and
made him selfe very strong. Now appeared Catoes predictions and forewarnings true unto Pompey, and began to
quicken his spirits which had slept so long, and made him
then to consider of the daunger, the which before he could
not be perswaded to beleve. But perceiving his slackenes
and feare withall, douting howe to proceede: to prevent
Cæsars practises, Cato determined to sue to be Consul, with
intent either to make him leave his army, or else to finde
out the practise he entended. Catoes competitors, they were
both of them very honest men also, of the which, Sulpitius
had received great honor and preferrement by Catoes credit
and authoritie: in respect whereof, many thought that it
was scant honestly done of Sulpitius, to shew himselfe so
unthankfull, as to stand against Cato in this sute. Howbeit
Cato never complained of the matter, but sayd, that it was
no marvell he would geve place to no man in that, sith it
was the greatest good happe that ever came unto him.
This notwithstanding he perswaded the Senate to make a
law, that from thence forth, such as sued for any office, they
should them selves be suters to the people, and not preferre
their sute by others. This caused the people to be more
offended with him, then before, bicause thereby he did not
only take away their fingering of money, which they got by
their voyces in elections: but tooke from them the meanes

Cato sued to
be Consull, to
resist Cæsar.

CATO
UTICAN
Cato was
denied the
Consulshippe.

they had also to pleasure many, bringing them now into povertie and contempt. He therefore having no face to flatter the people and to currie favor with them, but rather sticking to his grave maner and modest life, then to seeke the dignitie of a Consul by suche meanes : made sute him selfe in person, and would not suffer his frends to take the ordinary course which might win the peoples harts, whereupon he was put from his Consulshippe. This denyall was wont not only to have made the parties refused, very sorowfull, but their frendes and kinsemen also greatly ashamed a long time after. Howbeit Cato made no reckoning of that, but went the next morning, and played at tennis with his frends in the field of Mars, and after he had dyned, walked againe in the market place, as his maner was, without shooes on his feete, and coate. But Cicero blamed him much for

Cicero
blameth
Cato.

that, bicause the common wealth requiring then such a Consul as he, he had not carefully endevored him selfe by curtesie and gentle meanes to winne the favor of the people, neither woulde ever after make sute for it, although at an other time he sued to be Prætor. Thereunto Cato aunswered, that for the Prætorship, he was not denyed it by the good will of the people, but rather for that they were bribed with money. And for the election of the Consuls, where there was no deceit used, he knew plainly he went without it, for his maners which the people misliked : the which he thought were no wise mans parte to chaunge for any mans pleasure, nor yet by making the like sute again, to hazard the refusall. Furthermore, Cæsar making warre with very stowt nations, and having with no small daunger and travell subdued them : and having also set upon the Germaines, with whom the Romanes were at peace, and also slaine three hundred thowsand persons : his frends made sute that the people should do solemne sacrifice to geve thankes

Catoes
opinion
against
Cæsar.

unto the gods. But Cato in open Senate was of opinion, that they should deliver Cæsar into their handes, whome he had injured, to receive such punishment as they thought good : to thend the whole offence, for the breach of peace, might be cast upon him, that the citie might be no partaker of it, sith they could not do withall. Neverthelesse, sayd

158

he, we are to doe sacrifices unto the goddes, to geve them thankes, for that they turned not the revenge of the fury and rashnes of the Captaine, apon our poore souldiers which were in no fault, but have pardoned the common wealth. Cæsar being advertised thereof, wrote a letter unto the Senate, contayning many accusations against Cato. The letter being red, Cato rose, not as a man put in a chafe with choller, nor pricked with envie, but coldly and quietly (as if he had long before premeditated what he would say) declared that the accusations which Cæsar heaped against him in his letters, were but pretie mockes and sleytes which he had gathered together to make the people mery withall. But on thother side, when he beganne to unrippe his whole intents and practises from the beginning, not as if he had bene his enemie, but rather a confederate with him in his conspiracie, declaring that they were not the Germaines, nor the Gaules, which they were to be affrayed of, but of him selfe, if they were wise: he thereupon so offended the Senate, and made such sturre among them, that Cæsars frends repented them they had caused his letters to be red in the Senate, giving Cato thereby occasion justly to complaine of Cæsar, and to alleage much good matter against him. At that time therefore there was nothing decreed in the Senate against Cæsar, but this was sayed onely, that it were good reason to let him have a successor. Then Cæsars frends made sute that Pompey shoulde put away his army, and resigne up the provinces he kept, or else that they should compell Cæsar no more then him to doe it. Then Cato opened his mouth, and sayd, the thing was now come to passe, which he had ever told them of, and that Cæsar came to oppresse the common wealth, openly turning the armie against it, which deceitfully he had obtained of the same. All this prevailed not, neither could he thereby winne any thing of the Senate, bicause the people favored Cæsar, and would alwayes have him great: for the Senate did beleve all that he sayed, but for all that they feared the people. When newes was brought that Cæsar had wonne the citie of Ariminum, and was comming on with his armie towardes Rome: then every man looked apon Cato, and the

Cato inveyeth against Cæsar.

Cato prognosticated Cæsars tyrannie.

159

people and Pompey confessed, that he only from the beginning had found out the marke Cæsar shot at, and had hit
the white of his slie devise.   Then sayd Cato unto them, If
you would have beleved me, my Lordes, and followed my
counsell : you should not now have bene affrayd of one man
alone, neither should you also have put your only hope in
one man.   Pompey aunswered thereunto, that Cato in deede
had gessed more truely, howbeit that he also had delt more
frendly.   Thereuppon Cato gave counsell, that the Senate
should referre all unto Pompeys order : for, sayd he, they
that can doe great mischiefe, knowe also howe to helpe it.
Pompey perceiving that he had no army convenient about
him to tary Cæsars comming, and that the men also which
he had, were but faint harted : he forsooke the citie.   Cato

being determined to goe with him, sent his younger sonne
before unto Munatius, which laye in the contrie of the Bru-
tians, and tooke his eldest sonne with him.   Now, bicause
he was to provide a stay and governor of his house and
daughters, he tooke Martia againe, which was left a widowe
and verie riche, for that Hortensius dying, made her his
heire of all that he had.   Therein Cæsar upbraydeth Cato

much, reproving his covetousnes to marry for goodes.   For,
sayd he, if he had neede of a wife, why then did he before
graunt her unto an other ?   If he had no neede of a woman,
why then did he take her afterwards againe ?   Unlesse she
were before a bayte unto Hortensius, to keepe her whilest
she was young, that he might have her againe when she
was riche.   But against that, me thinkes it is sufficient to
recite these verses of Euripides :

> Unlikelyhoodes first I will disprove.   For why? what man can say,
> That ever feare made Hercules to turne his face away?

For I take it to be all one, to reprove Hercules cowardlines, and Catoes covetousnes.   But if his mariage be to be
reproved, peradventure it is in an other sorte.   For so soone
as he had maried Martia againe, he left his house and his
daughters to her government, and followed Pompey.   But
after that time, men reporte that he never polled his head,
clipped his beard, nor ware any garland, but to his dying

160

day, lamented, and bewailed in his hart, the miserie and calamitie of his contrie, whether they had victorie, or were overcome. So having the province of Sicile allotted to him, he went unto Syracusa. There understanding that Asinius Pollio was arrived at Messina, with men of warre from his enemies: Cato sent unto him, to knowe wherefore he came thither. Pollio againe asked of him, who was the causer of all this warre. Againe, when Cato was advertised that Pompey had forsaken Italie, and that he lay in campe beyond the sea, by the citie of Dyrrachium, then he sayd, he saw a marvelous great chaunge and incerteintie in the providence of the goddes: that when Pompey did all things beyond reason, and out of course, he was invincible: and now that he sought to preserve his contrie, he saw he lacked his former good happe. Nowe he knewe he was strong enough at that time, to drive Asinius Pollio out of Sicile if he would: but bicause there came a greater aide unto him, he would not plague that Iland, with the miserie of warre. Then after he had advised the Syracusans to take the stronger part, and to looke to their safety: he tooke the sea and went towards Pompey. When he was come unto him, he did alwaies counsel him to prolong the warre, hoping still of some treaty of peace: and would in no case they should come to fight any battell, where the weaker parte should of necessity be put to the sword, by the stronger. Therefore he perswaded Pompey and the counsellers about him, to establishe certaine lawes to this effect. That they should sacke no citie in this warre, the which belonged unto the Empire of Rome: and also, that they should kill no citizen of Rome, but in furie of battell, when their swordes were in their hands. Therby he wanne him selfe great honor, and brought many men to take Pompeys parte, by the lenity and clemency he used unto them that were taken. Thereupon Cato being sent into Asia, to aide them that had commission to presse shippes and men of warre, he tooke his sister Servilia with him, and the boy which Lucullus had by her: for all the time of her widowhoode, she had followed Cato, and thereby had worne out her ill name she had before, sith they saw she had so willingly geven her selfe to follow him in his

CATO UTICAN
Cato is sent into Sicile.

Cato leaveth Sicile.

Catoes lawes in Pompeys army.

5 : X

flying, and contented her selfe with his straight maner of life. This notwithstanding, Cæsar did not let to shame her to Cato. Pompeys Captaines had no neede of Cato any where, but at the Rhodes. For he wanne the people there with his curteous usage and perswasion, leaving with them Servilia and her litle sonne, and went from thence to Pompeys campe, who had leavied a great armie both by sea and land. There did Pompey most of all discover his minde and intent. For first he ment to have geven Cato the charge of the armie by sea, which were above five hundred shippes of warre, besides an infinite number of foystes and pinases, and such small bottomes uncovered : but sodainly consider-

ing better of it (or possibly being informed by some of his frends, that al Catoes regard and counsell in matters of government was, to deliver Rome from tyranny, and that if he had so great a charge under him, Cæsar being once overcome, he would also force Pompey to leave his army, and so make him subject to the law) he chaunged his minde, notwithstanding he had already moved it to Cato, and leaving him, gave Bibulus the charge of all his army by sea. But Cato therefore shewed no lesse good will unto Pompey, then before. For it is reported, that in a certaine skirmish and conflict before the city of Dyrrachium, Pompey encoraging his souldiers, and commaunding every Captaine also to do the like in his quarter : the souldiers gave but faint care unto them, and made no manner of show of men whose harts had bene any whit the more encoraged thereby. But when Cato after them all came and told them (as the time served) the reason of Philosophie, and the effect of libertie, manhoode, death, and honor, and that with a great vehement affection : and last of all ending his oration, calling apon the gods, turning his speache unto them, as if they had bene present to have scene how valliantly the souldiers fought for the libertie of their contry : they gave such a lustie crye, and had such a brave conceite and vehement desire to fight like men, that all the Captaines were filled with good hope, and so led them to battell, where they gave such a cruell charge and fierce onset apon their enemies, that they overthrewe them, and put them that day to flight. Howebeit Cæsars

162

good fortune tooke the finall ende of this victorie from
Pompey, by his overgreat feare and mistrust: who could
not tell how to take the benefit of his victorie, as we have
wrytten more amply in his life.   But when all the rest
rejoyced that they had done so noble an exployte, and
made their vawnts of the great advantage they had of their
enemies: Cato to the contrarie bewailed the calamitie of his
contrie, and lamented that cursed ambicion which caused so
many good and valliant citizens of one selfe citie, so to kill
and murther one an other.   After this overthrowe, Cæsar
taking his way into Thessalie, Pompey raised his campe to
followe him, and leaving a great power at Dyrrachium, of
men, armor, munition and frends: he gave Cato the charge
of them all, and fifteene ensignes of footemen besides.   The Why Pompey
left Cato at
Dyrrachium.
which he did for the feare and mistrust he had of him, being
assured, that if by ill fortune he should lose the battell, he
knew well enough that he could not commit them to a
trustier man then he: but on thother side if he wanne the
victory, he douted sore that he could not commaund as he
would, where Cato was.   There were also many other noble
men, as a man would say, cast away, and left at Dyrrachium,
with Cato.   In fine, the overthrow of the battell at Pharsalia
being blowen abroad, Cato resolved with himselfe if Pompey
were dead, that he would passe over all his men into Italie,
and then like a banished man would him selfe alone wander
as farre as he coulde from the tyrannie: and contrarily, if
he were alive, that then he would keepe his army together
for him, as long as he could.   With this determination, he
passed over the sea into the Ile of Corfu, where Pompeys
armie by sea lay.   There Cato finding Cicero, he would have
surrendered up his charge unto him, as to a man of greater
dignitie, for that he had bene Consul, and Cato only but
Prætor.   Howbeit Cicero would in no wise receive it, but
returned immediatly into Italy.   Cato then perceiving that Cato saveth
Ciceroes life,
from Pompeis
sonne.
Pompey the younger (sonne unto Pompey the great) of a
rash and hawty minde, would have punished all them that
went into Italie, and left the armie by sea, and that specially
he was bent first of all to begin with Cicero: Cato reproved
him privately for it, so that he certainly saved Ciceroes life,

163

and many other moe besides. Now Cato supposing that Pompey the great had saved him selfe in Ægypt, or in Africke, he determined to take the seas, to meete him with all his men: but before he tooke shippe, he gave all men leave to depart that were not willing to follow him.

Cato went into Africke.

Cato being arrived in Africke, sayling up and downe the coast there, he met with Sextus, the youngest sonne of Pompey, who first told him, that his father was slaine in Ægypt: when the souldiers heard it, they tooke it very heavily, and not one of them after the death of Pompey the great, would serve under any other Captaine then Cato. He therupon being ashamed, and thinking it pity also to leave so many noble and good men that had served so faithfully under him, without a Captaine, not knowing what way to take, nor whether to goe: at their request he was contented to take charge of them, and went first unto the citie of Cyrenes, where not many dayes before, the citizens had shut the gates against Labienus. Being there, it was told him that Scipio, Pompeys father in law, was gotten unto king Iuba, who had received him: and that Actius Varus, unto whome Pompey had geven the charge of the province of Africke, was in their company with an army, and determined to goe joyne with them. So he went by lande in the winter time, and had gotten a marvelous number of asses together, to cary water and vittels, which followed him with a great number of carts besides, and of those men, which

Psilles, be men which heale the stinging of serpents.

the Africanes call Psilles, to wit, they that doe heale the stinging of serpents, and doe sucke out the poyson with their mouthes, and doe furthermore charme and enchaunt the snakes, that they have no power to doe any hurt. He was seven dayes together marching continually, and went a foote as a guide unto his men, without helpe of horse or beast. From that day foorth, on the which he understoode of the battell lost at Pharsalia, he never supped, but sitting,*

*Men in olde time bathed and washed them selves, and then laied them downe in their bed to suppe.

and added that unto the rest of his sorrow, that he never layed him downe, but when he went to bedde for all night. Cato having passed the winter in Lybia, he brought his souldiers into the fielde, which were about tenne thowsand persons. The affaires on their side had but hard successe,

164

for the contencion and variance betwext Scipio, and Varus, for the which, they both flattered king Iuba to winne his favor: being a marvelous prowde man for his greatnes and riches: as he shewed the first time he spake with Cato. For when Cato came, he caused his owne chayre to be set betwext Scipio and Cato, to have the honor to be in the middest. But Cato perceiving it, tooke up his owne chaire, and set it on thother side by Scipio to put him in the middest, notwithstanding that he was his enemie, and had wrytten a shamefull booke against him. Many make no accompt of this facte of Cato, but reprove him, bicause that walking one day with Philostratus in Sicile, he gave him the upper hande, honoring him for his Philosophie. Thus Cato did pull downe the pride of the king at that time, who before had used Scipio, and Varus, as his noble men and subjects: howebeit Cato did reconcile them together againe. Furthermore, when all the companie prayed him to take charge of the whole armie, and that Scipio him selfe, and Varus both, did first geve him place, and willingly resigned unto him the honor to commaunde the whole campe: he aunswered them, he woulde not offende the lawe, sith he made warre onely to preserve the authoritie and priviledge thereof, neither would take upon him to commaunde all, him selfe being but Vicepraetor, where there was a Viceconsull present. For Scipio was created Proconsull, and furthermore, the people had a certayne confidence that their affaires woulde prosper the better, if they had but the name of a Scipio to leade them in Africke. Nowe when Scipio was Generall over them, he woulde straight for Iubaes sake, have put all the inhabitantes of the citie of Utica (without respect of age) unto the sworde, and have rased the houses to the grounde as those that had taken Caesars parte. Howebeit Cato woulde not suffer him, but protesting unto them that were present, and calling the gods to witnesse in open counsell, with great difficulty he saved the poore people of Utica from that cruell tragedy and slaughter. Afterwards, partly at the request of the people, and partly also at Scipioes instance, Cato tooke apon him to keepe the city, fearing least by treason, or against their wills, it should come into

CATO
UTICAN

The modestie and noble minde of Cato.

Cato joyneth with Scipio in Africke.

Cato was made Governor of the city of Utica.

Cæsars hands: bicause it was a strong place of scituacion, and well replenished with all things necessary for him that should kepe it. Cato did both furnish it, and also fortifie it. For he brought in great store of corne, he repaired the rampers of the walls, made great high towers, and cast depe trenches round about the city, paling them in: and betwext the trenches and the towne, he lodged all the young men of Utica, and compelled them to deliver up their armor and weapon and kept all the rest within the city it selfe, carefully providing, that never a man of them should be hurt by the Romanes, and besides, did also send corne, armor, munition and money unto the campe: so that the city of Utica was the staple and storehouse of the warres. Moreover, as he had before counselled Pompey not to come to battell, the like counsell he now gave also unto Scipio: not to hazard battel against a man of great skill and experience in warres, but to take time, whereby, by litle and litle, he should consume the power and strength of Cæsars tyranny.

But Scipio was so stowt, that he regarded not Catoes counsell, but wrote otherwhile unto him, twitting him with his cowardlines in this maner: that it was enough for him to be safe in a good city compassed about with walls, though otherwise he sought not to hinder men to be valliant, to execute any enterprise as occasion was offred. Cato wrote againe unto him, that he was ready to goe into Italie with his footemen and horsemen which he had brought into Africke to draw Cæsar from them, and to turne him against him. Scipio made but a sport at it. Then Cato shewed plainly, that he did repent him he had geven him the preferrement to be generall of the army, bicause he saw he would but fondly prosecute this warre: and also, that if he chaunced to overcome, he could not moderately use the victory against his contry men. Then he beganne to mistrust the good successe of this warre (and so he told his frendes) for the Generalls hastines and unskilfulnesse: and yet if beyonde expectation it fell out well, and that Cæsar were overthrown, he would never dwell at Rome any more, but would flye the crueltie and bitternes of Scipio, who even at that present time did prowdly threaten many. But in the ende, that fell out

166

GRECIANS AND ROMANES

sooner then looked for. For a poste came to him late that
night, who but three dayes before departed from the campe,
and brought newes that all was lost, in a great battell, by
the citie of Thapses, which Cæsar had wonne: that he had
taken both campes, that Scipio and king Iuba were fled with
a fewe men, and that all the rest of their armie was slaine.
These newes did put the citizens in such a feare and maze,
(and specially being in the warre, and in the night time)
that for very feare they could scant keepe them selves within
the walles of their citie. But Cato meeting with them, stayed
them that ranne up and downe crying in the streetes, and
did comfort them the best he could. Yet he tooke not all
their feare from them, though he brought them againe unto
them selves from the extasie they were in, declaring unto
them, that the losse was nothing so great as it was made,
and that it was a common matter to enlarge suche newes
with wordes enowe. By these perswasions, he somwhat pacified the tumult and uprore, and the next morning by breake
of day, he made proclamacion, that the three hundred men
which he had chosen for his counsellers, should come and
assemble in the temple of Iupiter, they all being citizens of
Rome, which for trafficke of marchaundise lay in Africke,
and all the Romane Senators and their children also. Nowe
whilest they gathered them selves together, Cato him selfe
went verie gravely with a set modest countenaunce, as if
no suche matter had happened, having a litle booke in his
hande, which he read as he went. This booke conteyned
the store and preparacion of municion he had made for this
warre, as corne, armor, weapons, bowes, slings and footemen.
When they were all assembled, he began greatly to commend
the good love and faithfulnes of these three hundred Romanes,
which had profitably served their contry with their persons,
money, and counsell, and did counsell them not to depart
one from an other, as men having no hope, or otherwise
seeking to save them selves scatteringly. 'For remeining
'together, Cæsar would lesse despise them, if they would
'make warre against him: and would also sooner pardon
'them, if they craved mercie of him. Therefore he coun-
'selled them to determine what they would do, and for his

CATO
UTICAN

Catoes con-
stancy in
extremity.

Catoes oration
unto the
Romanes at
Utica.

167

' owne parte, he sayed he would not mislike whatsoever they
' determined of: for if their mindes followed their fortune,
' he would thinke this chaunge to procede of the necessitie
' of time. But if they were resolved to withstande their
' misfortune, and to hazard them selves to defend their
' libertie: he then would not only commend them, but
' having their noble corage in admiration, would him selfe
' be their chieftaine and companion, even to prove the for-
' tune of their contrie to the uttermost. The which was not
' Utica, nor Adrumetum, but the citie selfe of Rome: the
' which oftentimes through her greatnes, had raised her selfe
' from greater daungers and calamities. Furthermore, that
' they had many waies to save them selves, and the greatest
' meane of all was this: that they should make warre with
' a man, who by reason of his warres was compelled to be in
' many places. For Spayne of the one side was up against
' him, and tooke parte with the younger Pompey: and the
' citie of Rome also not being used to be brideled with the
' snaffle of such insolencie, could not abide it, but would
' rather rise with any other chaunge. Furthermore, that
' they were not to refuse any daunger, but to take example
' of their enemy: who, to worke his mischievous intent,
' spareth not his person in any daunger. And contrarily
' also, that unto them, the incertaintie of the warre, if
' victorie followed, would make them happy: as also in
' being overthrowen, their death would turne to immortall
' glory. Notwithstanding, they were to thinke of the matter
' among themselves, and to make their praiers to the gods,
' that in recompence of their vertue and good service which
' they had shewed thitherunto, they would graunt them
' grace to determine for the best.' After Cato had ended
his oration, there were divers of them that were stirred up by
his lively perswasions, but the most part of them were incoraged by his constancy and noble minde, and also by his
kindnes: so that they presently forgate the daunger they
were in, and prayd him to commaund their persons, goods,
and weapons, as he thought good, taking him for their only
invincible Captaine, of whom fortune had no power, thinking
it better to dye obeying his counsell, then to save them

selves, forsaking so valliant and worthy a man. Then, when
one of the assembly made a motion that they shoulde make
their bondmen free, and that divers also did confirme it, Cato
sayd he would by no meanes suffer it, because it was neither
meete nor lawfull : howbeit if their maisters would manumise
them, that he was contented to receive them for souldiers,
that could weare any weapon. Divers promised him to do
it : and Cato commaunded their names should be enrolled
that would, and so went his way. Immediatly after, letters
were brought him from king Iuba, and Scipio : of the which,
king Iuba was hidden in a mountaine with few men with
him, who sent unto him to know what he would determine
to do. For if he ment to forsake Utica, he would tary
him there : and if otherwise he determined to kepe Utica,
then that he would come and helpe him with an army.
Scipio on thother side riding at ancker, at a point of the
land not farre from Utica, staid for the like aunswere. Then
Cato thought it best to stay the messengers which had
brought him their letters, till he saw what was the determination of the three hundred. For all they that were Senators of Rome, were verie glad men, and did presently make
their bondmen free, and gave them weapons. But the other
three hundred which were marchant venterers, and that lived
by usury and exchaunge, who had the most parte of their
goods in slaves and bondmen, did not long follow Catoes
counsell : but like men, whose bodies soone receive heate, and
are soone cold againe, when they are once gone from the fire :
even so those marchants, while Cato was present among them,
had some good prety will and desire : but when by them
selves they had cast their accompt, the feare they had of
Cæsar, made them forget the reverence they bare unto Cato,
and unto their duety. For, sayd they, what are we, and
what is he whom we disdaine to obey ? Is it not Cæsar
him selfe, who at this day is Lord and Emperor of Rome ?
Never a one of us is Scipio, Pompey, nor Cato : and yet now,
when all men for feare (and in maner compelled) do yeld and
submit them selves, we will nedes take upon us within the
wals of Utica to fight for the liberty of Rome against him,
for whom, Cato flying with Pompey, forsooke Italie : and we

now make our bondmen free to fight with Cæsar, having no better liberty our selves, then it pleaseth him to geve us. Let us therefore now know our selves whilest we have time, and crave mercie at his handes that is the stronger, and send unto him, to pray him to pardon us. The greatest and wisest men of those three hundred marchants, had this speache. But the most parte of them sought meanes how to entrappe the Senators, hoping the better of mercy at Cæsars hand, if they did deliver them unto him. Cato did looke for this chaunge in them, but yet uttered not that he thought, and returned the messengers backe againe unto king Iuba, and Scipio, and wrote unto them: that they should beware they came not neere Utica, bicause he did mistrust these three hundred marchants. Now there were a great number of horsemen which had escaped from the battell, who comming towards Utica, sent three of their company unto Cato, the which brought him not one selfe determination from all the company. For some of them went to go unto king Iuba, others also to joyne with Cato, and parte of them were affraid to come into Utica. These things being thus reported unto Cato, he commaunded Marcus Rubrius to take care of these three hundred men, and to receive the names of the bondmen which they willingly manumised, without compelling of any man. In the meane

time, Cato with all the Senators went out of Utica to meete with these horsemen, and there he spake to the Captaines, and praid them that they would not forsake so many noble-men and Senators of Rome as were there: and that they would not have king Iuba for their Captaine before Cato, but to come into Utica: where they might save them selves the citie was of suche strength, and besides, so well armed and vitteled for many yeres. The like request did the Senators also make unto them, with the teares running downe their cheekes. Thereupon the Captaines went and spake with their souldiers. Cato in the meane time sate him downe on a litle hill, with the Senators, tarying for aunswere. But then on the sodaine came Rubrius unto him in great hast, complaining of the tumult of these three hundred marchants, which went about to make the city to rebell:

GRECIANS AND ROMANES

whereupon, the rest their harts failing them, fell to bewaile their miserable fortune. But Cato sought to comfort them, and then sent unto the three hundred marchantes, to pray them to have a litle pacience. So the Captaines returned againe with unreasonable demaundes of the horsemen. For they sayd, that they cared not for king Iubaes pay, neither were they affrayed of Cæsars malice, so that they had Cato for their generall: yet to be pende up within the walls of a citie with Africanes, that were Phœnicians, and a traiterous nation as could be: that grieved them most of all. For, sayd they, though now they sturre not, and be quiet: yet when Cæsar comes, they will be the first that will betray us, and cut our throates. And therefore, if Cato woulde have them to joyne with him in this warre: that he should either kill or drive away all the Uticans out of the citie, and then that they would come into it, when it was cleere of all those barbarous people their enemies. Cato thought this a cruell and barbarous condicion, nevertheles he told them that he would talke with the three hundred: and so returning againe into Utica, he spake unto them. But they then not regarding the reverence unto Cato, dissembling no lenger, said openly, that they would not like of him whatsoever he were, that should compel them to make warre with Cæsar, both bicause they would not, nor could not doe it. Further, there were some of them that mumbled to them selves, that the Senators should be kept there, till Cæsar came. Cato overheard them, for in deede his hearing was not very quicke. At that very instant one came to him, and tolde him, that the horsemen were going their way. Cato therefore fearing least these three hundred marchants would lay hands apon the Senators: he went unto them him selfe with his frends, and perceiving they were gone a great way of, he tooke his horse and rode after them. They rejoycing to see him come, received him among them, and prayed him to save him selfe with them. But Cato prayed them againe to save the Senators, and that with such affection, as it forced teares in him, besides, he held up his hands unto them, tooke their horses by the bridles, and them selves by their weapons, that at length he obtained of them, that they woulde remaine there

Cato an earnest suter for the Senators.

171

CATO
UTICAN

one daye at the least, to helpe the Senators to save them selves. So Cato returning with them into the city, he appointed some of them to ward at the gates, and put others also in garrison into the castell: so that the three hundred marchants quaked for feare, least he would have bene revenged of them, bicause of their returne with him. Thereuppon they sent unto Cato, humbly to praye him to come unto them in any case. But the Senators flocking about him, would not suffer him to go, and said, that they would not cast away their savior and protector, to put him into traitors

The sinceritie
of Cato.

hands. Then doutles, all that were within Utica, plainly saw the vertue and simplicity of Cato, and found that there was no frawde nor deceite in him: who having long time resolved to kill him selfe, he only tooke that extreame paines and care for others that their lives being saved, he might then rid him selfe of his owne. For men might easely see, though he dissembled it, that he was resolved to dye. Whereupon, having comforted the Senators, he yeelded unto the requests of the three hundred marchants, and went him selfe alone unto them. Then they thanked him much for his comming, and prayed him to commaund them, and boldly to trust them : so that he would pardon them if they could not be all Catoes, and would take pity of their faint harts, though they were not so constant and noble minded as he. For they were determined to send unto Cæsar, specially to intreate him for him : and if that they could not obteine pardon for him, then they were assured they could have none for them selves, and therfore would fight for the safety of him, while they had any breath in their bodies. Cato thanking them for their good wills, answered : that they should send quickely to crave pardon for them selves,

Catoes minde
unconquer-
able.

but to aske none for him. For sayd he, men that be overcome, and have offended, it standeth them upon to make humble sute, and to crave pardon : but for him selfe, he was never overcome in his life, and yet had overcome as much as he desired, and had alwayes bene better then Cæsar in justice, who only (not him selfe) was now taken and overcome: the thing being apparantly proved in sight against him, which he had alwaies denied to have practised against his

172

GRECIANS AND ROMANES

contry. When he had made this answere unto the three
hundred marchants, he departed from them. Newes being
brought that Cæsar was in his way with all his armie,
comming towards Utica: O goddes, sayd he, then he
commeth against us, as against men. Then turning unto
the Senators, he gave them counsell quickely to save them
selves, whilest the horsemen were yet in the city. So shutting
all the gates of the city, saving that towards the haven: he
appointed shippes for them all, and set every thing at a stay,
without tumult or disorder, no man having injurie offered
him, and gave everie one money to make way for their
safetie. When Marcus Octavius (who came with two legions,
and camped hard by Utica) sent unto Cato, to determine
which of them two should be Generall: he made no aunswere,
but turning to his frends said: How can we wonder any Cato reprov-
more that all goeth to wracke with us, sith there is suche eth the
ambition amongst us for the government, even now, when we ambition
are at the last cast? In the meane time word was brought of men.
him, how the horsemen going their way were spoyling of the
citizens goods, as a lawfull pray in warre. He straight ran
thither him selfe, and the first he met withall, he tooke from
them that they had gotten. The rest, before he came unto
them, threw downe that they were carying away, and hanging downe their heades for shame, they went their way, and
said nothing. Then Cato calling all the citizens of Utica
together, prayed them not to incense nor move Cæsar against
the three hundred, but rather to crave of him pardon for
them all. Then he went againe to the peere, and there
imbracing his frends, and taking his leave of them all, he
brought them to their shippes. Now for his sonne, he did
not counsell him to go, neither did he thinke it mete to urge
him to forsake his father. Furthermore, there was one Statilius, a
Statilius a young man in his companie, of a noble corage, follower of
that was determined to follow the invincible constancy of Cato.
Cato: who counselled him to take the sea, and to saile away
with the rest, bicause he knew he was Cæsars mortall enemy.
Statilius said he would not go. Then Cato turning him
unto Apollonides a Stoick Philosopher, and unto Demetrius
a Peripatetick Philosopher, said: You must take this stowt

young man, to perswade him to obey unto necessitie. Cato him selfe in the meane time sent away the rest, and did minister justice unto them that required it: spending all that night, and the next day, about those matters. Then Lucius Cæsar, the kinseman of Iulius Cæsar the conqueror, being chosen by the three hundred, to goe and make sute unto him for them all, came and prayed Cato to help him to make his oration, which he should say unto Cæsar for them all: And as for thee, Cato, said he, I will kisse his hands, and fall downe on my knees before him to intreate him for thee.

Nay said Cato, thou shalt not do so. For if I would save my life by Cæsars grace, I could do it, if I would but go unto him: howbeit I will not be bound to a tyran for injustice. For it is an injustice in him to take upon him, as a Lord and soveraine to save a mans life, when him selfe hath no authoritie to commaund. But yet let us consider if thou wilt, what thou shalt say, to crave pardon for the three hundred. So they were a while together considering the matter, and in fine, Lucius Cæsar being ready to departe, Cato recommended his sonne and frendes unto him, and imbracing him, tooke his leave of him. Then he returned unto his lodging, and calling his sonne and frends before him, and talking of many matters: among others he charged his sonne in no case to meddle in thaffaires of the common wealth.

Cato forbad
his sonne to
meddle with
matters of
State in a
corrupt time.

For said he, to deale uprightly like Catoes sonne, the corruption of the time and state will not abide it: and contrarily, observing the time, thou canst not do like an honest man. Towards evening he went into his bath to washe him selfe, and as he was a bathing, thinking apon Statilius, he cried out alowde: Well Apollonides, thou hast at length yet perswaded Statilius, to goe his way and pulled downe his stowt courage he had: and is he gone without bidding us farewell? Howe, gone? sayd Apollonides. Nay, his hart is now more stowt and couragious then ever it was, notwithstanding all the perswasions we could use unto him: for he is determined to tary, and to take such part as thou doest. After he had bathed him selfe, he went to supper, and sate at his meate, as he had alwaies used after the battell at Pharsalia, and never lay, but when he went to bed. So

he had all his frends, and the chiefe Magistrats of Utica to
supper with him. After supper, they fell into grave talke
and matters of Philosophie: till at length they came unto
the straunge opinion of the Stoick Philosophers, which was
this: that only the good man is free, and all the evill be
slaves. The Peripateticke Philosopher that was present
there, was straight against it. But Cato was very earnest
against the Peripateticke, and argued the matter a long time,
with a vehement speach and contencion: insomuch as they
that heard him, found then that he was determined to ende
his life, and to rid him him selfe out of all those troubles.
But then when he had ended his argument, and sawe that
every man helde his peace, and looked sadly of it: to comfort
them againe, and to put the suspicion of his death out of
their heades: he beganne againe to fall in talke of their
affaires, and seemed to be carefull of them, as though he had
bene affrayed least some misfortune were come unto them
apon the sea, or unto them that were gone by land, bicause
they passed through desertes, where there was no water to
be had. Now when supper was done, and the straungers
gone, he walked as his manner was with his frends, and
having taken order with the Captaines of the watch for
matters of service, as the time required: going into his
chamber he embraced his sonne and his frendes more lovingly
then he was wont to doe, whereby he made them againe
suspect the execution of his determination. When he was
come into his chamber and layed in his bedde, he tooke
Platoes dialogues in his hand, treating of the soule, and red
the most parte of it. Then looking by his beds side, and
missing his sword (which his sonne had taken from him when
he was at supper) he called one of the groomes of his chamber
to him, and asked him who had taken his sword away: his
man made him no aunswere, and he fell againe to read his
booke. Then a prety while after, not seeming to be importunate, or overhastie of the matter, but as though he woulde
only know what became of it: he willed them to bring him
his sword againe. They taried long, and he had red over
all the booke, but yet his sword was not brought him againe.
Wherupon he called for all his men one after an other, and

very angrily asked them his sword, and gave one of them such a blow in the face, that his nose fell a bleeding, and his hand was all bloody withal, and cried out that his sonne and his servaunts would deliver him naked into the hands of his enemie: untill his sonne and frends at length ranne unto him, and falling downe on their knees, lamented, and besought him to be contented. Cato then rising out of his bedde, looked grimly upon them, and sayd unto them: O goddes, who ever saw me in this taking? Why doth no man by reason perswade me, if they see me out of the way: and not to kepe me from my determination by plucking my weapons from me? why doest thou not bind thy father (my sonne) his hands behinde him, that when Cæsar commeth, he may finde me in case not to defend my selfe? I doe not desire my sworde to hurte my selfe, for if I had any suche minde, I neede but hold my breath a litle, or geve but a knocke of my head against the wall onely, and dispatche my selfe quickely. When he had sayd thus, his sonne went out of his chamber weeping, and all his frends also, no man remayning with Cato, but Demetrius and Apollonides, unto whom he spake

more gently, and reasoned in this sorte: What, doe you thinke to keepe an old man as I am, alive by force? And have you taried behinde but to sit staring apon me, and say nothing unto me? If otherwise else, by reason you come to perswade me, that it shall be no shame for Cato, dispairing of the safetie of his life, to seeke it by the grace and mercy of his enemy: why then doe you not now tell me your reasons to perswade me, that forsaking all other fancies and determinations which hetherunto we have holden for good, being on a sodaine become wiser by Cæsars meanes, we should be bound the more therefore to geve him thankes? I do not tell you this that I have determined any thing of my life, but that it is in my power (if I list) to put the thing in execution I have determined: but yet I will consult with you, when I am so determined, to heare the reasons and opinion of your bookes, which your selves doe use in discourse and argument together. Goe your way therefore hardily unto my sonne, and tell him, that he must not thinke to compell his father unto that, which he can not prove good unto him by reason.

GRECIANS AND ROMANES

After this talke, Demetrius and Apollonides being nothing comforted, weeping, departed out of his chamber. Then his sword was brought him by a little boy. When he had it, he drew it out, and looked whether the point and edge of his sword was sharpe and woulde cut: when he saw it was well, O, sayd he, now I am where I would be, and so laying downe the sword naked by him, he tooke his booke againe in his hand, and red it over (as they say) twise together. Then he slept so soundly after it, that his men which were without his chamber heard him snort againe. About midnight, he called for two of his freemen, Cleanthes his Phisitian, and Butas, whom he chiefly employed in his weightiest affaires of the common wealth. So he sent him unto the haven to see, if all his men that were imbarked were under saile : and gave his hand unto the Phisitian to be bound up, bicause it was swollen with the blow he gave one of his slaves when he hit him on the face. All his servaunts were glad to heare of that, hoping then that he desired to live. Soone after came Butas backe againe from the haven, and brought him word that all were gone but Crassus, who stayed about some busines he had, and yet that he was going to take shippe : howbeit that the sea was very roughe, and winde exceeding great. Cato hearing this, sighed, being sory for them that were upon the sea : and sent Butas backe againe to the haven, to see if any man came backe for any matter they had to say unto him. The litle birdes began to chirpe, and Cato fel againe in a litle slumber. But thereuppon Butas returned, and brought him word that all was quiet in the haven, and there was no sturre. Then Cato bad him goe his way, and shut to the dore after him, and layed him downe in his bed, as though he had ment to have slept out all the rest of the night. Butas backe was no sooner turned, but Cato taking his naked sword in his hand, thrust it into his breast : howbeit the swelling of his hand made the blowe so weake, that it killed him not presently, but drawing on to his latter ende, he fell downe upon his bedde, and made such a noyse with his fall (overthrowing a litle table of geometry hard by his bedde) that his servaunts hearing the noyse, gave a great

CATO UTICAN

Cato considered his sworde wherewith he killed him selfe.

The death of Cato.

shreeke for feare. Thereuppon his sonne and his friendes ranne into the chamber, and found him all of a gore bloud, and the most part of his bowells comming out of his bodye, him selfe being yet alive, and seeing them. They were all striken with such sorow to behold it, that at the first they were so amazed, as they could not tel what to say to it. His Phisitian comming to him, he went about to put in his bowels againe which were not perished, and to sow up his wound. But Cato comming to him selfe, thrust backe the Phisitian, and tare his bowells with his owne handes, and made his wound very great, and immediatly gave up the ghost. Whereuppon the three hundred Romanes (in lesse time then a man would have thought Catoes owne houshold servaunts could have knowen of his death) were at his dores, and immediatly after, all the people of Utica also came thither, and with one voyce called Cato their benefactor and savior, and sayd he onely was a free man, and had an invincible minde: and this was done, when they heard say that Cæsar was not farre from Utica. Furthermore, nether feare of the present daunger, nor the desire to flatter the Conqueror, nether any private quarrell amongest them selves, could keepe them from honoring Catoes funeralls. For,

Catoes
funeralls.

sumptuously setting out his body, and honorably accompanying his funeralls as might be, they buryed him by the sea side, where at this present time is to be seene his image, holding a sworde in his hande. After that, they made their best way to save them selves and their citie. Nowe Cæsar beeing advertised by them that came unto him, howe Cato sturred not from Utica, nor fled not, but sent all others away, saving him selfe, and his sonne, and a few of his friends that remained there, being afraid of nothing: he could not devise what he ment by it. Therefore esteeming Cato much, he made haste with all the speede he could with his armie, to come thether. But when he understoode that Cato had slaine him selfe, writers doe reporte he sayd thus:

Cæsars saying unto Cato the dead.

O Cato, I envy thy death, sithe thou hast envied mine honor to save thy life. For in deede, had Cato beene contented Cæsar should have saved his life, he had not so much impaired his owne honor, as he had augmented Cæsars glory.

178

And yet what Cæsar would have done, men make it doubt-
ful, saving that they conjecture well of Cæsars clemencie.
Cato dyed when he was but eight and forty yeare old. For
his sonne, Cæsar never did him hurt: howbeit it is reported
of him, that he was very idlely given, and lascivious besides.
For when he lay in Cappadocia, in a noble mans house of
the kings bloud, called Maphradates, who had a fayre woman
to his wife : he taried longer there then he might well with
honestie, whereuppon he fell to be a laughing stocke to the
people, and in mockery they sayd, Cato will goe too morrow,
a thirty dayes hence. And further, that Maphradates and
Porcius are two good friendes, but they have but one minde.
And the reason was, bicause Maphradates wife was called
Psyche, which in the Greeke signifieth, minde and Cato is
a noble fellow, and hath a princely mind, howbeit his famous
death did stoppe this infamous speech. For he valiantly
fighting against Augustus, and Antonius, at the battell of
Philippes, for the libertie of his contry · their armie being
overthrowen and fled, he would neither flie nor hide him
selfe, but running in amongest his enemies, he made them
knowe what he was, by incoraging those of his side, which
yet did defend them selves, till he was slayne in the field, to
the great admiration of his valiantnes. Furthermore, Porcia,
the Daughter of Cato, gave no place unto her father, nether
for chastitie, nor greatnes of mind. For she being maried
unto Brutus, who sluc Cæsar, was of the conspiracie, and
slue her selfe as corageously as became the vertue and
nobilitie of her bloud from whence she came, as we have
more amply declared in the life of Brutus. Statilius also,
who had sayd he would ronne Catoes fortune (as we have
tolde you before) was kept from killing of him selfe by the
Philosophers, Demetrius, and Apollonides. But after that
tyme having shewed him selfe very faithfull and service-
able unto Brutus in all his affayres, he was slayne
in the field also at the battell of Philippes.

THE END OF CATOES LIFE

CATO
UTICAN

The sonne of
Cato what
conditions
he had.

Psyche,
signifieth
mind.

The death of
Porcia, the
Daughter of
Cato the
younger,
and wife of
Brutus

The death of
Statilius.

AGIS AND CLEOMENES

RUELY the fable of Ixion was not ill devised against ambicious persons: who imbracing a clowde for the goddesse Iuno, begot (as it is sayd) the Centauri. For even so ambicious men, imbracing glory for the true image of vertue, doe never any acte that is good nor perfect: but beeing caried away with divers fancies, and following others humors with desire to please the people, they may, as the herdmen in the tragedy of Sophocles (speaking of their cattell) say:

We wayt uppon their beasts, though we their Maisters bee,
And wheresoever they become, there also followe wee.

Such in deede are they compared to, that governe common weales, after peoples lust and fancy: who doubtles, are as their servaunts obedient at call, bicause they onely may enjoy the glorious title and name of an Officer. For like as in a shippe the Mariners that stande in the prowe, doe better see before them, then the Pilots that steere the helme in the poope, and yet lookes alwayes backe unto them to see what they commaunde: even so, they that governe in the common wealth for honors sake, are no better then honorable slaves of the people, having no more but the bare name of a governor. But in deede, the perfect good and honest man should never covet outward glory, but as a meane to bringe him to noble attempts, whereby he might procure the better credit of his doings. And for a younge man that coveteth honor by vertue, give him leave a litle to glory in his well doing: for, as Theophrastus sayth, vertue buddeth and florisheth in youth, and taketh fast roote by prayses given, as wit and corage groweth in them. But overmuch praise is daungerous in every person, but chiefly in ambicious governors. For if they be men of great power, it makes them

180

GRECIANS AND ROMANES

commit many desperat partes : for they wil not allow that
honor proceedes of vertue, but that honor is vertue it selfe.
But in deed they should say as Phocion did unto Antipater,
that requested an unlawfull matter of him : Thou canst not,
said he, have Phocion a friend and flatterer both. This, or
the very like, may be sayd unto the people : You can not
both have one, a Maister and a servaunt, that can commaunde and obey together. Or els the mischiefe spoken of
in the tale of the Dragon must needes happen, which was :
the taile on a time fell out with the head, and complained,
saying, it would an other while go before, and would not
alwaies come behind. The head graunted the taile, which
fell out very ill for it, not knowing howe to guide the heade,
and besides that the head thereby was tormented every way,
beeing compelled against nature to follow that part and
member, which could nether heare, nor see how to guide it.
The like matter have we seene happen unto many, which in
the administracion of the common wealth, did seeke to please
the humors of the multitude. For when they have once put
their heads under their girdles to please the common people,
which without cause and reason doe soone rebell : they can
by no possible meanes afterwards bridle their furie and insolencie. Now the reason that made us to enter into discourse against the ambition and vaine glorye amongest the
people : was the consideracion I had of their greate power,
remembring the misfortunes of Tiberius and Caius Gracchi :
bothe the which comming of a noble house, and having bene
marvelous well brought up, and maneging also the affayres
of the common wealth with a good desire, were notwithstanding in the ende cast away : not so much through
covetousnes of glorye, as for feare of dishonor, which came
also of no base mind. For they having received great
pleasures and friendships of the people, were ashamed to be
indetted to them, and therefore earnestly sought to exceede
the people in good will, by new decrees and devises, which
they preferred for common benefit : and the people also for
their partes contended to honor them the more, by how
much they strived to shewe them selves thankefull. So with
like strife on either side, they to gratifie the common people,

AGIS AND
CLEOMENES

Phocions
saying.

The fable of
the Dragons
head and
taile.

Plutarch
excuseth the
Gracchi.

181

LIVES OF THE NOBLE

and the people also to honor them, were unwares so entangled with publike causes, that they could no more follow the common proverbe, which sayth:

> Although our deedes discent from equitie,
> Yet can we not desist with honestie.

This thou shalt easily finde by the declaracion of the historie. With these we doe compare two other popular men, both kinges of Lacedæmon, Agis and Cleomenes. For they, as the Gracchi, seeking to increase the power of the common people, and to restore the just and honest government againe of the common wealth of Lacedæmon, which of long time had bene out of use: did in like manner purchase the hate of the nobilitie, which were loth to lose any part of their wonted covetousnes. In deed these two Laconians were no brethren borne, but yet did both follow one selfe course and forme of government, which had beginning in this sort. After that covetousnes of gold and silver crept againe into the citie of Sparta, and with riches, covetousnes also and miserie, and by use, voluptuousnes and licentious life: Sparta then was void of all honor and goodnes, and was long time drowned in shame and dishonor, untill king Agis and Leonidas came to raigne there. Agis was of the *The lynage of Agis.* house of the Eurytiontides, the sonne of Eudamidas, the sixt of lineall descent after Agesilaus, who had beene the greatest Prince of all Græce in his time. This Agesilaus had a sonne slaine in Italy by the Messapians, called Archidamus, before the citie of Mandonium. Archidamus had issue two sonnes, Agis, and Eudamidas that was king, who succeeded his brother Agis, whom Antipater slue before the citie of Megalipolis, and left no children behind him. Eudamidas begat Archidamus, which Archidamus begat another Eudamidas: which Eudamidas also begat Agis, whose life *The lynage of Leonidas.* we now write of. Leonidas also, the sonne of Cleonymus, was of the other familie of the Agiades, the eight of succession after Pausanias, who slue Mardonius, the kings Lieuetenant general of Persia, in a battell fought before the citie of Platees. This Pausanias had a sonne called Plistonax, and Plistonax also an other, called Pausanias: who flying

182

from Sparta unto the citie of Tegea, his eldest sonne Agesipolis was made king in his fathers roome, who dying without issue, his yonger brother Cleombrotus succeeded him in
the kingdom. Cleombrotus had two sonnes, Agesipolis and
Cleomenes: of the which, Agesipolis raigned not long king,
and dyed without issue. Then Cleomenes his brother, who
was king after him, had two sonnes, Acrotatus the elder,
that dyed in his fathers life time: and Cleonymus the yonger
which survived him, and was not king, but one Areus his
Nephewe, the sonne of Acrotatus. This Areus dyed before
the citie of Corinthe: who having an other Acrotatus to his
sonne, he succeeded him in the kingdome. He also dyed
at a battell before the citie of Megalipolis, and was slayne
there by the tyrant Aristodemus, leaving his wife great with
childe. She beeing brought to bedde after his death of a
sonne, whome Leonidas the sonne of Cleonymus taught and
brought up: the childe dying very young, the crowne by
his death was cast apon Leonidas him selfe. Howbeit his
maners and conditions never liked the people. For though
all men generally were corrupted through the common
wealth, and cleane out of order: yet Leonidas of all other
exceeded, deforming most the auncient Laconian life, bicause
he had bene long time brought up in Princes houses, and
followed also Seleucus Court, from whence he had brought
all the pride and pompe of those Courts into Græce, where
law and reason ruleth. Agis on the contrary part did not
onely farre excel Leonidas, in honor and magnanimitie of
mind: but all other almost also which had raigned in Sparta,
from the time of Agesilaus the great. So that when Agis
was not yet twenty yeare old, and being daintily brought up
with the finenes of two women, his mother Agesistrata, and
Archidamia his grandmother, which had more gold and
silver, then all the Lacedæmonians els: he began to spurne
against these womanish delights and pleasures, in making
him selfe fayer to be the better beliked, and to be fine and
trimme in his apparell, and to cast upon him a plaine Spanish
cape, taking pleasure in the dyet, bathes, and manner of the
auncient Laconian life: and openly boasted besides, that he
would not desire to be king, but onely for the hope he had

to restore the auncient Laconian life by his authority. Then began the state of Lacedæmon first to be corrupted, and to leave her auncient discipline, when the Lacedæmonians having subdued the Empire of the Athenians, stored them selves and contry both, with plenty of gold and silver. But yet reserving still the lands left unto them by succession from their fathers, according unto Lycurgus first ordinaunce and institucion, for division of the landes amongest them : which ordinaunce, and equalitie being inviolably kept amongest them, did yet preserve the common wealth from defamation of divers other notorious crimes. Until the time of the authoritie of Epitadeus, one of the Ephores, a seditious man, and of prowde conditions : who bitterly falling out with his own sonne, preferred a law, that every man might lawfully give his landes and goods whilest he lived, or after his death by testament, unto any man whom he liked or thought well of. Thus this man made this law to satisfie his anger, and others also did confirme it for covetousnes sake, and so overthrew a noble ordinaunce. For the riche men then began to buy lands of numbers, and so transferred it from the right and lawful heires : whereby a few men in short time being made very riche, immediatly after there fell out great povertie in the citie of Sparta, which made all honest sciences to cease, and brought in thereuppon unlawfull occupacions, who envyed them that were wealthy. Therefore, there remayned not above seven hundred naturall Citizens of Sparta in all, and of them, not above a hundred that had lands and inheritance : for all the rest were poore people in the citie, and were of no countenaunce nor calling, and besides that, went unwillingly to the warres against their enemies, looking every day for sturre and chaunge in the citie.

Agis therefore thinking it a notable good acte (as in deede it was) to replenish the citie of Sparta againe, and to bringe in the old equalitie, he moved the matter unto the Citizens. He found the youth (against all hope) to give good eare unto him, and very well given unto vertue, easily chaunging their garments and life, to recover their libertie againe. But the oldest men, which were now even rotten with covetousnes and corruption, they were

affraid to returne againe to the straight ordinaunces of
Lycurgus, as a slave and ronneagate from his Maister,
that trembleth when he is brought back againe unto him.
Therefore they reproved Agis, when he did lament before
them their present miserable estate, and wishe also for
the former auncient honor and true dignitie of Sparta.
Howbeit Lysander the sonne of Lybis, and Mandroclidas the
sonne of Ecphanes, and Agesilaus also, greatly commended
his noble desire, and perswaded him to goe forward withall.
This Lysander was of great authoritie and estimation
amongest them in the citie : Mandroclidas was also very
wise, and carefull, about any matter of counsell, and with
his wisedom and policy, very valiant : Agesilaus in like
manner, the kings Uncle, and an eloquent man, was very
effeminate and covetous, and yet prickt forward to give his
furtherance to this attempt as it appeared, by his sonne
Hippomedon, who was a notable good souldier, and could
doe very much, by meanes of the love and good will the
younge men did beare him. But in deede, the secret cause
that brought Agesilaus to consent unto this practise, was
the greatnes of his dette which he ought, of the which
he hoped to be discharged by chaunging of the state and
common wealth. Now when Agis had wonne him, he sought
by his meanes to drawe his mother also unto the matter,
which was Agesilaus sister. She could doe very much by
the number of her friendes, followers, and detters in the
citie, by whose meanes she ruled the most part of the
affayres of the citie after her owne pleasure. But the young
man Hippomedon making her privie unto it, at the first she
was amased withall, and bad him hold his peace if he were
wise, and not medle in matters unpossible and unprofitable.
But when Agesilaus had told her what a notable acte it
would be, and how easily it might be brought to passe, with
marvelous great profit : and that king Agis beganne also to
strayne her with great intreatie, that she would willingly
depart with her goods to winne her sonne honor and glory :
who, though he could not in money and riches come to be
like unto other kinges (bicause the slaves and factors onely
of the kinges Seleucus and Ptolomy, had more money then

AGIS AND
CLEOMENES
all the kings of Sparta had together that ever raigned) yet if in temperance, thriftines, and noble mind (exceeding all their vanities) he could come to restore the Lacedæmonians againe unto equalitie: that then in deede he should be counted a noble king. These women being stirred up with ambition by these perswasions of the younge man, seeing him so nobly bent, as if by the goddes their mindes had secretly bene inflamed with the love of vertue: did presently alter their mindes in such sort, that they them selves did pricke forward Agis, and sent for their friends to pray and intreate them to favor his enterprise: and furthermore, they brought on other women also, knowing that the Lacedæmonians did ever heare and beleve their wives, suffering them to understand more of the affayres of the state, then they them selves did of their private estate at home. Herein is to be considered, that the most part of the riches of Lacedæmon was in the handes of the women, and therefore they were against it, not onely bicause thereby they were cut of from their finenes and excesse, in the which being ignorant of the true good in deede, they put all their felicitie: but also, bicause they sawe their honor and authoritie which they had by their riches, cleane troden under foote. Therefore they comming to Leonidas, they did perswade him to reprove Agis, bicause he was elder man then he, and to let that this enterprise went not forward. Leonidas did what he could in favour of the riche, but fearing the common people, who desired nothing but alteracion, he durst not openly speake against him, but secretly he did the best he could to hinder Agis practise, talking with the Magistrates of the citie: and accusing Agis unto them, he told them how he did offer the riche mens goods unto the poore, the division of their landes, and the abolishing of all detts, for rewarde to put the tyrannie into his handes, and that thereby he got him a stronge gard unto him selfe, but not many Citizens unto Sparta. This notwithstanding, king Agis having procured Lysander to be chosen one of the Ephores, he presently preferred his lawe unto the counsell. The articles whereof were these: That such as were in debt, should be cleered of all their debts, and that the landes also should be divided into equall partes:

How loving
the Lacedæ-
monians were
unto their
wives.

Agis law.

186

so that from the valley of Pallena unto mount Taugetus, and unto the cities of Malea, and Selasia, there should be foure thowsand five hundred partes, and without those boundes, there should be in all the rest, fifteene thowsand partes, the which should be distributed unto their neighbours meete to cary weapon: and the rest unto the natural Spartans. The number of them should be replenished with their neighbours and straungers in like manner, which should be very well brought up, and be able men besides to serve the common wealth: all the which afterwards should be divided into fifteene companies, of the which, some should receive two hundred, and others foure hundred men, and should live according to the olde auncient institucion observed by their auncestors. This lawe being preferred unto the Senate, the Senators grewe to divers opinions apon it. Whereuppon Lysander him selfe assembled the great counsell of all the people, and there spake unto them him selfe, and Mandroclidas, and Agesilaus also, praying them not to suffer the honor of Sparta to be troden under foote, for the vanitie of a fewe: but that they would remember the auncient oracles of the goddes, warning them to beware of avarice, as of the plague and destruction of the common wealth: and of the late oracle also brought unto them, from the temple of Pasiphaé. The temple and oracle of Pasiphaé, was famous at the citie of Thalames: and some say, that Pasiphaé was one of the Daughters of Atlas, which was gotten with child by Iupiter, and was delivered of a sonne called Hammon. Other thinke that it was Cassandra, one of king Priamus Daughters that died there, which was surnamed Pasiphaé, bicause she gave all the aunswers and oracles of things to come. But Phylarchus writeth, that Daphné the Daughter of Amycla, flying from Apollo that would have ravished her, was turned into a lawrell tree, and honored by Apollo with the gift of prophecie. So, they said that this oracle of the god commaunded them, that the Spartans should againe returne unto their former auncient equalitie, stablished first by Lycurgus lawe. When every man els had spoken, king Agis rising up, briefly speaking unto the people, sayd: that he would bestowe great contri-

Pasiphaé, the Daughter of Atlas.

187

butions for the reformation of this common wealth, which he
was desirous to restore againe. For first of all, he would
make common all his errable and pasture he had, and besides
that, he would adde to six hundred talents in ready money,
and so much should his mother, grandmother, kinsemen and
friendes, all the which were the richest and wealthiest in
Sparta. When the people heard what he sayd, they marvelled much at the noble minde of this younge king, and were
very glad of it, saying : that for three hundred yeares space
together, the citie of Sparta had not so worthy a king as he.

But Leonidas contrarily assayed with all his power he could
to resist him, thinking with him selfe, that if king Agis
purpose tooke place, he should also be compelled to doe as
he did, and yet he should have no thankes, but king Agis:
bicause that all the Spartans indifferently should be compelled to make their goods in common, but the honor should
be his onely that first beganne it. So he asked Agis, whether
he thought Lycurgus had bene a good and just man or not.
Agis aunswered, that he had bene. Then replyed Leonidas,
Did you ever see that he had taken away and abolished any
detts, or had receyved straungers into the number of the
Citizens of Sparta? Who contrarily thought his common
wealth unperfect, if all straungers were not banished the
citie. Agis agayne aunswered him : that he marvelled not
that Leonidas beeing brought up in a straung contry, and
also maryed there in a noble mans house, he should be
ignorant of Lycurgus lawes, who banishing gold and silver
out of his citie, did therewithall exile dette and lending.
And for straungers, he hated them that woulde not conforme
them selves unto the manners and facions of life which he
instituted, and those they were which he banished : not for
any ill will he bare unto their persons, but bicause he feared
their manners of life, least that mingling them with the
Citizens, they should make them runne after vanitie and
covetousnes to be riche. For otherwise, Terpander, Thales,
and Pherecydes, which were all straungers, were marvelously
reverenced and honored in Sparta in olde tyme, bicause they
did singe in their writings, the selfe same thinges which
Lycurgus had established in his lawes. And thou thy selfe

also doest commend Ecprepes, being one of the Ephores, bicause he did cut with a hatchet the two stringes which Phrynis the Musitian had added unto the Citherne, more then the seven common stringes, and those also which did the like unto Timotheus: and yet thou reprovest me, bicause I goe about to roote out all excesse and pride out of Sparta, as though those men did not farre of prevent that these superfluous stringes of the musicke, delighting the Citizens mindes too much with their songes, should not cause them fall unto such trade and manner of life, as should make the citie at discord with it selfe. After this contencion, the common people did sticke unto king Agis, and the riche men followed Leonidas, praying and perswading him not to forsake them: and further, they did so intreate the Senators, in whom consisteth the chiefe authority, to determine and disgest all matters before they be propownded unto the people, that they overthrew the law, by the onely voice of one man more. Wherefore Lysander who was yet in office, attempted to accuse Leonidas by an auncient lawe, forbidding that none of the race of Hercules should mary with any straung woman, nor beget children of her: and sayde further, that no man upon payne of death should dwell any where, but in Sparta. When he had instructed others to object these thinges agaynst Leonidas, he with other of his colleagues observed a signe in the element, the ceremony wherof was in this sorte: Every nynenth yeare, the Ephori chusing a bright night without moonelight, did sit downe in some open place, and beheld the starres in the element, to see if they saw any starre shoote from one place to another: if they did, then they accused their kinges that they had offended the goddes, and did deprive them of their kingdom, untill some oracle came from Delphes or Olympus, to restore them againe. Lysander then declaring that he had seene a starre flie in the element, did therefore accuse king Leonidas, and brought forth witnesses against him: how he had maried a woman of Asia, the which one of king Seleucus Lieuetenants had given him in mariage, and that he had two children by her: and afterwards being forsaken of his wife that refused him, he returned againe into his contry against

King Leonidas accused by Lysander.

189

his will, and so had possessed the kingdom for lacke of lawful heire. So following his accusation in this manner against him, he allured Cleombrotus his sonne in law, being also of the kings blood, to make title to the crowne. Leonidas being affraid of the successe hereof, tooke sanctuary in the temple of Iuno, surnamed Chalceæcos, and his Daughter with him, who forsooke her husband Cleombrotus. Leonidas then being cited to appeare in person, and making default, they deposed him, and made Cleombrotus king. In the meane time Lysanders office expired, and the new Ephori which succeded him, did deliver Leonidas againe, and accused Lysander and Mandroclidas, bicause against the law, they had abolished all debts, and had againe made newe division of lands. When they sawe they were openly accused, they incensed both the kinges, that joyning together, they shoulde make the Ephores ordinaunces of no effect : declaring, that their authority was onely erected for the discord of the two kings, bicause they should give their voices unto that king that had the best judgement and reason, when the other would wilfully withstand both right and reason. And therfore, that they two agreing together, might lawfully do what they would, without controlment of any person : and that to resist the kings was a breaking of the lawe, sith that by right the Ephori had no other privileage and authority, but to be judges and arbitrators betwene them, when there was any cause of jarre or controversie. Both the kings being caried away by this perswasion, went into the market place accompanied with their frends, plucked the Ephores from their seates, and put others in their roomes, of the which Agesilaus was one. Furthermore, they armed a great number of yong men, and opening the prisons, did set the prisoners at liberty : the which made their adversaries affraid of them, doubting some great murther would have followed upon it, howbeit no man had any hurt. For Agesilaus being bent to kill Leonidas, who fled unto the city of Tegea, and having also laid men in waite for him by the way : king Agis hearing of it, sent thither other frends of his in whom he put great confidence, and they did accompany Leonidas, and brought him safely unto the city of Tegea. Thus their

GRECIANS AND ROMANES

purpose taking effect, and no man contrarying them: one man only Agesilaus overthrew all, and dashed a noble Laconian law by a shamful vice, which was covetousnes. For he being a great landed man, and having the best lands of any man in the contry, and owing a great summe of money besides: would nether pay his detts, nor let go his land. Wherfore he perswaded king Agis, that if he went about to stablish both together, he should raise a great uprore in the city, and withall, if he did first winne them that were landed men, preferring at the beginning the cutting of of dets only: then that they would easily and willingly also accept the law for partition of lands. Lysander was also of his opinion: wherby king Agis and he both were deceived by Agesilaus subtlety. So they commaunded al the creditors to bring their bonds, obligations, and bils of det (which the Lacedæmonians do cal Claria) into the market place, and there laying them on a heape together, they did set fire of them. When the usurers and creditors saw their writings obligatory afire, they departed thence with heavy harts: but Agesilaus mocking them said, he never saw a brighter fire in his life. The people then requiring that the lands also should be presently devided, and the kings likewise commaunding it: Agesilaus stil interposing some cause of let, delaied time, untill oportunitye served, that king Agis should go to the warres, for that the Achaians their confederats had praied aide of Lacedæmon, being bound thereunto by the league confirmed betwene them, bicause they looked daily that the Ætolians comming through the contry of Megara, would invade Peloponnesus. Aratus general of the Achaians had leavied a great army to withstand their invasion, and had also written unto the Ephores, that they should send them aide. Wheruppon, they presently sent king Agis, perceiving also the readines and good wil of the souldiers which were appointed to go with him. For the most of them were young men and needy, who seing them selves discharged of the feare of their dets, and hoping also at their return, that the lands likewise should be devided among them: they went with glad harts, and were obedient unto king Agis. So that the cities where through they passed, wondred how they

King Agis
deceived by
Agesilaus.

New lawes
stablished by
the Lacedæ-
monians.

Aratus, gene-
rall of the
Achaians.

King Agis
jorney into
Achaia.

191

came through all Peloponnesus, from the one side to the other, very quietly, without noyse or offence to any man. Likewise many Græcians calling to mind the auncient times, told one another, that it was a noble sight then to see the army of Lacedæmon, when they were led by Agesilaus, Lysander, and Leonidas, famous captaines: sith now they saw so great obedience unto Agis by his souldiers, who was in maner the yongest man of all his campe. Who also glorying to be content with litle, to away with paines, and not to be more costly apparelled and armed then any privat souldier he had : he wanne him self therby a marvelous love of the people. Howbeit the rich men liked not this chaung, and were affraid lest Agis should give other people example to rise also, and to do the like with theirs, as he had done. Agis meting with Aratus by the city of Corinthe, even as he was consulting whether he should fight with his enemy or not : shewed him self in his counsel, then no rash, but a resolute and valiant man. For he told him, that for his opinion he thought it better to fight, and not to suffer the warre to come any further, leaving the entry into Peloponnesus free to their enemy : nevertheles, that he would do what Aratus thought good, bicause he was the elder, and general also of the Achaians, whom he came not to commaund, but to aide them. But Baton Sinopian writeth, that king Agis would not fight, though Aratus was willing : howbeit he had not red that which Aratus had written for his excuse and justification, alleaging there, that the farmers and husbandmen having brought all the corne into their barnes, he thought it better to suffer the enemies to come further into the contry, rather then to hazard battel, to the losse of the whole contry of Peloponnesus, and that therfore he licenced al the confederats to depart, and brake up his army. So king Agis returned home again, greatly honored of al them that served with him in this jorney, finding the city of Sparta then in great broile and trouble. For Agesilaus at that time being one of the Ephores, finding him self rid of the feare which before kept him under : cared not what injury or mischief he did to any citizen, so he might get money. For amongest other things, that very yere he

*King Agis
gave place
unto Aratus.*

192

made them pay beyond al reason the tallages and taxes due
unto the common wealth for thirtene moneths, adding to the
thirtenth moneth, above the ordinary time of the yere.
Wherfore perceiving every man hated him, and being affraid
of them he had offended: he kept souldiers about him, armed
with their swords, and so came downe into the market place
among them. And for the two kings, he made no accompt
of the one: but of the other that was Agis, he semed out-
wardly to make good accompt, rather for kinreds sake, then
for his dignity of a king, and furthermore gave it out abroad,
that he would also be one of the Ephores the next yere
following. Wheruppon, his enemies spedely to prevent the
daunger, gathered force together, and openly brought king
Leonidas from Tegea, to restore him again to his kingdom.
The people were glad to see that, bicause they were angry
they had bene mocked in that sort, for that the landes were
not devided according unto promise. Furthermore, Hippomedon was so welbeloved for his valiantnes of every man,
that intreating the people for his father Agesilaus, he saved
his life, and got him out of the city. But for the two kings,
Agis tooke sanctuary in the temple of Iuno Chalceæcos.
And Cleombrotus the other king fled into the temple of
Neptune: for it semed that Leonidas being much more
offended with him, did let king Agis alone, and went
against him with certen soldiers armed. Then he sharply
taunted him, that being his sonne in law, he had conspired
against him to deprive him of his kingdom, and had driven
him out of his contry. But then Cleombrotus not having a
word to say, sate stil, and made him no answer. Wheruppon his wife Chelonis, the daughter of Leonidas, who before was offended for the injury they did her father, and had
left her husband Cleombrotus, that had usurped the kingdom
from him, to serve her father in his adversity, and while he was
in sanctuary tooke part with him also of his misery, and afterwards when he went unto the city of Tegea, ware blacks for
sorow, being offended with her husband: she contrarily then
chaunging her anger with her husbands fortune and misery,
became also an humble suter with him sitting down by him,
and imbracing him, having her two litle sonnes on either side

King
Leonidas re-
turneth from
exile into
Sparta.

The naturall
love of
Chelonis
Leonidas
daughter,
unto her
father and
husband.

5 : BB

of them. All men wondering, and weping for pity, to see the goodnes and natural love of this Lady, who shewing her mourning apparell, and heare of her head flaring about her eyes, bare headed: she spake in this sort unto her father:

' O father mine, this sorowfull garment and countenance is
' not for pity of Cleombrotus, but hath long remained with
' me, lamenting sore your former misery and exile : but now,
' which of the two should I rather choose, either to continue
' a mourner in this pitiful state, seing you again restored to
' your kingdom, having overcome your enemies: or els putting
' on my princely apparel, to see my husband slain, unto whom
' you maried me a maid? who, if he can not move you to take
' compassion of him, and to obtein mercy, by the teares of his
' wife and children : he shall then abide more bitter paine of
' his evil counsel, then that which you intend to make him
' suffer. For he shall see his wife die before him, whom he
' loveth more derely then any thing in the world. Also, with
' what face can I loke apon other ladies, when I could never
' bring my father to pity, by any intercession I could make
' for my husband, neither my husband, intreating him for my
' father : and that my hap is to be borne, a daughter and
' wife, alwaies most unfortunat, and despised of mine owne?
' And for my husband, if he had any reason to do that he did,
' I then tooke it from him, by taking your parte, and pro-
' testing against him : and contrarily, your selfe doth give
' him honest culler to excuse his faulte, when he seeth in you
' the desire of the kingdom so great, that for the love thereof,
' you thinke it lawfull to kill your sonnes in law, and also not
' to regard the children he hath gotten, for her sake.' Chelonis
pitifully complayning in this sorte, putting her face upon
Cleombrotus head, cast her swollen and blubbering eyes apon

the standers by. Wherefore Leonidas after he had talked a litle with his friendes, he commaunded Cleombrotus to get him thence, and to leave the citie as an exile : and prayed his Daughter for his sake to remayne with him, and not to forsake her father, that did so dearely love her, as for her sake he had saved her husbands life. This notwithstanding, she would not yeelde to his request, but rising up with her husband, gave him one of his sonnes, and her self tooke the other in her armes: and then making her prayer before the altar of the goddesse, she went as a banished woman away with her husband. And truely thexample of her vertue was so famous, that if Cleombrotus mind had not bene too much blinded with vain glory, he had cause to thinke his exile farre more happy, to enjoye the love of so noble a wife as he had, then for the kingdom which he possessed without her. Then Leonidas having banished king Cleombrotus out of the city, and removing the first Ephores, had substituted other in their place: he presently bethought him howe he might craftily come by king Agis. First, he perswaded him to come out of the sanctuary, and to governe the kingdom safely with him, declaring unto him that his citizens had forgiven him all that was past, bicause they knew he was deceived, and subtely circumvented by Agesilaus craft, being a young man, ambitious of honor. Agis would not leave the sanctuary for Leonidas cunning perswasion, but mistrusted all that he said unto him: wherefore, Leonidas would no more beguile him with faire words. But Amphares, Demochares, and Arcesilaus, did oftentimes go to visit king Agis, and otherwhile also they got him out of the sanctuary with them unto the bath, and brought him backe againe into the temple, when he had bathed. But Amphares having borrowed not long before, certein rich apparel and plate of Agesistrata, bicause he would not redeliver them againe, he determined to betray king Agis, his mother, and grandmother. And it is reported that he chiefly did serve Leonidas turne, and provoked the Ephores (of which number he was one) against Agis. Now therefore, Agis keping all the rest of his time within the temple, saving when he went apon occasion to the bath: they determined to intercept him by the way, and to take him when he was out of the sanctuary. So they watched him one day when he bathed, and came and saluted him as their maner was, and seemed to accompany him, sporting, and being mery with him, as with a young man their famillier. But when they came to the turning of a streete that went towardes the prison, Amphares laying hold on him, beeing one of the Ephores, said unto him: I arrest thee Agis, and wil bring thee before the Ephores, to give

AGIS AND CLEOMENES

The great vertue and love of Chelonis, to her husband Cleombrotus.

Amphares betrayed king Agis.

195

accompt of thy doings in the common wealth. Then Demochares, which was a great mighty man, cast his gowne over his eares, and pulled him forward: others also thrust him forward behind him, as they had agreed together. So no man being neare them to help Agis, they got him into prison. Then came Leonidas incontinently with a great number of souldiers that were straungers, and beset the prison round about. The Ephores went into the prison, and sent unto some of the Senate to come unto them, whom they knew to be of their mind: then they commaunded Agis, as if it had bene judicially, to give accompt of the alteracion he had made in the common wealth. The younge man laughed at their hypocrisie. But Amphares told him that it was no laughing sport, and that he should pay for his folly. Then another of the Ephores seeming to deale more favorably with him, and to shew him a way how he might escape the condemnation for his fault: asked him, if he had not bene intised unto it by Agesilaus, and Lysander. Agis aunswered, that no man compelled him, but that he onely did it to follow the steppes of the auncient Lycurgus, to bring the common wealth unto the former estate of his grave ordinaunce and institution. Then the same Senator asked him againe, if he did not repent him of that he had done. The younge man boldly aunswered him, that he would never repent him of so wise and vertuous an enterprise, though he ventred his life for it. Then they condemned him to death, and commaunded the Sergeants to cary him into the Decade, which was a place in the prison where they were strangled, that were condemned to dye. Demochares perceiving the Sergeaunts durst not lay hold of him, and likewise that the souldiers which were straungers, did abhorre to commit such a fact, contrary to the law of God and man, to lay violent hands upon the person of a king: he threatned and reviled them, and dragged Agis perforce into that place called the Decade. Now the rumor ranne straight through the citie, that king Agis was taken, and a multitude of people were at the prison dores with lights and torches. Thither came also king Agis mother and grandmother, shreeking out, and praying that the king of Sparta might yet be heard and

Note the
reverent re
gard of the
heathen, unto
the person of
a king,
abhorring to
lay violent
handes upon
him.

judged by the people. For this cause, they hastned his
death the sooner, and were afraid besides, least the people
in the night would take him out of their hands by force,
if there came any more people thither. Thus king Agis
being led to his death, spied a Sergeaunt lamenting and
weeping for him, unto whom he said: Good fellowe, I pray
thee weepe not for me, for I am honester man then they that
so shamefully put me to death, and with those words he
willingly put his head into the halter. Amphares then
going out of the prison into the street, found Agesistrata
there, king Agis mother, who straight fel downe at his
feete: but he taking her up againe, in old famillier maner, as
being her very friend, told her that they should doe king
Agis no hurt, and that she might if she would, goe and see
him. Then she prayed, that they would also let her mother
in with her. Amphares sayde, With a good will: and so put
them both into the prison house, and made the dores be
shut after them. But when they were within, he first gave King Agis,
Archidamia unto the Sergeaunts to be put to death, who his mother,
was a marvelous olde woman, and had lived more honorably and grand-
unto that age, then any Lady or Matrone beside her in the three
citie. She being executed, he commaunded Agesistrata also strangled.
to come in. Who when she sawe the bodye of her dead
sonne layed on the ground, and her mother also hanging on
the gallowes: she did her selfe helpe the hangman to plucke
her downe, and layed her body by her sonnes. Then having
covered her in decent manner, she layed her downe on the
ground by the corps of her sonne Agis, and kissing his
cheeke sayd: Out, alas my sonne, thy great modestie, goodnes
and clemencie, brought thee and us unto this deathe. Then
Amphares peeping in at the dore to see what was done,
hearing what she sayde, came in withall in a greate rage,
and sayde: I perceyve thou hast also beene of counsell with
thy sonne, and sithe it is so, thou shalt also followe him.
Then she rising likewise to be strangled, sayd: The goddes
graunt yet that this may profit Sparta. This horrible
murther beeing blowen abroad in the citie, and the three
dead bodies also brought out of prison: the feare though it
were great amongest the people, could not keepe them back

from apparant show of griefe, and manifest hate against
Leonidas and Amphares, thinking that there was never a
more wicked and crueller fact committed in Sparta, since
the Dorians came to dwell in Peloponnesus. For the very
enemies them selves in battell, would not willingly lay hands
upon the kings of Lacedæmon, but did forbeare as much as
they could possible, both for feare and reverence they bare
unto their majestie. For in many great battels and conflicts
which the Lacedæmonians had against the Græcians, there
was never any king of Lacedæmon slain, before Philips time,
but Cleombrotus only, who was slain with a dart at the
battell of Leuctres. Some write also, that the Messenians
hold opinion, that their Aristomenes slue king Theopompus:
howbeit the Lacedæmonians sayde, that he was but hurt,
not slayne. But hereof there are divers opinions: but it
is certain that Agis was the first king whom the Ephores
ever put to death: for that he had layd a plat of a noble
devise, and worthy of Sparta, being of that age when men
doe easily pardon them that offend: and was rather to be
accused of his friendes and enemies, bicause he had saved
Leonidas life, and had trusted other men, as the best natured
younge man that could be.

The enemies
did not will-
ingly kill
any king of
Lacedæmon.

Now Agis having suffered in this sort, Leonidas was not
quicke enough to take Archidamus his brother also, for he
fled presently. Yet he brought Agis wife out of her house
by force, with a litle boy she had by him, and maried her
unto his sonne Cleomenes, who was yet under age to marye:
fearing least this younge Ladye should be bestowed els
where, beeing in deede a great heire, and of a riche house,
and the Daughter of Gylippus, called by her name Agiatis,
besides that she was the fayrest woman at that tyme in all
Græce, and the vertuousest and best condicioned. Wherefore,
for divers respects she praied she might not be forced to it.
But now being at length maried unto Cleomenes, she ever
hated Leonidas to the death, and yet was a good and loving
wife unto her young husband: who immediatly after he
was maried unto her, fell greatly in fancy with her, and for
compassions sake (as it seemed) he thanked her for the love
she bare unto her first husband, and for the loving remem-

GRECIANS AND ROMANES

braunce she had of him: insomuch as he him selfe many times would fall in talke of it, and would be inquisitive how thinges had passed, taking great pleasure to heare of Agis wise counsell and purpose. For Cleomenes was as desirous of honor, and had as noble a minde as Agis, and was borne also to temperancie and moderation of life, as Agis in like manner was: howbeit, he had not that shamefast modestie and lenitie which the other had, but was somewhat more sturring of nature, and readier to put any good matter in execution. So he thought it greate honestie to bringe the Citizens if he could, to be contented to live after an honest sorte: but contrarily, he thought it no dishonestie to bringe them unto good life, by compulsion also. Furthermore, the manners of the Citizens of Sparta, giving them selves over to idlenes and pleasure, did nothing like him at all: neither that the king did suffer the common wealth to be ruled as they listed, so no man impeached his pleasure, and that they did let him alone: insomuch no man regarding the profit of the common wealth, every man was for him self, and his familie. And contrarily, it was not lawfull for any man to speake for the exercises of the youth, for their education in temperancie, and for the restoring againe of equality of life, the preferment whereof was the only cause of the late death of Agis. They say also, that Cleomenes being a young stripling, had heard some disputacion of Philosophie, when the Philosopher Sphærus, of the contry of Borysthenes came to Lacedæmon, and lovingly stayed there to teache younge men and children. He was one of the chiefest schollers of Zenon Citian, and delighted (as it seemed) in Cleomenes noble minde, and had a great desire to pricke him forward unto honor. For, as it is reported, that the auncient Leonidas beeing demaunded what Poet he thought Tyrtæus to be, aunswered he was good to flatter younge mens myndes: for he sette their hartes a fire by his verses, when they beganne to fight any battell, fearing no daunger, they were so incoraged by them. So the Stoicke discipline is somewhat daungerous, for the stowte and valiant myndes, which otherwise doth make them desperate: but when they are joyned unto a grave and gentle nature, first it lyfteth up his

199

hart, and then maketh him taste the profit thereof. Nowe
Leonidas (the father of Cleomenes) beeing deceased, and he
him selfe comen unto the crowne, finding that the Citizens
of Sparta at that tyme were very dissolute, that the riche
men followed their pleasure and profit taking no care of the
common weale, that the poore men also for very want and
neede went with no good life and courage to the warres,
nether cared for the bringing up of their children, and that
he him selfe had but the name of a king, and the Ephori
the absolute authoritie to doe what they listed: at his first
comming to his kingdome, he determined to alter the whole
state and government of the common wealth. Who having
a friend called Xenares, that had beene his lover in his
youth (which the Lacedæmonians called Empnistæ, as much
as inspired) he beganne to sownd his opinion, asking what
manner of man king Agis had bene, and by what reason, and
whose advise he had followed in his attempt for the reformation of the common wealth. Xenares at the first did not
willingly rehearse these things unto him, declaring every
thing what had passed. But when he found that Cleomenes
was affected unto king Agis intent, and still desired to heare
of it: then Xenares sharply and angrily reproved him, and
tolde him he was not wise, nor well advised, and at length
would no more come and talke with him as he was wont, yet
making no man privye why he absteyned from comming to
him, but told them that asked him, he knewe a cause well
enough why. Xenares nowe having thus refused him, and
thinking all the rest woulde doe the like: to bringe this
matter to passe, he tooke this resolution with him selfe.

Cleomenes
did set the
Lacedæ-
monians and
Achaians
together by
the eares. Bicause he thought he might the rather doe it in warre, then
in peace, he set the citie of Sparta and the Achaians at
variance together: who did them selves give the first occasion
to be complayned uppon. For Aratus beeing President and
chiefe of all the Achaians, had practised a longe tyme to
bringe all Peloponnesus into one bodye: and had therefore
onely susteyned great troubles in warres, and at home in
peace: thinking that there was no other waye to deliver them
from forreyne warres. Nowe when he had wonne all the
other people to be of his opinion: there remained no more

but the Elians, the Lacedæmonians, and a few of the
Archadians, which were subject unto the Lacedæmonians.
When king Leonidas was deade, Aratus beganne to invade
the Archadians, those specially that bordered apon the
Argives: to prove how the Lacedæmonians would take it,
making no accompt of Cleomenes, being but a young king,
and had no experience of warres. Thereuppon the Ephori
sent Cleomenes unto Athænium (a temple of Minerva hard
by the citie of Belbina) with an armie to take it: bicause it
was a passage and entry into the contry of Laconia, howbeit
the place at that time was in question betwixt the Megalo-
politanes, and the Lacedæmonians. Cleomenes got it, and
fortefied it. Aratus making no complaint otherwise of the
matter, stale out one night with his army to set apon the
Tegeans, and Orchomenians, hoping to have taken those
cities by treason. But the traitors that were of his con-
federacy, their harts failed them when they should have
gonne about it: so that Aratus returned, having lost his
jorney, thinking that this secret attempt of his was not discovered. But Cleomenes finely wrote unto him as his friend,
and asked him, whether he had led his armie by night:
Aratus returned aunswer againe, that understanding Cleomenes ment to fortifie Belbina, he went forth with his armye,
thinking to have let him. Cleomenes wrote againe unto him,
and said he did beleeve that which he spake was true: howbeit he earnestly requested him, (if it were no trouble to
him) to advertise him why he brought schaling ladders and
lightes after him. Aratus smiling at this mocke, asked what
this young man was. Democritus Lacedæmonian being a
banished man out of his contry, aunswered: If thou hast
any thing to doe against the Lacedæmonians, thou hadst
neede make haste, before this young Cockerel have on his
spurres. Then Cleomenes being in the field in the contry of
Archadia, with a few horsemen and three hundred footemen
onely: the Ephori being affraid of warres, sent for him to
returne againe. His backe was no sooner turned, obeying
their commaundement: but Aratus sodainly tooke the citie
of Caphyes. Thereuppon, the Ephori incontinently sent
Cleomenes backe again with his armie: who tooke the fort

AGIS AND
CLEOMENES

Cleomenes
jorney into
the coutry of
the Argives.

The victorie
of Cleomenes
against
Aratus.

The saying of
the kings of
Lacedæmon
touching their
enemies.

of Methydrium, and burnt the borders of the Argives. The
Achaians came against him with an army of twenty thowsand
footemen, and a thowsand horsemen, led by Aristomachus:
Cleomenes met with them by the city of Palantium, and
offred battell. But Aratus quaking at the hardines of this
young man, would not suffer Aristomachus to hazard battell,
but went his way, derided by the Achaians, and despised by
the Lacedæmonians: who in all were not above five thowsand
fighting men. Cleomenes corage beeing now lift up, and
bravely speaking to his citizens: he remembred them of a
saying of one of their auncient kings, that the Lacedæmonians never inquired what number their enemies were, but
where they were. Shortly after, the Achaians making warre
with the Elians, Cleomenes was sent to ayde them, and met
with the armie of the Achaians by the mountaine Lyceum,
as they were in their returne: he setting apon them, gave
them the overthrowe, slue a great number of them, and
tooke many also prisoners, that the rumor ranne through
Græce, how Aratus selfe was slaine. Cleomenes wisely
taking the occasion which this victory gave him: he went
straight to the citie of Mantinea, and taking it upon a
sodaine, when no man knew of his comming, he put a
strong garrison into it. Now the Lacedæmonians harts
failing them, and resisting Cleomenes enterprises, over-
wearying them with warres: he went about to sende for
Archidamus, king Agis brother, being then at Messena,
unto whom the kingdom of right belonged by the other
house, supposing that he shoulde easely weaken the power
of the Ephores, by the authoritie of the two kinges, if both
of them joyned together. Which when the murtherers of
king Agis understoode, being affraid that Archidamus returning from exile, he would be revenged of them: they
secretly received him into the citie, and founde the meanes
to bring him into Sparta. But when they had him, they
put him straight to death, whether it was unwitting to
Cleomenes (as Phylarchus plainly testifieth) or else with his
privitie, suffring them to make him away, by perswasion of
his frends. But it is a cleere case, the citie was burdened
withall, bicause probable matter fell out that they had com-

Archidamus
king Agis
brother slaine.

pelled Cleomenes to doe it. Neverthelesse, he holding still
his first determination, to alter the state of the common
wealth of Sparta, as soone as he could possible: he so fed
the Ephores with money, that he brought them to be contented he should make warre. He had also won many
other citizens by the meanes of his mother Cratesiclea, who
furnisht him with money, that he lacked not to honor him
withall: and further, maried as it is reported, (being otherwise not ment to mary) for her sonnes sake, unto one of the
wealthiest men of all the citie. So Cleomenes leading his
army into the field, wanne a place within the territorie
of Megalopolis, called Leuctra. The Achaians also being
quickly come to their aide, led by Aratus: they straight
fought a battell by the citie selfe, where Cleomenes had the
worst on the one side of his armie. Howbeit Aratus woulde
not suffer the Achaians to follow them, bicause of bogges
and quavemyres, but sounded the retreate. But Lysiadas
a Megalopolitan being angrie withall, caused the horsemen
he had about him to follow the chase, who pursued so
fiercely, that they came amongest vines, walls, and ditches,
where he was driven to disperse his men, and yet coulde not
get out. Cleomenes perceiving it, sent the light horsemen
of the Tarentins and Cretans against him: of whom Lysiadas
valliantly fighting was slaine. Then the Lacedæmonians
being couragious for this victorie, came with great cries,
and geving a fierce charge apon the Achaians, overthrew
their whole armie, and slue a marvelous number of them:
but yet Cleomenes at their request suffered them to take
up the dead bodies of their men to burie them. For
Lysiadas corps, he caused it to be brought unto him, and
putting a purple robe apon it, and a crowne on his head,
sent it in this aray unto the very gates of the city of Megalopolis. It was that selfe Lysiadas, who geving over the
tyranny and government of Megalopolis, made it a popular
state, and free city, and joyned it to the Achaians. After
this victorie, Cleomenes that determined greater matters and
attempts, perswaded him selfe that if he might once come to
stablishe the affaires of the common wealth at Sparta to his
mind, he might then easely overcome the Achaians: brake

Lysiadas
slaine.

Cleomenes
victorie of the
Achaians.

Lysiadas,
tyranne of
Megalopolis,
gave over his
tyrannie, and
made it a
popular state.

with his father in law Megistonus, and told him that it was
necessary to take away the authoritie of the Ephores, and
to make division of the landes among the Spartans, and
then being brought to equalitie, to encorage them to recover
the Empire of Græce againe unto the Lacedæmonians, which
their predecessors before them, held and enjoyed. Megistonus
graunting his good will and furtherance, joyned two or three
of his frendes more unto him. It chaunced at that time
that one of the Ephores lying in the temple of Pasiphaé,
had a marvelous dreame in the night. For he thought he
sawe but one chaire standing where the Ephori did use to
sit to geve audience, and that the other foure which were
wont to be there, were taken away : and that marvelling at
it, he heard a voyce out of the temple that said, that was
the best for Sparta. He declaring this dreame the next
morning unto Cleomenes, it somewhat troubled him at the
first, thinking that he came to feele him, for that he had
heard some inckling of his intent. But when he perswaded
him selfe that the other ment good faith, and lyed not unto
him, being bolder then before, he went forward with his purpose, and taking with him unto the campe all those Spartans
which he suspected to be against his enterprise, he went
and tooke the cities of Heræa and Alsea, confederats of the
Achaians, and vitteled Orchomena, and went and camped
before the citie of Mantinea. In fine, he so wearied and
overharried the Lacedæmonians by long jorneys, that at
length they besought him he would let them remaine in
Arcadia, to repose them selves there. In the meane time,
Cleomenes with his straungers which he had hyred, returned
againe unto Sparta, and imparted his intent by the way
unto them he trusted best, and marched at his owne ease,
that he might take the Ephores at supper. When he came
neere unto the city, he sent Euryclidas before, into the halle
of the Ephores, as though he brought them newes out of the
campe from him. After him, he sent also Thericion and
Phœbis, and two other that had bene brought up with him,
whom the Lacedæmonians called the Samothracians, taking
with them a fewe souldiers. Nowe whilest Euryclidas was
talking with the Ephores, they also came in apon them with
204

their swordes drawen, and did set apon the Ephores. Agesilaus was hurt first of all, and falling downe, made as though
he had bene slaine, but by litle and litle he crept out of the
halle, and got secretly into a chappell consecrated unto
Feare, the which was wont ever to be kept shut, but then by
chaunce was left open: when he was come in, he shut the
dore fast to him. The other foure of the Ephores were
slaine presently, and above tenne moe besides, which came
to defende them. Furthermore, for them that sate still and
sturred not, they killed not a man of them, neither did
keepe any man that was desirous to goe out of the citie:
but moreover, they pardoned Agesilaus, who came the next
morning out of the chappell of Feare. Amongest the Lacedæmonians in the citie of Sparta, there are not onely temples
of feare and death, but also of laughter, and of many other
such passions of the minde. They do worshippe Feare, not
as other spirites and devills that are hurtfull: but bicause
they are perswaded, that nothing preserveth a common
wealth better then feare. Wherefore the Ephori (as Aristotle witnesseth) when they are created, doe by publicke
proclamacion commaunde all the Spartans to shave their
chinnes, and to obey the law, least they should make them
feele the rigour of the law. They brought in the shav-
ing of their chinnes, in my opinion, to inure young men
to obey the Magistrates even in trifles. Moreover it
seemes that men in olde time did esteeme fortitude to be
no taking away of feare, but rather a feare and lothnes
to incurre shame. For commonly those that are most
affrayed to offend the law, are in the field most valliant
against their enemie: and shunne no perill to winne fame
and honest reputacion. And therefore it was wisely sayd
of one,

> That feare can not be without shamefastnes.

And so Homer in a certaine place made Hellen say unto
king Priamus:

> Of trueth I doe confesse deere father in law,
> You are the man of whom I stand in aw,
> And reverence most of all that ere I saw.

205

And in an other place, speaking of the Græcian souldiers, he sayeth thus:

For feare of their Captaines they spake not a word.

The chappell of feare, joyned to the halle of the Ephores.

For men do use to reverence them whom they feare. And this was the cause why the chapell of Feare was by the halle of the Ephores, having in maner a princely and absolute authoritie. The next morning Cleomenes banished by trompet, foure score citizens of Sparta, and overthrew all the chaires of the Ephores but one only, the which he reserved for him selfe to sit in to geve audience. Then calling the people to counsell, he gave them an account of his doings, and told them that Lycurgus had joyned the Senators with the kings, and how the citie had bene governed a long time by them, without helpe of any other officers. Notwithstanding, afterwards the city having great warres with the Messenians, the kings being alwaies employed in that warre, whereby they could not attend the affaires of the common wealth at home, did choose certaine of their frendes to sitte in judgement in their steades, to determine controversies of lawe: which were called Ephores, and did governe long time as the kinges ministers, howbeit that afterwards, by litle and litle, they tooke apon them absolute government by them selves. And for manifest proofe hereof, you see that at this present time when the Ephori do send for the king, the first and second time, they refuse to come, but the third time he riseth and goeth unto them. The first man that gave the Ephores this authoritie, was Aste-ropus, one of the Ephores many yeares after the first insti-tucion of the kinges: and yet if they had governed discreetely, peradventure they might have continued lenger. But they licentiously abusing their authoritie, by suppressing the law-full Governors instituted of old time, taking apon them to banish some of their kings, and putting other of them also to death, without law and justice, and threatning others that desire to restore that noble and former blessed government unto Sparta againe: all these things I say, are in no wise to be suffered any lenger. And therefore, if it had bene possible to have banished all these plagues of the common wealth out of Sparta, brought from forreine nations: (I meane, plea-

The oration of king Cleo-menes, touch-ing the first originall of the Ephores.

Asteropus, the first man that gave authority to the Ephores.

sures, pastimes, money, dets, and usuries, and others yet
more auncient, poverty and riches) he might then have
esteemed him selfe the happiest king that ever was, if like
a good Phisitian he had cured his contrie of that infection,
without griefe or sorrow. But in that he was constrained
to beginne with blood, he followed Lycurgus example:
who being neither king nor other Magistrate, but a private
citizen only, taking apon him the authoritie of the king,
boldly came into the market place with force and armed
men, and made king Charilaus that then raigned, so affrayed,
that he was driven to take sanctuarie in one of the temples.
But the king being a Prince of a noble nature, and loving
the honor of his contrie: tooke parte with Lycurgus, adding
to his advise and counsell, for the alteracion of the state of
the government of the common wealth, which he did confirme. Hereby then it appeareth, that Lycurgus saw it was
a hard thing to alter the common wealth without force and
feare: the which he notwithstanding had used with as great
modestie and discretion, as might be possible, banishing
them that were against the profit and wealth of Lacedæmon,
geving all the lands of the contrie also to be equally devided
amongest them, and setting all men cleere that were in dette.
And furthermore, that he would make a choyse and proofe
of the straungers, to make them free citizens of Sparta, whom
he knew to be honest men, thereby to defende their citie the
better by force of armes: to thend that from henceforth we
may no more see our contrie of Laconia spoyled by the
Ætolians and Illyrians, for lacke of men to defende them
selves against them. Then he beganne first him selfe to
make all his goods common, and after him Megistonus his
father in law, and consequently all his other frendes. Then
he caused the lands also to be devided, and ordeined every
banished man a part, whom he him selfe had exiled, promising that he would receive them againe into the city,
when he had established all things. So when he had replenished the number of the citizens of Sparta, with the
choycest honest men their neighbours: he made foure thowsand footemen well armed, and taught them to use their
pykes with both handes, in steade of their dartes with one

AGIS AND
CLEOMENES hande, and to carie their targets with a good strong handle, and not buckled with a leather thong. Afterwardes he tooke order for the education of children, and to restore the auncient Laconian discipline againe: and did all these things in maner by the helpe of Sphærus the Philosopher. Insomuch as he had quickely set up againe schoole houses for children, and also brought them to the old order of dyet: and all, but a very fewe, without compulsion were willing to fall to their old institucion of life. Then bicause the name of one king should not offend any man, he made his brother Euclidas king with him. But this was the first time that ever the two kings were of one house but then. Furthermore, understanding that the Achaians and Aratus were of opinion, that he durst not come out of Lacedæmon, for feare to leave it in perill of revolting, bicause of the late chaunge and alteracion in the common wealth: he thought it an honorable attempt of him, to make his enemies see the readines and good will of his armie. Thereupon he invaded the

Cleomenes invadeth the borders of the Megalopolitans.

territories of the Megalopolitans, and brought away a great praye and booty, after he had done great hurt unto his enemies. Then having taken certaine players and minstrells that came from Messina, he sette up a stage within the enemies contrie, made a game of 40 Minas for the victor, and sate a whole day to looke apon them, for no pleasure he tooke in the sight of it, but more to despite the enemies withall, in making them see how muche he was stronger then they, to make such a Mayegame in their owne contrie, in despite of them. For of all the armies otherwise of the Græcians, or kinges in all Græce, there was no armie onely but his, that was without players, minstrells, fooles and jugglers: for his campe only was cleane of such rabble and foolerie, and all the young men fell to some exercise of their bodies, and the old men also to teache them. And if they chaunced to have any vacant time, then they would pleasauntly be one merie with an other, in geving some pretie

King Cleomenes, the teacher and example of temperancy.

fine mocke after the Laconian manner. And what profit they got by that kinde of exercise, we have written it at large in Lycurgus life. But of all these things, the king him selfe was their schoolemaister and example, shewing him

208

selfe very temperate of life, and plaine without curiositie, no more then any private souldier of all his campe: the which were great helpes unto him in his enterprises he made in Græce. For the Græcians having cause of sute and negociacion with other kings and Princes, did not wonder so much at their pompe and riches, as they did abhorre and detest their pride and insolencie: so disdainfully they would aunswere them that had to doe with them. But contrarily when they went unto Cleomenes, who was a king in name and deede as they were, finding no purple robes nor stately mantells, nor rich imbrodered beddes, nor a Prince to be spoken to but by messengers, gentlemen ushers, and supplications, and yet with great a doe: and seeing him also come plainly apparelled unto them, with a good countenaunce, and curteously aunswering the matters they came for: he thereby did marvelously win their harts and good wills, that when they returned home, they said he only was the worthy king, that came of the race of Hercules. Now for his dyet at his bord, that was very straight and Laconian like, keping only three bords: and if he chaunced to feast any Ambassadors or other his frendes that came to see him, he then added to two other bords, and besides, made his men to see that his fare should be amended, not with pastrie and conserves, but with more store of meate, and some better wyne then ordinarie. For he one day reproved one of his frendes, that bidding straungers to supper, he gave them nothing but blacke broth, and browne bread only, according to their Laconian maner. Nay, said he, we may not use straungers so hardly after our maner. The bord being taken up, an other litle table was brought with three feete, whereupon they set a bolle of copper full of wyne, and two silver cuppes of a pottell a peece, and certaine other fewe silver pottes besides: so every man dranke what they listed, and no man was forced to drinke more then he woulde. Furthermore, there was no sporte, nor any pleasaunt song, soung, to make the companie merie, for it needed not. For Cleomenes selfe would entertaine them with some pretie questions, or pleasaunt tale: whereby, as his talke was not severe and without pleasure, so was it also pleasaunt without insolencie. For he

Cleomenes moderate dyet.

Cleomenes curteous entertainment at his bord.

was of opinion, that to winne men by gifts or money, as
other kings and Princes did, was but base and cloynelike:
but to seeke their good wills by curteous meanes, and pleasauntnes, and therewith to meane good faith, that he thought
most fit and honorable for a Prince. For this was his minde,
that there was no other difference betwext a frend and
hyerling: but that the one is wonne with money, and the
other with civility and good entertainment. The first
therefore that received king Cleomenes into their citie, were
the Mantinians, who opened him the gates in the night, and
helping him to drive out the garrison of the Achaians, they
yeelded them selves unto him. But he referring them to
the use and government of their owne lawes and libertie,
departed from thence the same day, and went unto the citie
of Tegea. Shortly after, he compassed about Arcadia, and
came unto Pheres in Arcadia determining one of the two,
Cleomenes
leadeth his
army against
Aratus, and
the Achaians. either to geve the Achaians battell, or to bring Aratus out of
favor with the people, for that he had suffred him to spoyle
and destroy their contry. Hyperbatas was at that time
Generall of the Achaians, but Aratus did beare all the sway
and authoritie. Then the Achaians comming into the field
with all their people armed, and encamping by the citie of
Dymes, neere unto the temple of Hecatombæum: Cleomenes
going thither, laye betwext the citie of Dymes that was
against him, and the campe of his enemies, which men
thought a verie unwise parte of him. Howebeit valliantly
provoking the Achaians, he procured them to the battell,
The victory
of Cleomenes
against the
Achaians. overthrew them, made them flie, and slue a great number in
the field, and tooke many of them also prisoners. Departing
from thence, he went and set apon the citie of Langon, and
drave the garrison of the Achaians out of it, and restored
the citie againe unto the Elians. The Achaians being then
in verie hard state, Aratus that of custome was wont to be
their Generall, (or at the least once in two yeares) refused
now to take the charge, notwithstanding the Achaians did
specially pray and intreate him: the which was an ill act of
him, to let an other steere the rudder, in so daungerous a
storme and tempest. Therefore the Achaians sent Ambassadors unto Cleomenes to treate peace, unto whome it

seemed he gave a verie sharpe aunswere. After that, he sent unto them, and willed them only to resigne the signiorie of Græce unto him: and that for all other matters he would deale reasonably with them, and presently deliver them up their townes and prisoners againe, which he had taken of theirs. The Achaians being glad of peace with these condicions, wrote unto Cleomenes that he shoulde come unto the citie of Lerna, where the dyet and generall assemblie shoulde be kept to consult thereupon. It chaunced then that Cleomenes marching thither, being very hotte, dranke cold water, and fell of suche a bleeding withall, that his voyce was taken from him, and he almost stifled. Wherefore he sent the Achaians their chiefest prisoners home againe, proroging the parlament till an other time, and returned backe to Lacedæmon. It is supposed certainly, that this let of his comming to the dyet, was the onely cause of the utter destruction of Græce: the which otherwise was in good way to have risen againe, and to have bene delivered from the present miseries, and extreame pride and covetousnes of the Macedonians. For Aratus, either for that he trusted not Cleomenes, or for that he was affrayed of his power, or that he otherwise envied his honor and prosperitie, to see him risen to such incredible greatnes in so short a time, and thinking it also too great shame and dishonor to him, to suffer this young man in a moment to deprive him of his great honor and power which he had possessed so long time, by the space of thirtie yeares together, ruling all Græce: first, he sought by force to terrifie the Achaians, and to make them breake of from this peace. But in fine, finding that they litle regarded his threats, and that he could not prevaile with them, for that they were affrayed of Cleomenes valliantnesse and corage, whose request they thought reasonable, for that he sought but to restore Peloponnesus into her former auncient estate againe: he fell then into a practise farre unhonest for a Græcian, verie infamous for him selfe, but most dishonorable for the former noble acts he had done. For he brought Antigonus into Græce, and in his age filled the contrie of Peloponnesus with Macedonians, whom he himselfe in his youth had driven thence, had taken from

them the castell of Corinthe, and had alwayes bene an
enemie of the kinges (but specially of Antigonus, of whom
before he had spoken all the ill he coulde, as appeareth in his
wrytings, saying that he tooke marvelous paines, and did put
him selfe into many daungers, to deliver the city of Athens
from the garrison of the Macedonians) and yet notwithstanding he brought them armed with his owne hands, not into
his contrie only, but into his owne house, yea even into the
Ladies chambers and closets: disdaining that the king of
Lacedæmon, discending of the blood royall of Hercules (who
setting up againe the auncient maner of life of his contrie,
did temper it as an instrument of musicke out of tune, and
brought it to the good, auncient and sober discipline and
Dorican life instituted by Lycurgus) should be called and
wrytten, king of the Sicyonians, and of the Triccæians. And
furthermore, flying them that were contented with browne
bread, and with the plaine course capes of the Lacedæmonians, and that went about to take awaye riches (which
was the chiefest matter they did accuse Cleomenes for) and to
provide for the poore: he went and put him selfe and all
Achaia into the crowne and diadeame, the purple robe, and
prowde imperious commaundementes of the Macedonians,
fearing least men should thinke that Cleomenes coulde commaunde him. Furthermore his follie was such, that having
garlands of flowers on his head, he did sacrifice unto Antigonus, and sing songs in praise of his honor, as if he had bene
a god, where he was but a rotten man, consumed away.
This that we have written of Aratus (who was indued with
many noble vertues, and a worthy Græcian) is not so much
to accuse him, as to make us see the frayelty and weakenes
of mans nature: the which, though it have never so excellent
vertues, can not yet bring forth such perfit frute, but that
it hath ever some mayme and bleamishe. Now, when the
Achaians were met againe in the citie of Argos, to hold
the session of their parlament before proroged, and Cleomenes also being come from Tegea, to be at that parlament: everie man was in hope of good peace. But
Aratus then, who was agreed before of the chiefest articles of
the capitulacions with Antigonus, fearing that Cleomenes

by fayre words or force would bring the people to graunt that he desired: sent to let him understand, that he should but come him selfe alone into the citie, and for safetie of his person, they would geve him three hundred ostages: or otherwise, if he would not leave his armie, that then they would geve him audience without the citie, in the place of exercises, called Cyllarabium. When Cleomenes had heard their aunswere, he told them that they had done him wrong: for they should have advertised him of it before he had taken his jorney, and not now when he was almost hard at their gates, to sende him backe againe, with a flea in his eare. Thereuppon he wrote a letter unto the counsell of the Achaians, altogether full of complaintes against Aratus. On thother side also, Aratus in his oration to the counsell, inveyed with bitter wordes against Cleomenes. Thereuppon Cleomenes departing with speede, sent a Herauld to proclaime warres against the Achaians, not in the city of Argos, but in the city of Ægion, as Aratus wryteth, meaning to set apon them being unprovided. Hereuppon all Achaia was in an uprore: for divers cities did presently revolt against the Achaians, bicause the common people hoped after the division of lands, and the discharging of their dettes. The noble men also in many places were offended with Aratus, bicause he practised to bring the Macedonians into the contrie of Peloponnesus. Cleomenes therefore hoping well for all these respectes, brought his armie into Achaia, and at his first comming tooke the citie of Pallena, and drave out the garrison of the Achaians: and after that, wanne also the cities of Pheneum, and Pentelium. Now the Achaians fearing some treason in Corinthe and Sycione, sent certaine horsemen out of the citie of Argos, to keepe those cities. The Argives in the meane time, attending the celebracion of the feast at the games Nemeea, Cleomenes thinking (which fell out true) that if he went to Argos, he should finde the citie full of people that were come to see the feastes and games, and that assailing them uppon the sodaine, he shoulde put them in a marvelous feare: brought his armie in the night hard to the walls of the citie of Argos, and at his first comming wanne a place they call Aspis, a verie strong place

Cleomenes winneth the citie of Argos.

above the Theater, and ill to come unto. The Argives were
so amazed at it, that no man would take apon him to
defende the citie, but received Cleomenes garrison, and gave
him twentie ostages, promising thenceforth to be true confederates unto the Lacedæmonians, under his charge and
conduct. The which doubtles wanne him great fame, and
increased his power: for that the auncient kings of Lacedæmon, could never before with any policie or devise, winne
King Pyrrhus the citie of Argos. For king Pyrrhus one of the most
slaine at the valliantest and warlikest Prince that ever was, entring the
citie of Argos. citie of Argos by force, could not keepe it, but was slaine
there, and the most parte of his armie: wherby, every man
wondred greatly at the diligence and counsell of Cleomenes.
And where every man did mocke him before, when Cleomenes
sayd that he would follow Solon, and Lycurgus, in making
the citizens goods common, and discharging all dets: they
were then clerely perswaded that he onely was the cause and
meane of that great chaunge, which they sawe in the corage
of the Spartans: who were before so weake and out of hart,
that they having no corage to defend them selves, the
Ætolians entring Laconia, with an armie, tooke away at one
time, fiftie thowsand slaves. Whereuppon an old man of
Sparta pleasauntly sayd at that time, that their enemies had
done them a great pleasure, to ridde their contrie of Laconia
The force of of suche a rabble of rascalls. Shortly after, they being entred
Lycurgus againe into the former auncient discipline of Lycurgus, as if
lawes. Lycurgus selfe had bene alive to have trained them unto it:
they shewed them selves verie valliant, and obedient also
unto their Magistrates, whereby they recovered againe the
commaundement of all Græce, and the contrie also of Peloponnesus. After Cleomenes had taken the citie of Argos,
the cities also of Cleones, and Phliunta, did yeelde them
selves unto him. Aratus in the meane time remayned at
Corinthe, and there did busily accuse them which were suspected to favor the Lacedæmonians. But when newes was
brought him that Argos was taken, and that he perceived
also the citie of Corinthe did leane unto Cleomenes parte,
and drave away the Achaians: he then calling the people to
counsell in Corinthe, secretly stale to one of the gates of the
214

citie, and causing his horse to be brought unto him, tooke
his backe, and gallopped for life unto the citie of Sicyone.
When the Corinthians heard of it, they tooke their horse-
backes also, striving who shoulde be there soonest, and posted
in suche hast unto Cleomenes at the citie of Argos, that
many of them (as Aratus wryteth) killed their horses by the
waye: howebeit Cleomenes was verie muche offended with
them, for that they had let him scape their handes. But
Aratus sayth further, that Megistonus came unto him from
Cleomenes, and offered him a great summe of money to
deliver him the castell of Corinthe, wherein there was a
great garrison of the Achaians. But he aunswered againe,
that thinges were not in his power, but rather that he was
subject to their power. Now Cleomenes departing from the
city of Argos, overcame the Trœzenians, the Epidaurians,
and the Hermionians. After that, he came unto Corinthe,
and presentlie entrenched the castell there rounde about, and
sendinge for Aratus frendes and factors, commaunded them
to keepe his house and goodes carefullie for him, and sent
Tritymallus Messenian againe unto him, to praye him to
be contented that the castell might be kept indifferentlie
betwext the Achaians and Lacedæmonians, promisinge him
privately to double the pencion that kinge Ptolomy gave
him. But Aratus refusinge it, sent his sonne unto Antigonus
with other ostages, and perswaded the Achaians to deliver
uppe the castell of Corinthe, unto Antigonus handes. Cleomenes understandinge it, entred with his armie into the
contrie of the Sicyonians, and destroyed it as he went, and
tooke Aratus goodes and money, of the gift of the Corinthians by decree. Nowe Antigonus in the meane tyme,
beinge passed the mountayne of Gerania with a greate power:
Cleomenes determined not to fortifie the Isthmus or straight
of Peloponnesus, but the wayes of the mountaynes Onienes,
determininge to keepe everie one of them against the Macedonians, with intent to consume them rather by tyme, then
to fight a battell with an armie, so good souldiers and well
trayned as they were. Cleomenes followinge this determination, did putte Antigonus to greate trouble, bicause he
had not in time provided for corne: and coulde not winne

the passage also by force, for that Cleomenes kept it with
suche garde and souldiers. Then Antigonus stealinge
secretely into the haven of Lechæum, he was stowtly repulsed, and lost a number of his men: whereuppon Cleomenes
and his men beinge couragious for this victorie, went quietly
to supper. Antigonus on thother side fell into dispaire, to
see him selfe brought by necessitie into suche harde termes.
Wherefore he determined to goe to the temple of Iuno, and
from thence to passe his armie by sea into the citie of
Sicyone, the which required a longe tyme, and great preparacion. But the same night there came some of Aratus
frendes of the Argives, who comminge from Argos by sea,
brought newes that the Argives were rebelled against Cleomenes. The practiser of this rebellion, was one Aristoteles,
who easelie brought the people unto it, that were alreadie
offended with Cleomenes, that had promised to passe a lawe
for the clearinge of dettes, but performed it not accordinge
to their expectacion. Wherefore, Aratus with a thowsande
five hundred men which Antigonus gave him, went by sea
unto Epidaurum. Howebeit Aristoteles taried not his comminge, but takinge them of the citie with him, went and
besieged the garrison of the Lacedæmonians within the
castell, beinge ayded by Timoxenus, with the Achaians that
came from Sicyone. Cleomenes receivinge advertisement
hereof, about the seconde watche of the night, sent for
Megistonus in haste, and commaunded him in anger speedilie
to go and ayde their men that were in the citie of Argos.
For it was Megistonus him selfe that promised Cleomenes
the fidelitie of the Argives, and that kept him from drivinge
them out of the citie, which he suspected. So sendinge him
awaye foorthwith with two thowsande men, he attended
Antigonus, and comforted the Corinthians the best he
coulde: advertisinge them that it was but a litle mutinie
of a fewe, that chaunced in the citie of Argos. Megistonus
beinge come to Argos, and slayne in battell, fightinge for
the Lacedæmonians in garrison there (who beinge in greate
distresse, scant able to keepe the castell against the enemies)
sent sundrie messengers unto Cleomenes, to praye him to sende
them immediate ayde. Cleomenes then beinge affrayed that

the enemies havinge taken Argos, woulde stoppe his way to returne backe into his contrie, who havinge oportunitie safelie to spoyle Laconia, and also to besiege the citie selfe of Sparta, that had but a fewe men to defende it : he departed with his armie from Corinthe. Immediatly after came Antigonus, and tooke it from him, and put a stronge garrison into it. When Cleomenes came before the citie of Argos, he scaled the walles, and breakinge the vawtes and arches of the place called Aspis, entred into the citie, and joyned with his garrison there, which yet resisted the Achaians : and takinge other partes of the same also, assaulted the walles, and cleared the streetes in suche sorte, that not an enemie durst be seene, for feare of the archers of the Cretans. In the meane time, when he sawe Antigonus a farre of, comminge downe the hilles into the valley with his footemen, and that his horsemen also came apon the spurre into the citie : dispayringe then that he coulde any lenger keepe it, he gathered all his men together, and safelie goinge downe by the walles retyred without losse of any man. So, when in shorte tyme he had conquered muche, and had almost wonne all within Peloponnesus : in shorter space also, he lost all againe. For, of the confederates that were in his campe, some did presentlie forsake him : others also immediatly after surrendered up the townes unto Antigonus. Cleomenes beinge thus oppressed with the fortune of warre, when he came backe to Tegea with the rest of his armie, newes came to him in the night from Lacedæmon, which grieved him as muche as the losse of all his conquestes : for he was advertised of the death of his wife Agiatis, whome he loved so dearelie, that in the middest of his chiefest prosperitie and victories, he made often jorneys to Sparta to see her. It coulde not but be a marvelous griefe unto Cleomenes, who beinge a younge man, had loste so vertuous and fayer a younge Ladie, so dearelie beloved of him : and yet he gave not place unto his sorowe, neither did griefe overcome his noble courage, but he used the selfe same voyce, apparell, and countenaunce, that he did before. Then taking order with his private Captaines, about his affayres, and havinge provided also for the safetie of the Tegeans : he went the

Cleomenes lost the citie of Corinthe.

Cleomenes lost the citie of Argos.

The death of Agiatis, king Cleomenes wife.

next morninge by breake of daye unto Sparta. After he had
privately lamented the sorowe of his wives death, with his
mother and children: he presentlie bent his minde againe to
publike causes. Nowe Cleomenes had sent unto Ptolomy
kinge of Ægypt, who had promised him ayde, but apon
demaunde, to have his mother and children in pledge. So
he was a longe tyme before he woulde for shame make his
mother privie unto it, and went oftentymes of purpose to
lette her understande it: but when he came, he had not the
harte to breake it to her. She first suspectinge a thinge,
asked Cleomenes frendes, if her sonne had not somewhat to
saye unto her, that he durst not utter. Whereuppon, in
fine he gave the venter, and brake the matter to her. When

she hearde it, she fell a laughinge, and tolde him: Why,
howe commeth it to passe, that thou hast kept it thus long,
and wouldest not tell me? Come, come, sayed she, put me
straight into a shippe, and sende me whither thou wilt, that
this bodie of myne may doe some good unto my contrie, before
crooked age consume my life without profitte. Then all
thinges beinge prepared for their jorney, they went by lande,
accompanied with the armie, unto the heade of Tænarus.
Where Cratesiclea beinge readie to imbarke, she tooke Cleomenes aside into the temple of Neptune, and imbracinge and
kissinge him, perceivinge that his harte yerned for sorowe
of her departure, she sayed unto him: O kinge of Lacedæmon, lette no man see for shame when we come out of
the temple, that we have wept and dishonored Sparta. For
that onely is in our power, and for the rest, as it pleaseth
the goddes, so lette it be. When she had spoken these

Cleomenes
sendeth his
mother and
children
hostages unto
Ptolomy king
of Ægypt.
wordes, and facioned her countenaunce againe: she went
then to take her shippe, with a litle sonne of Cleomenes, and
commaunded the maister of the shippe to hoyse sayle. Nowe
when she was arrived in Ægypt, and understoode that kinge
Ptolomy received Ambassadours from Antigonus, and were
in talke to make peace with him: and hearinge also that
Cleomenes beinge requested by the Achaians to make peace
with them, durst not hearken to it, and ende that warre,
without king Ptolomyes consent, and bicause of his mother:
she wrote unto him, that he shoulde not spare to doe any

thinge that shoulde be expedient for the honour of Sparta, without feare of displeasing Ptolomy, or for regarde of an olde woman, and a younge boye. Suche was the noble minde of this worthie Ladie in her sonne Cleomenes adversitie. Furthermore, Antigonus having taken the citie of Tegea, and sacked the other cities of Orchomenum, and Mantinea: Cleomenes seeinge him selfe brought to defende the borders onely of Laconia, he did manumise all the Ilotes (which were the slaves of Lacedæmon) payinge five Attica Minas a man. With that money he made the summe of five hundred talentes, and armed two thowsande of these freed slaves after the Macedonian facion to fight against the Leucaspides: (to witte, the white shieldes of Antigonus) and then there fell into his minde a marvelous greate enterprise, unlooked for of every man. The citie of Megalipolis at that time being as great as Sparta, and having the aide of the Achaians, and Antigonus at hand, (whom the Achaians as it seemed had brought in, chiefly at the request of the Megalopolitans) Cleomenes determininge to sacke this citie, and knowing that to bring it to passe, nothing was more requisite then celeritie · he commaunded his souldiers to vittell them selves for five dayes, and marching with the choyce of all his armie towardes Selasia, as though he had ment to have spoyled the Argives, sodainly turning from thence, he invaded the contrie of the Megalopolitans, and supping by Roetium, went straight by Elicunta unto the citie. When he was come neere unto it, he sent Panteas before with speede, with two bandes of the Lacedæmonians, and commaunded him to take a certeine pece of the wall betwene two towers, which he knewe was not kept nor garded: and he followed him also with the rest of his armie coming on fayer and softly. When Panteas came thither, finding not onely that place of the wall without gard or watche which Cleomenes had told him of, but also the most parte of that side without defence · he tooke some parte of the wall at his first comming, and manned it, and overthrew an other pecce of it also, putting them all to the sword that did defend it, and then came Cleomenes, and was within the citie with his armie, before the Megalopolitans knewe of his

Cleomenes
wanne the
citie of Megalipolis.

219

comming. At length, the citizens understanding that the citie was taken, some fled in hast, conveying suche light things as came to hande, in so great a feare: and the others also arming them selves, ranne together to resist the enemies. But though they valliantly fought to repulse them out of the citie, and yet prevayled not: they gave the rest leisure thereby to flye and save them selves, so that there remayned not behinde, above a thowsande men. For all the rest were fled with their wives and children, into the citie of Messena. The most parte of them also that fought with the enemies, saved them selves, and verie fewe were taken, the chiefest whereof were Lysandridas, and Thearidas, the noblest persons that were amongest the Megalopolitans: wherefore when the souldiers had taken them, they brought them unto Cleomenes. Lysandridas, when he saw Cleomenes a good way of, cried out alowde unto him: O king of Lacedæmon, this day thou hast an occasion offered thee to doe a more famous princely acte, then that which thou hast alreadie done, and that will make thy name also more glorious. Cleomenes musing what he woulde request: Well (quoth he) what is that thou requirest? One thing I will tell thee before hande, thou shalt not make me restore your citie to you againe. Yet, quoth Lysandridas, lette me request thus muche then, that ye doe not destroy it, but rather replenishe it with frendes and confederates, which hereafter will be true and faithfull to you: and that shall you doe, geving the Megalopolitans their citie againe, and preserving suche a number of people as have forsaken it.

Cleomenes pawsing a while, aunswered, it was a hard thing to beleve that: But yet quoth he, let honor take place with us, before profit. After that he sent a Heraulde straight unto Messena unto them that were fledde thither, and tolde them that he was contented to offer them their citie againe, so that they would become good frendes and confederates of the Lacedæmonians, forsaking the alliance of the Achaians. Philopœmen would by no meanes suffer the Megalopolitans to accept this gracious offer of Cleomenes, nor also to leave their alliance with the Achaians: telling them, that he ment not to geve them their citie againe, but to take them also with their citie: and therefore drave Thearidas and Lysan-

dridas out of Messena, that moved this practise. It was
that Philopœmen that afterwardes was the chiefest man of
the Achaians, and that wanne suche fame and honor among
the Græcians, as we have particularly declared in his life.
This worde being brought to Cleomenes, who had kept the
city from spoyling untill that time: he was then so thorowly
offended, that he gave the goods in praye to the souldiers,
sent away their goodly tables, images, and pictures unto
Sparta, and defaced the chiefest partes of the citie, and then
returned home againe, being affrayed of Antigonus, and the
Achaians. Howebeit they sturred not, bicause of the parlament that was kept at that time in the citie of Ægium,
where Aratus being in the pulpit for orations, and holding
his gowne a long time before his face, the people marvelling
at it, willed him to tell what he ayled: he answered them,
Megalipolis is taken, and rased by Cleomenes. The Achaians _Cleomenes_
being amazed at the sodainnes of this great losse, straight _rased the_
brake of their parlament and assemblie. But Antigonus _citie of Mega-_
thinking to ayde them, sent presently for all his garrisons, _lipolis._
who being long a comming, he willed them to stay where
they were, and he him selfe taking a fewe souldiers with him,
went unto the citie of Argos. Therefore the seconde enterprise of Cleomenes, seemeth at the first sight a verie rashe
and desperate attempt: howebeit Polybius wryteth, that it
was an attempt of greate wisedome and policie. For Cleo- _Cleomenes_
menes understanding that the Macedonians were dispersed in _stratageame._
garrisons in divers places, and that Antigonus lay all the
winter in the citie of Argos, with a certeyne number of
footemen that were straungers: he invaded the contrie of
the Argives with his armie, perswading him selfe, that
either Antigonus woulde for shame come and fight with
him, or if he did not, that then he shoulde put him in disgrace with the Argives: which in deede came so to passe.
The Argives seeinge their contrie spoyled by Cleomenes,
were in a marvelous rage, and gatheringe together at Antigonus lodginge, they cryed out unto him, either to goe into
the fielde, and fight with the enemie: or else if he were
affrayed, to resigne his office of Generall of Græce, unto
others that were vallianter than him selfe. But Antigonus

AGIS AND
CLEOMENES
A wise Cap-
taine should
not rashly put
him selfe in
hazard.

like a wise and excellent Captayne, thinkinge it a dishonour to him rashely to put him selfe in daunger, and his frendes also, though he were provoked with many injuries and opprobrious wordes: woulde not goe into the fielde, but stoode constant in his first determination.   Then Cleomenes having brought his armie hard to the walles of the citie of Argos, and spoyled and destroyed the contrie rounde about: without lette or daunger he safely returned home againe. Within a while after, Cleomenes beinge advertised that Antigonus was come unto Tegea, with intent to invade the contrie of Laconia: he goinge an other way with his armie, (unwitting to his enemies) they wondered when they saw him in the morning by the citie of Argos, spoylinge their contrie, and cuttinge downe their corne, not with sickles and knyves as other doe use, but with long poles in forme of Sythes, that the souldiers as they went sportingewise, did overthrowe and spoyle it.   But when they came to the place of exercises in the suburbes, called Cyllabaris, certaine of the

The modera-
cion of Cleo-
menes to his
enemies.

souldiers goinge about to have sette it afire, Cleomenes woulde not suffer them, and tolde them, that what he had done at Megalipolis, it was rather angrily then honestlie done. Now Antigonus, presentlye returninge backe againe, beinge minded first to have gone directly to the citie of Argos, but sodainely alteringe his minde, did campe upon the toppe of hilles and mountaynes.   Cleomenes seeminge not to be affrayed of him, sent Herauldes to him to desire the keyes of the temple of Iuno, and then after he had done sacrifice, he woulde departe his waye.   Thus mockinge Antigonus, after he had sacrificed unto the goddesse, under the temple that was shut up, he sent his armie unto Phliunta, and havinge driven awaye the garrison out of Ologunta, he came unto the citie of Orchomenum, havinge not onely incouraged his citizens, but gotten even amongest the enemies them selves, a fame also to be a noble Captaine, and worthie to manage greate affaires.   For everie man judged him to be a skillfull souldier, and a valliant Captaine, that with the power of one onely citie, did mainteine warre against the kingdom of Macedon, against all the people of Peloponnesus, and against the treasure of so greate a king: and withall, not onely to

keepe his owne contrie of Laconia unfoyled, but farre otherwise to hurte his enemies contries, and to take so many
greate cities of theirs. But he that sayed first, that money
was the sinewe of all thinges, spake it chiefly in my opinion,
in respect of the warres. Demades the Orator sayed on
a time, when the Athenians commaunded certaine gallies
shoulde be put out of the arsenall into the sea, and presently
rigged and armed with all possible speed, though they lacked
money: He that rules the prowe, must first see before him.
Meaning, munition and vittells must be provided, before the
shippes be sette out. And it is reported also, that the
auncient Archidamus, when the confederates of the Lacedæmonians at the beginninge of the warre of Peloponnesus
required, that they might be sessed at a certeine rate,
aunswered: The charges of warre have no certeyne stinte.
For like as wrestlers that exercise their bodies continuallie in
games, are better able to wrestle, and overthrowe them with
tyme, that have no strength, but onely arte and slight: even
so Kinge Antigonus, who by the greatnesse of his kingdome
did defraye the charge of this warre, did wearie and overcome Cleomenes at the length, bicause he lacked money
bothe to paye the straungers that served him, and also to
mayntayne his owne citizens. For otherwise, doubtlesse the
time served his turne well, bicause the troubles that fell
apon Antigonus in his realme, did make him to be sent for
home. For the barbarous people his neighbours, in his
absence did spoyle and destroye the realme of Macedon, and
speciallie the Illyrians of the high contrie that came downe
then with a greate armie: whereupon, the Macedonians
being spoyled and harried on all sides by them, they sent
poste unto Antigonus, to pray him to come home. If these
letters had bene brought him but a litle before the battell,
as they came afterwardes: Antigonus had gone his waye,
and left the Achaians. But fortune, that alwayes striketh
the stroke in all weightiest causes, gave suche speede and
favour unto time: that immediatly after the battell was
fought at Selasia, (where Cleomenes lost his armie and citie)
the verie messengers arrived that came for Antigonus
to come home, the which made the overthrowe of king

Cleomenes so muche more lamentable. For if he had delayed battell but two dayes lenger, when the Macedonians had bene gone, he might have made what peace he would with the Achaians: but for lacke of money, he was driven (as Polybius wryteth) to geve battell, with twentie thowsande men, against thirtie thowsande: where he shewed him selfe an excellent and skilfull Captaine, and where his citizens also fought like valliant men, and the straungers in like case did shewe them selves good souldiers. But his onely overthrowe was, by the manner of his enemies weapons, and the force of their battell of footemen. But Phylarchus wryteth, that treason was the cause of his overthrowe. For Antigonus had appointed the Acarnanians, and the Illyrians which he had in his armie, to steale uppon the winge of his enemies armie, where Euclidas, king Cleomenes brother was, to compasse him in behinde, whilest he did sette the rest of his men in battell. When Cleomenes was got up upon some hill to looke about him, to see the countenaunce of the enemie, and seeing none of the Acarnanians, nor of the Illyrians: he was then affrayed of Antigonus, that he went about some stratageame of warre. Wherefore he called for Demoteles, whose charge was to take heede of stratageames and secret ambushes, and commaunded him to looke to the rerewarde of his armie, and to be verie circumspect all about. Demoteles, that was bribed before (as it is reported) with money, tolde him that all was cleere in the rerewarde, and bad him looke to overthrowe his enemies before him. Cleomenes trusting this reporte, sette forward against Antigonus, and in the ende, his citizens of Sparta which he had about him, gave suche a fierce charge apon the squadron of the Macedonian footemen, that they drave them backe five furlonges of. But in the meane time, Euclidas his brother, in the other wing of his armie, being compassed in behinde, Cleomenes turning him backe, and seeing the overthrowe, cried out alowde: Alas, good brother, thou art but slaine, yet thou dyest valliantlie, and honestlie, and thy death shall be a worthie example unto all posteritie, and shall be song by the praises of the women of Sparta. So Euclidas and his men being slaine, the enemies came straight to sette upon Cleomenes

Battell betwext Cleomenes and Antigonus at Selasia.

The treason of Demoteles.

winge. Cleomenes then seeing his men discouraged, and that they durst no lenger resist the enemie, fledde, and saved him selfe Many of the straungers also that served him, were slaine at this battell : and of sixe thowsande Spartans, there were left alive but onely two hundred. Now Cleomenes being returned unto Sparta, the citizens comming to see him, he gave them counsell to yeeld them selves unto Antigonus the conqueror : and for him selfe, if either alive or dead he could doe any thing for the honor and benefit of Sparta, that he would willingly doe it. The women of the citie also, comming unto them that flying had escaped with him, when he saw them unarme the men, and bring them drinke to refresh them with : he also went home to his owne house. Then a maide of the house, which he had taken in the citie of Megalipolis (and whom he had enterteined ever since the death of his wife) came unto him as her maner was, to refresh him comming hot from the battell : howbeit he would not drinke though he was extreame drie, nor sit being verie wearie, but armed as he was, layed his arme a crosse apon a piller, and leaning his head apon it, reposed himselfe a litle, and casting in his minde all the wayes that were to be thought of, he tooke his frendes with him, and went to the haven of Gythium, and there having his shippes which he had appointed for the purpose, he hoysed sayle, and departed his way. Immediatly after his departure, came Antigonus into the citie of Sparta, and curteously intreated the citizens and inhabitants he found, and did offend no man, nor prowdly despise the auncient honor and dignitie of Sparta : but referring them to their owne lawes and government, when he had sacrificed to the goddes for his victorie, he departed from thence the thirde daye, newes being brought him that the warre was verie great in Macedon, and that the barbarous people did spoyle his contrie. Now a disease tooke him, whereof he dyed afterwards, which appeared a tisicke, mixt with a sore catarre but yet he yeelded not to his disease, and bare it out, that fighting for his contrie, and obteyning a famous victorie, with great slaughter of the barbarous people, he might yet dye honorably, as in deede he did, by Phylarchus testimonie, who

Cleomenes overthrowen by Antigonus.

Antigonus wanne the citie of Sparta.

The death of Antigonus the sonne of Demetrius, king of Macedon

AGIS AND
CLEOMENES
sayth, that with the force of his voyce, fiercely crying out in
the middest of his fight, he tare his lunges and lightes, worse
then they were before. Yet in the schooles it is sayd, that
after he had wonne the battell, he was so joyfull of it, that
crying out, O blessed day : he brake out into a great
bleeding at the mouth, and a great fever tooke him withall,
that he dyed of it. Thus much touching Antigonus. Now

Cleomenes
flieth out of
Pelopon-
nesus.
Cleomenes departing out of the Isle of Cythera, went and
cast ancker in an other Iland, called Ægialia. Then determining to saile over to the citie of Cyrena, Therycion, one of
Cleomenes frendes (a man that in warres shewed him selfe
verie valliant, but a boaster besides of his owne doinges)

The oration
of Therycion,
unto Cleo-
menes,against
death.
tooke Cleomenes aside, and sayd thus unto him : ‘ Truely O
‘ king, we have lost an honorable occasion to dye in battell,
‘ though every man hath heard us vaunt and say, that Anti-
‘ gonus should never overcome the king of Sparta alive, but
‘ dead. A seconde occasion yet is offered us to dye, with
‘ much lesse honor and fame notwithstanding, then the first.
‘ Whether doe we saile to no purpose ? Why doe we flie the
‘ death at hand, and seeke it so farre of ? If it be no shame
‘ nor dishonor for the posteritie and race of Hercules to
‘ serve the successors of Philip and Alexander : let us save
‘ then our labor, and long daungerous sailing, and goe yeelde
‘ our selves unto Antigonus, who in likelyhoode will better
‘ use us then Ptolomy, bicause the Macedonians are farre
‘ more nobler persons then the Ægyptians. And if we
‘ disdaine to be commaunded by them which have over-
‘ commen us in battell, why then will we make him Lord of
‘ us, that hath not overcomen us : in steade of one, to make
‘ us inferior unto both, flying Antigonus, and serving king
‘ Ptolomy ? Can we say that we goe into Ægypt, in respect
‘ to see your mother there ? A joyfull sight no doubt, when
‘ she shall shew king Ptolomyes wives her sonne, that before
‘ was a king, a prisoner, and fugitive now. Were it not
‘ better for us, that having yet Laconia our contrie in sight,
‘ and our swordes besides in our owne hands, to deliver us
‘ from this great miserie, and so doing to excuse our selves
‘ unto them that are slaine at Selasia, for defence of Sparta :
‘ then cowardly loosing our time in Ægypt, to inquire whom

GRECIANS AND ROMANES

' Antigonus left his Lieutenaunt and Governor in Lacedæ-
' mon ? ' Therycion ending his oration, Cleomenes aunswered
him thus : 'Doest thou thinke it a glorie for thee to seeke
' death, which is the easiest matter, and the presentest unto
' any man, that can be : and yet, wretche that thou art :
' thou fliest now more cowardly and shamefully, then from
' the battell.   For divers valliant men, and farre better then
' our selves, have often yeelded unto their enemies, either
' by some misfortune, or compelled by greater number and
' multitude of men : but he say I, that submitteth him
' selfe unto paine and miserie, reproache and praise of men,
' he can not but confesse that he is overcome by his owne
' unhappinesse.   For, when a man will willingly kill him
' selfe, he must not doe it to be rid of paynes and labour,
' but it must have an honorable respect and action.   For,
' to live or dye for his owne respect, that can not but be
' dishonorable : the which now thou perswadest me unto,
' to make me flie this present miserie we are in, without
' any honor or profitte in our death.   And therefore, I am
' of opinion, that we shoulde not yet cast of the hope we
' have to serve our contrie in time to come : but when all
' hope fayleth us, then we may easely make our selves awaye
' when we list.'   Thereunto Therycion gave no aunswere, but
as soone as he founde oportunitie to slippe from Cleomenes,
he went to the sea side, and slewe him selfe.   Cleomenes
hoysinge sayle from the Ile of Ægialia, went into Africke,
and was brought by the kinges servauntes unto the citie
of Alexandria.   King Ptolomy at his first comming, gave
Cleomenes no speciall good, but indifferent intertainment :
but after that he had shewed him selfe to be of great wisedom
and judgement, and that Ptolomy saw in the simplicity of
his Laconian life he had also a noble disposition and corage,
nothing degenerating from the princely race and blood of
Hercules, and that he yelded not to his adversitie : he tooke
more delight in his company, then in all the company of
his flatterers and hangers on him : and then repented him
greatly, that he had made no more account of him before,
but had suffered him to be overthrowne by Antigonus, who
through the victory of him, had marvelously enlarged his

*Cleomenes
oration of
death.*

*Willing
death, must
have honor-
able respect.*

*Cleomenes
flieth into
Ægypt unto
king Ptolomy.*

honor and power. Then he began to comfort Cleomenes, and doing him as great honor as could be, promised that he would send him with shippes and money into Græce, and put him againe into his kingdom : and further, gave him an annuall pencion in the meane time, of foure and twenty talents, with the which he simply and soberly enterteyned him selfe and his men about him : and bestowed all the rest apon his contry men that came out of Græce into Ægypt. But now, old king Ptolomy deceasing before he could per-forme the promise he made unto Cleomenes, to send him into Græce : the Realme falling then into great lasciviousnes, dronckennes, and into the government of women, his case and miserie was cleane forgotten. For the young king his sonne was so given over to women and wine, that when he was most sober, and in his best witts, he most disposed him selfe to make feastes and sacrifices, and to have the taber playing in his Court, to gather people together, like a stage player or jugler, whilest one Agathoclea his lemman, and her mother, and Oenanthes a bawde, did rule all the affayres of the state. But when he came to be king, it appeared he had neede of Cleomenes : bicause he was affraid of his brother Megas, who by his mothers meanes, was very wel esteemed of among souldiers. Wherefore he called Cleomenes to him, and made him of his privy counsel, where he devised by practise, which way to kill his brother. All other his friends that were of counsell with him, did counsell him to do it : but Cleomenes onely vehemently disswaded him from it, and tolde him, that if it were possible, rather moe brethren should be begotten unto the king for the safetie of his person, and for deviding of the affayres of the kingdome betweene them. Amongest the kinges familliers that was chiefest about him, there was one Sosibius that said unto Cleomenes : so long as his brother Magas lived, the souldiers that be straungers, whom the king entertayned, would never be true to him. Cleomenes aunswered him, for that matter there was no daunger : for sayth he, of those hiered straungers, there are three thowsand Peloponnesians, which he knewe at the twinckling of an eye, would be at his commaundement, to come with their armor and weapon where he would appoynt them. These words of Cleomenes at that tyme shewed his fayth and good will he bare unto the king, and the force he was of besides. But afterwards, Ptolomyes fearefulnes increasing his mistrust: (as it commonly hapneth, that they that lacke wit, thinke it the best safetie to be fearefull of every wagging of a strawe, and to mistrust every man) the remembrance of Cleomenes wordes made him much suspected of the Courtiers, understanding that he could doe so much with the souldiers that were straungers: insomuch as some of them sayd, See (meaning Cleomenes) there is a lyon amongest sheepe. In deede, considering his facions and behavior, they might well say so of him: for he would looke thorough his fingers as though he saw nothing, and yet saw all what they did. In fine, he required an armie and ships of the king and understanding also that Antigonus was dead, and that the Achaians and Ætolians were at great warres together, and that the affaires of his contry did call him home, all Peloponnesus being in armes and uprore, he prayed that they would licence him to depart with his friends. But never a man would give eare unto him, and the king also heard nothing of it, bicause he was continually entertained among Ladies, with banckets, dauncing, and maskes. But Sosibius that ruled all the Realme, thought that to keepe Cleomenes against his wil, were a hard thing, and also daungerous: and to let him goe also, knowing that he was a valiant man, and of a sturring minde, and one that knew the vices and imperfections of their government: he thought that also no safe way, sithe no giftes nor presents that could be offered him, could soften him. For as the holy bull (which they call in Ægypt Apis) that is ful fed in goodly pasture, doth yet desire to followe his naturall course and libertie, to runne and leape at his pleasure, and plainely sheweth that it is a griefe to him to be kept stil by the Priest: even so the courtly pleasures did nothing delight Cleomenes, but as Homer writeth of Achilles:

> It irkt his noble hart to sit at home in slothfull rest,
> When martiall matters were in hand, the which he liked best.

Nowe Cleomenes standing in these tearmes, there arrived in

Nicagoras
Messenian,
an enemy to
Cleomenes.

Alexandria one Nicagoras Messenian, who maliced Cleomenes in his hart, but yet shewed as though he loved him. This Nicagoras on a time had sold Cleomenes certein land, but was not payed for it, either bicause he had no present money, or els by occasion of the warres which gave him no leasure to make payment. Cleomenes one day by chaunce walking upon the sandes, he sawe Nicagoras landing out of his shippe, being newly arrived, and knowing him, he curteously welcomed him, and asked what wind had brought him into Ægypt. Nicagoras gently saluting him againe, tolde him that he had brought the king excellent horse of service. Cleomenes smiling, told him, Thou haddest bene better have brought him some curtisans and daunsers, for they would have pleased the king better. Nicagoras faintly laughed at his aunswer, but within few dayes after he did put him in remembraunce of the land he sold him, and prayed him then that he would helpe him to money, telling him that he would not have prest him for it, but that he had susteyned losse by marchandise. Cleomenes aunswered him, that all his pension was spent he had of the king. Nicagoras being offended with this aunswer, he went and told Sosibius of the mocke Cleomenes gave the king. Sosibius was glad of this occasion, but yet desiring further matter to make the king offended with Cleomenes, he perswaded Nicagoras to write a letter to the king agaynst Cleomenes, as though he had conspired to take the citie of Cyrena, if the king had given him shippes, money, and men of warre. When Nicagoras had written this letter, he tooke shippe, and hoysed sayle. Foure dayes after his departure, Sosibius brought his letter to the king, as though he had but newly received

Cleomenes
committed to
prison in
Alexandria.

it. The king apon sight of it was so offended with Cleomenes, that he gave present order he should be shut up in a great house, where he should have his ordinary dyet allowed him, howbeit that he should keepe his house. This grieved Cleomenes much, but yet he was worse affraid of that which was to come, by this occasion: Ptolomy the sonne of Chrysermus, one of the kings familliers, who had oftentimes before bene very conversant and famillier with Cleomenes, and did franckly talke together in all matters: Cleomenes

230

one daye sent for him, to praye him to come unto him. Ptolomy came at his request, and familliarly discoursing together, went about to disswade him from all the suspicions he had, and excused the king also for that he had done unto him : so taking his leave he left him, not thinking that Cleomenes followed him (as he did) to the gate, where he sharply tooke up the souldiers, saying, that they were very negligent and careles in looking to such a fearefull beast as he was, and so ill to be taken, if he once scaped their handes. Cleomenes heard what he sayd, and went into his lodging againe, Ptolomy knowing nothing that he was behind him : and reported the very wordes againe unto his friendes. Then all the Spartans converting their good hope into anger, determined to be revenged of the injurie Ptolomy had done them, and to dye like noble Spartans not tarying til they should be brought to the shambles like fat weathers, to be sold and killed. For it would be a great shame and dishonor unto Cleomenes, having refused to make peace with Antigonus, a noble Prince and warrier : to tary the kinges pleasure till he had left his dronckennes and daunsing, and then to come and put him to death. They beeing fully resolved hereof, as you have heard : king Ptolomy by chaunce went unto the citie of Canobus, and first they gave out in Alexandria, that the king minded to set Cleomenes at libertie. Then Cleomenes friendes observing the custom of the kings of Ægypt, when they ment to set a prisoner at libertie (which was, to send the prisoners meate, and presents before to their supper) did send unto him such manner of presents, and so deceived the souldiers that had the keeping of him, saying, that they brought those presents from the king. For Cleomenes him selfe did sacrifice unto the goddes, and sent unto the souldiers that kept him, parte of those presents that were sent unto him, and supping with his friendes that night, made mery with them, every man being crowned with garlands. Some say, that he made the more haste to execute his enterprise, sooner then he would have done, by meanes of one of his men that was privye unto his conspiracie : who went every night to lye with a woman he kept, and therefore was affraid lest he would bewray

Cleomenes practiseth to kill king Ptolomy.

them. Cleomenes about noone, perceiving the souldiers had
taken in their cuppes, and that they were a sleepe: he put
on his coate, and unripping it on the right shoulder, went
out of the house with his sword drawen in his hand, accompanied with his friends, following him in that sort, which
were thirty in all. Amongest them there was one called
Hippotas, who being lame, went very lively out with them
at the first: but when he saw they went faier and softly
bicause of him, he prayed them to kil him, bicause they
should not hinder their enterprise for a lame man, that
could doe them no service. Notwithstanding, by chaunce
they met with a townes man a horsebacke, that came hard
by their dore, whome they pluckt from his horse, and cast
Hippotas uppon him: and then ranne through the citie,
and cryed to the people, Libertie, libertie. Now the people
had no other corage in them, but onely commended Cleomenes, and wondred at his valiantnes: but otherwise to
follow him, or to further his enterprise, not a man of them
had any hart in them. Thus running up and downe the
towne, they met with Ptolomy (the same whome we sayde
before was the sonne of Chrysermus) as he came out of the
Court: whereuppon three of them setting on him, slue
him presently. There was also another Ptolomy that was
governor and Lieuetenant of the citie of Alexandria: who
hearing a rumor of this sturre, came unto them in his coche.
They went and met him, and first having driven away his
garde and souldiers that went before him, they pluckt him
out of his coche, and slue him also. After that they went
towards the castell, with intent to set all the prisoners there
at libertie to take their part. Howbeit the gaylers that
kept them had so strongly locked up the prison dores, that
Cleomenes was repulsed, and put by his purpose. Thus
wandring up and downe the citie, no man neither came to
joyne with him, nor to resist him, for every man fled for
feare of him. Wherefore at length being weary with going
up and downe, he turned him to his friends, and sayd unto
them: It is no marvell though women commaund such a
cowardly people, that flye in this sort from their libertie.
Thereuppon he prayed them all to dye like men, and like

232

those that were brought up with him, and that were worthy
of the fame of his so noble deedes.   Then the first man that
made him selfe be slayne, was Hippotas, who dyed of a
wound one of the younge men of his company gave him
with a sword at his request.   After him every man slue
them selves, one after another, without any feare at all,
saving Panteas, who was the first man that entred the citie
of Megalipolis.   He was a faier younge man, and had bene
very well brought up in the Laconian discipline, and better
then any man of his yeares.   Cleomenes did love him
dearely, and commaunded him that when he should see
he were dead, and all the rest also, that then he should
kill him selfe last of all.   Now they all being layed on the
ground, he searched them one after another with the poynt
of his sword, to see if there were any of them yet left alive.
and when he had pricked Cleomenes on the heele amongest
others, and saw that he did yet knit his browes, he kissed
him, and sate downe by him.   Then perceiving that he had
yelded up the ghost, imbracing him when he was dead,
he also slue him selfe, and fell upon him.   Thus Cleomenes
having raigned king of Sparta sixteene yeares, being the
same manner of man we have described him to be · he ended
his dayes in this sort as ye heare.   Now, his death being
presently bruted through the citie, Cratesiclea his mother,
though otherwise she had a noble minde, did notwithstanding a litle forget her greatnes, through thextreame sorow
she felt for the death of her sonne: and so imbracing Cleomenes sonnes, she fell to bitter lamentacion.   But the eldest
of his sonnes, (no man mistrusting any such matter) found
meanes to get out of her handes, and running up to the
toppe of the house, cast him selfe headlong downe to the
ground, that his head was all broken and splitted, yet died
not, but was taken up crying, and angry with them, that
they would not suffer him to dye.   This newes being brought
to king Ptolomy, he commaunded they should first flea
Cleomenes, and then hange up his body, and also, that they
should put his children, his mother, and all her women
wayting on her to death: among the which was Panteas
wife, one of the fayrest and curteousest women in her tyme.

The ende and
death of Cleo-
menes and his
friendes.

The corage of
Panteas

They had not beene longe maried before, when these mischieves lighted apon them, at what tyme their love was then in greatest force. Her parents then would not let her depart, and imbarke with her husband, but had locked her up, and kept her at home by force. Howbeit shortly after she found the meanes to get her a horse, and some money, and stale away in the night, and gallopped towards the haven of Tænarus, where finding a shippe ready bound for Ægypt, she imbarked, and went to seeke her husband, with whome she gladly and lovingly ledde her life, forsaking her owne contry, to live in a straunge Realme. Now when the Sergeaunts came to take Cratesiclea to put her to death, Panteas wife led her by the arme, carying up her traine, and did comfort her, although Cratesiclea otherwise was not affraid to dye, but onely asked this favor, that she might dye before her litle children. This notwithstanding, when they came to the place of execution, the hangman first slue her children before her eyes, and then her selfe afterwards, who in such great griefe and sorowe, sayd no more but thus: Alas, my poore children, what is become of you? And Panteas wife also, being a mighty tall woman, girding her clothes to her, tooke up the slayne bodies one after another, and wrapped them up in such things as she could get, speaking never a word, nor shewing any signe or token of griefe: and in fine, having prepared her self to dye, and plucked of her attyre her selfe, without suffering any other to come neare her, or to see her, but the hangman that was appoynted to stryke of her head. In this sorte she dyed as constantly, as the stowtest man living could have done, and had so covered her body, that no man needed after her death to touche her: so carefull was she to her ende, to keepe her honestie, which she had alwayes kept in her life, and in her death was mindefull of her honor, wherewith she decked her body in her life tyme. Thus these Lacedæmon Ladies playing their partes in this pitifull tragedie, contending at the time of death, even with the corage of the slayne Spartans their contrymen, which of them should dye most constantly: left a manifest proofe and testimonie, that fortune hath no power over fortitude and corage.

GRECIANS AND ROMANES

Shortly after, those that were appoynted to keepe the body of king Cleomenes that hong upon the crosse, they spied a great Serpent wreathed about his head, that covered all his face, insomuch as no ravening fowle durst come neare him to eate of it: whereuppon the king fell into a supersticious feare, being affrayd that he had offended the goddes. Hereuppon, the Ladyes in his Court began to make many sacrifices of purification, for the cleering of this sinne: perswading them selves, that they had put a man to death, beloved of the gods, and that he had something more in him then a man. The Alexandrinians thereuppon went to the place of execution, and made their prayers unto Cleomenes, as unto a demy god, calling him the sonne of the goddes. Untill that the learned men brought them from that error, declaring unto them, that like as of oxen being dead and rotten, there breede bees, and of horse also come waspes, and of asses likewise bitels: even so mens bodies, when the marie melteth and gathereth together, doe bringe forth Serpents. The which comming to the knowledge of the auncients in olde tyme, of all other beastes they did consecrate the Dragon to Kinges and Princes, as proper unto man.

Cleomenes hanging upon a crosse, had a Serpent wreathed about his head.

Living things breeding of the corruption of dead beasts.

Why the Dragon is consecrated unto Princes.

THE END OF THE LIFE OF AGIS AND CLEOMENES

TIBERIUS AND CAIUS GRACCHI

OW that we have declared unto you the historie of the lives of these two Græcians, Agis, and Cleomenes aforesayd: we must also write the historie of two Romanes, the which is no lesse lamentable for the troubles and calamities that chaunced unto Tiberius and Caius, both of them the sonnes of Tiberius Gracchus. He having bene twise Consul, and once Censor, and having had the honor of two triumphs: had notwithstanding more

235

Tiberius
Gracchus the
father, maried
Cornelia, the
Daughter of
Scipio
African.

The tender
love of Tibe-
rius to his wife
Cornelia.

The praise
of Cornelia,
mother of the
Gracchi.

honor and fame onely for his valiantnes, for the which he was thought worthy to marye with Cornelia, the daughter of Scipio, who overcame Hanniball after the deathe of his father: though while he lived he was never his friend, but rather his enemy. It is reported, that Tiberius on a tyme found two snakes in his bed, and that the Soothsayers and wysards having considered the signification thereof, did forbid him to kill them both, and also to let them both escape, but one onely: assuring him that if he killed the male, he should not live long after: and if he killed the female, that then his wife Cornelia shoulde dye. Tiberius then loving his wife dearely, thinking it meeter for him also, that he being the elder of both, and she yet a younge woman, should dye before her: he slue the male, and let the female escape, howbeit he dyed soone after, leaving twelve children alive, all of them begotten of Cornelia. Cornelia after the death of her husband, taking upon her the rule of her house and children, led such a chast●●●, was so good to her children, and of so noble a mi●●●hat every man thought Tiberius a wise man for that ●●d, and left her behind him. She remayning widow, king Ptolomy made sute unto her, and would have made her his wife a●● Queene. But she refused, and in her widowehed lost all her children, but one Daughter, (whome she bestowed upon the younger Scipio African) and Tiberius and Caius, whose lives we presently write. Those she so carefully brought up, that they being become more civill, and better conditioned, then any other Romanes in their time: every man judged, that education prevailed more in them, then nature. For, as in the favors and pictures of Castor and Pollux, there is a certaine difference discerned, whereby a man may know that the one was made for wrestling, and the other for running: even so betwene these two young brethren, amongest other the great likenes betwene them, being both happely borne to be valiant, to be temperate, to be liberall, to be learned, and to be nobly minded, there grew notwithstanding great difference in their actions and doings in the common wealth: the which I thinke convenient to declare, before I proceede any farther. First of all, for the favor of the face, the looke

236

GRECIANS AND ROMANES

and moving of the bodye, Tiberius was much more milde and tractable, and Caius more hotte and earnest. For the first in his orations was very modest, and kept his place: and the other of all the Romanes was the first, that in his oration jetted up and downe the pulpit, and that plucked his gowne over his showlders: as they write of Cleo Athenian, that he was the first of all Orators that opened his gowne, and clapped his hand on his thighe in his oration. Furthermore, Caius wordes, and the vehemencie of his perswasion, were terrible and full of passion: but Tiberius wordes in contrary manner, were mild, and moved men more to compassion, beeing very propper, and excellently applyed, where Caius wordes were full of finenes and curiositie. The like difference also was betwene them in their fare and dyet. For Tiberius alwayes kept a convenient ordinarie: and Caius also in respect of other Romanes, lived very temperately, but in respect of his brothers fare, curiously and superfluously. Insomuch as Drusus on a tyme reproved him, bicause he had bought certayne Dolphyns of silver, to the value of a thousand two hundred and fiftie Drachmas for every pownd waight. And now, as touching the manners and naturall disposition of them both, agreeing with the diversitie of their tongues, the one being milde and plausible, and the other hotte and chollerike: insomuch that otherwhile forgetting him selfe in his oration, agaynst his will he would be very earnest, and strayne his voice beyond his compasse, and so with great uncomelines confound his wordes. Yet finding his owne fault, he devised this remedye. He had a servaunt called Licinius, a good wise man, who with an instrument of Musicke he had, by the which they teache men to ryse and fall in their tunes, when he was in his oration, he ever stoode behinde him: and when he perceyved that his Maisters voyce was a litle too lowde, and that through choller he exceeded his ordinary speache: he played a softe stoppe behinde him, at the sownde whereof Caius immediatly fell from his extreamitie, and easily came to him selfe agayne. And here was the diversitie betweene them. Otherwise, for their hardines against their enemies, the justice unto their tennaunts, the care and paynes in their

237

TIBERIUS
AND CAIUS
GRACCHI
offices of charge, and also their continencie against voluptuousnes : in all these they were both alike. For age, Tiberius
was elder by nyne yeares, by reason whereof their severall
authoritie and doings in the common wealth fell out at
sundry times. And this was one of the chiefest causes why
their doings prospered not, bicause they had not both authoritie in one selfe time, nether could they joyne their power
together : the which if it had mette at one selfe time, had
bene of great force, and peradventure invincible. Wherefore we must write perticularly of them both, but first of all
we must begin with the elder. He, when he came to mans
state, had such a name and estimacion, that immediatly they
made him fellow, in the colledge of the Priests, which at

Tiberius
made Augure.
Rome are called Augures : (being those that have the charge
to consider of signes and predictions of things to come) more
for his valiantnes, then for nobility. The same doth Appius
Clodius witnesse unto us, one that hath bene both Consul
and Censor, and also President of the Senate, and of greater
authoritie then any man in his time. This Appius at a
supper when all the Augures were together, after he had
saluted Tiberius, and made very much of him, he offered him

Tiberius
maried
Appius
Clodius
daughter.
his daughter in mariage. Tiberius was very glad of the
offer, and therewithall the mariage was presently concluded
betwene them. Thereuppon Appius comming home to his
house, at the threshold of his dore he called a lowd for his
wife, and told her : Antistia, I have bestowed our Daughter
Clodia. She wondring at it, O goddes sayd she, and what
needed all this haste ? what couldest thou have done more,
if thou haddest gotten her Tiberius Gracchus for her husband ? I know that some refer this historie unto Tiberius,
father of these two men we write of, and unto Scipio the
African : but the most part of writers agree with that we
write at this present. And Polybius him selfe also writeth,
that after the death of Scipio African, his friendes beeing
met together, they chose Tiberius before all the other younge
men of the citie, to marye him unto Cornelia, being free, and
unpromised, or bestowed apon any man by her father. Now
Tiberius the yonger being in the warres in Africke under
Scipio the second, who had maryed his sister : lying in his
238

GRECIANS AND ROMANES

tent with him, he found his Captaine indued with many noble giftes of nature, to allure mens harts to desire to follow his valiantnes. So in a short tyme he did excell all the younge men of his tyme, aswell in obedience, as in the valiantnes of his person: insomuch that he was the first man that scaled the walles of the enemies, as Fannius reporteth, who sayeth that he scaled the walles with him, and did helpe him in that valiant enterprise. So that being present, all the campe were in love with him: and when he was absent, every man wished for him againe. After this warre was ended, he was chosen Treasorer, and it was his chaunce to goe against the Numantines, with Caius Mancinus one of the Consuls, who was an honest man, but yet had the worst lucke of any Captaine the Romanes had. Notwithstanding, Tiberius wisedome and valiantnes, in this extreame ill lucke of his Captaine, did not onely appeare with great glorye to him, but also most wonderfull, the great obedience and reverence he bare unto his Captaine: though his misfortunes did so trouble and grieve him, that he could not tell him selfe, whether he was Captaine or not. For when he was overthrowen in great foughten fieldes, he departed in the night, and left his campe. The Numantines hearing of it, first tooke his campe, and then ranne after them that fled, and setting upon the rereward, slue them, and envyronned all his armye. So that they were driven into straight and narrowe places, where out they could by no meanes escape. Thereuppon Mancinus dispayring that he could get out by force, he sent a Herauld to the enemyes to treate of peace. The Numantines made aunswer, that they would trust no man but Tiberius onely, and therefore they willed he shoulde bee sent unto them. They desired that, partly for the love they bare unto the vertues of the younge man, bicause there was no talke of any other in all this warre but of him: and partly also, as remembring his father Tiberius, who making warres in Spayne, and having there subdued many nations, he graunted the Numantines peace, the which he caused the Romanes after-wardes to confirme and ratifie. Hereuppon Tiberius was sent to speake with them, and partly obteynung that he desired, and partly also graunting them that they required . he con-

TIBERIUS AND CAIUS GRACCHI

Tiberius Gracchus souldierfare.

Tiberius Gracchus chosen Quæstor.

Tiberius Gracchus concludeth peace with the Numantines.

239

cluded peace with them, whereby assuredly he saved the lives of twenty thowsande Romane Citizens, besides slaves and other stragglers that willingly followed the campe. This notwithstanding, the Numantines tooke the spoyle of all the goods they founde in the Romanes campe, amonge the which they founde Tiberius bookes of accompt touching the money disbursed of the treasure in his charge. Tiberius beeing marvailous desirous to have his bookes agayne, returned backe to Numantia with two or three of his friendes onely, though the armye of the Romanes were gone farre on their waye. So comming to the towne, he spake unto the governors of the citie, and prayed them to redeliver him his bookes of accompt, bicause his malicious enemies should not accuse him, calling him to accompt for his doings. The Numantines were very glad of this good happe, and prayed them to come into the towne. He standing still in doubt with him selfe what to doe, whether he should goe into the towne or not: the governors of the citie came to him, and taking him by the hande, prayed he would thinke they were not his enemies, but good friendes, and that he would trust them. Whereuppon Tiberius thought best to yeelde to their perswasion, beeing desirous also to have his bookes agayne, and the rather, for feare of offending the Numantines, if he shoulde have denyed and mistrusted them. When he was brought into the citie, they provided his dynner, and were very earnest with him, intreating him to dyne with them. Then they gave him his bookes againe, and offered him moreover to take what he woulde of all the spoyles they had gotten in the campe of the Romanes. Howebeit of all that he woulde take nothing but frankensence, which he used, when he did any sacrifice for his contry: and then taking his leave of them, with thankes he returned. When he was returned to Rome, all this peace concluded was utterly misliked, as dishonorable to the majestie of the Empire of Rome. Yet the parents and friendes of them that had served in this warre, making the greatest part of the people: they gathered about Tiberius, saying that what faultes were committed in this service, they were to impute it unto the Consul Mancinus, and not unto Tiberius, who had saved such a number of Romanes lives. Notwithstanding, they that were offended with this dishonorable peace, would that therein they should follow the example of their forefathers in the like case. For they sent backe their Captaines naked unto their enemies, bicause they were contented the Samnits should spoyle them of that they had, to escape with life. Moreover, they did not onely send them the Captaines and Consuls, but all those also that bare any office in the fielde, and had consented unto that condition: to the ende they might lay all the perjurie and breache of peace apon them. Herein therefore did manifestly appeare, the love and good will the people did beare unto Tiberius. For they gave order, that the Consul Mancinus should be sent naked, and bound unto the Numantines, and for Tiberius sake, they pardoned all the rest. I thinke Scipio, who bare great sway at that time in Rome, and was a man of greatest accompt, did helpe him at that pinche: who notwithstanding was ill thought of, bicause he did not also save the Consul Mancinus, and confirme the peace concluded with the Numantines, considering it was made by Tiberius his friend and kinsman. But these mislikings grew chiefly through the ambition of Tiberius friendes, and certein learned men, which stirred him up against Scipio. But yet it fell not out to open malice betwene them, neither followed there any hurte apon it. And surely I am perswaded, that Tiberius had not fallen into those troubles he did afterwards, if Scipio African had bene present, when he passed those thinges he preferred. But Scipio was then in warres at the seege of Numantia, when Tiberius apon this occasion passed these lawes. When the Romanes in olde tyme had overcomen any of their neighbours, for raunsom they tooke oftentymes a great deale of their land from them, parte whereof they solde by the cryer, for the benefite of the common wealth, and parte also they reserved to their state as demeane, which afterwards was let out to farme for a small rent yearely, to the poore Citizens that had no lands. Howbeit the riche men inhaunsed the rents, and so began to thrust out the poore men. Thereuppon was an ordinance made, that no Citizen of Rome should have above five hundred acres lande. This lawe for a tyme did bridle the covetousnes of the riche men, and did

TIBERIUS AND CAIUS GRACCHI

The peace broken with the Numantines.

Why Tiberius preferred the law Agraria.

Iugera.

5 : HH   241

ease the poore also that dwelt in the contry, apon the farmes they had taken up of the common wealth, and so lived with their owne, or with that their Auncestors had from the beginning. But by pioces of time, their riche neighbours, by names of other men, got their farmes over their heads, and in the end, the most of them were openly seene in it in their own names. Whereuppon, the poore people being thus turned out of all, went but with faint corage afterwards to the warre, nor cared any more for bringing up of children: so that in short time, the free men left Italy, and slaves and barbarous people did replenish it, whom the rich men made to plough those landes, which they had taken from the Romanes. Caius Lælius, one of Scipioes friends, gave an

attempt to reforme this abuse: but bicause the chiefest of the citie were against him, fearing it would breake out to some uprore, he desisted from his purpose, and therefore he was called Lælius the wise. But Tiberius being chosen

Tribune, he did forthwith preferre the reformation aforesayd, being allured unto it (as divers writers report) by Diophanes the Orator, and Blossius the Philosopher: of the which, Diophanes was banished from the citie of Mitylene, and Blossius the Italian from the citie of Cumes, who was scholler and famillier unto Antipater of Tarsus at Rome, by whome he was honored by certaine workes of Philosophie he dedicated unto him. And some also do accuse their mother Cornelia, who did twit her sonnes in the teeth, that the Romanes did yet call her Scipioes mother-in law, and not the mother of the Gracchi. Other say it was Spurius Posthumius, a companion of Tiberius, and one that contended with him in eloquence. For Tiberius returning from the warres, and finding him farre beyond him in fame and reputacion, and well beloved of every one: he sought to excell him by attempting this noble enterprise, and of so great expectacion. His owne brother Caius in a certaine booke, wrote, that as he went to the warres of Numantia, passing through Thuscan, he founde the contrye in manner unhabited: and they that did followe the ploughe, or keepe beastes, were the moste of them slaves, and barbarous people, comen out of a straunge contrie. Whereuppon ever after it ranne

242

in his minde to bringe this enterprise to passe, which brought great troubles to their house. But in fine, it was the people onely that moste set his harte afire to covet honor, and that hastened his determinacion: first bringing him to it by bylles sette uppe on every wall, in every porche, and uppon the tombes, praying him by them to cause the poore Citizens of Rome to have their landes restored, which were belonging to the common wealth. This notwithstanding he him selfe made not the lawe alone of his owne head, but did it by the counsell and advise of the chiefest men of Rome, for vertue and estimation: amonge the which, Crassus the high Bishoppe was one, and Mutius Scævola the Lawyer, that then was Consul, and Appius Clodius his father in lawe. And truely it seemeth, that never lawe was made with greater favor, then that which he preferred against so great injustice, and avarice. For those that should have bene punished for transgressing the lawe, and should have had the landes taken from them by force, which they unjustly kept against the lawe of Rome, and that should also have bene amersed for it: he ordeyned that they should be payed by the common wealth to the value of the landes, which they held unjustly, and so should leave them to the poore Citizens againe that had no land, and lacked helpe and reliefe. Now, though the reformation established by this lawe, was done with such great favor: the people notwithstanding were contented, and would forget all that was past, so that they might have no more wronge offred them in time to come. But the rich men, and men of great possessions, hated the law for their avarice, and for spight and selfwill (which would not let them yeeld) they were at deadly foode with the Lawyer that had preferred the lawe, and sought by all devise they could to disswade the people from it: telling them that Tiberius brought in this law Agraria againe, to disturbe the common wealth, and to make some alteracion in the state. But they prevailed not. For Tiberius defending the matter, which of it selfe was good and just, with such eloquence as might have justified an evill cause, was invincible: and no man was able to argue against him to confute him, when speaking in the behalfe of the poore

Side notes:

TIBERIUS AND CAIUS GRACCHI

Counsellers to Tiberius for preferring the law.

Lex Agraria.

Tiberius orations.

243

Citizens of Rome, (the people being gathered round about the pulpit for orations) he told them, that the wild beastes through Italy had their dennes and caves of abode, and that the men that fought, and were slaine for their contry, had nothing els but ayer and light, and so were compelled to wander up and downe with their wives and children, having no resting place nor house to put their heads in : and that the Captaines do but mocke their souldiers, when they encorage them in battel to fight valiantly for the graves, the temples, their owne houses, and their predecessors. For, said he, of such a number of poore Citizens as there be, there can not a man of them shew any auncient house or tombe of their auncestors : bicause the poore men doe go to the warres, and be slaine for the rich mens pleasures and wealth : besides they falsely cal them Lordes of the earth, where they have not a handfull of ground, that is theirs. These and such other like wordes being uttered before all the people with such vehemency and trothe, did so move the common people withall, and put them in such a rage, that there was no adversarye of his able to withstand him. Therefore, leaving to contrary and deny the lawe by argu-
Marcus
Octavius
Tribune, did
withstand
Tiberius lawe. ment, the rich men did put all their trust in Marcus Octavius, colleague and fellow Tribune with Tiberius in office, who was a grave and wise young man, and Tiberius very famil|lier friend. So that the first time they came to him, to oppose him against the confirmation of this lawe : he prayed them to holde him excused, bicause Tiberius was his very friend. But in the ende, being compelled unto it through the great number of the riche men that were importunate with him : he did withstande Tiberius lawe, the which was enoughe to overthrowe it. For if any one of the Tribunes speake against it, though all the other passe with it, he overthroweth it : bicause they all can doe nothing, if one of them be against it. Tiberius being very much offended with it, proceeded no further in this first favorable law, and in a rage preferred an other more gratefull to the common people, as also more extreme against the riche. In that law he ordeyned, that whosoever had any lands contrary to the auncient lawes of Rome, that he should presently depart

The modest contention betwixt Tiberius and Octavius.

from them. But theruppon there fel out continual brawles in the pulpit for orations, against Octavius: in the which, though they were very earnest and vehement one against another, yet there passed no fowle words from them, (how hot soever they were one with another) that should shame his companion. Whereby it appeareth, that to be well brought up, breedeth such a stay and knowledge in a man, not onely in things of pleasure to make him regard his credit, both in word and deede: but in passion and anger also, and in their greatest ambition of glory. Thereuppon Tiberius finding that this lawe among others touched Octavius, bicause he enjoyed a great deale of lande that was the common wealthes: he prayed him secretly to contend no more against him, promising him to give him of his owne, the value of those lands which he should be driven to forsake, although he was not very able to performe it. But when he sawe Octavius would not be perswaded, he then preferred a law, that all Magistrats and Officers should cease their authoritie, till the law were either past, or rejected, by voices of the people: and thereuppon he set his own seale upon the dores of the temple of Saturne, where the cofers of the treasure lay, bicause the treasorers them selves during that time, should neither take out nor put in any thing, apon great pennalties to be forfited by the Prætors or any other Magistrat of authority, that should breake this order. Hereuppon, all the Magistrates fearing this pennaltie, did leave to exercise their office for the time. But then the riche men that were of great livings, chaunged their apparell, and walked very sadly up and downe the market place, and layed secret wayte to take Tiberius, having hyered men to kill him: which caused Tiberius him selfe, openly before them all, to weare a shorte dagger under his longe gowne, properly called in Latine, *Dolon.* When the day came that this lawe should be established, Tiberius called the people to give their voyces: and the riche men on thother side, they tooke away the pots by force, wherein the papers of mens voyces were throwen, so that there was like to fall out great sturre upon it. For the faction of Tiberius was the stronger side, by the number of people that were gathered about him for that purpose: had it not bene for Manlius and Fulvius, both the which had ben Consuls, who went unto him, and besought him with the teares in their eies, and holding up their hands, that he would let the lawe alone. Tiberius thereuppon, foreseeing the instant daunger of some great mischief, as also for the reverence he bare unto two such noble persons, he stayed a litle, and asked them what they would have him to doe. They made aunswer, that they were not able to counsel him in a matter of so great waight, but they praied him notwithstanding, he would be contented to referre it to the judgement of the Senate. Thereuppon he graunted them presently. But afterwards perceiving that the Senate sate apon it, and had determined nothing, bicause the rich men were of too great authoritie: he entred into another devise that was nether honest nor meete, which

was, to deprive Octavius of his Tribuneship, knowing that otherwise he could not possibly come to passe the law. But before he tooke that course, he openly intreated him in the face of the people with curteous words, and tooke him by the hand, and prayed him to stand no more against him, and to doe the people this pleasure, which required a matter just and reasonable, and onely requested this final recompence for the great paines they tooke in service abroad for their contry. Octavius denied him plainely. Then said Tiberius openly, that both of them being brethren in one selfe place and authoritie, and contrary one to another in a matter of so great waight, this contencion could not be possibly ended, without civill warre · and that he could see no way to remedy it, unles one of them two were deposed from their office. Thereuppon he bad Octavius begin first with him, and he would rise from the benche with a good will, and become a private man, if the people were so contented. Octavius would doe nothing in it. Tiberius then replyed, that he would be doing with him, if he altered not his mind, apon a better breathe and consideration: and so dismissed the assemblye for that daye. The next morning the people being againe assembled, Tiberius going up to his seate, attempted agayne to perswade Octavius to leave of. In fine, finding him still a man unremoveable, he referred the matter to the voyce of the people, whether they were contented Octavius should be deposed from his office. Nowe there were five and thirtie trybes of the people, of the which, seventeene of them had already passed their voyces agaynst Octavius, so that there remayned but one trybe more to put him out of his office. Then Tiberius made them staye for proceeding any further, and prayed Octavius agayne, imbracing him before all the people, with all the intreatye possible: that for selfewill sake he would not suffer such an open shame to be done unto him, as to be put out of his office: neither also to make him the occasion and instrument of so pitifull a deede. They saye that Octavius at this last intreatie was somewhat moved and wonne by his perswasions, and that weeping, he stayed a longe tyme, and made no aunswer. But when he looked apon the riche men that stoode in a great company together, he was ashamed (I thinke) to have their ill willes, and rather betooke him selfe to the losse of his office, and so bad Tiberius doe what he would. Thereuppon he beeing deprived by voyces of the people, Tiberius commaunded one of his infranchised bondmen to pull him out of the pulpit for orations: for he used his infranchised bondmen in steede of Sergeaunts. This made the sight so much more lamentable, to see Octavius thus shamefully pluckt away by force. Yea furthermore, the common people would have ronne apon him, but the riche men came to rescue him, and woulde not suffer him to doe him further hurte. So Octavius saved him selfe ronning away alone, after he had bene rescued thus from the fury of the people. Moreover, there was a faithfull servaunt of Octavius, who stepping before his Maister to save him from hurt, had his eyes pulled out, against Tiberius minde, who ranne to the rescue with all speede when he heard the noyse

After that, the lawe Agraria passed for division of landes, and three Commissioners were appoynted to make inquirie and distribution thereof. The Commissioners appoynted were these: Tiberius him selfe: Appius Clodius his father in lawe, and Caius Gracchus his brother: who was not at that tyme in Rome, but in the campe with Scipio African, at the seege of the citie of Numantia. Thus Tiberius very

Tiberius preferreth the law Agraria.

quietly passed over these matters, and no man durst withstand him : and furthermore, he substituted in Octavius place no man of qualitie, but onely one of his followers, called Mutius. Wherewith the noble men were so sore offended with him, that fearing the increase of his greatnes, they being in the Senate house did what they could possible to doe him despyte and shame. For when Tiberius demaunded a tent at the charge of the common wealth, when he should goe abroad to make division of these landes, as they usually graunted unto others, that many tymes went in farre meaner commissions. they flatly denyed him, and through the procurement of P. Nasica (who being a great landed man in his contry, shewed him selfe in this action his mortall enemie, taking it greevously to be compelled to depart from his land) onely graunted him nyne of their obuli a day, for his ordinarye allowance. But the people on thother side were all in an uprore against the riche. Insomuch as one of Tiberius friendes beeing deade uppon the sodaine, uppon whose body beeing deade there appeared very ill signes · the common people ranne sodainely to his buriall, and cryed out that he was poysoned. And so taking uppe the beere whereon his bodie laye uppon their showlders, they were present at the fire of his funeralls, where immediatly appeared certaine signes to make them suspect, that in deede there was vehement cause of presumption he was poysoned. For his belly burst, whereout there issued such aboundance of corrupt humors, that they put out the first fire, and made them fetche another, the which also they could not make to burne, until that they were compelled to cary the bodie into some other place, where notwithstanding they had much a doe to make it burne. Tiberius seeing that, to make the common people mutyne the more, he put on mourning apparell, and brought his sonnes before them, and besought the people to be good unto them and their mother, as one that dispayred of his health and safetie.

King Attalus
made the
people of
Rome his
heire.
About that tyme dyed Attalus, surnamed Philopater, and Eudemus Pergamenian brought his will to Rome, in the which he made the people of Rome his heires. Wherefore Tiberius, still to encrease the good wil of the common people

towards him, preferred a law immediatly, that the ready
money that came by the inheritaunce of this king shoulde
bee distributed amonge the poore Citizens, on whose lot it
should fall to have any parte of the division of the landes of
the common wealth, to furnishe them towardes house, and
to set uppe their tillage. Furthermore, he sayd, that concerning the townes and cities of the kingdome of Attalus,
the Senate had nothing to doe to take any order with them,
but that the people were to dispose of them, and that he
him selfe would put it out. That made him againe more
hated of the Senate then before, insomuch as there was
one Pompey a Senator, that standing up, sayde: that he
was next neighbour unto Tiberius, and that by reason of
his neighbourhed he knew that Eudemus Pergamenian had
given him one of king Attalus royall bands, with a purple
gowne besides, for a token that he should one day be king of
Rome. And Quintus Metellus also reproved him, for that
his father being Censor, the Romanes having supped in the
towne, and repayring every man home to his house, they did
put out their torches and lights, bicause men seeing them
returne, they should not thinke they taryed too long in
companie bancketing: and that in contrary maner, the
seditious and needy rabble of the common people did light
his sonne home, and accompany him all night long up
and downe the towne. At that tyme there was one Titus
Annius, a man that had no goodnes nor honestie in him,
howbeit taken for a great reasoner, and for a suttell questioner and aunswerer. He provoked Tiberius to aunswer
him, whether he had not committed a shamefull facte to his
companion and brother Tribune, to defame him, that by the
lawes of Rome should have bene holy, and untouched. The
people tooke this provocation very angrily, and Tiberius
also comming out, and having assembled the people, commaunded them to bringe this Annius before him, that he
might be endyted in the market place. But he finding
him selfe farre inferior unto Tiberius, both in dignitie and
eloquence, ranne to his fine suttill questions, to take a man
at his worde: and prayed Tiberius before he did proceede
to his accusation, that he would first aunswer him to a

TIBERIUS
AND CAIUS
GRACCHI
Tiberius law,
for deviding
of Attalus
money.

Titus Annius
a suttile
questioner
and aunswerer
of thinges.

question he would ask him. Tiberius bad him saye what
he would. So silence being made, Annius asked him· If
thou wouldest defame me, and offer me injurie, and that I
called one of thy companions to helpe me, and he should
ryse to take my parte, and anger thee : wouldest thou
therefore put him out of his office ? It is reported that
Tiberius was so gravelled with this question, that though
he was one of the readiest speakers, and the boldest in his
orations of any man : yet at that tyme he held his peace,
and had no power to speake, and therefore he presently
dismissed the assemblie. Afterwards, understanding that of
al the things he did, the deposing of Octavius from his office
was thought (not onely of the nobilitie, but of the common
people also) as fowle and wilfull a parte as ever he played,
for that thereby he had imbased, and utterly overthrowen
the dignitie of the Tribunes, the which was alwayes had in
great veneration untill that present tyme : to excuse him
selfe therefore, he made an excellent oration to the people,
whereby shall appeare unto you some special poyntes thereof,
to discerne the better the force and effect of his eloquence.

The oration
of Tiberius
Gracchus,
touching the
power and
authoritie
of the
Tribune.

‘ The Tribuneship sayd he, in deede was a holy and sacred
‘ thing, as perticularly consecrated to the people, and estab-
‘ lished for their benefit and safetie : where contrariwise, if
‘ the Tribune doe offer the people any wronge, he thereby
‘ minisheth their power, and taketh away the meanes from
‘ them to declare their wills by voyces, besides that, he doth
‘ also imbase his owne authoritie, leaving to doe the thing for
‘ the which his authority first was given him. Or otherwise
‘ we could not choose but suffer a Tribune, if it pleased him,
‘ to overthrow the Capitoll, or to set fire on the arsenall : and
‘ yet notwithstanding this wicked part, if it were committed,
‘ he should be Tribune of the people still, though a lewde
‘ Tribune. But when he goeth about to take away the
‘ authoritie and power of the people, then he is no more a
‘ Tribune. Were not this against all reason, thinke you,
‘ that a Tribune when he list, may take a Consul, and
‘ commit him to prison : and that the people should not
‘ withstand the authoritie of the Tribune, who gave him the
‘ same, when he would use his authoritie to the prejudice

250

' of the people? for the people are they that doe choose,
' both Consul and Tribune. Furthermore, the kingly dignitie
' (bicause in the same is conteyned the absolute authoritie
' and power of all other kindes of Magistrates and offices
' together) is consecrated with very great and holy cere-
' monies, drawing very neare unto the godhed: and yet the
' people expulsed king Tarquin, bicause he used his autho-
' ritie with crueltie, and for the injurie he offered one man
' onely, the most aunciente rule and government, (by the
' which the foundacion of Rome was first layed) was utterly
' abolished. And who is there in all the citie of Rome to
' be reckoned so holy as the Vestall Nunnes, which have the
' custodie and keeping of the everlasting fire? and yet if
' any of these be taken in fornication, she is buried alive for
' her offence: for when they are not holy to the goddes,
' they lose the libertie they have, in respect of serving the
' goddes. Even so also it is unmeete, that the Tribune if
' he offend the people, should for the peoples sake be rever-
' enced any more: seeing that through his owne folly he
' hath deprived him selfe of that authoritie they gave him.
' And if it be so that he was chosen Tribune by the most
' parte of the trybes of the people: then by greater reason
' is he justly deprived, that by all the whole trybes together
' is forsaken and deposed. There is nothing more holy nor
' inviolate, then thinges offered up unto the goddes: and
' yet it was never seene that any man did forbid the people
' to take them, to remove and transport them from place
' to place, as they thought good. Even so, they may as
' lawfully transferre the office of the Tribune unto any
' other, as any other offring consecrated to the goddes.
' Furthermore, it is manifest that any Officer or Magistrate
' may lawfully depose him selfe: for, it hath bene often
' seene, that men in office have deprived them selves, or
' otherwise have sued to be discharged.' This was the effect
of Tiberius purgation. Now his friendes perceiving the
threats the riche and noble men gave out against him,
they wished him for the safetie of his person, to make
sute to be Tribune againe the next yeare. Whereuppon
he began to flatter the common people againe afresh, by

new lawes which he preferred: by the which he tooke
away the time and number of yeares prescribed, when every
citizen of Rome was bound to goe to the warres being called,
and his name billed. He made it lawfull also for men to
appeale from sentence of the Iudges unto the people, and
thrust in also amongst the Senators (which then had absolute
authoritie to judge among them selves) a like number of the
Romane Knightes, and by this meanes sought to weaken and
imbase the authority of the Senate, increasing also the power
of the people, more of malice then any reason, or for any
justice or benefit to the common wealth. Furthermore, when
it came to the gathering of the voyces of the people for the
confirmacion of his new lawes, finding that his enemies were
the stronger in the assembly, bicause all the people were not
yet come together: he fell a quarrelling with his brethren
the Tribunes, alwayes to winne time, and yet in the end
brake up the assembly, commaunding them to returne the
next morning. There he would be the first man in the
market place apparelled all in blacke, his face beblubbered
with teares, and looking heavely upon the matter, praying
the people assembled to have compassion upon him, saying,
that he was affrayed least his enemies would come in the
night, and overthrow his house to kill him. Thereupon the
people were so moved withall, that many of them came and
brought their tentes, and lay about his house to watche it.

Unluckie
signes unto
Tiberius.
At the breake of the day, the keeper of the chickins, by
signes of the which they doe divine of thinges to come,
brought them unto him, and cast them downe meate before
them. None of them would come out of the cage but one
only, and yet with much a doe, shaking the cage· and when
it came out, it would eate no meate, but only lift up her left
wing, and put forth her legge, and so ranne into the cage
againe. This signe made Tiberius remember an other he
had had before. He had a marvelous fayer helmet and very
riche, which he ware in the warres: under it were crept two
snakes unwares to any, and layed egges, and hatched them.
This made Tiberius wonder the more, bicause of the ill signes
of the chickins: notwithstanding, he went out of his house,
when he heard that the people were assembled in the Capitoll,

but as he went out, he hit his foote such a blow against a stone at the thresshold of the dore, that he brake the nayle of his great toe, which fell in suche a bleeding, that it bled through his shooe. Againe, he had not gone farre, but he saw upon the toppe of a house on his left hand, a couple of ravens fighting together: and notwithstanding that there past a great number of people by, yet a stone which one of these ravens cast from them, came and fell hard at Tiberius foote. The fall thereof staied the stowtest man he had about him. But Blossius the Philosopher of Cumes that did accompany him, told him it were a great shame for him, and enough to kill the harts of all his followers: that Tiberius being the sonne of Gracchus, and nephew of Scipio the African, and the chiefe man besides of all the peoples side, for feare of a raven, should not obey his citizens that called him: and how that his enemies and ill willers would not make a laughing sporte of it, but would plainly tell the people that this was a tricke of a tyran that raigned in dede, and that for pride and disdaine did abuse the peoples good wills. Furthermore, divers messengers came unto him, and sayd that his frends that were in the Capitoll, sent to pray him to make hast, for all went well with him. When he came thither, he was honorably received: for the people seeing him comming, cried out for joy to welcome him, and when he was gotten up to his feate, they shewed them selves both carefull and loving towardes him, looking warely that none came neere him, but such as they knew well. While Mutius beganne againe to call the tribes of the people to geve their voyces, he could not procede according to the accustomed order in the like case, for the great noyse the hindmost people made, thrusting forward, and being driven backe, and one mingling with an other. In the meane time, Flavius Flaccus, one of the Senators, got up into a place where all the people might see him, and when he saw that his voyce coulde not be heard of Tiberius, he made a signe with his hande that he had some matter of great importance to tell him. Tiberius straight bad them make a lane through the prease. So, with much a doe, Flavius came at length unto him, and tolde him, that the riche men in open Senate,

Flavius Flaccus bewraieth the conspiracy against Tiberius.

when they could not frame the Consull to their wills, determined them selves to come and kill him, having a great
number of their frendes, and bondmen armed for the purpose.
Tiberius immediatly declared this conspiracy unto his frends
and followers: who straight girte their long gownes unto
them, and brake the sergeaunts javelins which they caried
in their handes to make roome among the people, and tooke
the tronchions of the same to resist those that would set apon
them. The people also that stoode furdest of, marveled at
it, and asked what the matter was. Tiberius by a signe to
tell them the daunger he was in, layed both his hands on his
head, bicause they coulde not heare his voyce for the great
noyse they made. His enemies seeing the signe he gave,
ranne presently to the Senate, crying out, that Tiberius
required a royall bande or diadeame of the people, and that
it was an evident signe, bicause they sawe him clappe his
handes apon his head. This tale troubled all the companie.
Whereupon Nasica besought the Consul, chiefe of the Senate,
to help the common wealth, and to take away this tyran.
The Consul gently aunswered againe, that he would use no
force, neither put any citizen to death, but lawfully condemned: as also he would not receive Tiberius, nor protect
him, if the people by his perswasion or commaundement,
should commit any acte contrarie to the law. Nasica then

rising in anger, Sith the matter is so, sayd he, that the
Consull regardeth not the common wealth: all you then,
that will defende the authoritie of the law, follow me.
Thereupon he cast the skirt of his gowne over his head, and
went straight to the Capitoll. They that followed him also
tooke their gownes, and wrapt them about their armes, and
layed at as many as they might, to make them geve way:
and yet very few of the people durst meete with such states
as they were to stay them, bicause they were the chiefest men
of the citie, but every man flying from them, they fell one
on an others necke for hast They that followed them, had
brought from home great leavers and clubbes, and as they
went, they tooke up feete of trestles and chaires which the
people had overthrowen and broken, running away, and hyed
them a pace to meete with Tiberius, striking at them that

stoode in their way: so that in short space they had dispersed all the common people, and many were slaine flying. Tiberius seeing that, betooke him to his legges to save him selfe, but as he was flying, one tooke him by the gowne, and stayed him: but he leaving his gowne behinde him, ranne in his coate, and running fell upon them that were downe before. So, as he was rising up againe, the first man that strake him, and that was plainly seene strike him, was one of the Tribunes his brethren, called Publius Satureius: who gave him a great rappe on the head with the foote of a chaire, and the second blow he had, was geven him by Lucius Rufus that boasted of it, as if he had done a notable acte. In this tumult, there were slaine above three hundred men, and were all killed with staves and stones, and not one man hurt with any iron. This was the first sedition among the citizens of Rome, that fell out with murder, and bloodshed, since the expulsion of the kinges. But for all other former dissentions (which were no trifles) they were easily pacified, either partie geving place to other: the Senate for feare of the commoners, and the people for reverence they bare to the Senate. And it seemeth, that Tiberius him selfe woulde easely have yeelded also, if they had proceeded by faire meanes and perswasion, so they had ment good faith, and would have killed no man: for at that time he had not in all, above 3000 men of the people about him. But surely it seemes this conspiracie was executed against him, more for very spite and malice the rich men did beare him, then for any other apparant cause they presupposed against him. For proofe hereof may be alleaged, the barbarous cruelty they used to his body being dead. For they would not suffer his owne brother to have his bodie to burie it by night, who made earnest sute unto them for it: but they threw him amongest the other bodies into the river, and yet this was not the worst. For, some of his frends they banished without forme of law, and others they put to death, which they coulde meete withall. Among the which, they slue Diophanes the Orator, and one Caius Billius, whom they inclosed in a pype among snakes and serpentes, and put him to death in this sorte. Blossius also the Philosopher of Cumes, was brought before the Consuls,

TIBERIUS AND CAIUS GRACCHI

Tiberius Gracchus the Tribune slaine

Tiberius frends slaine.

The cruell death of Caius Billius.

255

and examined about this matter: who boldly confessed
unto them, that he did as much as Tiberius commaunded
him.   When Nasica did aske him, And what if he had commaunded thee to set fire on the Capitoll? he made him
aunswere, that Tiberius would never have geven him any
suche commaundement.   And when divers others also were
still in hand with him about that question: But if he had
commaunded thee? I would sure have done it, said he: for
he would never have commaunded me to have done it, if it
had not bene for the commoditie of the people.   Thus he
scaped at that time, and afterwards fled into Asia unto Aristonicus, whom misfortune having overthrowen, he slue him
selfe.   Now, the Senate to pacifie the people at that present
time, did no more withstand the law Agraria, for division of
the lands of the common wealth, but suffered the people to
appoint an other Commissioner for that purpose, in Tiberius
place.   Thereupon Publius Crassus was chosen, being allied
unto Tiberius, for Caius Gracchus (Tiberius brother) had
maried his daughter Licinia.   Yet Cornelius Nepos sayth,
that it was not Crassus daughter, Caius maried, but the
daughter of Brutus, that triumphed for the Lusitanians.
Howbeit the best wryters and authority, agree with that
we wryte.   But whatsoever was done, the people were marvelously offended with his death, and men might easely per-
ceive, that they looked but for time and oportunity to be
revenged, and did presently threaten Nasica to accuse him.
Whereupon the Senate fearing some trouble towards him,
devised a way upon no occasion, to sende him into Asia.
For the common people did not dissemble the malice they
bare him when they met him, but were verie round with
him, and called him tyran, and murderer, excommunicate,
and wicked man, that had imbrued his hands in the blood
of the holy Tribune, and within the most sacred temple of
all the citie.   So in the ende he was inforced to forsake
Rome, though by his office he was bounde to solemnise all
the greatest sacrifices, bicause he was then chiefe Bishoppe
of Rome   Thus, travelling out of his contrie like a meane
man, and troubled in his minde: he dyed shortly after, not
farre from the citie of Pergamum.   Truely it is not greatly

GRECIANS AND ROMANES

to be wondred at, though the people so much hated Nasica,
considering that Scipio the African him selfe (whom the
people of Rome for juster causes had loved better then any
man else whatsoever) was like to have lost all the peoples
good wils they bare him, bicause that being at the siege of
Numantia, when newes was brought him of Tiberius death,
he rang out this verse of Homer.

> Such end upon him ever light,
> Which in such doings doth delight.

Scipioes sentence of the death of Tiberius Gracchus.

Furthermore, being asked in thassembly of the people, by
Caius, and Fulvius, what he thought of Tiberius death : he
aunswered them, that he did not like his doinges. After
that the people handled him very churlishly, and did ever
breake of his oration, which they never did before : and he
him self also would revile the people even in the assembly.
Now Caius Gracchus at the first, bicause he feared the
enemies of his deade brother, or otherwise for that he
sought meanes to make them more hated of the people : he
absented him selfe for a time out of the common assembly,
and kept at home and meddled not, as a man contented
to live meanely, without busying him selfe in the common
wealth : insomuch as he made men thinke and reporte both,
that he did utterly mislike those matters which his brother
had preferred. Howbeit he was then but a young man, and
nine yeares younger then his brother Tiberius, who was not
thirty yeare old when he was slaine. But in processe of
time, he made his manners and condicions (by litle and litle)
appeare, who hated sloth and curiositie, and was least of all
geven unto any covetous minde of getting : for he gave him
selfe to be eloquent, as preparing him wings afterwardes to
practise in the common wealth. So that it appeared plainely,
that when time came, he would not stand still, and looke on.
When one Vectius a frende of his was sued, he tooke apon
him to defend his cause in courte. The people that were
present, and heard him speake, they leaped for joy to see
him : for he had such an eloquent tongue, that all the
Orators besides were but children to him. Hereuppon the
riche men began to be affrayed againe, and whispered among

Caius Gracchus maners.

5 KK

TIBERIUS
AND CAIUS
GRACCHI

Caius
Gracchus
Quæstor in
Sardinia.

them selves, that it behoved them to beware he came not to be Tribune. It chaunced so that he was chosen Treasorer, and it was his fortune to goe into the Ile of Sardinia, with the Consul Orestes. His enemies were glad of that, and he him selfe was not sory for it. For he was a martiall man, and as skilfull in armes, as he was else an excellent Orator : but yet he was affrayed to come into the pulpit for Orations, and misliked to deale in matters of state, albeit he could not altogether deny the people, and his frends that prayed his furtherance. For this cause therfore he was very glad of this voyage, that he might absent him selfe for a time out of Rome : though divers were of opinion, that he was more popular, and desirous of the common peoples good will and favor, then his brother had bene before him. But in deede he was cleane contrarie for it appeared that at the first he was drawen rather against his will, then of any speciall desire he had to deale in the common wealth. Cicero the Orator also sayth, that Caius was bent altogether to flie from office in the common wealth, and to live quietly as a privat man. But Tiberius (Caius brother) appeared to him in his sleepe, and calling him by his name, sayd unto him : Brother, why doest thou prolong time, for thou canst not possiblie escape? For we were both predestined to one maner of life and death, for procuring the benefite of the people. Now when Caius arrived in Sardinia, he shewed all the proofes that might be in a valliant man, and excelled all the young men of his age, in hardines against his enemies, in justice to his inferiors, and in love and obedience towards the Consul his Captaine : but in temperaunce, sobrietie, and in painfulnes, he excelled all them that were elder then he. The winter by chaunce fell out very sharpe, and full of sickenes in Sardinia : whereupon the Consul sent unto the cities to helpe his souldiers with some clothes : but the townes sent in poste to Rome, to pray the Senate they might be discharged of that burden. The Senate found their allegacion reasonable, whereuppon they wrote to the Consul to finde some other meanes to clothe his people. The Consul coulde make no other shift for them, and so the poore souldiers in the meane time smarted for it. But Caius Gracchus went

Caius
Gracchus
vision and
dreame.

258

GRECIANS AND ROMANES

him selfe unto the cities and so perswaded them, that they of them selves sent to the Romanes campe such thinges as they lacked. This being caried to Rome, it was thought straight it was a pretie beginning to creepe into the peoples favor, and in dede it made the Senate also affrayed. In the necke of that, there arrived Ambassadors of Africke at Rome, sent from king Micipsa, who told the Senate that the king their maister, for Caius Gracchus sake, had sent their armie corne into Sardinia. The Senators were so offended withall, that they thrust the Ambassadours out of the Senate, and so gave order that other souldiers shoulde be sent in their places that were in Sardinia: and that Orestes should still remaine Consul there, meaning also to continue Caius their Treasorer. But when he hearde of it, he straight tooke sea, and returned to Rome in choller. When men saw Caius returned to Rome unlooked for, he was reproved for it not onely by his enemies, but by the common people also: who thought his returne verie straunge before his Captaine, under whom he was Treasorer. He being accused hereof before the Censors, prayed he might be heard. So, aunswering his accusation, he so turned the peoples mindes that heard him, that they all sayd he had open wrong. For he told them, that he had served twelve yeares in the warres, where others were enforced to remaine but ten yeres: and that he had continued Treasorer under his Captaine, the space of three yeares, where the law gave him libertie to returne at the end of the yeare. And that he alone of all men else that had bene in the warres, had caried his purse full, and brought it home empty: where others having dronke the wyne which they caried thither in vessells, had afterwardes brought them home full of gold and silver. Afterwards they went about to accuse him as accessarie to a conspiracie, that was revealed in the citie of Fregelles. But having cleared all that suspicion, and being discharged, he presently made sute to be Tribune: wherein he had all the men of qualitie his sworne enemies. On thother side also he had so great favor of the common people, that there came men out of all partes of Italie to be at his election, and that such a number of them, as there was no lodging to be had for them all. Furthermore, the field of Mars not being large enough to hold such a multitude of people, there were that gave their voyces upon the toppe of houses. Nowe the noble men coulde no otherwise let the people of their will, nor prevent Caius of his hope, but where he thought to be the first Tribune, he was only pronounced the

fourth. But when he was once possest officer, he became immediatly the chiefe man, bicause he was as eloquent as any man of his time. And furthermore, he had a large occasion of calamity offred him: which made him bolde to speake, bewailing the death of his brother. For what matters soever he spake of, he always fell in talke of that, remembring them what matters had passed: and laying before them the examples of their auncesters: who in olde time had made warre with the Phalisces, by the meanes of one Genutius Tribune of the people, unto whom they had offered injurie: who also did condemne Caius Veturius to death, bicause that he onely woulde not geve a Tribune place, comming through the market place. Where these sayd he, that standing before you in sight, have slaine my brother Tiberius with staves, and have dragged his bodie from the mount of the Capitoll, all the citie over, to throw it into the river: and with him also have most cruellie slaine all his frendes they coulde come by, without any lawe or justice at all. And yet by an auncient custome of long time observed in this citie of Rome, when any man is accused of treason, and that of duety he must appeare at the time appointed him: they doe notwithstanding in the morning sende a trompet to his house, to summone him to appeare: and moreover the Iudges were not wont to condemne him, before this ceremony was performed: so carefull and respective were our predecessors, where it touched the life of any Romane. Now Caius having first stirred up the people with these perswasions (for he had a marvelous lowde voyce) he preferred two lawes.

The first, that he that had once bene put out of office by the people, should never after be capable of any other office.

The seconde, that if any Consul had banished any citizen

without lawefull accusation, the sentence and hearing of the matter should perteine to the people.

The first of these two lawes did plainly defame Octavius, whom Tiberius his brother had by the people deposed from the Tribunshippe. The seconde also touched Popilius, who being Prætor, had banished his brother Tiberius frendes: whereuppon he stayed not the triall, but willingly exiled him selfe out of Italie. And touching the first law, Caius him selfe did afterwards revoke it, declaring unto the people, that he had saved Octavius at the request of his mother Cornelia. The people were verie glad of it, and confirmed it, honoring her no lesse for respect of her sonnes, then also for Scipioes sake her father. For afterwards they cast her image in brasse, and set it up with this inscription: 'Cornelia the mother of the Gracchi.' Many common matters are found written touching Cornelia his mother, and eloquently pleaded in her behalfe, by Caius against her adversaries. As when he sayd unto one of them: How darest thou presume to speake evill of Cornelia, that had Tiberius to her sonne? And the other partie also that slandered her, being sorely suspected for a Sodomite: And art thou so impudent, sayd he, to shew thy face before Cornelia? Hast thou brought foorth children as she hath done? And yet it is wel knowen to all men in Rome, that she being but a woman, hath lived longer without a man, than thou that art a man. Thus were Caius words sharpe and stinging, and many such like are to be gathered out of his wrytinges. Furthermore he made many other lawes afterwardes to increase the peoples authoritie, and to imbase the Senates greatnes.

The first was, for the restoring of the Colonies to Rome, in dividing the landes of the common wealth unto the poore citizens that should inhabite there.

The other, that they shoulde apparell the souldiers at the charge of the common wealth, and that it should not be deducted out of their paye: and also, that no citizen should be billed to serve in the warres, under seventeene yeares of age at the least.

An other law was, for their confederats of Italie: that through all Italie they shoulde have as free voyces in the election of any Magistrate, as the naturall citizens of Rome it selfe.

An other setting a reasonable price of the corne that should be distributed unto the poore people.

An other touching judgement, whereby he did greatly minish the authority of the Senate. For before, the Senators were onely Iudges of all matters, the which made them to be the more honored and feared of the people, and the Romane Knights : and now he joyned three hundred Romane Knights unto the other three hundred Senators, and brought it so to passe, that all matters judiciall shoulde be equally judged, among those six hundred men   After he had passed this law, it is reported he was verie curious in observing all other thinges, but this one thing specially : that where all other Orators speaking to the people turned them towards the pallace where the Senators sate, and to that side of the market place which is called Comitium : he in contrarie manner when he made his Oration, turned him outwardes towardes the other side of the market place, and after that kept it constantly, and never failed. Thus, by a litle turning and altering of his looke only, he removed a great matter. For he so transferred all the government of the common wealth from the Senate, unto the judgement of the people : to teach the Orators by his example, that in their Orations they should behold the people, not the Senate.

Now, the people having not only confirmed the law he made touching the Iudges, but geven him also full power and authoritie to choose amonge the Romane Knightes suche Iudges as he liked of : he founde thereby he had absolute power in his owne hands, insomuche as the Senators them selves did aske counsell of him. So did he ever geve good counsell, and did preferre matters meete for their honor. As amongest others, the lawe he made touching certaine wheate that Fabius Viceprætor had sent out of Spayne : which was a good and honorable acte. He perswaded the Senate that the corne might be solde, and so to send backe againe the money therof unto the townes and cities from whence the corne came : and therewithall to punish Fabius for that he made the Empire of Rome hatefull and intoller-

GRECIANS AND ROMANES

matter wanne him great love and commendacion of all the
provinces subject to Rome. Furthermore, he made lawes
for the restoring of the decayed townes, for mending of
high wayes, for building of garners for provision of corne.
And to bring all these things to passe, he him selfe tooke
apon him the only care and enterprise, being never wearied
with any paines taken in ordering of so great affaires. For,
he followed all those thinges so earnestly and effectually, as
if he had had but one master in hand: insomuch that they
who most hated and feared him, wondred most to see his
diligence and quicke dispatche in matters. The people also
wondred muche to beholde him only, seeing alwaies suche a
number of laborers, artificers, Ambassadors, officers, souldiers,
and learned men, whom he easely satisfied and dispatched,
keping still his estate, and yet using great curtesie and
civilitie, entertaining every one of them privately: so that
he made his accusers to be found lyers, that said he was a
stately man, and very cruell. Thus he wanne the good will
of the common people, being more popular and familiar in
his conversation and deedes, then he was otherwise in his
Orations But the greatest paines and care he tooke apon
him was, in seeing the high wayes mended, the which he
woulde have as well done, as profitablie done. For he would
cast the cawcies by the lyne in the softest ground in the
fields, and then woulde pave them with hard stone, and
cast a great deale of gravell upon it, which he caused to
be brought thither. When he found any low or waterie
places which the rivers had eaten into, he raised them up,
or else made bridges over them, with an even height equall
to either side of the cawcie · so that all his worke caried a
goodly leavell withall even by the lyne or plummet, which
was a pleasure to beholde it. Furthermore, he devided
these high wayes by myles, every myle conteining eight
furlonges, and at every myles ende he set up a stone for a
marke. At either end also of these high wayes thus paved,
he set certaine stones of convenient height, a prety way a
sunder, to helpe the travellers by to take their horse backes
againe, without any helpe. The people for these things

TIBERIUS
AND CAIUS
GRACCHI
Other lawes
of Caius
Gracchus.

The Italian
myle con-
teineth eight
furlong.

263

highly praising and extolling him, and being readie to make shew of their love and good will to him any maner of way: he told them openly one day in his Oration, that he had a request to make unto them, the which if it would please them to graunt him, he woulde thinke they did him a marvelous pleasure: and if they denied him also, he cared not muche. Then everie man thought it was the Consulshippe he ment to aske, and that he woulde sue to be Tribune and Consul together. But when the day came to choose the Consuls, every man looking attentively what he would doe: they marveled when they sawe him come downe the fielde of Mars, and brought Caius Fannius with his frends, to further his sute for the Consulshippe. Therein he served Fannius turne, for he was presently chosen Consul: and Caius Gracchus was the seconde time chosen Tribune againe, not of his owne sute, but by the good will of the people. Caius perceiving that the Senators were his open enemies, and that Fannius the Consul was but a slacke frende unto him, he began againe to currie favor with the common people, and to preferre new lawes, setting forth the lawe of the Colonies, that they should send of the poore citizens to replenishe the cities of Tarentum and Capua, and that they should graunt all the Latines the freedom of Rome. The Senate perceiving his power grew great, and that in the end he would be so strong that they coulde not withstande him: they devised a new and straunge way to plucke the peoples good will from him, in graunting them things not altogether very honest. There was one of the Tribunes, a brother in office with Caius, called Livius Drusus, a man noblely borne, and as well brought up as any other Romane · who for wealth and eloquence was not inferior to the greatest men of estimacion in Rome. The chiefest Senators went unto him, and perswaded him to take parte with them against Caius, not to use any force or violence against the people to withstand them in any thing, but contrarily to graunt them those things which were more honestie for them to deny them with their ill will. Livius offering to pleasure the Senate with his authority, preferred lawes neither honorable nor profitable to the common wealth, and were to no other ende, but

contending with Caius, who should most flatter the people
of them two, as plaiers do in their common plaies, to shew
the people pastime. Wherby the Senate shewed, that they
did not so much mislike Caius doings, as for the desire they
had to overthrow him and his great credit with the people.
For where Caius preferred but the replenishing of the two
cities, and desired to send the honestest citizens thither:
they objected against him, that he did corrupt the common
people. On the other side also they favored Drusus, who
preferred a law that they should replenish twelve Colonies,
and should send to every one of them three thowsande of
the poorest citizens. And where they hated Caius for that
he had charged the poore citizens with an annual rent for
the lands that were devided unto them: Livius in contrary
maner did please them by disburdening them of that rent
and payment, letting them have the lands scotfree. Furthermore also, where Caius did anger the people, bicause he gave
all the Latines the fredom of Rome to geve their voyces in
choosing of Magistrates as freely as the naturall Romanes:
when Drusus on thother side had preferred a law that
thencefoorth no Romane should whip any souldier of the
Latines with rods to the warres, they liked the law, and
past it. Livius also in every law he put forth, said in all his
orations, that he did it by the counsell of the Senate, who
were very carefull for the profit of the people: and this was
all the good he did in his office unto the common wealth.
For by his meanes the people were better pleased with the
Senate, and where they did before hate all the noble men of
the Senate, Livius tooke away that malice, when the people
saw that all that he propounded, was for the preferment and
benefit of the common wealth, with the consent and further-
aunce of the Senate. The only thing also that perswaded
the people to thinke that Drusus ment uprightly, and that
he only respected the profit of the common people was:
that he never preferred any law for him selfe, or for his
owne benefit. For in the restoring of these Colonies which
he preferred, he alwaies sent other Commissioners, and gave
them the charge of it, and would never finger any money
him selfe: where Caius tooke apon him the charge and care

5 : LL

TIBERIUS
AND CAIUS
GRACCHI of all things him selfe, and specially of the greatest matters. Rubrius also an other Tribune, having preferred a law for the reedifying and replenishing of Carthage againe with people, the which Scipio had rased and destroyed: it was Caius happe to be appointed one of the Commissioners for it. Whereupon he tooke shippe, and sailed into Afrike. Drusus in the meane time taking occasion of his absence, did as much as might be to seeke the favor of the common people, and specially by accusing Fulvius, who was one of the best frends Caius had, and whom they had also chosen Commissioner with him for the division of these landes among the citizens, whom they sent to replenish these **Fulvius** Colonies. This Fulvius was a seditious man, and therefore **Commissioner** marvelously hated of the Senate, and withall suspected also **with Caius, a** of them that tooke parte with the people, that he secretly **veriesediotious** practised to make their confederats of Italie to rebell. But **man.** yet they had no evident proofe of it to justifie it against him, more then that which he himselfe did verifie, bicause he semed to be offended with the peace and quietnes they enjoyed. And this was one of the chiefest causes of Caius overthrow, bicause that Fulvius was partely hated for his **The death of** sake For when Scipio African was found dead one morning **Scipio African** in his house, without any manifest cause how he should **the lesse.** come to his death so sodainly: (saving that there appeared certaine blinde markes of stripes on his body that had bene geven him: as we have declared at large in his life) the most parte of the suspicion of his death was layed to Fulvius, being his mortall enemy, and bicause the same day they had bene at great wordes together in the pulpit for orations. So was Caius Gracchus also partly suspected for it. Howsoever it was, such a horrible murder as this, of so famous and worthy a man as any was in Rome, was yet notwithstanding never revenged, neither any inquirie made of it: bicause the common people would not suffer the accusacion to goe forward, fearing least Caius would be found in fault, if the matter should go forward. But this was a great while before. Now Caius at that time being in Africk about the reedifying and replenishing of the city of Carthage againe, the which he named Iunonia: the voyce goeth that

GRECIANS AND ROMANES

he had many ill signes and tokens appeared unto him. For
the staffe of his ensigne was broken with a vehement blast of
wind, and with the force of the ensigne bearer that held it
fast on thother side. There came a flaw of winde also that
caried away the sacrifices upon the aulters and blew them
quite out of the circuite which was marked out for the
compasse of the city. Furthermore, the woulves came and
tooke away the markes which they had set downe to limite
the bonds of their circuite, and caried him quite away.
This notwithstanding, Caius having dispatched all things
in the space of three score and ten daies, he returned incontinently to Rome, understanding that Fulvius was oppressed
by Drusus, and that those matters required his presence.
For Lucius Hostilius that was all in all for the nobility, and
a man of great credit with the Senate, being the yeare before
put by the Consulshippe, by Caius practise, who caused
Fannius to be chosen : he had good hope this yere to speede,
for the great number of frends that furthered his sute. So
that if he could obtaine it, he was fully bent to set Caius
beside the saddle, and the rather, bicause his estimacion and
countenaunce he was wont to have among the people, began
now to decay, for that they were ful of such devises as his
were : bicause there were divers others that preferred the
like to please the people withal, and yet with the Senates
great good will and favor. So Caius being returned to
Rome, he removed from his house, and where before he
dwelt in mount Palatine, he came now to take a house
under the market place, to shew him selfe therby the lowlier
and more popular, bicause many of the meaner sorte of
people dwelt thereaboutes. Then he purposed to goe forward with the rest of his lawes, and to make the people to
establish them, a great number of people repairing to Rome
out of all parts for the furtherance thereof. Howbeit the
Senate counselled the Consul Fannius to make proclamacion,
that al those which were no natural Romanes, resident and
abiding within the city self of Rome · that they should
depart out of Rome. Besides all this, there was a straunge
proclamacion made, and never seene before · that none of all
the frends and confederats of the Romanes, for certaine daies

Unluckie
signes ap-
pearing unto
Caius.

This man
is named
afterwardes
Opimius.

should come into Rome. But Caius on the thother side set up bills on every post, accusing the Consul for making so wicked a proclamacion : and further, promised the confederates of Rome to aide them, if they would remaine there against the Consuls proclamacion. But yet he performed it not. For when he saw one of Fannius sergeaunts cary a frend of his to prison, he held on his way, and would see nothing, neither did he helpe him : either of likelyhoode bicause he feared his credit with the people, which began to decay, or else bicause he was loth (as he said) to picke any quarrell with his enemies, which sought it of him. Furthermore, he chaunced to fall at variance with his brethren the Tribunes, about this occasion. The people were to see the pastime of the sword plaiers or fensers at the sharp, within the very market place, and there were divers of the officers that to see the sport, did set up scaffoldes rounde about, to take money for the standing. Caius commaunded them to take them downe again, bicause the poore men might see the sport without any cost. But not a man of them would yeeld to it. Wherefore he staid till the night before the pastime should be, and then he tooke all his laborers he had under him, and went and overthrew the scaffolds every one of them : so that the next morning all the market place was clere for the common people, to see the pastime at their pleasure. For this fact of his, the people thanked him marvelously, and tooke him for a worthie man. Howbeit his brethren the Tribunes were very much offended with him, and tooke him for a bold presumptuous man. This seemeth to be the chiefe cause why he was put from his third Tribuneship, where he had the most voices of his side : bicause his colleagues, to be revenged of the part he had plaied them, of malice and spight, made false report of the voices. Howbeit there is no great troth in this. It is true that he was very angry with this repulse, and it is reported he spake somwhat too prowdly to his enemies, that were mery with the matter, and laughed him to scorne : that they laughed a Sardonians laugh, not knowing how darkely his deedes had wrapt them in. Furthermore, his enemies having chosen Opimius Consul, they began imme-

268

diatly to revoke divers of Caius lawes: as among the rest,
his doings at Carthage for the reedifying of that city, procuring thus all the waies they could to anger him, bicause
they might have just occasion of anger to kil him. Caius
notwithstanding did paciently beare it at the first: but
afterwards his frends, and specially Fulvius, did encorage
him so, that he began againe to gather men to resist the
Consul. And it is reported also, that Cornelia his mother did
help him in it, secretly hyring a great number of straungers
which she sent unto Rome, as if they had bene reapers or
harvest men. And this is that she wrote secretly in her
letter, unto her sonne in ciphers. And yet other write to the
contrary, that she was very angry he did attempt those things.
When the day came that they should proceede to the re- Sedition be-
vocation of his lawes, both parties met by breake of day at twext Caius
the Capitoll. There when the Consul Opimius had done Gracchus and
sacrifice, one of Caius sergeaunts called Quintus Antyllius, the Senate.
carying the intrals of the beast sacrificed, said unto Fulvius,
and others of his tribe that were about him: Give place to
honest men, vile citizens that ye be. Some say also, that
besides these injurious wordes, in skorne and contempt he
held out his naked arme to make them ashamed. Where- Antillius,
upon they slue him presently in the field with great botkins C. Gracchus
to wryte with, which they had purposely made for that sergeaunt
intent. Hereupon the common people were marvelously slaine.
offended for this murther, and the chiefe men of both sides
also were diversly affected. For Caius was very sory for it,
and bitterly reproved them that were about him, saying,
that they had given their enemies the occasion they looked
for, to set upon them. Opimius the Consul in contrary
maner, taking this occasion, rose apon it, and did stirre
up the people to be revenged. But there fell a shower of
raine at that time that parted them. The next morning
the Consul having assembled the Senate by breake of day,
as he was dispatching causes within, some had taken the
body of Antyllius and layed it naked upon the beere, and
so caried it through the market place (as it was agreed
upon before amongst them) and brought it to the Senate
dore: where they began to make great mone and lamen-

tacion, Opimius knowing the meaning of it, but yet he dissembled it, and seemed to wonder at it. Wherupon the Senators went out to see what it was, and finding this beere, in the market place, some fell a weeping for him that was dead, others cried out that it was a shamefull act, and in no wise to be suffred. But on the other side, this did revive the old grudge and malice of the people, for the wickednes of the ambitious noble men : who having themselves before slaine Tiberius Gracchus that was Tribune, and within the Capitoll it selfe, and had also cast his body into the river, did now make an honorable show openly in the market place, of the body of a sergeaunt Antyllius (who though he were wrongfully slaine, yet had himselfe geven them the cause that slue him, to do that they did) and all the whole Senate were about the beere to bewaile his death, and to honor the funeralls of a hyerling, to make the people also kill him, that was only left the protector and defender of the people. After this, they went againe unto the Capitoll, and there made a decree, wherby they gave the Consul Opimius extraordinary power and authority, by absolute power to provide for the safety of the common wealth, to preserve the city, and to suppresse the tyrans. This decree being established, the Consul presently commaunded the Senators that were present there, to go arme them selves : and appointed the Romane Knights, that the next morning betimes every man should bring two of their men armed with them. Fulvius on the other side, he prepared his force against them, and assembled the common people together. Caius also returning from the market place, stayd before the image of his father, and looked earnestly apon it without ever a word speaking, only he burst out a weeping, and fetching a great sigh, went his way. This made the people to pitie him that saw him · so that they talked among them selves, that they were but beasts and cowards at such a straight to forsake so worthy a man. Therupon they went to his house, stayed there all night and watched before his gate : not as they did that watched with Fulvius, that passed away the night in guseling and drinking drunke, crying out, and making noyse, Fulvius him selfe being dronke first

of all, who both spake and did many thinges farre unmeete
for his calling. For they that watched Caius on thother
side, were very sorowfull, and made no noyse, even as in a
common calamitie of their contrie, devising with them selves
what would fall out apon it, waking, and sleeping one after
an other by turnes. When the day brake, they with Fulvius
did awake him, who slept yet soundly for the wine he dranke
over night, and they armed them selves with the spoiles of
the Gaules that hong rounde about his house, whom he had
overcome in battell the same yeare he was Consul · and with
great cries, and thundering threats, they went to take the
mount Aventine. But Caius would not arme him selfe, but
went out of his house in a long gowne, as if he woude have
gone simply into the market place according to his wonted
maner, saving that he caried a short dagger at his girdel
under his gowne. So as he was going out of his house, his
wife stayed him at the dore, and holding him by the one
hand, and a litle child of his in her other hand, she sayd
thus unto him: 'Alas Caius, thou doest not now goe as The words
' thou wert wont, a Tribune into the market place to speake of Licinia to
' to the people, neither to preferre any new lawes: neither her husband
' doest thou goe unto an honest warre, that if unfortunately Gracchus.
' that shoulde happen to thee that is common to all men, I
' might yet at the least mourne for thy death with honor.
' But thou goest to put thy selfe into bloodie butchers
' handes, who most cruelly have slaine thy brother Tiberius:
' and yet thou goest, a naked man unarmed, intending rather
' to suffer, then to doe hurt. Besides, thy death can bring
' no benefit to the common wealth. For the worser part
' hath now the upper hand, considering that sentence passeth
' by force of sword. Had thy brother bene slaine by his
' enemies, before the citie of Numantia: yet had they geven
' us his bodie to have buried him. But such may be my
' misfortune, that I may presently go to pray the river or
' sea to geve me thy bodie, which as thy brothers they have
' likewise throwen into the same. Alas, what hope or trust
' is left us now, in lawes or gods, sithence they have slaine
' Tiberius?' As Licinia was making this pitiefull mone unto
him, Caius fayer and softly pulled his hand from her, and

left her, geving her never a word, but went on with his frends. But she reaching after him to take him by the gowne, fell to the ground, and lay flatling there a great while, speaking never a word: untill at length her servaunts tooke her up in a swoone, and caried her so unto her brother Crassus. Now Fulvius, by the perswasion of Caius, when all their faction were met: sent his younger sonne (which was a prety fayer boy) with a Heraulds rodde in his hand for his safetie. This boy humbly presenting his duetie, with the teares in his eyes, before the Consul and Senate, offred them peace. The most of them that were present thought verie well of it. But Opimius made aunswere saying, that it became them not to send messengers, thinking with fayer wordes to winne the Senate: but it was their duetie to come them selves in persons, like subjects and offendors to make their triall, and so to crave pardon, and to seeke to pacifie the wrath of the Senate. Then he commaunded the boy he should not returne againe to them, but with this condicion he had prescribed. Caius (as it is reported) was ready to go and cleare him selfe unto the Senate: but the residue would not suffer him to go. Wheruppon Fulvius sent his sonne backe againe unto them, to speake for them as he had done before But Opimius that was desirous to fight, caused the boy to be taken, and committed him in safe custodie, and then went presently against Fulvius with a great number of footemen well armed, and of Cretan archers besides: who with their arrowes did more trouble and hurt their enemies, then with any thing else, that within a while they all began to flie Fulvius on the other side fled into an old hottehouse that no body made reckoning of, and there being found shortly after, they slue him, and his eldest sonne. Now for Caius, he fought not at all, but being mad with him selfe, and grieved to see such bloodshed: he got him into the temple of Diana, where he would have killed him selfe, had not his very good frends Pomponius and Licinius saved him. For both they being with him at that time, tooke his sword from him, and counselled him to flie. It is reported that then he fell downe on his knees, and holding up both his hands unto the goddesse, he besought

Fulvius sent
his sonne to
the Consull
with a
Heraulds
rodde to offer
peace.

The death of
Fulvius and
his eldest
sonne.

her that the people might never come out of bondage, to
be revenged of this their ingratitude and treason. For the
common people (or the most parte of them) plainly turned
their coats, when they heard proclamacion made, that all
men had pardon graunted them, that woulde returne. So
Caius fled apon it, and his enemies followed him so neere,
that they overtooke him apon the wodden bridge, where
two of his frends that were with him stayed, to defende him
against his followers, and bad him in the meane time make
shift for him selfe, whilest they fought with them apon the
bridge: and so they did, and kept them that not a man got
the bridge of them, untill they were both slaine. Nowe
there was none that fled with Caius, but one of his men
called Philocrates: notwithstanding, everie man did still encorage and counsell him, as they do men to winne a game,
but no man would helpe him, nor offer him any horse, though
he often required it, bicause he sawe his enemies so neere
unto him. This notwithstanding, by their defence that were
slaine apon the bridge, he got ground on them so, that he
had leasure to crepe into a litle grove of wodde which was
consecrated to the furies. There his servaunt Philocrates
slue him, and then slue him selfe also, and fell dead upon
him. Other write notwithstanding, that both the maister
and servaunt were overtaken, and taken alive: and that his
servaunt did so straight imbrace his maister that none of the
enemies could strike him for all the blowes they gave, before
he was slaine him selfe. So one of the murderers strake of
Caius Gracchus head to carie to the Consul. Howbeit one
of Opimius frendes called Septimuleius, tooke the head from
the other by the way, bicause proclamacion was made before
they fought by trompet, that whosoever brought the heades
of Fulvius and Caius, they should be payed the weight of
them in gold. Wherefore this Septimuleius caried Caius
head upon the toppe of his speare unto Opimius: whereuppon the skales being brought to wey it, it was found that
it weyed seventeene pounde weight and two third partes of
a pound, bicause Septimuleius besides the horrible murder
he had committed, had also holpen it with this villanie, that
he had taken out his braine, and in liew thereof had filled

TIBERIUS
AND CAIUS
GRACCHI his scull with lead. Now the other also that brought Fulvius head, bicause they were poore men, they had nothing. The bodies of these two men, Caius Gracchus and Fulvius, and of other their followers (which were to the number of three thowsand that were slaine) were all throwen into the river, their goods confiscate, and their widowes forbidden to mourne for their death. Furthermore, they tooke from Licinia Caius wife, her joynter: but yet they delt more cruelly and beastly with the young boy, Fulvius sonne: who had neither lift up his hand against them, nor was in the fight among them, but only came to them to make peace before they fought, whom they kept as prisoner, and after the battell ended,
The temple of
concord built
by Opimius
the Consul. they put him to death. But yet that which most of all other grieved the people, was the temple of concorde, the which Opimius caused to be built: for it appeared that he boasted, and in maner triumphed, that he had slaine so many citizens of Rome. And therefore there were that in the night wrote under the inscription of the temple these verses:

A furious fact and full of beastly shame,
This temple built, that beareth concordes name.

Opimius the
first Consul,
usurping the
power of the
Dictator. This Opimius was the first man at Rome, that being Consul, usurped the absolute power of the Dictator: and that without law or justice condemned three thowsand citizens of Rome, besides Fulvius Flaccus, (who had also bene Consul, and had received the honor of triumphe) and Caius Gracchus a young man in like case, who in vertue and reputacion excelled all the men of his yeares. This notwithstanding, coulde not keepe Opimius from theverie
Opimius
bribed with
money of
Iugurthe, and
condemned. and extorcion. For when he was sent Ambassador unto Iugurthe king of Numidia, he was bribed with money: and therupon being accused, he was most shamefully convicted, and condemned. Wherefore he ended his dayes with this reproch and infamy, hated, and mocked of all the people:
The Gracchi
were marvel-
ously desired
of the people. bicause at the time of the overthrow he delt beastly with them that fought for his quarrell. But shortly after, it appeared to the world, how much they lamented the losse of the two brethren of the Gracchi. For they made images

GRECIANS AND ROMANES

and statues of them, and caused them to be set up in an
open and honorable place, consecrating the places where
they had bene slaine and many of them also came and
offred to them, of their first frutes and flowers, according
to the time of the yere, and went thither to make their
prayers on their knees, as unto the temples of the gods.
Their mother Cornelia, as writers report, did beare this
calamity with a noble hart: and as for the chappels which
they built and consecrated unto them in the place where
they were slaine, she said no more, but that they had such
graves, as they had deserved. Afterwardes she dwelt continually by the mount of Misene, and never chaunged her
manner of life. She had many frends, and bicause she was
a noble Ladie, and loved ever to welcome straungers, she
kept a very good house, and therefore had always gieat
repaire unto her, of Græcians and learned men: besides,
there was no king nor Prince, but both received giftes from
her, and sent her againe They that frequented her company, delighted marvelously to heare her report the dedes
and maner of her fathers life, Scipio African: but yet they
wondred more, to heare her tell the actes and death of her
two sonnes, Tiberius and Caius Gracchi, without sheading
teare, or making any shew of lamentacion or griefe, no more
then if she had told an history unto them that had requested
her. Insomuch some writers report, that age, or her great
misfortunes, had overcomen and taken her reason and sence
from her, to feele any sorowe. But in deede they were
senselesse to say so, not understandinge, howe that to be
noblie borne, and vertuouslie brought up, doth make men
temperatly to disgest sorow, and that fortune oftentimes
overcomes vertue, which regardeth honestie in all respectes, but yet with any adversity she can not take
away the temperaunce from them, whereby
they paciently beare it

275

LIVES OF THE NOBLE

THE COMPARISON OF
TIBERIUS AND CAIUS GRACCHI WITH
AGIS AND CLEOMENES

OW that we be come to the end of this history, we are to compare the lives of these two men the one with the other. First, as touching the two Gracchi : their enemies that most hated them, and spake the worst they could of them, could not deny but that they were the best geven to vertue, and as well taught and brought up, as any Romanes that were in their time. But yet it appeareth, that nature had the upper hand of them, in Agis and Cleomenes. For they having bene very ill brought up, both for learning and good manners, for lacke whereof the oldest men were almost spoyled : yet did they notwithstandinge make them selves the first maisters and example of sobrietie, temperaunce, and simplicitie of life. Furthermore, the two first having lived in that time, when Rome florished most in honor and vertuous desires : they were more then ashamed to forsake the vertues inherited from their auncesters. These two last also being borne of fathers that had a cleane contrarie disposicion, and finding their contrie altogether without any order, and infected with dissolute life : were not therefore any whit the more moved with desire to do well. Furthermore, the greatest praise they gave unto the two Gracchi, was, their abstinence and integritie from taking of money all the time they were in office, and delt in matters of state, ever keeping their handes cleane, and tooke not a pennie wrongfully from any man. Where Agis on thother side was offended if any man praised him, for that he tooke nothing from an other man : seeing that he dispossessed him selfe of his owne goods, and gave it to his citizens, which

276

GRECIANS AND ROMANES

amounted in readie coyne to the value of six hundred talents. Whereby men may easely judge, how grievous a sinne he thought it to take any thing wrongfully from any man. seeing that he thought it a kinde of avarice, lawfully to be richer then others. Furthermore, there was marvelous great difference in their alteracions, and renuing of the state, which they did both preferre. For the actes of the two Romanes were to mend high wayes, and to reedifie and replenish decayed townes: and the worthiest acte Tiberius did, was the lawe Agraria, which he brought in for dividing of the lands of the common wealth amongest the poore Citizens. And the best acte his brother Caius also did, was the mingling of the Iudges: adding to the three hundred Senators, three hundred Romane knightes to be indifferent Iudges with them. Whereas Agis and Cleomenes in contrary manner were of opinion, that to reforme smal faults, and to redresse them by litle and litle, was (as Plato sayd) to cut of one of the Hydraes heads, of the which came afterwards seven in the place: and therefore they tooke apon them a chaunge and innovation, even at once to roote out all the mischiefs of their contry, (or to speake more truely, to take away the disorder which brought in all vice and mischief to the common wealth) and so to restore the citie of Sparta againe to her former auncient honorable estate. Nowe this may be said againe, for the government of the Gracchi · that the chiefest men of Rome were ever against their purposes. Where, in that that Agis attempted, and Cleomenes ended, they had the noblest ground that could be, and that was the auncient lawes and ordinances of Sparta, touching temperance and equalitie: the first, instituted in old time by Lycurgus, the other confirmed by Apollo. Furthermore, by the alteracions of the first, Rome became no greater then it was before. Where, by that which Cleomenes did, all Græce in short time sawe that Sparta commaunded all the rest of Peloponnesus, and fought at that time against those that were of greatest power in all Græce, for the signiorie thereof. Whereby their onely marke and purpose was, to rid all Græce from the warres of the Gaules and Illyrians, and to restore it againe to the honest

TIBERIUS AND CAIUS GRACCHI AND AGIS AND CLEOMENES

The Actes of the Gracchi did litle profit Rome.

277

government of the race and lyne of Hercules. Their deathes, me thinkes, doe shew great difference of their corages. For the Gracchi fighting with their owne Citizens, were slaine flying. Of these two also, Agis, bicause he would put never a Citizen to death, was slayne in manner voluntarily: and Cleomenes receiving injurie stoode to his defence, and when he had no oportunitie to doe it, he stowtly killed him selfe. And so may it be said on thother side, that Agis did never any noble acte of a Captaine or souldier, bicause he was slayne before he could come to it. And for the victories of Cleomenes on thother side, may be opposed the scaling of the walls of Carthage, where Tiberius was the first man that at the assault got up upon the wall, which was no small exployte: and the peace which he made also at the seege of Numantia, whereby he saved twenty thowsand fighting men of the Romanes, the which had no meanes otherwise to save their lives. And Caius also in the selfe same warre, at the seege of Numantia, and afterwards in Sardinia, did many noble feates of warre: so that there is no doubt, but if they had not bene slaine so soone as they were, they might have bene compared with the excellentest Captaines that ever were in Rome. Again, touching their doings in civill pollicie, it appeareth that Agis delt more slackly, being abused by Agesilaus: who likewise deceived the poore Citizens of the division of the landes which he had promised them. In fine, for lacke of corage, bicause he was very young, he left the thinges undone which he had purposed to have performed. On thother side, Cleomenes went too rowndly to worke to renew the auncient government of the common wealth againe, by killing the Ephores with too much crueltie, whom he might easily have wonne, or otherwise by force have gotten the upper hande. For it is not the parte of a wise Phisition, nor of a good governor of a common weale to use the sword, but in great extreamitie, where there is no other helpe nor remedie: and there lacked judgement in them both, but worst of all in the one, for injury is ever joyned with crueltie. The Gracchi on thother side, nether the one nor the other, began to embrew their hands in the blood of their Citizens. For it is reported,

278

that though they did hurt Caius, yet he would never defend him selfe : and where it was knowen that he was very valliant in battell with his sword in his hand against the enemie, he shewed him selfe as cold againe in the uprore against his Citizens. For he went out of his house unarmed, and fled when he saw them fight : being more circumspect not to doe hurt, then not to suffer any. Therefore they are not to be thought cowards for their flying, but rather men fearefull to offend any man. For they were driven, either to yeeld to them that followed them, or els if they stayed, to stande to their defence, bicause they might keepe them selves from hurt. And where they accuse Tiberius for the faults he committed, the greatest that ever he did, was when he deposed Octavius his colleague from the Tribuneship, and that he him selfe made sute for the second. And as for Caius, they falsely accused him for the death of Antyllius the Sergeaunt, who in deede was slayne unknowen to him, and to his great griefe. Where Cleomenes on thother side, although we should forget the murder he committed upon the Ephores, yet he set slaves at libertie, and ruled the kingdom in manner him selfe alone : but yet for manners sake onely he joyned his owne brother with him, which was of the selfe same house. And when he had perswaded Archidamus, (who was next heire to the kingdom of the other royall house) to be bold to returne home from Messena unto Sparta he suffered him to be slayne, and bicause he did not revenge his death, he did confirme their opinion that thought he was consenting to his death. Lycurgus on the other side, whose example he did counterfeate to followe, bicause he did willingly resigne the kingdom unto his brothers sonne Charilaus, and being afrayd also, that if the young child should chaunce to miscary, they would suspect him for his death · he exiled him selfe out of his owne contry a long time, travelling up and downe, and returned not to Sparta againe, before Charilaus had gotten a sonne to succeede him in his kingdom. But we can not set another Græcian by Lycurgus comparable unto him. We have declared also that amongest Cleomenes deedes, there were many other greater altcracions then these, and also many other breaches

TIBERIUS
AND CAIUS
GRACCHI
AND
AGIS AND
CLEOMENES
of the lawe. So they that doe condemne the manners of the one and the other, say, that the two Græcians from the beginning had an aspyring minde to be tyrannes, still practising warres. Whereas the two Romanes onely, even by their most mortall enemies, could be blamed for nothing els, but for an extreame ambition, and did confesse that they were too earnest and vehement above their nature, in any strife or contencion they had with their adversaries, and that they yelded unto that choller and passion, as unto ill windes, which brought them to doe those thinges they did in the ende. For what more just or honest intent could they have had, then the first was: had not the riche men (even through stowtnes and authoritie to overthrow the lawes) brought them against their wills into quarrell: the one to save his life, the other to revenge his brothers death, who was slayne without order, justice, or the authoritie of any officer? Thus thou maiest thy selfe see the difference, that was betwene the Græcians and Romanes: and nowe to tell you plainly my opinion of both, I think that Tiberius was the stowtest of the foure, that the younge king Agis offended least, and that for boldnes and corage, Caius came nothing neare unto Cleomenes.

THE LIFE OF DEMOSTHENES

E that made the litle booke of the praise of Alcibiades, touching the victorie he wanne at the horse rase of the Olympian games, (were it the Poet Euripides as some thinke, or any other) my friende Sossius: sayde, that to make a man happy, he must of necessitie be borne in some famous citie. But to tell you what I thinke hereof, douteles, true happines chiefly consisteth in the vertue and qualities of the minde, being a matter of no

moment, whether a man be borne in a pelting village, or in a famous citie: no more then it is for one to be borne of a fayer or fowle mother. For it were a madnes to thinke that the litle village of Iulide, being the least part of the Ile of Ceo (the whole Iland of it selfe being but a small thing) and that the Ile of Ægina (which is of so smal a length, that a certaine Athenian on a time made a motion it might be taken away, bicause it was but as a strawe in the sight of the haven of Piræa) could bring forth famous Poets, and excellent Comediants: and not breede an honest, just, and wise man, and of noble corage. For, as we have reason to thinke that artes and sciences which were first devised and invented to make some thinges necessary for mens use, or otherwise to winne fame and credit, are drowned, and cast away in litle poore villages: so are we to judge also, that vertue, like a strong and frutefull plant, can take roote, and bringe forth in every place, where it is graffed in a good nature, and gentle person, that can patiently away with paines. And therefore if we chaunce to offend, and live not as we should: we can not accuse the meanenes of our contry where we were borne, but we must justly accuse our selves. Surely he that hath taken upon him to put forth any worke, or to write any historie, into the which he is to thrust many straunge things unknowen to his contry, and which are not ready at his hand to be had, but dispersed abroad in divers places, and are to be gathered out of divers bookes and authorities: first of all, he must needes remaine in some great and famous citie throughly inhabited, where men doe delight in good and vertuous thinges, bicause there are commonly plenty of all sortes of bookes: and that perusing them, and hearing talke also of many things besides, which other Historiographers peradventure have not written of, and which will cary so much more credit, bicause men that are alive may presently speake of them as of their owne knowledge, whereby he may make his worke perfect in every poynt, having many and divers necessary things conteyned in it. But I my selfe that dwell in a poore litle towne, and yet doe remayne there willingly least it should become lesse: whilest I was in Italy, and at Rome, I had no leysure to study

DEMOS-
THENES

True happines consisteth in the minde and manners of man, not in any place or contry.

Expedient for an Historiographer to be in a famous citie.

Plutarkes contry very litle.

5 : NN

and exercise the Latine tongue, aswell for the great busines
I had then to doe, as also to satisfie them that came to
learne Philosophie of me: so that even somewhat too late,
and now in my latter time, I began to take my Latine
bookes in my hand. And thereby, a straunge thing to tell
you, but yet true: I learned not, nor understood matters so
much by the words, as I came to understand the words, by
common experience and knowledge I had in things. But
furthermore, to knowe howe to pronownce the Latin tongue
well, or to speake it readily, or to understand the signification, translations, and fine joyning of the simple words one
with another, which doe bewtifie and set forth the tongue:
surely I judge it to be a marvailous pleasant and sweete
thing, but withall it requireth a long and laborsome study,
meete for those that have better leysure then I have, and
that have young yeares on their backes to follow such
pleasure. Therefore, in this present booke, which is the fift
of this work, where I have taken upon me to compare the
lives of noble men one with another: undertaking to write
the lives of Demosthenes and Cicero, we will consider and
examine their nature, manners and condicions, by their acts
and deedes in the government of the common wealth, not
meaning otherwise to conferre their workes and writings of
eloquence, nether to define which of them two was sharper
or sweeter in his oration. For, as the Poet Ion sayth,

> In this behalfe a man may rightly say,
> The Dolphynes in their proper soyle doe play.

The which Cæcilius litle understanding, being a man very
rashe in all his doings, hath unadvisedly written and set
forth in print, a comparison of Demosthenes eloquence, with
Ciceroes. But if it were an easie matter for every man to
know him selfe, then the goddes needed have given us no
commaundement, nether could men have said that it came
from heaven. But for my opinion, me thinks fortune even
from the beginning hath framed in maner one self mowld of
Demosthenes and Cicero, and hath in their natures facioned
many of their qualities one like to the other: as, both of
them to be ambitious, both of them to love the libertie of

their contry, and both of them very feareful in any daunger of warres. And likewise their fortunes seeme to me, to be both much alike. For it is harde to finde two Orators againe, that being so meanely borne as they, have comen to be of so great power and authoritie as they two, nor that have deserved the ill will of kings and noble men so much as they have done, nor that have lost their Daughters, nor that have bene banished their contries, and that have bene restored againe with honor, and that againe have fled, and have bene taken againe, nor that have ended their lives with the libertie of their contry. So that it is hard to be judged, whether nature have made them liker in manners, or fortune in their doings, as if they had both like cunning workemaisters strived one with the other, to whome they should make them best resemble. But first of all we must write of the elder of them two.

Demosthenes the father of this Orator Demosthenes, was as Theopompus writeth, one of the chiefe men of the citie, and they called him Machæropœus, to wete, a maker of sworde blades, bicause he had a great shoppe where he kept a number of slaves to forge them. But touching Æschynes, the Orators report of his mother, who said that she was the Daughter of one Gelon (that fled from Athens beeing accused of treason) and of a barbarous woman that was her mother: I am not able to say whether it be true, or devised of malice to doe him despite. Howsoever it was, it is true that his father died, leaving him seven yeare olde, and left him reasonable wel: for his goods came to litle lesse then the value of fifteene talents. Howbeit his gardians did him great wronge: for they stale a great parte of his goods them selves, and did let the rest runne to naught, as having litle care of it, for they would not pay his schoolemaisters their wages. And this was the cause that he did not learne the liberall sciences which are usually taught unto honest mens sonnes: and to further that want also, he was but a weakling, and very tender, and therefore his mother would not much let him goe to schoole, nether his masters also durst keepe him too hard to it, bicause he was but a sickly childe at the first, and very weake. And it is reported also,

The parentage of Demosthenes.

The patrimony left Demosthenes.

DEMOS-
THENES

Demosthenes
why he was
called
Battalus.

Demosthenes,
why sur-
named Argas.

Callistratus
the Orator.

The earnest
desire of
Demosthenes
to learne
eloquence.

that the surname of Battalus was given him in mockery by other schooleboyes his companions, bicause of his weaknes of bodye. This Battalus (as divers men doe report) was an effeminate player on the flute, against whom the Poet Antiphanes to mocke him, devised a litle play. Others also doe write of one Battalus, a dissolute Orator, and that wrote lascivious verses : and it seemeth that the Athenians at that time did call a certaine part of mans body uncomely to be named, Battalus. Now for Argas (which surname men say was also given him) he was so called, either for his rude and beastly maners, (bicause some Poets doe call a snake Argas) or els for his maner of speech, which was very unpleasant to the eare: for Argas is the name of a Poet, that made alwayes bawdy and ill favored songs. But hereof enough as Plato said. Furthermore, the occasion (as it is reported) that moved him to give him selfe to eloquence, was this. Calistratus the Orator was to defend the cause of one Oropus before the Iudges, and every man longed greatly for this daye of pleading, both for the excellencie of the Orator, that then bare the bell for eloquence : as for the matter, and his accusation, which was manifestly knowen to all. Demosthenes hearing his schoolemasters agree together to goe to the hearing of this matter, he prayed his schoolemaster to be so good, as to let him goe with him. His Maister graunted him, and being acquainted with the keepers of the hal dore where this matter was to be pleaded, he so intreated them, that they placed his scholler in a very good place, where being set at his ease, he might both see and heare all that was done, and no man could see him. Thereuppon, when Demosthenes had heard the case pleaded, he was greatly in love with the honor which the Orator had gotten, when he sawe howe he was wayted upon home with such a trayne of people after him : but yet he wondred more at the force of his great eloquence, that could so turne and convey all thinges at his pleasure. Thereuppon he left the studie of all other sciences, and all other exercises of witte and bodye, which other children are brought up in : and beganne to labor continually, and to frame him selfe to make orations, with intent one day to be an Orator amonge the rest. His

Maister that taught him Rethoricke was Isæus, notwithstanding that Isocrates also kept a schoole of Rethoricke at
that time: either bicause that beeing an orphane he was not
able to paye the wages that Isocrates demaunded of his
schollers, which was ten Minas· or rather for that he founde
Isæus manner of speeche more propper for the use of the
eloquence he desired, bicause it was more finer, and sutler.
Yet Hermippus writeth notwithstanding, that he had red
certayne bookes, having no name of any author, which
declared that Demosthenes had bene Platoes scholler, and
that by hearing of him, he learned to frame his pronunciation and eloquence. And he writeth also of one Ctesibius,
who reporteth that Demosthenes had secretly redde Isocrates
workes of Rethoricke, and also Alcidamus bookes, by meanes
of one Callias Syracusan, and others. Wherefore when he
came out of his wardeshippe, he beganne to put his gardians
in sute, and to write orations and pleas against them: who
in contrary manner did ever use delayes and excuses, to save
them selves from giving up any accompt unto him, of his
goods and patrimony left him. And thus, following this
exercise (as Thucydides writeth) it prospered so well with
him, that in the ende he obtayned it, but not without great
paynes and daunger· and yet with all that he could doe, he
could not recover all that his father left him, by a good deale.
So having now gotten some boldnes, and being used also to
speake in open presence, and withall, having a feeling and
delight of the estimation that is wonne by eloquence in
pleading: afterwardes he attempted to put forward him
selfe, and to practise in matters of state. For, as there
goeth a tale of one Laomedon an Orchomenian, who having
a grievous paine in the splene, by advise of the Phisitions
was willed to runne long courses to helpe him. and that
following their order, he became in the end so lusty and
nymble of body, that afterwards he would needes make one
to ronne for games, and in deede grew to be the swiftest
runner of all men in his time. Even so the like chaunced
unto Demosthenes. For at the first, beginning to practise
oratorie for recoverie of his goods, and thereby having gotten
good skill and knowledge how to pleade he afterwards

A remedie for
the paine of
the splene.

Demosthenes
mocked of the
people for his
long orations.

Demosthenes
impediments
of nature.

tooke apon him to speake to the people in assemblies, touching the government of the common wealth, even as if he should have contended for some game of price, and at length did excell all the Orators at that time that got up into the pulpit for orations: notwithstanding that when he first ventred to speake openly, the people made such a noyse, that he could scant be heard, and besides they mocked him for his manner of speeche that was so straunge, bicause he used so many long confused peryods, and his matter he spake of was so intricate with arguments one apon another, that they were tedious, and made men weary to heare him. And furthermore, he had a very soft voice, an impediment in his tongue, and had also a short breath, the which made that men could not well understand what he ment, for his long periods in his oration were oftentimes interrupted, before he was at the ende of his sentence. So that at length, perceiving he was thus rejected, he gave over to speake any more before the people, and halfe in dispaire withdrew him selfe into the haven of Piræa. There Eunomus the Thessalian beeing a very olde man, founde him, and sharpely reproved him, and told him that he did him selfe great wronge, considering, that having a manner of speeche much like unto Pericles, he drowned him selfe by his faynt harte, bicause he did not seeke the way to be bolde against the noyse of the common people, and to arme his body to away with the paines and burden of publike orations, but suffering it to growe feebler, for lacke of use and practise. Furthermore, being once againe repulsed and whistled at, as he returned home, hanging downe his heade for shame, and utterly discouraged: Satyrus an excellent player of comedies, being his famillier friende, followed him, and went and spake with him. Demosthenes made his complaynt unto him, that where he had taken more paynes then all the Orators besides, and had almost even worne him selfe to the bones with studie, yet he coulde by no meanes devise to please the people: whereas other Orators that did nothing but bybbe all day long, and Maryners that understoode nothing, were quietly heard, and continually occupied the pulpit with orations: and on thother side that they made no accompt of

him. Satyrus then aunswered him, Thou sayest true Demosthenes, but care not for this, I will helpe it straight, and
take away the cause of all this: so thou wilt but tell me
without booke certaine verses of Euripides, or of Sophocles.
Thereuppon Demosthenes presently rehearsed some unto
him, that came into his minde. Satyrus repeating them
after him, gave them quite another grace, with such a pronunciation, comely gesture, and modest countenance be-
comming the verses, that Demosthenes thought them cleane
chaunged. Whereby perceiving how much the action (to
wete, the comely manner and gesture in his oration) doth
give grace and comlines in his pleading : he then thought it
but a trifle, and almost nothing to speake of, to exercise to
pleade well, unles therewithall he doe also study to have a
good pronunciation and gesture. Thereuppon he built him
a celler under the ground, the which was whole even in my
time, and he would daily goe downe into it, to facion his
gesture and pronunciation, and also to exercise his voice,
and that with such earnest affection, that oftentimes he
would be there two or three monethes one after an other,
and did shave his heade of purpose, bicause he durst not goe
abroade in that sorte, although his will was good. And yet
he tooke his theame and matter to declame apon, and to
practise to pleade of the matters he had had in hande
before, or els upon occasion of such talke as he had with
them that came to see him, while he kept his house. For
they were no sooner gone from him, but he went downe into
his celler, and repeated from the first to the last all matters
that had passed betwene him and his friendes in talke together,
and alleaged also both his owne and their aunswers. And if
peradventure he had bene at the hearing of any long matter,
he would repeate it by him selfe : and would finely cowche
and convey it into propper sentences, and thus chaunge and
alter every way any matter that he had heard, or talked
with others. Thereof came the opinion men had of him,
that he had no very quicke capacitie by nature, and that his
eloquence was not naturall, but artificially gotten with extreame labor. And for proofe hereof, they make this probable reason, that they never sawe Demosthenes make any

Demosthenes
seldom
pleaded on
the suddein.

oration on the suddein, and that oftentymes when he was sette in the assemblie, the people would call him by his name, to say his opinion touching the matter of counsell then in hand : howbeit that he never rose upon their call, unles he had first studied the matter well he would speake of. So that all the other Orators would many times give him a tawnte for it : as Pytheas among other, that tawnting him on a tyme, tolde him, his reasons smelled of the lampe. Yea, replyed Demosthenes sharply againe : so is there great difference, Pytheas, betwixt thy labor and myne by lampelight. And him selfe also speaking to others, did not altogether deny it, but told them plainly, that he did not alwaies write at length all that he would speake, nether did he also offer to speake, before he had made briefes of that he would speake. He sayd furthermore, that it was a token the man loved the people well, that he would be carefull before what he would say to them. For this preprative (quoth he) doth shewe that he doth honor and reverence them. In contrary manner also, he that passeth not how the people take his words, it is a plaine token that he despiseth their authoritie, and that he lacketh no good will (if he could) to use force against them, rather then reason and perswasion. But yet further to enlarge the proofes, that Demosthenes had no hart to make any oration on the suddein, they doe alleage this reason : that Demades many times rose upon the sodaine to mainteyne Demosthenes reasons, when the people otherwhile did reject him : and that Demosthenes on thother side did never rise to make Demades words good, which he had spoken in his behalfe. But now might a man aske againe : If Demosthenes was so timerous to speake before the people upon the sodaine : what ment Æschines then to say, that he was marvelous bold in his words? And how chaunceth it, that he rising upon the sodaine, did presently aunswer the Orator Python Bizantine in the field, that was very lusty in speech, (and rough like a vehement running streame) against the Athenians? And how chaunced it that Lamachus Myrrinæian, having made an oration in the praise of Philip and Alexander, kings of Macedon, in the which he spake all the

Demosthenes
in his oration
studieth to
please the
people.

ill he could of the Thebans, and of the Olynthians, and when he had red and pronownced it in the open assembly of the Olympian games: Demosthenes apon the instant rising up on his feete, declared, as if he had red some historie, and poynted as it were with his finger unto all the whole assembly, the notable great service and worthy deedes the which the Chalcidians had done in former times, for the benefit and honor of Græce. And in contrary maner also, what mischief and inconvenience came by meanes of the flatterers, that altogether gave them selves to curry favor with the Macedonians? With these and such like perswasions, Demosthenes made such sturre amongest the people, that the Orator Lamachus being affraid of the sodaine uprore, did secretly convey him selfe out of the assembly. But yet to tell you what I thinke, Demosthenes in my opinion facioning him selfe even from the beginning, to followe Pericles steppes and example, he thought that for other qualities he had, they were not so requisite for him, and that he would counterfeate his gravitie and sober countenance, and to be wise, not to speake over lightly to every matter at all adventures: judging, that by that manner of wisedom he came to be great. And like as he would not let slippe any good occasion to speake, where it might be for his credit. so would he not likewise over rashely hazard his credit and reputacion to the mercy of fortune. And to prove this true, the orations which he made uppon the sodaine without premeditacion before, doe shewe more boldnes and courage, then those which he had written, and studied long before: if we may beleeve the reports of Eratosthenes, Demetrius Phalerian, and of the other comicall Poets. For Eratosthenes sayd, that he would be often caried away with choller and furie. Demetrius also sayth, that speaking one daye to the people, he sware a great othe in ryme, as if he had bene possessed with some divine spirit, and sayd,

> By sea and land, by rivers, springes, and Ponds.

There are also certaine comicall Poets that doe call him Ropoperperethra, as who would say, a great babbler that

Οὕτως ἀπέ-
λαβεν ὥσπερ
ἔλαβεν.
Μὴ λαμβάνειν
ἀλλὰ ἀπολαμ-
βάνειν παρὰ
Φιλίππου.

The naturall
eloquence of
Demades the
Orator.

Theophrastus
judgement of
Orators.

Phocion
called the
axe of
Demosthenes
orations.

Demosthenes
by industry
reformeth
his defects
of nature.

speaketh all thinges that commeth to his tongues ende. Another mocked him for too much affecting a figure of Rethoricke called, Antitheton : which is, opposicion, with saying, 'Sic recepit sicut cepit,' (which signifieth, He tooke it as he found it.) In the use of this figure Demosthenes much pleased him selfe, unles the poet Antiphanes speaketh it of pleasure, deriding the counsel he gave the people, not to take the Ile of Halonesus of king Philip, as of gift : but to receive it as their owne restored. And yet every body did graunt, that Demades of his owne naturall wit, without arte, was invincible : and that many times speaking upon the sodaine, he did utterly overthrow Demosthenes long studied reasons. And Aristo, of the Ile of Chio, hath written Theophrastus judgement of the Orators of that time. Who being asked what maner of Orator he thought Demosthenes : he aunswered, Worthy of this citie. Then again, how he thought of Demades : Above this citie, said he. The same Philosopher writeth also, that Polyeuctus Sphettian, (one of those that practised at that time in the common wealth) gave this sentence : that Demosthenes in deede was a great Orator, but Phocions tongue had a sharper understanding, bicause in fewe wordes, he comprehended much matter. And to this purpose, they say that Demosthenes him selfe said also, that as oft as he saw Phocion get up into the pulpit for orations to speake against him, he was wont to say to his friends : See, the axe of my words riseth. And yet it is hard to judge, whether he spake that in respect of his tongue, or rather for the estimacion he had gotten, bicause of his great wisedome : thinking (as in deede it is true) that one word only, the twinckling of an eye, or a nod of his head of such a man (that through his worthines is attained to that credit) hath more force to perswade, then all the fine reasons and devises of Rethoricke. But now for his bodily defects of nature, Demetrius Phalerian writeth, that he heard Demosthenes him selfe say, being very olde, that he did helpe them by these meanes. First, touching the stammering of his tongue, which was very fat, and made him that he could not pronounce all syllables distinctly : he did helpe it by putting of litle pybble stones into his mouth, which he found upon the sands by the rivers side, and so pronounced with open mouth the orations he had without booke. And for his smal and soft voice, he made that lowder, by running up steepe and high hills, uttering even with full breath some orations or verses that he had without booke. And further it is reported of him, that he had a great looking glasse in his house, and ever standing on his feete before it, he would learne and exercise him selfe to pronounce his orations. For proofe hereof it is reported, that there came a man unto him on a time, and prayed his helpe to defend his cause, and tolde him that one had beaten him: and that Demosthenes sayd agayne unto him, I doe not beleeve this is true thou tellest me, for surely the other did never beate thee. The playntif then thrusting out his voyce alowde, sayde: What, hath he not beaten me? Yes, in deede, quoth Demosthenes then: I beleeve it now, for I heare the voyce of a man that was beaten in deede. Thus he thought, that the sound of the voyce, the pronunciation or gesture in one sort or other, were thinges of force to beleeve or discredit that a man sayth. His countenaunce when he pleaded before the people, did marvailously please the common sorte: but the noble men, and men of understanding, found it too base and meane, as Demetrius Phalerius sayde, amonge others. And Hermippus writeth, that one called Æsion, beeing asked of the auncient Orators, and of those of his tyme, aunswered: That every man that had seene them, would have wondred with what honor, reverence, and modestie, they spake unto the people: howbeit that Demosthenes orations (whosoever red them) were too artificiall and vehement. And therefore we may easily judge, that the orations Demosthenes wrote are very severe and sharpe. This notwithstanding, otherwhile he would give many pleasant and witty aunswers apon the sodain. As when Demades one day sayd unto him, Demosthenes will teach me: after the common proverbe, The sowe will teach Minerva. He aunswered straight againe: This Minerva not long since, was in Collytus streete, taken in adulterie. A certein theefe also called Chalcus (as much to say, as of copper) stepping forth to saye somewhat of Demos-

Demosthenes countenance and gesture mishked of the nobilitie.

Demosthenes witty answers.

thenes late sitting up a nights, and that he wrote and studied the most part of the night by lampe light: In deede, quoth Demosthenes, I know it grieves thee to see my lampe burne all night. And therefore, you, my Lords of Athens, me thinkes you should not wonder to see such robberies in your citie, considering we have theeves of copper, and the walles of our houses be but of claye. We could tell you of divers others of his like wittie and pleasant aunswers, but these may suffice for this present: and therefore we will proceede to consider further of his nature and conditions, by his actes and deedes in the affaires of the common wealth.

The time of
Demosthenes
comming to
practise in
the affayres
of the state.

Now Demosthenes first beginning when he came to deale in the affaires of the state, was in the time of the warre made with the Phocians, as him selfe reporteth: and as appeareth further in his orations which he made against Philip: of the which, the last were made after the warre was ended, and the first doe touch also some particuler doings of the same.

Displeasure
betwixt
Demosthenes
and Midias.

He made the oration against Midias, when he was but 32 yeare old, and was of small countenance and reputacion in the common wealth: the want whereof was the chiefest cause (as I thinke) that induced him to take money for the injury he had done him, and to let his action fall against him.

He was not of a meeld and gentle mind,
But feerce and hastie to revenge by kind.

But, knowing that it was no small enterprise, nor that could take effect by a man of so small power and authoritie as him selfe, to overthrow a man so wealthy, so befriended, and so eloquent as Midias: he therfore yelded him selfe unto those, that did speake and intreate for him. Nether do I think that the three thowsand Drachmas which he received, could have brideled the bitternes of his nature, if otherwise he had seene any hope or likelihood that he could have pre-

Demosthenes,
an enemy to
the Mace-
donians.

vailed against him. Now at his first comming unto the common wealth, taking a noble matter in hand to speake against Philip, for the defence and maintenance of the lawes and liberties of the Græcians, wherein he handled him self so worthely: that in short space he wanne him marvelous

fame for his great eloquence and plaine manner of speech.
Thereby he was marvelously honored also through all Græce,
and greatly esteemed with the king of Persia: and Philip
him self made more accompt of him, then of all the Orators
in Athens, and his greatest foes which were most against
him, were driven to confesse that they had to doe with
a famous man. For, in the orations which Æschines and
Hyperides made to accuse him, they write thus of him.
And therefore I marvell what Theopompus ment, when he
wrote that Demosthenes had a suttell, unconstant mind, and
could not long continue with one kind of men, nor in one
mind for matters of state. For in contrary maner, in my
judgement, he continued constant still to the end, in one
selfe maner and order, unto the which he had betaken him
self at the beginning: and that not only he never chaunged
all his life time, but to the contrary he lost his life, bicause he
would be no chaungeling. For he did not like Demades, who
to excuse him self for that he had oft turned coate in matters
of government, said, that he went oftentimes against his own
sayings, as matters fel out: but never against the benefit
of the common wealth. And Melanopus also, who was ever
against Callistratus, having his mouth stopped many times
with money, he would up to the pulpit for orations, and tel
the people, that in deede Callistratus, which mainteineth the
contrary opinion against me, is mine enemy, and yet I yeld
unto him for this time: for, the benefit of the common
wealth must cary it. And another also, Nicodemus Messenian, who being first of Cassanders side, toke part afterwards with Demetrius, and then said, that he did not speake
against him selfe, but that it was meete he should obey his
superiors. They can not detect Demosthenes with the like,
that he did ever halt or yeld, either in word or deed: for
he ever continued firme and constant in one mind in his
orations. Insomuch that Panætius the Philosopher sayth,
that the most part of all his orations are grounded upon
this maxime and principle: that for it selfe, nothing is to be
taken or accepted, but that which is honest. As, the oration
of the crowne, the which he made against Aristocrates: that
also which he made for the franches and freedom · and in

Side notes:

DEMOS-
THENES

The con-
stancy of
Demosthenes
defended
against
Theopompus.

Note the
inconstancy
and suttell
evasion of
these Orators

Demosthenes
preferreth
honesty, as
a speciall
rule in his
orations.

fine, all his orations against Philip of Macedon. And in all those he doth not perswade his contry men to take that which is most pleasant, easiest, or most profitable: but he proveth that oftentimes honestie is to be preferred above

safetie or health. So that, had he in all his orations and doings, joyned to his honestie, curtesie, and francke speeche, valliantnes in warres, and cleane hands from briberye: he might deservedly have bene compared, not with Myrocles, Polyeuctus, Hyperides and such other Orators: but even with the highest, with Cimon, Thucydides, and Pericles. For Phocion, who tooke the worst way in government of the common wealth, bicause he was suspected that he tooke part with the Macedonians: yet for valliantnes, wisedom and justice, he was ever thought as honest a man, as Ephialtes, and Aristides. But Demosthenes on thother side (as Demetrius sayth) was no man to trust to for warres, nether had he any power to refuse gifts and bribes. For, though he would never be corrupted with Philip king of Macedon, yet he was bribed with gold and silver that was brought from the cities of Susa and Ecbatana, and was very ready to praise and commend the deedes of their auncestors, but not to follow them. Truely, yet was he the honestest man of all other Orators in his time, excepting Phocion. And

besides, he did ever speake more boldely and plainely to the people then any man els, and would openly contrary their mindes, and sharpely reprove the Athenians for their faultes, as appeareth by his orations. Theopompus also writeth, that the people on a time would have had him to accuse a man, whome they would needes have condemned. But he refusing to doe it, the people were offended, and did mutine against him. Thereuppon he rising up, sayd openly unto them: My Lordes Athenians, I will alwayes counsell ye to that which I thinke best for the benefit of the common wealth, although it be against your mindes: but falsely to accuse one, to satisfie your minds, though you commaund me, I wil not do it. Furthermore, that which he did against Antiphon, sheweth plainly, that he was no people pleaser, and that he did leane more unto the authoritie of the Senate. For when Antiphon was quit by the people in an assemblie

of the citie: Demosthenes notwithstanding tooke him, and
called him againe into the Court of the Areopagites, and did
not passe upon the peoples ill will, but there convinced him
for promising Philip of Macedon to burne the arsenall of
Athens: so by sentence of that court he was condemned,
and suffred for it. He did also accuse the Nunne Theorides
for many lewd parts committed, and amongst others, for
that she taught slaves to deceive their maisters: and so following the matter against her to death, she was condemned,
and executed. It is thought also, that he made the oration
Apollodorus spake against the Prætor Timotheus, and proved
thereby that he was a detter to the common wealth, and so
a naughty man: and that he wrote those orations also intituled unto Formio and Stephanus, for the which he was
justly reproved. For Formio pleaded against Apollodorus
with the oration which Demosthenes selfe had made for
him: which was even alike, as if out of one selfe cutlers
shoppe, he had solde his enemies swords one to kil another.
And for his knowen orations, those which he made against
Androtion, Timocrates, and Aristocrates he caused them
to give them unto others, when he had not yet delt in
matters of state. For in deede when he did put them forth,
he was not passing seven or eight and twenty yeare olde.
The oration which he made against Aristogiton, and the
other also of libertie, against Ctesippus the sonne of Cabrias,
he spake them, as he saith him selfe, (or as others write)
openly unto the people, bicause he intended to mary Chabrias mother. Howbeit he did not, but maried a Samian
woman, as Demetrius Magnesius writeth in his booke he
made intituled *Synonyma*, and in that he wrote against
Æschines. where he accuseth him that he delt falsely when
he was Ambassador. It is not knowen whether it was ever
recited or not, although Idomeneus writeth, that there lacked
but thirtye voices onely to have quit Æschines. But in this
me thinkes he spake not truely, and doth but conjecture it,
by that the one and the other have sayd in their orations
against the crowne, in the which, nether the one nor the
other doe say precisely, that this accusation proceeded
to judgement. But let other that lyst decide this doubt.

Now before the warre beganne, it was evident enough, to which parte Demosthenes would incline in the common wealth : for, he would never leave to reprove and withstand Philippes doings. Therefore he being more spoken of in Philippes Court, then any man els, he was sent unto him the tenth person with nyne others in ambassade. Philippe gave them all audience one after an other : howbeit he was more carefull and circumspect to aunswer Demosthenes oration, then all the rest. But otherwise out of that place, he did not Demosthenes so much honor, nor gave him so good entertainment, as to his other companions. For Philip shewed more kindnes, and gave better countenance unto Æschines, and Philocrates, then unto him. Wherefore when they did highly praise Philip, and sayd that he was a well spoken Prince, a fayer man, and would drinke freely, and be pleasant in company : Demosthenes smyled at it, and turned all those thinges to the worst, saying, that those qualities were nothing commendable nor meete for a king. For, the first was a qualitie meete for a pleader, the second for a woman, and the third for a sponge. In fine, warres falling out betwene them, because Philip of the one side could not live in peace, and the Athenians on the other side were stil incensed and stirred up by Demosthenes daily orations. Whereupon, the Athenians first sent into the Ile of Eubœa, (the which by meanes of certaine private tyrannes that had taken the townes, became subject againe unto Philip) follow-ing a decree Demosthenes had preferred, and so went to expulse the Macedonians againe. After that also he caused them to send ayde unto the Bizantines, and unto the Perin-thians, with whom Philip made warre. For he so perswaded the Athenians, that he made them forget the malice they did beare unto those two nations, and the faults which either of both the cities had committed against them in the warres, touching the rebellion of their confederats : and he caused them to send them ayde, which kept them from Philips force

and power. Furthermore, going afterwards unto all the great cities of Græce as Ambassador, he did so solicite and perswade them, that he brought them all in manner to be against Philip. So that the army which their tribe should

find at their common charge, was fifteene thowsand footemen, all straungers, and two thowsand horsemen, besides the
Citizens of every citie which should also serve in the warres
at their charge: and the money leavied for the maintenance
of this warre, was very willingly disbursed. Theophrastus
writeth, that it was at that tyme their confederats did pray
that they would set downe a certaine summe of money,
what every citie shoulde paye: and that Crobylus an Orator
shoulde make aunswer, that the warre had no certaine
maintenance: inferring that the charges of warre was
infinite. Now all Græce being in armes, attending what
should happen, and all these people and cities being unite
in one league together: as, the Eubœians, the Athenians,
the Corinthians, the Megarians, the Leucadians, and the
Corcyriæians: the greatest matter Demosthenes had to do,
was to perswade the Thebans also to enter into this league,
bicause their contry confined and bordered with Attica ·
besides, their force and power was of great importance, for
that they caried the fame of all Græce at that time, for the
valliantest souldiers. But it was no trifling matter to winne
the Thebans, and to make them breake with Philip, who
but lately before had bound them unto him by many great
pleasures which he had done to them, in the warre of the
Phocians · besides also that betwixt Athens and Thebes, by
reason of vicinitie, there fell out daily quarells and debates,
the which with every litle thing were soone renued. This
notwithstanding, Philippe being prowde of the victorie he
had wonne by the citie of Amphisse, when he came and invaded the contry of Elatia, and was entred into Phocide:
the Athenians were then so amased with it, that no man
durst occupie the pulpit for orations, neither could they tell
what way to take Thus the whole assemblie standing in a
doubt with great silence, Demosthenes onely stept up, and
did agayne give them counsell to seeke to make league and
alliance with the Thebans. and so did further encourage the
people, and put them in good hope, as he was alwayes wont
to doe. Then with others he was sent Ambassador unto
Thebes: and Philippe also for his parte, sent Ambassadors
unto the Thebans, Amyntas and Clearchus, two gentlemen

DEMOS-
THENES
Demosthenes
force of
eloquence
joyned the
Thebans with
the Athen-
ians, and
wanne them
from Philippe
king of
Macedon.

Macedonians, and with them, Daochus, Thessalus, and Thra-sydæus, to aunswer and withstande the perswasions of the Athenian Ambassadors. Thereuppon the Thebans beganne to advise them selves for the best, and layd before their eyes the miserable frutes and calamities of warre, their woundes being yet greene and uncured, which they gotte by the warres of Phocide. Notwithstanding, the great force of Demosthenes eloquence (as Theopompus writeth) did so in-flame the Thebans courage with desire of honor, that it trode under their feete all manner of considerations, and did so ravishe them with the love and desire of honestie: that they cast at their heeles, all feare of daunger, all remembrance of pleasures received, and all reason perswading the contrary. This acte of an Orator was of so great force, that Philippe forthwith sent Ambassadors unto the Græcians, to intreate for peace, and all Græce was uppe, to see what would become of this sturre. Thus, not onely the Captaines of Athens obeyed Demosthenes, doing all that he commaunded them but the governors also of Thebes, and of all the contry of Bœotia besides. And the assemblies also of the counsell of Thebes were as well governed by him, as the assemblies of Athens, being alike beloved both of the one and the other, and having a like authoritie to commaund both, and not undeservedly, as Theopompus sayth, but by just desert. But some fatall destinie, and the revolucion of times had determined the finall ende of the libertie of Græce at that time, cleane contrary to his purpose and intent. There were also many celestiall signes that did foreshewe and prognosticate what ende should ensue thereof. And amonge others, Apolloes Nunne gave these dreadful oracles : and this olde prophecie of the Sibyls was commonly song in every bodies mouth :

The over-
throw of the
Græcians
foreshewed
at Chæronea,
by signes
and auncient
oracles.

What time the bluddy battell shall be fought at Thermodon,
God graunt I may be farre away, or els (to looke theron)
Have Egles wings to sore above, among the clowdes on hye.
For there the vanquisht side shall weepe, and Conquerer shall dye

Men do report that this Thermodon is a litle river of our contry of Chæronea, the which falleth into the river of

Cephisus · howbeit at this present time there is never a
river nor brook in all our contry, that I know, called
Thermodon. And I thinke, that that river which we call
now Hæmon, was in old time Thermodon. for it runneth
by the temple of Hercules, where the Græcians lay in campe.
And it may be, that bicause it was filled with dead bodies,
and that it ranne bloud at the day of the battel, it chaunged
her name, and was surnamed Hæmon, bicause *Hœma* in the
Greeke tongue, signifieth bloud. Yet Duris writeth notwithstanding, that this Thermodon was no river, but that certaine
men setting up their tent, and trenching it about, found a
litle image of stone, whereuppon were engraven these letters,
whereby it appeareth that it was a man called Thermodon,
who caried an Amazon hart in his armes, and that for this
image of Thermodon, they doe sing such another olde oracle
as this:

> Ye Ernes and Ravens tary till the field of Thermodon:
> There will be store of carkesses of men to feede upon.

This notwithstanding, it is very hard to tell the trothe of
these things. But Demosthenes trusting to the valliantnes
and power of the Græcians, and being marvelously incoraged
to see such a great number of valliant and resolute men, so
willing to fight with the enemy. he bad them be of good
corage, and not to busse about such oracles, and to give
eare to those prophecies. And furthermore, he told them
plainly, that he did mistrust the Nunne Pythia did leane
unto Philip, as favoring him, and did put the Thebans in
mind of their Captaine Epaminondas, and the Athenians of
Pericles, and perswaded them, that those two famous men
were alwaies of opinion, that such prophecies were no other,
but a fine cloke for cowards, and that taking no heede to
them, they did dispatch their matters according to their owne
discretion. Until this present time, Demosthenes shewed
him selfe alwaies an honest man: but when it came to the
battel, he fled like a coward, and did no valliant acte any
thing aunswerable to the orations whereby he had perswaded
the people. For he left his ranck, and cowardly cast away
his weapons to ronne the lighter, and was not ashamed at

Margin notes:

DEMOS-
THENES
The river of
Thermodon,
or Hæmon, in
the contry of
Chæronea

Another
opinion of
Thermodon.

Demosthenes
flieth from
the battell.

DEMOS-
THENES
Demosthenes
word and
devise upon
his shield.

al, as Pythias said, of the words written upon his shield in golden letters, which were, 'Good Fortune' Now Philip having wonne the battell, he was at that present so joyfull, that he fell to commit many fond parts. For after he had droncke well with his friends, he went into the place where the overthrow was given, and there in mockery began to sing the beginning of the decree which Demosthenes had preferred, (by the which, the Athenians accordingly proclaimed warres against him) rising and falling with his voyce, and dauncing it in measure with his foote:

> Demosthenes, the sonne of Demosthenes Pæanian did put forth this.

But afterwards beginning to waxe sober, and leaving his dronckennes, and that he had remembred him selfe what daunger he had bene in: then his heare stood bolt upright upon his head, considering the force and power of such an Orator, that in a peece of a day had inforced him to hazard his Realme and life at a battell. Now Demosthenes fame was so great, that it was caried even to the great king of Persiaes court, who wrote unto his Lieuetenants and governors, that they should feede Demosthenes with money, and should procure to entertaine him above all the men in Græce, as he that could best withdraw Philip, and trouble him with the warres and tumults of Græce. And this was afterwards proved by letters found of Demosthenes him selfe, the which came to king Alexanders hands in the citie of Sardis, and by other writings also of the governors and Lieuetenants of the king of Persia: in the which were named directly the expresse sommes of money which had bene sent and given unto him. Now, the Græcians being thus overthrowen by battel, the other Orators, adversaries unto Demosthenes in the common wealth, began to set apon him, and to prepare to accuse him. But the people did not onely cleere him of all the accusations objected against him, but did continue to honor him more then before, and to call him to assemblies, as one that loved the honor and benefit of his contry. So that when the bones of their contry men which were slayne at the battell

GRECIANS AND ROMANES

of Chæronea, were brought to be openly buried according to the custom. the people gave him the honor to make the funeral oration in praise of the dead, and made no shew of sorow or griefe for the losse they had received: (as Theopompus witnesseth, and doth nobly declare) but rather in contrary manner shewed that they did not repent them in following of his counsel, but did honor him that gave it. Demosthenes then did make the funerall oration. But afterwards in all the decrees he preferred to the people, he would never subscribe any, to prevent the sinister lucke and misfortune of his name, but did passe it under his friends names one after another, untill he grew coragious againe, shortly after that he understoode of the death of Philip, who was slaine immediatly after the victorie he wanne at Chæronea. And it seemeth this was the meaning of the prophecie or oracle in the two last verses:

> The vanquished bewayles his lucklesse lot,
> And he that winnes, with life escapeth not.

Now Demosthenes hearing of Philips death, before the newes were openly known, to prevent them, he would put the people again into a good hope of better lucke to come. Thereupon he went with a cheerfull countenance into the assembly of the counsel, and told them there, that he had had a certain dreame that promised great good hap, and that out of hand unto the Athenians: and immediatly after, the messengers arrived that brought certain newes of king Philips death. Thereupon the Athenians made sacrifices of joy to the goddes for this happie newes, and appointed a crowne unto Pausanias that had slaine him. Demosthenes also came abroade in his best gowne, and crowned with flowers, seven dayes after the death of his daughter, as Æschines reporteth: who reproveth him for it, and noteth him to be a man having litle love or charitie unto his owne children. But in deede Æschines selfe deserveth more blame, to have such a tender womanish hart, as to beleve, that weeping, and lamenting, are signes of a gentle and charitable nature, condemning them that with pacience and constancie doe passe away such misfortunes. But now to the

Demosthenes preferreth the joy of his contrie, before the sorow of his owne daughter.

Æschines reproved by Plutarch for his fonde beleefe, that blubbering and sorowing are signes of love and charitie.

301

Athenians againe. I can neither thinke nor say that they
did wisely to shew such open signes of joy, as to weare
crownes and garlands upon their heads, nor also to sacrifice
to the goddes for the death of a Prince, that behaved him
selfe so Princely and curteously unto them in the victories
he had won of them. For, though in dede all cruelty be
subject to the revenge of the goddes, yet is this an act of a
vile and base minde, to honor a man, and while he lived to
make him free of their citie, and now that an other hath
slaine him, they to be in such an exceeding jolitie withall,
and to exceede the bondes of modestie so farre, as to rampe
in maner with both their feete upon the dead, and to sing
songes of victorie, as if they them selves had bene the men
that had valliantly slaine him. In contrarie manner also, I
praise and commend the constancie and corage of Demosthenes, that he leaving the teares and lamentacion of his
home trouble unto women, did him selfe in the meane time
that he thought was for the benefite of the common wealth:
and in my opinion, I thinke he did therein like a man of
corage, and worthy to be a governor of a common wealth,
never to stowpe nor yeeld, but alwayes to be found stable
and constant, for the benefit of the common wealth, reject-
ing all his troubles, cares, and affections, in respect of the
service of his contrie, and to keepe his honor much more
carefully, then common players use to doe, when they play
the partes of Kings and Princes, whom we see neither weepe
nor laugh when they list, though they be on the stage: but
when the matter of the play falleth out to geve them just
occasion. But omitting those reasons, if there be no reason
(as in deede there is not) to leave and forsake a man in his
sorow and trouble, without geving him some wordes of comfort, and rather to devise some matter to asswage his sorow,
and to withdraw his minde from that, to thinke upon some
pleasaunter thinges: even as they should keepe sore eyes
from seeing bright and glaring colours, in offering them
greene and darker. And from whence can a man take
greater comfort for his troubles and grieves at home, when
the common wealth doth well: then to joyne their private
grieves with common joyes, to the end, that the better may

Plutarch
praiseth
Demosthenes
constancie, for
leaving of his
mourning, to
rejoyce for
his common
contrie
benefit.

302

obscure and take away the worse? But thus farre I disgressed
from my historie, enlarging this matter, bicause Æschines
in his Oration touching this matter, did move the peoples
hartes too muche to womanish sorow. But now to the rest.
The cities of Græce being againe stirred up by Demosthenes,
made a new league againe together. and the Thebans also
having armed them selves by his practise, did one day set
upon the garrison of the Macedonians within their city, and
slue many of them. The Athenians prepared also to maintaine warre on the Thebans behalfe, and Demosthenes was
dayly at all the assemblies of counsell, in the pulpit, perswading the people with his Orations· and he wrote also
into Asia unto the king of Persiaes Lieutenaunts and Captaines, to make warre with Alexander on their side, calling
him child, and Margites, as muche to say, as foole. But
after that Alexander having set all his things at stay within
his realme, came him selfe in person with his armie, and invaded the contrie of Bœotia: then fell the pride of the
Athenians greatly, and Demosthenes also plied the pulpit
no more as he was wont. At length, the poore Thebans
being left unto them selves, forsaken of everie man they
were compelled them selves alone to beare the brunte of
this warre, and so came their city to utter ruine and destruction. Thereby the Athenians being in a marvelous
feare and perplexitie, did sodainly choose Ambassadors to
send unto this young king, and Demosthenes chiefly among
others. who being affrayed of Alexanders furie and wrath,
durst not goe to him, but returned from mount Cytheron,
and gave up the Ambassade. But Alexander sent to summone the Athenians, to send unto him ten of their Orators,
as Idomeneus and Duris both doe write: or eight, as the
most writers and best historiographers doe reporte, which
were these· Demosthenes, Polyeuctus, Ephialtes, Lycurgus,
Myrocles, Damon, Callisthenes, and Charidemus. At which
time, they wryte that Demosthenes told the people of Athens,
the fable of the sheepe and woulves, how that the woulves
came on a time, and willed the sheepe, if they woulde have
peace with them, to deliver them their mastives that kept
them. And so he compared him selfe, and his companions

Demosthenes
raiseth up the
Græcians
against
Alexander.

Alexander
required cer-
taine Orators
of Athens.

Demosthenes
tale of the
sheepe and
woulves.

303

LIVES OF THE NOBLE

that travelled for the benefit of the contrie, unto the dogges
that kepe the flocks of sheepe, and calling Alexander the
woulfe. And so forth, sayd he, like as you see these corne
maisters bringing a sample of their corne in a dish or
napkin to shew you, and by that litle doe sell all that they
have: so I thinke you will all wonder, that delivering of us,
you will also deliver your selves into the handes of your
enemies. Aristobulus of Cassandra reporteth this matter
thus. Now the Athenians being in consultacion, not knowing how to resolve: Demades having taken five talents of
them whom Alexander demaunded, did offer him selfe, and
promised to goe in this Ambassade unto Alexander, and to
intreate for them, either bicause he trusted in the love the
king did beare him, or else for that he thought he hoped he
shoulde finde him pacified, as a Lyon glutted with the blood
of beastes which he had slaine. Howsoever it happened, he
perswaded the people to send him unto him, and so handled
Alexander, that he got their pardon, and did reconcile him
with the citie of Athens. Thereuppon Alexander being
retyred, Demades and his fellowes bare all the sway and
authoritie, and Demosthenes was under foote. In deede
when Agis king of Lacedæmon, came with his armie into
the field, he began a litle to rowse him selfe, and to lift up
his head: but he shrunke choller againe soone after, bicause
the Athenians woulde not rise with the Lacedæmonians, who
were overthrowen, and Agis slaine in battell. At that time

was the cause of the crowne pleaded against Ctesiphon, and
the plea was written a litle before the battell of Chæronea,
in the yeare when Charondas was Provost of Athens: howbeit
no sentence was given but ten yeres after that Aristophon
was Provost. This was such an open judgement, and so
famous, as never was any, as well for the great fame of the
Orators that pleaded in emulacion one of the other, as also
for the worthines of the Iudges that gave sentence thereof:
who did not leave Demosthenes to his enemies, although in
deede they were of greater power then he, and were also
supported with the favor and good will of the Macedonians:
but they did notwithstanding so well quit him, that Æschines
had not so muche as the fift parte of mens voyces and

304

opinions in his behalfe. Wherefore immediatly after sentence geven, he went out of Athens for shame, and travelled into the contrie of Ionia, and unto the Rhodes, where he did teache Rethoricke. Shortly after, Harpalus flying out of Alexanders service, came unto Athens, being to be charged with many fowle matters he had committed by his exceeding prodigalitie : and also bicause he feared Alexanders furie, who was growen severe and cruell, unto his chiefest servauntes.

Harpalus a
great money
man came to
Athens, flying
from Alex-
ander.

He comming now amongest the Athenians, with store of gold and silver, the Orators being greedie and desirous of the golde and silver he had brought : beganne straight to speake for him, and did counsell the people to receive and protect a poore suter that came to them for succour. But Demosthenes gave counsell to the contrarie, and bad them rather drive him out of the citie, and take heede they brought not warres apon their backes, for a matter that not onely was not necessarie, but furthermore meerely unjust. But within fewe daies after, inventory being taken of all Harpalus goods, he perceiving that Demosthenes tooke great pleasure to see a cuppe of the kings, and considered verie curiously the facion and workemanshippe upon it : he gave it him in his hand, to judge what it weyed. Demosthenes peasing it, wondered at the great weight of it, it was so heavie : so he asked how many pownd weight it weyed. Harpalus smiling, answered him : It will wey thee twentie talents. So when night was come, he sent him the cuppe, with the twentie talentes. This Harpalus was a verie wise man, and found straight by Demosthenes countenaunce that he loved money, and coulde presently judge his nature, by seeing his pleasaunt countenaunce, and his eyes still upon the cuppe. So Demosthenes refused not his gift, and being overcomen withall, as if he had received a garrison into his house, he tooke Harpalus parte. The next morning, he went into the assemblie of the people, having his necke bound up with wolle and rolles. So when they called him by his name to steppe up into the pulpit, to speake to the people as he had done before : he made a signe with his head, that he had an impediment in his voyce, and that he could not speake. But wise men laughing at his fine excuse, tolde

LIVES OF THE NOBLE

**DEMOS-
THENES**

*This conceit
can hardly be
expressed in
any other lan-
guage, then
in Greeke.
For he sayth,
οὐκ ἀκούσατε
τοῦ τὴν κυλίκα
ἔχοντος :
alluding to
the verbe
κυλειν, which
signifieth to
delight by
pleasaunt
speeche or
sound

Demosthenes
banishment.

him it was no sinanche that had stopped his wesill that night, as he would make them beleve : but it was Harpalus argent-synanche which he had received, that made him in that case. Afterwardes when the people understoode that he was corrupted, Demosthenes going about to excuse him selfe, they would not abide to heare him : but made a noyse and exclamacion against him.   Thereuppon there rose up a pleasaunt conceited man, that sayd : Why my maisters, do ye refuse to heare a man that hath * such a golden tongue? The people thereuppon did immediatly banishe Harpalus, and fearing least king Alexander would require an accompt of the gold and silver which the Orators had robbed and pilfred away among them. they made very diligent searche and inquirie in every mans house, excepting Callicles house, the sonne of Arrenidas, whose house they would have searched by no meanes, bicause he was but newly maried, and had his newe spowse in his house, as Theopompus wryteth. Nowe Demosthenes desiring to shewe that he was in fault, preferred a decree, that the court of the Areopagites should heare the matter, and punish them that were found faultie, and therewithall straight offered him selfe to be tried. Howbeit he was one of the first whom the court condemned in the summe of fiftie talents, and for lacke of payment, they put him in prison : where he could not endure long, both for the shame of the matter for the which he was condemned, as also for his sickely body. So he brake prison, partly without the privitie of his keepers, and partely also with their consent. for they were willing he should make a scape. Some doe report that he fled not farre from the citie : where it was told him that certaine of his enemies followed him, whereuppon he would have hidden him selfe from them. But they them selves first called him by his name, and comming to him, prayed him to take money of them, which they had brought him from their houses to helpe him in his banishment : and that therefore they ran after him. Then they did comfort him the best they could, and perswaded him to be of good cheere, and not to dispaire for the misfortune that was comen unto him. This did pearce his hart the more for sorow, that he aunswered them : Why, would you not have

306

me be sorie for my misfortune, that compelleth me to forsake the citie where in deede I have so curteous enemies,
that it is hard for me to finde any where so good frends?
So he tooke his banishment unmanly, and remained the
most parte of his banishment in the citie of Ægina, or at
the citie of Trœzen, where oftentimes he would cast his
eyes towards the contrie of Attica, and weepe bitterly. And
some have written certeine words he spake, which shewed no
minde of a man of corage, nor were aunswerable to the noble
thinges he was wont to perswade in his Orations. For it is
reported of him, that as he went out of Athens, he looked
backe againe, and holding up his handes to the castell, sayd
in this sorte: O Ladie Minerva, Ladie patronesse of this
city· why doest thou delight in three so mischievous beastes
the owle, the draggon, and the people? Besides, he perswaded the young men that came to see him, and that were
with him, never to meddle in matters of state, assuring
them, that if they had offred him two wayes at the first,
the one to goe into the assembly of the people, to make
Orations in the pulpit, and the other to be put to death
presently, and that he had knowen as he did then, the
troubles a man is compelled to suffer that medleth with the
affaires of the state, the feare, the envie, the accusacions,
and troubles in the same: he would rather have chosen
the way to have suffered death. So, Demosthenes continuing in his exile, king Alexander dyed, and all Græce was up
againe: insomuch as Leosthenes being a man of great valure,
had shut up Antipater in the citie of Lamea, and there kept
him straightly besieged. Then Pytheas and Callimedon,
surnamed Carabos, two Orators, and both of them banished
from Athens, they tooke parte with Antipater, and went
from towne to towne with his Ambassadors and frendes,
perswading the Græcians not to sturre, neither to take
parte with the Athenians. But Demosthenes in contrarie
maner, joyning with the Ambassadors sent from Athens into
everie quarter, to solicite the cities of Græce, to seeke to
recover their libertie: he did aide them the best he coulde,
to solicite the Græcians, to take armes with the Athenians,
to drive the Macedonians out of Græce. And Phylarchus

DEMOS-
THENES

Demosthenes
tooke his
banishment
grievously.

Three mis-
chievous
beasts.

Antipater be-
sieged of the
Athenians.

307

writeth, that Demosthenes encountered with Pytheas wordes
in an open assemblie of the people in a certaine towne of
Arcadia. Pytheas having spoken before him, had said: Like
as we presume alwaies that there is some sickenesse in the house
whether we doe see asses milke brought: so must that towne
of necessitie be sicke, wherein the Ambassadors of Athens
doe enter. Demosthenes aunswered him againe, turning his
comparison against him: that in deede they brought asses
milke, where there was neede to recover health: and even
so, the Ambassadors of Athens were sent, to heale and cure
them that were sicke. The people at Athens understanding
what Demosthenes had done, they so rejoyced at it, that
presently they gave order in the fielde, that his banishment

should be revoked. He that perswaded the decree of his
revocation, was called Dæmon, Pæanian, that was his nephew:
and thereupon the Athenians sent him a galley to bring him
to Athens, from the city of Ægina. So Demosthenes being
arrived at the haven of Piræa, there was neither Governor,
Priest, nor almost any townes man left in the city, but went
out to the haven to welcome him home. So that Demetrius
Magnesian wryteth, that Demosthenes then lifting up his
handes unto heaven sayed, that he thought him selfe happie
for the honor of that jorney, that the returne from his
banishment was farre more honorable, then Alcibiades returne in the like case had bene. For Alcibiades was called
home by force: and he was sent for with the good will of
the citizens. This notwithstanding, he remained still condemned for his fine: for by the law, the people coulde not
dispence withall, nor remit it. Howbeit they devised a way
to deceive the lawe: for they had a manner to geve certaine
money unto them that did prepare and sette out the aulter
of Iupiter savior, for the day of the solemnitie of the sacrifice, the which they did yearely celebrate unto him: so they

gave him the charge to make this preparacion for the summe
of fifty talents being the summe of the fine aforesayd
wherin he was condemned. Howbeit, he did not long enjoy
the good happe of his restitucion to his contry and goodes.
For the affaires of the Græcians were immediatly after
brought to utter ruine. For the battell of Cranon which

they lost, was in the moneth Munichyon (to wit, Iulie) and
in the moneth Boedromion next ensuing, (to wit, August)
the garrison of the Macedonians entred into the forte of
Munichya. And in the moneth Pyanepsion (to wit, the
October following) Demosthenes died in this maner. When
newes came to Athens, that Antipater and Craterus were
comming thither with a great armie, Demosthenes and his
frends got out of the towne a litle before they entred, the
people, by Demades perswasion, having condemned them to
dye. So, every man making shift for him selfe, Antipater
sent souldiers after them to take them . and of them Archias
was Captaine, surnamed Phygadotheras, as muche to say,
as a hunter of the banished men. It is reported that this
Archias was borne in the citie of Thuries, and that he had
bene sometimes a common player of tragedies · and that
Polus also who was borne in the citie of Ægines, (the excellentest craftes maister in that facultie of all men) was his
scholler. Yet Hermippus doth recite him amongest the
number of the schollers of Lacritus the Orator. And
Demetrius also wryteth, that he had bene at Anaximenes
schoole. Now, this Archias having founde the Orator
Hyperides in the citie of Ægina, Aristonicus Marathonian,
and Himeræus the brother of Demetrius the Phalerian,
which had taken sanctuary in the temple of Ajax : he tooke
them out of the temple by force, and sent them unto Antipater, who was at that time in the citie of Cleones, where he
did put them all to death . and some say, that he did cut of
Hyperides tongue. Furthermore, hearing that Demosthenes
had taken sanctuarie in the Ile of Calauria, he tooke litle
pinnasies, and a certaine number of Thracian souldiers, and
being comen thither, he sought to perswade Demosthenes
to be contented to goe with him unto Antipater, promising
him that he should have no hurt. Demosthenes had a
straunge dreame the night before, and thought that he had
played a tragedie contending with Archias, and that he
handled him selfe so well, that all the lookers on at the
Theater did commende him, and gave him the honor to be
the best player : howbeit that otherwise he was not so well
furnished, as Archias and his players, and that in all manner

DEMOS-
THENES

Archias Phy-
gadotheras, a
hunter of the
banished men.

Demosthenes
dreame

309

DEMOS-
THENES

of furniture he did farre exceede him. The next morning when Archias came to speake with him, who using gentle wordes unto him, thinking thereby to winne him by fayer meanes to leave the sanctuarie: Demosthenes looking him full in the face, sitting still where he was, without removing, sayd unto him : O Archias, thou diddest never perswade me when thou playedst a play, neither shalt thou nowe perswade me, though thou promise me. Then Archias began to be angrie with him, and to threaten him. O, sayd Demosthenes, now thou speakest in good earnest, without dissimulacion, as the Oracle of Macedon hath commaunded thee : for before, thou spakest in the clowdes, and farre from thy thought. But I pray thee stay a while, till I have written somewhat to my frendes. After he had sayd so, he went into the temple as though he would have dispatched some letters, and did put the ende of the quill in his mouth which he wrote withall, and bit it as his maner was when he did use to write any thing, and held the ende of the quill in his mouth a pretie while together : then he cast his gowne over his head, and layed him downe. Archias souldiers seeing that, being at the dore of the temple, laughing him to scorne (thinking he had done so for that he was affrayed to dye) called him coward, and beast. Archias also comming to him, prayed him to rise, and beganne to use the former perswasions to him, promising him that he would make Antipater his frende. Then Demosthenes feeling the poyson worke, cast open his gowne, and boldly looking Archias in the face, sayd unto him : Nowe when thou wilt, play Creons parte, and throwe my bodie to the dogges, without further grave or buriall. For my parte, O god Neptune, I do goe out of thy temple being yet alive, bicause I will not prophane it with my death : but Antipater, and the Macedonians, have not spared to defile thy sanctuarie with blood, and cruell murder. Having spoken these wordes, he prayed them to stay him up by his armeholes, for his feete began alreadie to faile him, and thinking to goe forward, as he past by the aulter of Neptune, he fel downe, and geving one gaspe, gave up the ghost. Now touching the poyson, Aristo reporteth, that he sucked and drewe it up into his

Demosthenes taketh poyson to kill him selfe, in the temple of Neptune, in the Ile of Calauria.

The death of Demosthenes.

310

mouth out of his quill, as we have sayd before. But one
Pappus, (from whom Hermippus has taken his historie)
wryteth, that when he was layed on the ground before the
aulter, they founde the beginning of a letter which sayd:
Demosthenes unto Antipater, but no more. Nowe his death
being thus sodaine, the Thracian souldiers that were at the
temple dore, reported that they sawe him plucke the poyson
which he put into his mouth, out of a litle cloth he had, thinking to them that it had bene a pece of gold he had swallowed
downe. Howbeit a maide of the house that served him,
being examined by Archias about it : tolde him that he had
caried it about him a long time, for a preservatife for him.
Eratosthenes writeth, that he kept this poyson in a litle
boxe of gold made hollow within, the which he ware as
a bracelet about his arme. There are many writers also
that do reporte his death diversly, but to recite them all it
were in vaine : saving that there was one called Demochares
(who was Demosthenes verie frende) sayd, that he dyed not
so sodainly by poyson, but that it was the speciall favor of the
gods (to preserve him from the crueltie of the Macedonians)
that so sodainly tooke him out of his life, and made him
feele so litle paine. Demosthenes dyed the sixteenth day
of the moneth Pynepsion (to wit, October) on the which
day they doe celebrate at Athens the feast of Ceres, called
Tesmophoria, which is the dolefullest feast of all the yeare.
on the which day also, the women remaine all day longe
in the temple of the goddesse, without meate or drinke.
Shortly after, the Athenians to honor him according to his
desertes, did cast his image in brasse, and made a lawe
besides, that the oldest man of his house shoulde for ever
be kept within the pallace, at the charge of the common
wealth : and ingraved these verses also apon the base of his
image :

> Hadst thou Demosthenes had strength according to thy hart,
> The Macedons should not have wrought the Greekes such woe and
> smart.

For they that thinke, that it was Demosthenes him selfe
that made the verses in the Ile of Calauria, before he tooke

Marginal notes:

DEMOS-
THENES

The time of
Demosthenes
death.

The Athen-
ians honored
Demosthenes
after his
death.

his poyson: they are greatly deceived. But yet a litle before my first comming to Athens, there went a reporte that such a thing happened. A certaine souldier being sent for to come unto his Captaine, did put such pecces of gold as he had into the handes of Demosthenes statue, which had both his hands joyned together: and there grew hard by it a great plane tree, divers leaves whereof either blowen of by winde by chaunce, or else put there of purpose by the souldier, covered so this golde, that it was there a long time, and no man found it: untill such time as the souldier came againe, and found it as he left it. Hereuppon this matter running abroade in everie mans mouth, there were divers wise men that tooke occasion of this subject, to make epigrammes in the praise of Demosthenes, as one who in his life was never corrupted. Furthermore, Demades did not long enjoy the honor he thought he had newly gotten. For the justice of the goddes, revenger of the death of Demosthenes, brought him into Macedon, to receive just punishment by death, of those whom he dishonestly flattered: being before growen hatefull to them, and afterwardes committed a fault whereby he coulde not escape. For there were letters of his

taken, by the which he did perswade, and pray * Perdiccas, to make him selfe king of Macedon, and to deliver Græce from bondage, saying that it hong but by a threde, and yet it was halfe rotten, meaning thereby, Antipater. Dinarchus Corinthian accused him, that he wrote these letters the which so grievously offended Cassander, that first he slewe his owne sonne in his armes, and then commaunded that

they should afterwards kill Demades, making him feele then by those miseries (which are the cruellest that can happen unto man) that traitors betraying their owne contrie do first of all betray them selves. Demosthenes had often fore-
warned him of his end, but he would never beleve
him. Thus, my frend Sossius, you have what we
can deliver you, by reading, or reporte, touching
Demosthenes life and doings.

GRECIANS AND ROMANES

THE LIFE OF
MARCUS TULLIUS CICERO

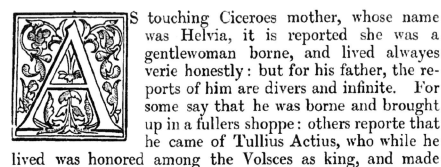

touching Ciceroes mother, whose name Ciceroes was Helvia, it is reported she was a parentage. gentlewoman borne, and lived alwayes verie honestly: but for his father, the reports of him are divers and infinite. For some say that he was borne and brought up in a fullers shoppe: others reporte that he came of Tullius Actius, who while he lived was honored among the Volsces as king, and made verie sharpe and cruell warres with the Romanes. But surely it seemes to me, that the first of that name called Cicero, was some famous man, and that for his sake his ofspring continued still that surname, and were glad to keepe it, though many men scorned it, bicause *Cicer* in English signifieth a riche pease. That Cicero had a thing Cicero, why upon the tippe of his nose, as it had bene a litle wart, so called. muche like to a riche pease, whereuppon they surnamed him Cicero. But this Cicero, whose life we write of nowe, nobly aunswered certaine of his frendes on a time geving him counsell to chaunge his name, when he first made sute for office, and beganne to practise in matters of state: that he woulde endevour him selfe to make the name of the Ciceroes more noble and famous, then the Scauri, or Catuli. After Cicero that, Cicero beinge made Treasorer in Sicile, he gave an Quæstor. offering of certeine silver plate unto the goddes, and at large engraved on it his two first names, Marcus Tullius: and in place of his third name, he pleasauntly commaunded the workeman to cut out the forme and facion of a riche pease. Thus muche they wryte of his name. Nowe Ciceroes for his birth, it was sayed that his mother was brought a birth. bedde of him without any paine, the third daye of Ianuarie: on which day the Magistrates and Governours of Rome doe

: RR   313

An image
appeared to
Ciceroes
nurse.

Ciceroes
towardnes
and wit.

use at this present, yearely to make solemne prayers and
sacrifices unto the goddes, for the health and prosperitie of
the Emperour. Further, it is reported, that there appeared
an image to his nurse, that did prognosticate unto her she
gave a childe sucke, which in time to come shoulde doe great
good unto all the Romanes. Nowe though such thinges
may seeme but dreames and fables unto many, yet Cicero
him selfe shortly after proved this prophecie true : bicause
that when he came of age to learne, he grewe so toward, and
wanne suche fame among the boyes, for his excellent wit and
quicke capacitie. For thereuppon came the other boyes
fathers them selves to the schoole to see his face, and to be
eye witnesses of the reporte that went of him, of his sharpe
and quicke witte to learne. But others of the rude and
baser sorte of men were offended with their sonnes, bicause
to honor Cicero, they did alwayes put him in the middest
betwene them, as they went in the streetes. Cicero in deede
had suche a naturall witte and understanding, as Plato
thought meete for learning, and apt for the studie of Philosophie. For he gave him selfe to all kinde of knowledge,
and there was no arte, nor any of the liberall sciences, that
he disdained : notwithstanding in his first young yeares he
was apter, and better disposed to the studie of Poetrie, then

Cicero a
notable Poet.

any other. There is a pretie poeme of his in verses of eight
staves, called *Pontius Glaucus*, extant at this day, the which
he made when he was but a boye. After that, being geven
more earnestlie unto this studie, he was not onely thought
the best Orator, but the best Poet also of all the Romanes in
his time : and yet doth the excellencie of his eloquence, and
commendacion of his tongue continewe, even to this daye,
notwithstanding the great alteracion and chaunge of the
Latine tongue. But his Poetrie hath lost the name and
estimacion of it, bicause there were many after him that

Cicero,
Philoes
scholler, the
Academicke
Philosopher.

became farre more excellent therein then he. After he had
left his childishe studies, he became then Philoes scholler,
the Academicke Philosopher, the onely scholler of all Clitomachus schollers, whome the Romanes esteemed so muche for
his eloquence, and loved more for his gentle behaviour and
conversation. He gave him selfe also to be a follower of

GRECIANS AND ROMANES

Mutius Scævola, who at that time was a greate man in
Rome, and Prince of the Senate, and who did also instruct
Cicero in the lawes of Rome.   He did also followe Sylla for
a time, in the warres of the Marsians.   But when he sawe
that the common wealth of Rome fell to civill warres, and
from civill warres to a monarchie : then he returned againe
to his booke and contemplative life, and frequented the
learned men of Græce, and alwayes studied with them, untill
Sylla had gotten the upper hande, and that he saw all the
common wealth againe at some stay.   About that time,
Sylla causing the goods of one that was sayd to be slaine,
to be solde by the crier : (beinge one of the outlawes and
proscriptes, to witte, banished by billes sette up on postes)
Chrysogonus, one of Syllaes freed bondemen, and in great
favour with his maister, bought them for the summe of two
thowsande Drachmes.   Therewithall the sonne and heire of
the deade person called Roscius, being marvelouslie offended,
he shewed that it was too shamefull an abuse . for his
fathers goodes amounted to the summe of two hundred and
fiftie talentes.   Sylla finding him selfe thus openlie touched
with publike fraude and deceite, for the onely gratifyinge of
his man : he procured Chrysogonus to accuse him, that he
had killed his owne father.   Never an Orator durst speake in
Roscius behalfe to defende his cause, but shronke colour,
fearing Syllaes crueltie and severitie.   Wherefore poore
Roscius the younge man, seeinge everie man forsake him, had
no other refuge but to goe to Cicero, whome his frendes did
counsell and perswade boldly to take upon him the defence
of Roscius cause : for he shoulde never have a happier
occasion, nor so noble a beginning to bring him selfe into
estimacion, as this.   Thereuppon Cicero determined to take
his cause in hande, and did handell it so well, that he
obteyned the thing he sued for · whereby he wanne him
greate fame and credit.   But yet being affrayed of Syllaes
displeasure, he absented him selfe from Rome, and went into
Græce, gevinge it out that his travell was for a disease he
had uppon him.   In deede Cicero was dogge leane, a litle
eater, and woulde also eate late, bicause of the greate weakenesse of his stomacke . but yet he had a good lowde voyce,

315

though it was somewhat harshe, and lacked grace and comelynesse. Furthermore he was so earnest and vehement in his Oration that he mounted still with his voyce into the highest tunes: insomuche that men were affrayed it woulde one daye put him in hazard of his life. When he came to Athens, he went to heare Antiochus of the citie of Ascalona, and fell in greate likinge with his sweete tongue, and excellent grace, though otherwise he misliked his newe opinions in Philosophie. For Antiochus had then forsaken the opinions of the newe Academicke Philosophers, and the sect of the Carneades: being moved thereunto, either through the manifest proofe of thinges, or by his certaine judgement, or (as some say) for that of an ambition or dissention against the schollers and followers of Clitomachus and Philo, he had reproved the resolucions of the Academickes, which he had of long time defended, onely to leane for the moste parte to the Stoickes opinions. Howebeit Cicero had most affection unto the Academickes, and did studie that sect more then all the rest, of purpose, that if he sawe he were forbidden to practise in the common wealth at Rome, he woulde then goe to Athens (leaving all pleaes and Orators in the common wealth) to bestowe the rest of his time quietly in the studie of Philosophie. At length, when he hearde newes of Syllaes death, and sawe that his bodie was growen to good state and health by exercise, and that his voyce became dayly more and more to fill mens eares with a sweete and pleasaunt sounde, and yet was lowde enough for the constitucion of his bodie: receiving letters dayly from his frendes at Rome, that prayed him to returne home, and moreover, Antiochus selfe also earnestlie perswadinge him to practise in the common wealth: he beganne againe to fall to the studie of Rethoricke, and to frame him selfe to be eloquent, being a necessarie thing for an Orator, and did continuallie exercise him selfe in making Orations uppon any speache or proposicion, and so frequented the chiefe Orators and masters of eloquence that were at that time. To this ende therefore he went into Asia unto Rhodes, and amongest the Orators of Asia, he frequented Xenocles Andramettin, and Dionysius Magnesian, and studied also with Menippus

GRECIANS AND ROMANES

Carian: at Rhodes he hearde Apollonius Molon, and the Philosopher Posidonius. And it is reported also, that Apollonius wanting the Latine tongue, he did pray Cicero for exercise sake, to declame in Græke. Cicero was verie well contented with it, thinkinge that thereby his faultes shoulde be the better corrected. When he had ended his declamacion, all those that were present were amazed to heare him, and everie man praised him one after an other. Howebeit Apollonius all the while Cicero spake, did never shewe any glad countenaunce: and when he had ended, he stayed a greate while and sayed never a worde. Cicero misliking withall, Apollonius at length sayed unto him: As for me Cicero, I doe not onely praise thee, but more then that, I wonder at thee: and yet I am sorie for poore Græce, to see that learning and eloquence (which were the two onely giftes and honor left us) are by thee obtained with us, and caried unto the Romanes. Nowe Cicero being verie well disposed, to goe with good hope to practise at Rome, he was a litle discouraged by an Oracle that was tolde him. For, inquiring of the god Apollo Delphian, howe he might doe to winne fame and estimacion: the Nunne Pythias aunswered him he shoulde obtayne it, so that in his doinges he woulde rather followe the disposicion of his owne nature, then the opinion of the common people. Wherefore when he came to Rome, at the first he proceeded verie warely, and discreetely, and did unwillinglie seeke for any office, and when he did, he was not greatlie esteemed: for they commonlie called him the Græcian, and scholler, which are two wordes, the which the artificers, (and suche base mechanicall people at Rome,) have ever readie at their tongues ende. Nowe he beinge by nature ambicious of honour, and prickt forward also by the perswasion of his father and frendes: in the ende he beganne to pleade, and there obteyned not the chiefest place by litle and litle, but so soone as he fell to practise, he was immediatly esteemed above all the other Orators and pleaders in his time, and did excell them all. Yet it is reported notwithstanding, that for his gesture and pronunciacion, having the selfe same defectes of nature at the beginning, which Demosthenes had: to reforme them, he carefully studied to counterfeate

317

CICERO
Roscius and
Æsopus
common
players.

Roscius, an excellent commediant, and Æsope also a player of tragedies. Of this Æsope men wryte, that he playing one day Atrius parte upon a stage (who determined with him selfe how he might be revenged of his brother Thyestes) a servaunt by chaunce having occasion to runne sodainly by him, he forgetting him selfe, striving to shewe the vehement passion and furie of this king, gave him suche a blowe on his head with the scepter in his hand, that he slue him dead in the place. Even so Ciceroes words were of so great force to perswade, by meanes of his grace and pronunciacion. For he mocking the Orators that thrust out their heades, and cried in their Orations, was wont to say that they were like to lame men, who were driven to ryde, bicause they coulde not goe a foote: Even so (sayd he) they crie out, bicause they can not speake. Truely pleasaunt tawntes doe grace an Orator, and sheweth a fine witte but yet Cicero used them so commonly, that they were offensive unto many, and brought him to be counted a malicious scoffer and spightfull man. He was chosen Treasorer in the time of dearth, when there was great scarcetie of corne at Rome: and the province of Sicile fell to his lotte. At his first comming thither, the Sicilians misliked him verie muche, bicause he compelled them to sende corne unto Rome · but after they had founde his diligence, justice, and lenitie, they honored him above any Governor that ever was sent from Rome. Nowe there were divers young gentlemen of Rome of noble houses, who being accused for sundrie faultes committed in warres against their honor, and martiall discipline, had bene sent backe againe unto the Prætor of Sicile: for whome Cicero pleaded, and did so excellently defende their cause, that they were pardoned everie man. Thereuppon, thinking well of him selfe, when his time expired, he went to Rome, and by the way there happened a prety feast unto him. As he passed through the contrie of Campania, (otherwise called the lande of labor) he met by chaunce with one of the chiefest Romanes of all his frends. So falling in talke with him, he asked him what they sayd of him at Rome, and what they thought of his doinges: imagining that all Rome had bene full of the glorie of his name and

Side notes

CICERO
Roscius and
Æsopus
common
players.

Cicero, a fine
Tawnter.

Cicero chosen
Quæstor.

Ciceroes diligence, justice,
and lenitie

deedes His frende asked him againe · And where hast thou
bene Cicero all this while, that we have not seene thee at
Rome? This killed his hart straight, when he sawe that
the reporte of his name and doinges, entring into the citie
of Rome as into an infinite sea, was so sodainely vanquished
away againe, without any other fame or speach. But after
that, when he looked into him selfe, and sawe that in reason
he tooke an infinite labor in hande to attaine to glorie,
wherein he sawe no certaine ende whereby to attaine unto
it it cut of a great parte of the ambicion he had in his
head. And yet the great pleasure he tooke to heare his Cicero,
ambitious,
and desirous
of praise.
owne praise, and to be overmuche geven to desire of honor
and estimacion : those two thinges continued with him
even to his dying day, and did eftsoones make him swarve
from justice. Furthermore, when he beganne thorowely to
practise in the affaires of the state, he thought it an ill
thing that artificers and craftes men shoulde have many
sortes of instrumentes and tooles without life, to knowe the
names of everie one of them, the places where they shoulde
take them, and the use whereto they shoulde employ them ·
and that a man of knowledge and qualitie (who doth all
thinges with the helpe and service of men) shoulde be slothfull, and carelesse, to learne to knowe the names of his
citizens Therefore he gave him selfe to knowe, not onely Cicero geven
to know mens
names, their
landes, and
frendes.
mens names of qualitie, but the streetes also they dwelt in,
what parte of the citie soever it was : their goodly houses in
the contrie, the frendes they made of, and the neighbours
whome they companied with. So that when he went abroade
into Italie, wheresoever he became, Cicero coulde shewe and
name his frendes houses. He was not verie riche, and yet
he had enough to serve his turne : the which made men
muse the more at him, and they loved him the better,
bicause he tooke no fee nor gifte for his pleading, what
cause soever he had in hande, but then speciallie, when he
defended a matter against Verres. This Verres had bene Ciceroes
doings
against
Verres.
Prætor of Sicilia, and had committed many lewde partes
there, for the which the Sicilians did accuse him. Cicero
taking apon him to defende their cause, made Verres to be
condemned, not by pleading, but in manner without plead-

ing, and in this sorte. The Prætors being his Iudges, and favoring Verres, had made so many rejornementes and delayes, that they had driven it of to the laste day of hearing. Cicero perceiving then he shoulde not have day light to speake all that he had to say against him, and that thereby nothing shoulde be done and judged: he rose up, and sayed, that there needed no further plea in this matter, but onely brought foorth the witnesses before the Iudges, and having caused their deposicions to be taken, he prayed they woulde proceede to sentence, according to their evidence geven on that behalfe. Yet some doe reporte, that Cicero gave many pleasaunt tawntes and girdes, in pleading the accusacion of the Sicilians against Verres. The Romanes doe call a bore, Verres. There was one Cæcilius, the sonne of a freed bondman, who was suspected to holde with the supersticion of the Iewes. This Cæcilius woulde have put by the Sicilians from following the accusacion of Verres, and woulde have had the matter of his accusacion only referred to him, for the prosecuting of it against him. Cicero skorning his sute,

sayd unto him: What hath a Iewe to doe with a swine? This Verres had a sonne somewhat above twentie yeares of age, who (as the reporte went) had a verie ill name for his beawtie. And therefore when Verres one day thought to mocke Cicero, saying that he was too womanly: His children (sayd he) are to be reproved of that secretly at home. In this accusacion, Hortensius the Orator durst not directly defende Verres: but touching the condemnacion of his fine, he was then contented to aunswere for him, for he had a Sphinx of Yvory geven him by Verres for his reward. Thereuppon Cicero gave him a pretie nippe by the way: but Hortensius not understanding him, sayd he coulde no skill of darke speaches. Well, sayd Cicero, yet hast thou a sphinx in thy house. In the ende Verres being condemned, and a fine sette on his heade to the value of seventie five Myriades, Cicero notwithstandinge was suspected to be bribed with money for agreeing to cast him in so small a summe. But

yet when he came to be Ædilis, the Sicilians to shew them selves thankefull to him, both brought and sent him many presentes out of Sicile. Of all that he tooke nothing to his

320

owne use, but onely bestowed their liberalitie in bringing
downe the prises of vittells at Rome. He had a goodly
house within the confines of the citie of Arpos, a farme also
by Naples, and an other about the citie of Pompeii. but all
these were no great thinges. Afterwardes also he had the
joynter of his wife Terentia, which amounted to the summe
of twelve Myriades, and besides all this, there came to him
by inheritaunce, eleven Myriades of their Denarii. Thereuppon he lived verie honestly and soberly, without excesse,
with his familiar frendes that loved him, both Græcians and
Romanes, and woulde never goe to supper till after sunne
set, not so muche for any great businesse he had, as for
the weakenesse of his stomake. But otherwise he was verie
curious, and carefull of his person, and woulde be rubbed and
noynted, and he would use also to walke a certaine number
of turnes by proporcion : and so exercising his bodie in that
sorte, he was never sicke, and besides was alwayes verie
strong and lustie of bodie, able to abide great paines and
sorowes which he fell into afterwardes. He gave his fathers
chiefe mansion house to his brother, and went to dwell
him selfe in the mount Palatine : bicause suche as came to
waite upon him to doe him honor, shoulde not take the
paines to goe so farre to see him. For, he had as many
men dayly at his gate everie morning, as either Crassus had
for his wealth, or Pompey for his estimacion among the
souldiers, both of them being at that time the chiefest
men of Rome. Yea furthermore, Pompeys selfe came unto
Cicero, bicause his Orations stoode him to great purpose,
for thincrease of his honor and authoritie. Nowe when
Cicero came to make sute to be Prætor (which is, to be
as an ordinarie judge) though he had many competitors, and
fellowe suters with him, yet was he first chosen affore them
all · and he did so honestly behave him selfe in that office,
that they did not so muche as once suspect him of briberie
or extorcion. And for proofe hereof, it is reported, that
Licinius Macer (a man that of him selfe was of great power,
and yet favored and supported besides by Crassus) was accused before Cicero of theft and extorcion in his office · but
he trustinge muche to his supposed credit, and to the greate

CICERO
Ciceroes
riches.

Ciceroesgreat
curtesie and
resorte.

Cicero chosen
Prætor.

sute and labour his frendes made for him, went home to his house before sentence proceeded against him (the Iudges being yet to geve their opinions) and there speedely trimmed his beard, and put a newe gowne uppon his backe, as though he had bene sure to have bene quitte of his accusacion, and then returned againe into the market place. But Crassus went to meete him, and tolde him all the Iudges had condemned him. Licinius Macer tooke suche a griefe and conceite upon it, that he went home to his house againe, layed him downe on his bedde, and never rose after. This judgement wanne Cicero greate fame, for they praised him exceedingly for the great paines he tooke, to see justice duely executed. An other called also Vatinius, (a bedlem fellowe, and one that behaved him selfe verie unreverently to the Magistrates in his pleadinge, and besides had a swollen necke) came verie arrogantly one day unto Cicero being in his Prætoriall seate, and asked him a thing which Cicero woulde not graunte him there, but woulde thinke of it at better leasure. Thereuppon Vatinius tolde him, that he would not be scrupulous to graunt that, if he were Prætor. Cicero turning to him, aunswered him againe: No more have I (sayd he) suche a swollen necke as thou hast. Towardes the ende of his office, two or three dayes before his time expired, there was one accused Manilius before him, that he also had robbed the common wealth. This Manilius was verie well beloved of the common people, who were perswaded that he was put in sute, not for any fault he had committed, but onely to despight Pompey with, whose familiar frende he was. So he required certaine dayes to aunswere the matter he was accused of; but Cicero woulde geve him no further respit, but to aunswere it the next day. The people therewith were marvelously offended, bicause the other Prætors in suche like cases were wont to geve tenne dayes respit to others. The next morninge when the Tribunes had brought him before the Iudges, and also accused him unto them: he besought Cicero to heare him pacientlie. Cicero made him aunswere, that havinge alwayes used as muche favour and curtesie as he possiblie might by lawe, unto those that were accused, he thought he shoulde

offer Manilius too great wrong, if he shoulde not doe the
like to him: wherefore, bicause he had but one day more
to continewe Prætor in office, he had purposely geven him
that day to make his aunswere before him. For he thought
that to leave his accusacion to the hearing of an other
Prætor, he coulde not have bene thought a man that had
borne him good will, and ment to pleasure him. These
wordes did marvelouslie chaunge the peoples opinion and
affection towardes him, and everie man speaking well of him,
they prayed him to defend Manilius cause. He willingly
graunted them: and comming from the benche, standing
at the barre like an Orator to pleade for him, he made a
notable Oration, and spake both boldly and sharpely against
the chiefe men of the citie, and those speciallie that did
envie Pompey. This notwithstanding, when he came to
sue to be Consul, he founde as great favour amongest the
Nobilitie, as he did with the communaltie. For they did
further his sute, for the common wealthes sake, upon this
occasion. The chaunge and alteracion of government the
which Sylla brought in, was thought straunge at the first
among the people: but nowe men by processe of time being
used to it, it was throughly established, and no man misliked it. At that time many men practised to subvert the
government, not for the benefit of the common wealth, but
to serve their owne covetous mindes. For Pompey being
then in the East partes, made warres with the kings of
Pontus and Armenia, and had not left sufficient force at
Rome to oppresse these seditious persons, that sought nothing
but rebellion. These men had made Lucius Catilina their
Captaine: a desperate man to attempt any great enterprise,
suttle, and malicious of nature. He was accused before
(besides many other vile faultes) for deflowering of his owne
daughter, and killinge his brother: and being affrayed to
be put in sute for it, he prayed Sylla to put his brother
amongest the number of the outlawes (or proscriptes) as
if he had bene then alive. These wicked rebells havinge
chosen them suche a Captaine, were sworne and bounde one
to an other in this manner. They killed a man, and did
eate of his fleshe together, and had besides corrupted the

most parte of all the youth. For Catiline their Captaine suffered everie man to take his pleasure, as his youth was inclined unto: as to banket, to followe harlottes, and gave them money largelie to bestowe in these vayne expences. Furthermore all Thuscan beganne to rise, and the most parte of Gaule also, lying betwene the Alpes and Italie. The citie of Rome it selfe was also in great daunger of rising, for the inequalitie of the goods of the inhabitauntes. For the noble men, and of greatest corage, had spent all their landes in playes and feasts, or in buildings and common workes, which they built at their owne charge, to currie favour with the common people, that they might obtaine the chiefe offices: so that thereby they became verie poore, and their goodes were in the handes of meane men and wretches. Thus the state of Rome stoode in great hazard of uprore, the which any man might easely have procured, that durst have taken uppon him any change or alteracion of government, there was then suche division among them in the state. Catiline notwithstanding, to provide him of a strong bullwarke to prosecute his intent, came to sue to be Consul, hoping that he should be chosen with Caius Antonius, a man that of him selfe was apt neither to doe any great good, nor much hurt, and yet that could be a great strength and aide unto him that woulde attempt any thing. Divers noble and wise men foreseeing that, did procure Cicero to sue for the Consulshippe. The people accepted him, and rejected Catiline. Antonius and Cicero thereuppon were created Consuls, although that Cicero of all the suters for the Consulship was but only a Knightes sonne, and not the sonne of a Senator of Rome. Nowe, though the common people understoode not the secret practise and meaning of Catiline: yet at the beginning of Ciceroes Consulshippe, there fell out great trouble and contencion in the common wealth. For they of the one side, whom Sylla had by his ordinaunces deposed from their dignities and offices in Rome (who were no small men, neither fewe in number) beganne to creepe into the peoples good will, alleaging many true and just reasons against the tyrannicall power of Sylla: howebeit spoken in ill time, when

C. Antonius, and M. T. Cicero created Consuls.

Great troubles at Rome, in the time of Ciceroes Consulshippe.

324

it was out of time to make any chaunge or alteracion in the
common wealth. The Tribunes on the other side preferred
lawes and ordinaunces to further this devise. They preferred
the lawe to choose the Decemviri, with soveraine power and
authoritie through all Italie and Syria, and also through all
the contries and provinces which Pompey had newly conquered to the Empire of Rome: to sell, and release all the
landes belonging to the state of Rome, to accuse any man
whome they thought good, to banishe any man, to restore
the Colonies with people, to take what money they woulde
out of the treasurie, to leavie men of warre, and to keepe
them in pay as long as they thought good. For this great
and absolute power of the Decemviri, there were many men
of great accompt that favored this law, but Antonius chiefly,
being colleague and fellowe Consul with Cicero, for he had
good hope to be chosen one of these ten Commissioners ·
and furthermore, it was thought that he was privie unto
Catilines conspiracie, and that he misliked it not, because
he was so muche in det. And this was it that the noble
men most feared of all other thinges. Thereuppon Cicero,
to provide first to prevent this daunger, graunted him the
province of the realme of Macedon: and the province of
Gaule being offered unto him selfe, he refused it. By this
good turne, he wanne Antonius like a hiered player, making
him to promise him that he would assist and aide him for
the benefit of the common wealth, and that he would say
no more, then he shoulde will him. When he had brought
him to this, and had wonne him to his minde: he then
beganne to be the bolder, and more stowtly to resist them
that were authors of this innovation and new lawes. Cicero
therefore in open Senate, did one day sharply reprove, and
invey against this law of the Decemviri, which the Tribunes
would have established. But thereby he did so terrifie the
authors thereof, that there was not one man durst speake
against him. This notwithstanding, the Tribunes afterwardes attempted once againe to have it to passe, and
appointed the Consuls to appeare before the people. Howbeit Cicero being nothing abashed at it, he commaunded
the Senate to follow him. So he did not only overthrow

CICERO

A law pre-
ferred for the
creacion and
authority of
the Decem-
viri.

325

this law of the Decemviri, which the Tribunes did preferre: but furthermore they were utterly discoraged and out of hope to bring any of their matters to passe they intended, he strooke them so dead with his eloquence. For Cicero onely of all men in Rome made the Romanes know, how muche eloquence doth grace and beawtifie that which is honest, and how invincible right and justice are, being eloquently set forth: and also how that a man that will be counted a wise Governor of a comman weale, should always in his doinges rather preferre profit, than to seeke to currie favor with the common people: yet so to use his words, that the thing which is profitable, may not

be also unpleasant. And to prove his sweete and pleasant tongue, may be alleaged that which he did in the time of his Consulship, touching the placing of men at the Theater to see the pastimes. For before, the knights of Rome did sit mingled one with another amongst the common people, and tooke their place as they came. The first that made the difference betwene them, was *Marcus Otho, at

that time Prætor: who made a law, by the which he ap-poynted severall seates for the knights, where they might from thenceforth see the pastimes. The people tooke this grievously, as a thing done to discountenance them: inso-much that Otho comming afterwards into the Theater, all the common people fel a whistling at him, to shame him withal. The knights also in contrariwise made him roome amongst them, with great clapping of hands, in token of honor. Therewith the people fell a whistling lowder then before, and the knights in like manner to clapping of their handes, and so grew to wordes one with another: that all the Theater was straight in uprore with it. Cicero under-standing it, went thither him selfe, and calling the people to the temple of the goddesse Bellona, he there so sharpely reproved them, and therewith so perswaded them, that re-turning presently to the Theater, they did then welcome and receive Otho with clapping of their handes, and con-tended with the knights which of them should doe him greatest honor. But now againe, the rebells of Catilines conspiracie (who were pretily cooled at the first for the feare they stoode in) began to be lustie againe, and to gather together, boldely incoraging one another to broache their practise, before Pompey returned, who was sayd to be on the way towards Rome with his armye. But besides them, those souldiers that had served before in the warres under Sylla, being dispersed uppe and downe Italy (but specially the best souldiers among them dwelling in the good townes of Thuscan) did stirre up Catiline to hasten the enterprise, perswading them selves that they should once againe have goods enough at hand, to spoyle and ransacke at their pleasure. These souldiers having one Manlius to their Captaine, that had borne office in the field under Sylla, conspyred with Catilin, and came to Rome to assist him in his sute: who purposed once againe to demaund the Consulship, being determined at the election to kill Cicero, in the tumult and hurly burly. The goddes also did plainly shewe by earthquakes, lightning and thunder, and by vision of spirits that did appeare, the secret practise and conspiracie: besides also, there fell out manifest conjectures and proofes by men that came to reveale them, howbeit they had not power sufficient to encownter so noble a man, and of great power as Catilin was. Cicero therefore deferring the day of election, called Catilin into the Senate, and there did examine him of that which was reported of him. Catiline supposing there were many in the Senate that had good wills to rebell, and also bicause he would shewe him self ready unto them that were of his conspiracie: he gave Cicero a gentle aunswer, and said thus, What doe I offend, sayd he, if that beeing two bodies in this towne, the one leane and weake, and throughly rotten, and hath a head: and the other being great, strong, and of power, having no head, I doe give it one? meaning under this darke aunswer, to signifie the people and Senate. This aunswer being made, Cicero was more affrayd then before, insomuch that he put on a brigantine for the safetie of his body, and was accompanied with the chiefest men of Rome, and a great number of younge men besides, going with him from his house unto the fielde of Mars, where the elections were made: and had of purpose left open his jacket lose at the choller, that his brigantyne

327

he had on might be seene, thereby to let every man that saw him, know the daunger he was in. Every man misliked it when they saw it, and came about him to defend him, if any offered to assayle him. But it so came to passe, that by voyces of the people, Catilin was againe rejected from

the Consulship, and Syllanus and Muræna chosen Consuls. Shortly after this election, the souldiers of Thuscan being joyned, which should have come to Catilin, and the day appoynted being at hande to broache their enterprise : about midnight there came three of the chiefest men of Rome to Ciceroes house (Marcus Crassus, Marcus Marcellus, and Scipio Metellus) and knocking at his gate, called his porter, and bad him wake his maister presently, and tell him how they three were at the gate to speake with him, about a matter

of importance. At night after supper, Crassus porter brought his maister a packet of letters, delivered him by a straunger unknowen, which were directed unto divers persons, amonge the which one of them had no name subscribed, but was onely directed unto Crassus him self. The effect of his letter was, that there should be a great slaughter in Rome made by Catilin, and therefore he prayed him that he would depart out of Rome to save him selfe. Crassus having red his owne letter, would not open the rest, but went forthwith unto Cicero, partly for feare of the daunger, and partly also to cleere him selfe of the suspition they had of him for the friendship that was betwixt him and Catiline. Cicero counselling with them what was to be done, the next morning assembled the Senate very earely, and carying the letters with him, he did deliver them according to their direction, and commaunded they should read them out alowde. All these letters, and every one of them particulerly, did bewray the conspiracie. Furthermore, Quintus Arrius, a man of authoritie, and that had bene Prætor, tolde openly the souldiers and men of warre that were leavied in Thuscan. And it was reported also, that Manlius was in the fielde with a great number of souldiers about the cities of Thuscan, gaping daily to heare newes of some chaunge at Rome. All these thinges being throughly considered, a decree passed by the Senate, that they should referre the care of the common

wealth unto the Consuls, to thend that with absolute authoritie they might (as well as they could) provide for the
safetie and preservation thereof. Such manner of decree
and authoritie, was not often seene concluded of in the
Senate, but in time of present feare and daunger. Now
Cicero having this absolute power, he referred all forreine
matters to Quintus Metellus charge, and did him self take
uppon him the care and government of all civill affayres
within Rome. On the day time when he went up and
downe the towne, he had such a trowpe of men after him,
that when he came through the great market place, he
almost filled it with his trayne that followed him. Thereuppon Catiline would no lenger delay time, but resolved to
goe him selfe unto Manlius where their armie lay. But
before he departed, he had drawen into his confederacie one
Martius, and another called Cethegus, whome he commaunded
betimes in the morning to goe to Ciceroes house with short
daggers to kil him, pretending to come to salute him, and
to give him a good morow. But there was a noble woman Fulvia
of Rome, called Fulvia, who went over night unto Cicero, bewrayeth
and bad him beware of that Cethegus, who in deede came Catilines
the next morning betimes unto him : but being denied to intent to
be let in, he began to chafe and raile before the gate. This kill Cicero.
made him the more to be suspected. In thend Cicero com-
ming out of his house, called the Senate to the temple of
Iupiter Stator, (as much to say, a stayer) which standeth
at the upper end of the holy streete as they goe to the
Mount Palatine. There was Catiline with others, as though
he ment to cleere him selfe of the suspition that went of
him howbeit there was not a Senator that would sit downe
by him, but they did all rise from the benche where Catiline
had taken his place. And further, when he began to speake,
he could have no audience for the great noyse they made
against him. So at length Cicero rose, and commaunded
him to avoid out of Rome . saying, that there must needes
be a separacion of walles betweene them two, considering
that the one used but words, and the other force of armes. Catiline
Catiline thereuppon immediatly departing the citie with three departed
hundred armed men, was no sooner out of the precinct of Rome.

the walles, but he made his Sergeaunts cary axes and bundells of roddes before him, as if he had beene a Consul lawfully created, and did display his ensignes of warre, and so went in this order to seeke Manlius. When they were joyned, he had not much lesse then twenty thowsand men together, with the which he went to practise the townes to rebell. Nowe open warre beeing thus proclaimed, Antonius, Ciceroes colleage and fellowe Consul, was sent against him to fight with him. In the meane space, Cornelius Lentulus surnamed Sura (a man of a noble house, but of a wicked disposition, and that for his ill life was put of the Senate) assembled all the rest which were of Catlines conspiracie, and that remained behind him in Rome, and bad them be affraid of nothing. He was then Prætor the second time, as the manner is when any man comes to recover againe the dignitie of a Senator

which he had lost. It is reported that this surname of Sura was given him upon this occasion. He being Treasorer in Syllaes Dictatorship, did fondly waste and consume a marvelous summe of money of the common treasure. Sylla being offended with him for it, and demaunding an accompt of him before the Senate. he carelesly and contemptuously stepped forth, saying he could make him no other accompt, but shewed him the calfe of his legge, as children doe, when they make a fault at tennys. And thereof it came that ever after that they called him Sura, bicause *Sura* in Latin signifieth, the calfe of the legge. Another time also being accused for a lewde part he had committed, he bribed some of the Iudges with money, and being onely quit by two voyces more which he had in his favor, he sayd he had lost his money he had given to one of those two Iudges, bicause it was enough for him to be cleered by one voice more. This man being of this disposition, was first of all incensed by Catiline, and lastly marred by certaine wisards and false prognosticators that had mocked him with a vaine hope, singing verses unto him which they had fayned and devised, and false prophecies

also, which they bare him in hande they had taken out of Sybilles bookes of prophecie, which sayd: that there should raigne three Cornelii at Rome, of the which, two had already fulfilled the prophecie, Cinna and Sylla, and for the

330

GRECIANS AND ROMANES

third, fortune layd it upon him, and therefore bad him goe
thorow withall, and not to dreame it out losing oportunitie
as Catiline had done. Now this Lentulus undertooke no
small enterprise, but had an intent with him to kil all the
whole Senate, and as many other Citizens as they could
murther, and to set fire of Rome, sparing none but Pompeys
sonnes, whome they would reserve for pledges, to make their
peace afterwards with Pompey. For the rumor was very
great and certein also, that he returned from very great
warres and conquests which he had made in the East
contryes. So they layed a plat to put their treason in
execution, in one of the nights of Saturnes feastes. Further,
they had brought flaxe and brimstone, and a great number
of armors and weapons into Cethegus house. Besides all
this provision, they had appoynted a hundred men in an
hundred partes of the citie, to the ende that fire being
raysed in many places at one tyme, it should the sooner
ronne through the whole citie. Other men also were appoynted to stoppe the pypes and water conduits which
brought water to Rome, and to kill those also that came
for water to quench the fire. In all this sturre, by chaunce
there were two Ambassadors of the Allobroges, whose contry
at that tyme did much mislike of the Romanes, and were
unwilling to be subject unto them. Lentulus thought these
men very fit instruments to cause all Gaule to rebell. Thereuppon practising with them, he wanne them to be of their
conspiracie, and gave them letters directed to the counsell
of their contrie, and in them did promise them fredom. He
sent other letters also unto Catilin, and perswaded him to
proclaime libertie to all bondmen, and to come with all the
speede he could to Rome: and sent with them one Titus of
the citie of Crotona, to cary these letters. But all their
counsells and purposes (like fooles that never met together
but at feastes, drincking droncke with light women) were
easily found out by Cicero: who had a carefull eye upon
them, and very wisely and discreetely sawe thorow them.
For he had appoynted men out of the citie to spie their
doings, which followed them to see what they intended.
Furthermore he spake secretly with some he trusted, (the

CICERO

*Great treason
practised in
Rome by
C. Lentulus,
and Cethegus.*

331

which others also tooke to be of the conspiracie) and knewe
by them that Lentulus and Cethegus had practised with the
Ambassadors of the Allobroges, and drawen them into their
conspiracie.   At length he watched them one night so narrowly, that he tooke the Ambassadors, and Titus Crotonian
with the letters he caried, by helpe of the Ambassadors of
the Allobroges, which had secretly informed him of all
before. The next morning by breake of day, Cicero assembled the Senate in the temple of Concorde, and there openly
red the letters, and heard the evidence of the witnesses.
Further, there was one Iunius Syllanus a Senator that gave
in evidence, that some heard Cethegus say they should kill
three Consuls, and foure Prætors. Pisa a Senator also, and
that had bene Consul, tolde in manner the selfe same tale.
And Caius Sulpitius a Prætor, that was sent into Cethegus
house, reported that he had found great store of darts,
armor, daggers and swordes new made.   Lastly, the Senate
having promised Titus Crotonian he should have no hurt, so
he would tell what he knew of this conspiracie: Lentulus
thereby was convinced, and driven to give uppe his office of
Prætor before the Senate, and chaunging his purple gowne,
to take another meete for his miserable state.   This being
done, Lentulus and his consorts were committed to warde,
to the Prætors houses. Now growing towards evening, the
people waiting about the place where the Senate was assembled, Cicero at length came out, and told them what they
had done within. Thereuppon he was conveyed by all the
people unto a friendes house of his hard by: for that his
owne house was occupied by the Ladies of the citie, who
were busy solemnly celebrating a secret sacrifice in the honor
of the goddesse, called of the Romanes the good goddesse,
and of the Græcians Gynæcia, to wit feminine: unto her
this yearely sacrifice is done at the Consuls house, by the
wife or mother of the Consul then being, the Vestal Nunnes
being present at it.   Now Cicero being comen into his
neighbours house, beganne to bethinke him what course
he were best to take in this matter. For, to punish the
offenders with severitie, according to their deserts, he was
afraid to do it: both bicause he was of a curteous nature, as

also for that he would not seeme to be glad to have occasion to shew his absolute power and authoritie, to punish (as he might) with rigour, Citizens that were of the noblest houses of the citie, and that had besides many friends. And contrariwise also, being remisse in so waightie a matter as this, he was affraid of the daunger that might ensue of their rashnes, mistrusting that if he should punish them with lesse then death, they would not amend for it, imagining they were well rid of their trouble, but would rather become more bold and desperate then ever they were · adding moreover the styng and spight of a newe malice unto their accustomed wickednes, besides that he him selfe should be thought a coward and tymerous man, whereas they had already not much better opinion of him. Cicero being perplexed thus with these doubts, there appeared a miracle to the Ladies, doing sacrifice at home in his house. For the fire that was thought to be cleane out upon the aulter where they had sacrificed, there sodainely rose out of the imbers of the ryend or barkes which they had burnt, a great bright flame, which amased all the other Ladies. Howbeit the Vestall Nunnes willed Terentia (Ciceroes wife) to go straight unto her husband, and to bid him not to be affraid to execute that boldly which he had considered of, for the benefit of the common wealth : and that the goddesse had raised this great flame, to shewe him that he should have great honor by doing of it. Terentia, that was no timerous nor faint harted woman, but very ambitious, and furthermore had gotten more knowledge from her husband of the affayres of the state, then otherwise she had acquainted him with her housewivery in the house, as Cicero him selfe reporteth : she went to make report thereof unto him, and prayed him to doe execution of those men. The like did Quintus Cicero his brother, and also Publius Nigidius, his friend and fellow student with him in Philosophie, and whose counsell also Cicero followed much in the government of the common wealth. The next morning, the matter being propounded to the arbitrement of the Senate, how these malefactors should be punished : Syllanus being asked his opinion first, said that they should be put in prison, and from thence to suffer execution. Others likewise that followed him, were all of that minde, but Caius Cæsar, that afterwards came to be Dictator, and was then but a young man, and began to come forward, but yet such a one, as by his behavior and the hope he had, tooke such a course, that afterwards he brought the common wealth of Rome into an absolute Monarchie. For at that time, Cicero had vehement suspicions of Cæsar, but no apparant proofe to convince him.

Cæsar privie to Catilines conspiracie.

And some say, that it was brought so neare, as he was almost convicted, but yet saved him selfe. Other write to the contrary, that Cicero wittingly dissembled, that he either heard or knew any signes which were told him against Cæsar, being affraid in deede of his friends and estimation. For it was a cleere case, that if they had accused Cæsar with the rest, he undoubtedly had sooner saved all their lives, then he should have lost his owne. Nowe when Cæsar came

Cæsars opinion for the punishment of the conspirators.

to deliver his opinion touching the punishment of these prisoners : he stoode up and sayde, that he did not thinke it good to put them to death, but to confiscate their goods : and as for their persons, that they should bestow them in prison, some in one place, some in another, in such cities of Italy, as pleased Cicero best, untill the warre of Catilin were ended. This sentence being very mild, and the author thereof marvelous eloquent to make it good : Cicero him self added thereunto a counterpease, inclining unto either of both the opinions, partly allowing the first, and partly also the opinion of Cæsar. His friends thinking that Cæsars opinion was the safest for Cicero, bicause thereby he should deserve lesse blame for that he had not put the prisoners to death : they followed rather the second. Whereuppon Syllanus also recanted that he had spoken, and expounded his opinion : saying, that when he spake they should be put to death, he ment nothing so, but thought the last punishment a Senator of Rome could have, was the prison. But the first that contraried this opinion, was Catulus Luctatius, and after him Cato, who with vehement wordes enforced Cæsars suspition, and furthermore filled all the Senate with wrath and corage : so that even upon the instant it was decreed by most voyces, that they should

GRECIANS AND ROMANES

suffer death. But Cæsar stept up again, and spake against the confiscation of their goods, misliking that they should reject the gentlest part of his opinion, and that contrariwise they should sticke unto the sevearest onely: howbeit bicause the greatest number prevailed against him, he called the Tribunes to ayde him, to the ende they should withstand it: but they would give no eare unto him. Cicero thereupon yelding of him self, did remit the confiscation of their goods, and went with the Senate to fetche the prisoners: who were not all in one house, but every Prætor had one of them. So he went first to take C. Lentulus, who was in the Mount Palatine, and brought him through the holy streete and the market place, accompanied with the chiefest men of the citie, who compassed him round about, and garded his person. The people seeing that, quaked and trembled with feare, passed by, and sayd never a word: and specially the younge men, who thought it had bene some solemne misterie for the health of their contry, that was so accompanied with the chiefe Magistrate, and the noble men of the citie, with terror and feare. So when he had passed through the The execu- market place, and was come to the prison, he delivered tion of the Lentulus into the handes of the hangman, and commaunded conspirators. him to doe execution. Afterwardes also Cethegus, and then all the rest one after another, whome he brought to the prison him selfe, and caused them to be executed. Further- more, seeing divers of their accomplices in a trowpe together in the market place, who knewe nothing what he had done, and watched onely till night were come, supposing then to take away their companions by force from the place where they were, thinking they were yet alive: he turned unto them, and spake alowd, They lived. This is a phrase of They lived: speeche which the Romanes use sometyme, when they will A word finely convey the hardnes of the speeche, to say He is dead. usurped for When night was comen, and that he was going homeward, the dead. as he came through the market place, the people did wayte upon him no more with silence as before, but with great cryes of his praise, and clapping of handes in every place he Ciceroes went, and called him Savior, and second fownder of Rome. praise. Besides all this, at every mans dore there were lynckes and

335

torches lighted, that it was as light in the streetes, as at noone dayes. The very women also did put lights out of the toppes of their houses to doe him honor, and also to see him so nobly brought home, with such a long trayne of the chiefest men of the citie, (of the which many of them had ended great warres for the which they had triumphed, and had obteyned many famous conquests to the Empire of Rome, both by sea and land) confessing betwene them selves one to another, that the Romanes were greatly bound to many Captaines and generalls of armies in their time, for the wonderfull riches, spoyles, and increase of their power which they had wonne: howbeit that they were to thanke Cicero onely, for their health and preservation, having saved them from so great and extreme a daunger. Not for that they thought it so wonderfull an acte to have striken dead the enterprise of the conspirators, and also to have punished the offenders by death: but bicause the conspiracie of Catilin being so great and daungerous an insurrection as ever was any, he had quenched it, and pluckt it up by the rootes, with so small hurt, and without uprore, trouble, or actuall sedition. For, the most part of them that were gathered together about Catiline, when they heard that Lentulus and all the rest were put to death, they presently forsooke him:

and Catiline him selfe also fighting a battell with them he had about him, against Antonius the other Consul with Cicero, he was slayne in the fielde, and all his armie defeated. This notwithstanding, there were many that spake ill of

Cicero for this facte, and ment to make him repent it, having for their heades Cæsar, (who was already chosen Prætor for the yeare to come) Metellus and Bestia, who should also be chosen Tribunes. They, so soone as they were chosen Tribunes, would not once suffer Cicero to speake to the people, notwithstanding that he was yet in his office of Consul for certaine dayes. And furthermore, to let him that he should not speake unto the people, they did set their benches upon the pulpit for orations, which they call at Rome, *Rostra*: and would never suffer him to set foote in it, but onely to resigne his office, and that done, to come downe againe immediatly. He graunted thereunto, and went up to the pulpit upon that condition. So silence being made him, he made an othe, not like unto other Consuls othes when they resigne their office in like manner, but straunge, and never heard of before: swearing, that he had saved the citie of Rome, and preserved all his contry and the Empire of Rome from utter ruine and destruction. All the people that were present, confirmed it, and sware the like othe. Wherewithall Cæsar and the other Tribunes his enemies were so offended with him, that they devised to breede him some new sturre and trouble. and amongest others, they made a decree, that Pompey should be sent for with his army to bridle the tyranny of Cicero. Cato, (who at that time was also Tribune) did him great pleasure in the furtherance of the common wealth, opposing him selfe against all their practises, with the like authoritie and power that they had, being a Tribune and brother with them, and of better estimation then they. So that he did not onely easily breake all their devises, but also in a goodly oration he made in a full assembly of the people, he so highly praised and extolled Ciceroes Consulship unto them, and the thinges he did in his office: that they gave him the greatest honors that ever were decreed or graunted unto any man living. For by decree of the people he was called, father of the contry, as Cato him selfe had called him in his oration: the which name was never given to any man, but onely unto him, and also he bare greater swaye in Rome at that time, than any man beside him. This notwithstanding, he made him selfe envyed and misliked of many men, not for any ill acte he did, or ment to doe: but onely bicause he did too much boast of him selfe. For he never was in any assembly of people, Senate, or judgement, but every mans head was full still to heare the sound of Catulus and Lentulus brought in for sporte, and filling the bookes and workes he compiled besides full of his owne prayses: the which made his sweete and pleasant stile, tedious, and troublesom to those that heard them, as though this misfortune ever followed him to take away his excellent grace But nowe, though he had this worme of ambition, and extreme covetous desire of honor in his head, yet did he

Ciceroes Consulship praised by Cato

Cicero the first man called, Father of the contry.

Cicero too much given to praise him self

not malice or envy any others glory, but would very franckly praise excellent men, as well those that had bene before him, as those that were in his time. And this appeareth plainly in his writings. They have written also certaine notable wordes he spake of some auncient men in olde time, as of Aristotle: that he was like a golden flowing river: and of Plato, that if Iupiter him selfe would speake, he would speake like him: and of Theophrastus, he was wont to call him his delight: and of Demosthenes orations, when one asked him on a time which of them he liked best: The longest saide he. There be divers writers also, who to shewe that they were great followers of Demosthenes, doe followe Ciceroes saying in a certaine epistle he wrote unto

one of his friends, wherein he said that Demosthenes slept in some of his orations: but yet they forget to tel how highly he praised him in that place, and that he calleth the orations which he wrote against Antonius (in the which he tooke great paines, and studied more then all the rest) Philippians: to followe those which Demosthenes wrote against Philip king of Macedon. Furthermore, there was not a famous man in all his tyme, either in eloquence, or in learning, whose fame he hath not commended in writing, or otherwise in honorable speech of him. For he obteyned of Cæsar, when he had the Empire of Rome in his handes, that Cratippus the Peripateticke Philosopher was made Citizen of Rome. Further, he procured that by decree of the court of the Areopagites, he was intreated to remaine at Athens, to teach and instruct the youth there: for that he was a great honor and ornament unto their city. There are extant also of Ciceroes epistles unto Herodes, and others unto his sonne, willing him to follow Cratippus in his studie and knowledge. He wrote an other letter also unto Gorgias the Rethoritian, and forbad him his sonnes company: bicause he understood he intised him to dronkennes, and to other great dishonestie. Of all his epistles he wrote in Greeke, there is but that onely written in choller, and another which he wrote unto Pelops Byzantine. And for that he wrote to Gorgias, he had great reason to be offended with him, and to tawnt him in his letter: bicause (as it

338

seemed) he was a man of very lewde life and conversation. But in contrary manner, writing as he did to Pelops, finding him selfe greved with him, for that he was negligent in procuring the Byzantines to ordeine some publike honors in his behalfe : that me thinkes proceeded of overmuch ambition, the which in many things made him too much forget the part of an honest man, and onely bicause he would be commended for his eloquence. When he had on a time pleaded Munatius cause before the Iudges, who shortly after accused Sabinus a friend of his : it is reported that he was so angry with him, that he told him, What Munatius, hast thou forgotten that thou wert discharged the last day of thine accusation, not for thine innocency, but for a miste I cast before the Iudges eies, that made them they could not discerne the fault ? An other tyme also, having openly praysed Marcus Crassus in the pulpit, with good audience of the people : shortly after he spake to the contrary, all the evill he could of him, in the same place. Why, how now, sayde Crassus : didest thou not thy selfe highly prayse me in this place, the last day ? I can not deny it, sayd Cicero. but in deede I tooke an ill matter in hand to shewe mine eloquence. An other time Crassus chaunced to say in an open assembly, that none of all the Crassi of his house that ever lived above lx. yeares : and afterwards againe repenting him selfe, he called it in againe, and sayde, Sure I knewe not what I did, when I sayd so. Cicero aunswered him againe : Thou knewest well enough the people were glad to heare it, and therefore spakest it to please them. Another time Crassus liking the opinion of the Stoicke Philosophers, that sayd the wise man was ever riche : Cicero aunswered him, and bad him consider whether they ment not thereby, that the wise man had all thinges. Crassus covetousnes was defamed of every man. Of Crassus sonnes, one of them did much resemble Actius, and therefore his mother had an ill name by him : one daye this sonne of Crassus made an oration before the Senate, which divers of them commended very muche. So, Cicero beeing asked how he liked it : Me thinkes, sayde he, it is *Actius of Crassus. About this tyme, Crassus being ready to take his jorney

Ciceroes subtile and pleasant sayings.

The Stoickes opinion : A wise man is ever riche.

*Ἄξιος Κράσσου. Actius, is a

339

into Syria, he desired to have Cicero his friend, rather then his enemy. Therefore one night making muche of him, he tolde Cicero that he would come and suppe with him. Cicero sayde he should be welcome. Shortly after some of his friendes told him of Vatinius, how he was desirous to be made friendes with him, for he was his enemy. What, quoth Cicero, and will he come to supper too? Thus he used Crassus. Now this Vitinius having a swollen necke, one daye pleading before Cicero: he called him the swollen Orator. Another tyme when he heard say that he was dead, and then that he was alive againe: A vengeance on him, sayde he, that hath lyed so shamefully. Another tyme when Cæsar had made a lawe for the deviding of the lands of Campania unto the souldiers: divers of the Senate were angry with him for it, and among other, Lucius Gellius (a very olde man) said, he would never graunt it while he lived. Cicero pleasauntly aunswered againe, Alas, tary a litle, the good olde man will not trouble you long. Another tyme there was one Octavius, supposed to be an *African borne. He when Cicero on a time pleaded a matter, saide that he heard him not. Cicero presently aunswered him againe, And yet hast thou a hole bored through thine eare. Another time Metellus Nepos told him, that he had overthrowen moe men by his witnes, then he had saved by his eloquence. I graunt said Cicero, for in deede I have more faith, then eloquence in me. So was there also a younge man that was suspected to have poysoned his father with a tarte, that boasted he would revile Cicero: I had rather have that of thee, quoth Cicero, then thy tarte. Publius Sextius also having a matter before the Iudges, enterteyned Cicero, with other of his Counsellers: but yet he would speake all him selfe, and give none of the Orators leave to say any thing. In the ende, when they sawe plainely that the Iudges would discharge him, being ready to give sentence: Cicero saide unto him, Besturre thee hardily to day for to morrowe Sextius thou shalt be a private man. Another, one Publius Scotta, who would fayne have bene thought a wise Lawyer, and yet had litle witte and understanding: Cicero appealed to him as a witnes in a matter,

340

and being examined, he aunswered he knewe nothing of it. Cicero replied to him againe: Thou thinkest peradventure they aske thee touching the law. Againe, Metellus Nepos, in a certaine disputacion he had with Cicero, did many times repeate, Who is thy father? Cicero aunswered him againe: Thy mother hath made this question harder for thee to aunswer. This Nepos mother was reported to be a light housewife, and he as suttle witted and unconstant. For he being Tribune, left in a geere the exercise of his office, and went into Syria to Pompey, upon no occasion: and as fondly againe he returned thence, upon a sodaine. His Schoolemaister Philager also being dead, he buried him very honestly, and set a crowe of stone upon the toppe of his tombe. Cicero finding it, tolde him, Thou hast done very wisely: for thy Maister hath taught thee rather to flie, then to speake. Another time Appius Clodius pleading a matter, saide in his preamble that his friende had earnestly requested him to employe all his knowledge, diligence, and faith upon this matter. O goddes, saide Cicero, and hast thou shewed thy selfe so harde harted to thy friende, that thou hast performed none of all these he requested thee? Nowe to use these fine tawnts and girds to his enemies, it was a parte of a good Orator: but so commonly to girde every man to make the people laughe, that wanne him greate ill will of many, as shall appeare by some examples I will tell you Marcus Aquinius had two sonnes in lawe, who were both banished: Cicero therefore called him Adrastus. Lucius Cotta by chaunce also was Censor at that tyme, when Cicero sued to be Consul: and beeing there at the daye of the election, he was a thyrst, and was driven to drinke. But while he dranke, all his friendes stoode about him, and after he had dronke, he saide unto them: It is well done of ye, sayde he, to be affrayed least the Censor shoulde be angry with me, bicause I drinke water: for it was reported the Censor loved wine well. Another tyme Cicero meeting one Voconius, with three fowle Daughters of his with him, he cryed out alowd:

This man hath gotten children in despight of Phœbus.

It was thought in Rome that Marcus Gellius was not borne

341

of free parents by father and mother, who reading certaine letters one daye in the Senate very lowde: Cicero sayde unto them that were about him, Wonder not at it, quoth he, for this man hath beene a cryer in his dayes. Faustus, the sonne of Sylla Dictator at Rome, which sette uppe billes outlawing divers Romanes, making it lawefull for any man to kill them without daunger where they founde them: this man after he had spent the moste parte of his fathers goods, was so sore in debt, that he was driven to sell his houshold stuffe, by billes sette up on every poste. Cicero when he sawe them, Yea mary saide he, these billes please me better, then those which his father sette uppe. These tawntes and common quippes without purpose, made divers men to malice

him. The great ill will that Clodius bare him, beganne uppon this occasion. Clodius was of a noble house, a younge man, and very wilde and insolent. He being in love with Pompeia Cæsars wife, founde the meanes secretly to gette into Cæsars house, apparelled like a younge singing wenche, bicause on that daye the Ladyes of Rome did solemnly celebrate a secret sacrifice in Cæsar's house, which is not lawefull for men to be present at. So there was no man there but Clodius, who thought he shoulde not have bene knowen, bicause he was but a younge man without any heare on his face, and that by this meanes he might come to Pompeia amongest the other women. He beeing gotten into this great house by night, not knowing the roomes and chambers in it: there was one of Cæsars mothers maydes of her chamber called Aurelia, who seeing him wandring up and downe the house in this sorte, asked him what he was, and how they called him. So being forced to aunswer, he saide he sought for Aura, one of Pompeias maides. The maide perceived straight it was no womans voice, and therewithal gave a great shriche, and called the other women: the which did see the gates fast shut, and then sought every corner up and downe, so that at length they found him in the maides chamber, with whom he came in. His offence was straight blowen abroad in the citie, whereuppon Cæsar put his wife away: and one of the Tribunes also accused Clodius, and burdened him that he had prophaned the holy

ceremonies of the sacrifices. Cicero at that time was yet
his friend, beeing one that had very friendly done for him
at all times, and had ever accompanied him to garde him, if
any man would have offered him injurie in the busie time
of the conspiracie of Catiline. Clodius stowtly denied the
matter he was burdened with, and saide that he was not in
Rome at that time, but farre from thence. Howbeit Cicero
gave evidence against him, and deposed, that the selfe same
daye he came home to his house unto him, to speake with him
about certaine matters. This in deede was true, though it
seemeth Cicero gave not this evidence so muche for the
truthes sake, as to please his wife Terentia: for she hated
Clodius to the deathe, bicause of his sister Clodia that
would have maried Cicero, and did secretly practise the
mariage by one Tullius, who was Ciceroes very friende, and
bicause he repayred very often to this Clodia that dwelt
harde by Cicero, Terentia beganne to suspect him. Terentia
beeing a cruell woman, and wearing her husbandes breeches:
allured Cicero to sette uppon Clodius in his adversitie, and
to witnesse agaynst him, as many other honest men of the
citie also did: some that he was perjured, others that he
committed a thowsande lewde partes, that he brybed the
people with money, that he had intised and deflowred many
women. Lucullus also brought forthe certayne Maydens
which deposed that Clodius had deflowred the youngest
of his owne sisters, she beeing in house with him, and
maryed. And there went out a greate rumor also, that he
knewe his two other sisters, of the which the one was called
Terentia,* and maried unto king Martius: and the other
Clodia, whome Metellus Celer had maried, and whom they
commonly called Quadrantaria: bicause one of her Para-
mours sent her a purse ful of quadrynes (which are litle
peeces of copper money) in stead of silver. Clodius was
slaundered more by her, then with any of the other two.
Notwithstanding, the people were very much offended with
them, that gave evidence against him, and accused him.
The Iudges being affrayed of it, got a great number of
armed men about them, at the day of his judgement, for
the safetie of their persons: and in the tables where they

wrote their sentences, their letters for the most part were confusedly set downe. This notwithstanding, it was found that he was quit by the greatest number: and it was reported also that some of them were close fisted. Catulus therefore meeting with some of them going home, after they had given their sentence, told them: Surely ye had good reason to be well garded for your safetie, for you were affraid your money should have bene taken from you, which you tooke for bribes. And Cicero sayd unto Clodius, who reproved him that his witnes was not true he gave against him: Cleane contrary, quoth Cicero, for five and twenty of the Iudges have beleved me, beeing so many that have condemned thee, and the thirty would not beleeve thee, for they would not quit thee before they had fingered money. Notwithstanding, in this judgement Cæsar never gave evidence against Clodius· and said moreover, that he did not think his wife had committed any adultery, howbeit that he had put her away, bicause he would that Cæsars wife should not only be clean from any dishonesty, but also void of all suspition. Clodius being quit of this accusation and trouble, and having also found meanes to be chosen Tribune: he beganne straight to persecute Cicero, chaunging all thinges, and stirring up all manner of people against him. First he wanne the good will of the common people by devising of newe lawes which he preferred, for their benefit and commoditie to both the Consuls he graunted great and large provinces. unto Piso, Macedon, and to Gabinius, Syria. He made also many poore men free Citizens, and had alwayes about him a great number of slaves armed. At that present tyme there were three notable men in Rome, which caried all the swaye: Crassus, that shewed him selfe an open enemie unto Cicero: Pompey the other, made muche both of the one and the other: the third was Cæsar, who was prepared for his joiney into Gaule with an armie. Cicero did leane unto him, (though he knewe him no fast friende of his, and that he mistrusted him for matters past in Catilines conspiracie) and prayed him that he might goe to the warres with him, as one of his Lieuetenants. Cæsar graunted him. Thereuppon Clodius perceiving that by

CICERO
Clodius quit, and found not guilty.

Cæsars wordes of the putting away his wife Pompeia.

Clodius chosen Tribune of the people.

Piso and Gabinius Consuls.

Crassus, Pompey, and Cæsar, three of the greatest men in Rome, tooke part with Clodius against Cicero.

344

this meanes he got him out of the daunger of his office of
Tribuneship for that yeare, he made fayer weather with
him (as though he ment to reconcile him selfe unto him)
and tolde him that he had cause rather to thinke ill of
Terentia, for that he had done against him, then of him
selfe, and alwayes spake very curteously of him as occasion
fell out, and sayde he did thinke nothing in him, nether
had any malice to him, howbeit it did a litle grieve him,
that being a friend, he was offered unkindnes by his friend.
These sweete wordes made Cicero no more affraied, so that
he gave up his Lieuetenancie unto Cæsar, and beganne againe
to pleade as he did before. Cæsar tooke this in such disdaine, that he hardened Clodius the more against him, and
besides, made Pompey his enemie. And Cæsar him selfe
also sayd before all the people, that he thought Cicero had
put Lentulus, Cethegus, and the rest, unjustly to death, and
contrary to lawe, without lawfull tryall and condemnation.
And this was the fault for the which Cicero was openly
accused. Thereuppon Cicero seeing him selfe accused for
this facte, he chaunged the usuall gowne he wore, and put
on a mourning gowne: and so suffering his beard and heare
of his head to growe without any coeming, he went in this
humble manner, and sued to the people. But Clodius was
ever about him in every place and streete he went, having
a sight of raskalls and knaves with him that shamefully
mocked him for that he had chaunged his gowne and countenance in that sort, and oftentimes they cast durt and
stones at him, breaking his talke and requests he made unto
the people. This notwithstanding, all the knights of Rome The knights
of Rome
and Senate
chaunged
garments for
Ciceroes sake
did in manner chaunge their gownes with him for companie,
and of them there were commonly twenty thowsand younge
gentlemen of noble house which followed him with their
heare about their eares, and were suters to the people for
him. Furthermore, the Senate assembled to decree that the
people should mourne in blacks, as in a common calamitie:
but the Consuls were against it. And Clodius on thother
side was with a band of armed men about the Senate, so
that many of the Senators ranne out of the Senat, crying,
and tearing their clothes for sorow. Howbeit these men

seeing all that, were nothing the more moved with pity and shame: but either Cicero must needes absent him selfe, or els determine to fight with Clodius. Then went Cicero to intreat Pompey to ayde him: but he absented him selfe of purpose out of the citie, bicause he would not be intreated, and laye at one of his houses in the contry, neare unto the citie of Alba. So he first of all sent Piso his sonne in lawe unto him to intreate him, and afterwardes went him selfe in person to him. But Pompey beeing tolde that he was come, had not the harte to suffer him to come to him, to looke him in the face: for he had bene past all shame to have refused the request of so worthy a man, who had before shewed him suche pleasure, and also done and sayde so many thinges in his favor. Howbeit Pompey being the sonne in lawe of Cæsar, did unfortunately (at his request) forsake him at his neede, unto whome he was bownde for so many infinite pleasures, as he had receyved of him afore: and therefore when he hearde saye he came to him, he went out at his backe gate and woulde not speake with him. So Cicero seeing him selfe betrayed of him, and nowe having no other refuge to whome he might repayre unto: he put him selfe into the handes of the two Consuls. Of them two, Gabinius was ever cruell, and churlishe unto him. But Piso on thother side spake alwayes very curteously unto him, and prayed him to absent him selfe for a tyme, and to give place a litle to Clodius furie, and paciently to beare the chaunge of the tyme: for in so doing, he might come agayne another tyme to be the preserver of his contry, which was nowe for his sake in tumult and sedition. Cicero upon this aunswer of the Consul, consulted with his friendes: amonge the which Lucullus gave him advise to tary, and sayd that he should be the stronger. But all the rest were of contrary opinion, and would have him to get him away with speede: for the people would shortly wishe for him agayne, when they had once bene beaten with Clodius furie and folly. Cicero liked best to followe this counsell. Whereuppon having had a statue of Minerva a long tyme in his house, the which he greatly reverenced: he caried her him selfe, and gave her to the Capitoll with this inscription:

346

GRECIANS AND ROMANES

'Unto Minerva, Protector of Rome.' So, his friends having given him safe conduct, he went out of Rome about midnight, and tooke his way through the contry of Luke by lande, meaning to goe into Sicile. When it was knowen in Rome that he was fledde, Clodius did presently banishe him by decree of the people, and caused billes of inhibition to be sette uppe, that no man should secretly receive him within five hundred myles compasse of Italy. Howbeit divers men reverencing Cicero, made no reckoning of that inhibition. but when they had used him with all manner of curtesie possible, they did conduct him besides at his departure, saving one citie onely in Luke, called at that tyme Hipponium, and nowe Vibone: where a Sicilian called Vibius, (unto whome Cicero before had done many pleasures, and specially amonge others, had made him Maister of the workes in the yeare that he was Consul) would not once receyve him into his house, but promised him he woulde appoynt him a place in the contry that he might goe unto. And Caius Virgilius also, at that tyme Prætor and governor of Sicile, who before had shewed him selfe his very greate friende wrote then unto him, that he shoulde not come neare unto Sicile. This grieved him to the harte. Thereuppon he went directly unto the citie of Brundusium, and there imbarked to passe over the sea unto Dyrrachium, and at the first had winde at will · but when he was in the mayne sea, the winde turned, and brought him backe agayne to the place from whence he came. But after that, he hoysed sayle agayne, and the reporte went, that at his arryvall at Dyrrachium when he tooke lande, the earth shooke under him, and the sea gave backe together Whereby the Soothesayers enterpreted, that his exile shoulde not be longe, bicause both the one and the other was a token of chaunge. Yet Cicero, notwithstanding that many men came to see him for the goodwill they bare him, and that the cities of Græce contended who shoulde most honor him, he was alwayes sadde, and could not be merie, but cast his eyes still towardes Italy, as passioned lovers doe towardes the women they love: shewing him selfe faynte harted, and tooke this adversitie more basely,

Hipponium, alîas Vibone: a city in Luke.

A wonder shewed unto Cicero in his exile.

Ciceroes faint hart in his exile.

347

then was looked for of one so well studied and learned as
he. And yet he oftentimes praied his friends, not to call
him Oratoi, but rather Philosopher saying, that Philosophie
was his chiefest profession, and that for his eloquence he did
not use it, but as a necessary instrument to one that pleadeth

in the common wealth. But glory, and opinion, hath great
power to take mans reason from him, even like a culler, from
the minds of them that are common pleaders in matters of
state, and to make them feele the selfe same passions that
common people doe, by dayly frequenting their companie :
unles they take great heede of them, and that they come to
practise in the common wealth with this resolute minde, to
have to doe with the like matters that the common people
have, but not to entangle them selves with the like passions
and moodes, by the which their matters doe rise. Nowe
Clodius was not contented that he had banished Cicero out
of Italy, but further he burnt all his houses in the contry,
and his house also in Rome standing in the market place, of
the which he built a temple of libertie, and caused his goods
to be solde by the cryer · so that the cryer was occupied all
daye long crying the goods to be sold, and no man offered
to buye any of them. The chiefest men of the citie beginning to be afrayd of these violent parts, and having the
common people at his commaundement, whom he had made
very bold and insolent · he beganne to invey against Pompey,
and spake ill of his doings in the time of his warres, the

which every man els but him self did commend Pompey
then was very angry with him selfe that he had so forsaken
Cicero, and repented him of it, and by his friendes procured
all the meanes he could to call him home againe from his
banishment. Clodius was against it all he could. The
Senate notwithstanding with one full consent ordeyned, that
nothing should be established for the common wealth, before
Ciceroes banishment were first repealed. Lentulus was at

that tyme Consul, and there grewe such an uprore and
sturre apon it, that some of the Tribunes were hurt in the
market place, and Quintus Cicero (the brother of Cicero)
was slayne and hidden under the deade bodies. Then the
people beganne to chaunge their mindes. And Annius Milo,

one of the Tribunes, was the first man that durst venter upon Clodius, and bringe him by force to be tryed before the Iudges. Pompey him selfe also having gotten a great number of men about him, aswell of the citie of Rome as of other townes adjoyning to it, beeing strongly garded with them: he came out of his house, and compelled Clodius to get him out of the market place, and then called the people to give their voyces, for the calling home agayne of Cicero. It is reported that the people never passed thinge with so great good will, nor so wholy together, as the returne of Cicero. And the Senate for their partes also, in the behalfe of Cicero, ordeyned that the cities which had honored and received Cicero in his exile, shoulde be greatly commended: and that his houses which Clodius had overthrowen and rased, should be reedified at the charge of the common wealth. So Cicero returned the sixtenth moneth after his banishment, and the townes and cities he came by, shewed them selves so joyfull of his returne, that all manner of men went to meete and honor him, with so great love and affection, that Ciceroes reporte thereof afterwardes came in deede short of the very truth as it was. For he sayde, that Italy brought him into Rome upon their shoulders. Insomuch as Crassus him selfe, who before his banishment was his enemie, went then with very good will unto him, and became his friende, saying: that he did it for the love of his sonne, who loved Cicero with all his hart. Nowe Cicero beeing returned, he found a tyme when Clodius was out of the citie, and went with a good companie of his friendes unto the Capitoll, and there tooke away the tables, and brake them, in the which Clodius had written all his actes that he had passed and done in the tyme of his Tribuneship. Clodius would afterwardes have accused Cicero for it: but Cicero aunswered him, that he was not lawfully created Tribune, bicause he was of the Patricians, and therefore all that he had done in his Tribuneship was voyde, and of none effect. Therewith Cato was offended, and spake against him, not for that he liked any of Clodius doings: (but to the contrary, utterly misliked all that he did) but bicause he thought it out of all reason, that the Senate shoulde cancell all those thinges

Cicero called home from banishment.

Cicero taketh away the tables of Clodius actes out of the Capitoll.

which he had done and passed in his Tribuneship, and specially, bicause amongest the rest that was there which he him selfe had done in the Ile of Cyprus, and in the citie of Byzantium. Hereuppon there grewe some straungenes betwixt Cicero and Cato, the which notwithstanding brake not out to open enmitie: but onely to an abstinence of their wonted familiaritie, and accesse one to another. Shortly

Clodius the Tribune, slain by Milo. after, Milo slue Clodius. Milo beeing accused of murder, prayed Cicero to pleade his cause. The Senate fearing that this accusation of Milo, (who was a hardie man, and of qualitie besides) woulde move some sedition and uprore in the citie: they gave commission to Pompey to see justice executed aswell in this cause, as in other offences, that the citie might be quiet, and judgement also executed with safetie Thereuppon Pompey the night before tooke the highest places of the market place, by his souldiers that were armed, whome he placed thereabout Milo fearing that Cicero woulde bee affraied to see suche a number of harnest men about him, beeing no usuall matter, and that it might peradventure hinder him to pleade his cause well he prayed him he woulde come betymes in the morning in his litter into the market place, and there to staye the

Cicero feare- comming of the Iudges, till the place were full. For Cicero
full in warres, was not onely fearefull in warres, but timerous also in plead-
and timerous ing. For in deede he never beganne to speake, but it was
in pleading in feare: and when his eloquence was come to the best proofe and perfection, he never left his trembling and timerousnes. Insomuch that pleading a case for Mutius Muræna (accused by Cato,) striving to excell Hortensius, whose pleading was very well thought of· he tooke no rest all night, and what through watching, and the trouble of his minde he was not very well, so that he was not so well

Cicero plead- liked for his pleading, as Hortensius. So, going to defend
eth Miloes Miloes cause, when he came out of his litter, and sawe
case. Pompey set aloft as if he had beene in a campe, and the market place compassed about with armed men, glistering in every corner: it so amated him, that he could scant facion him selfe to speake, all the partes of him did so quake and tremble, and his voyce could not come to him.

But Milo on the other side stoode boldly by him selfe, without any feare at all of the judgement of his cause, nether did he let his heere growe, as other men accused did. nether did he weare any mourning gowne, the which was (as it seemed) one of the chiefest causes that condemned him. Yet many held opinion that this timerousnes of Cicero came rather of the goodwill he bare unto his friends, then of any cowardly minde of him selfe. He was also chosen one of the Priestes of the Soothesayers, which they call Augures, in the roome of P. Crassus the younger, who was slayne in the Realme of Parthia. Afterwardes, the province of Cilicia being appoynted to him, with an armie of twelve thowsand footemen, and two thowsand five hundred horsemen, he tooke the sea to goe thither. So when he was arrived there, he brought Cappadocia agayne into the subjection and obedience of king Ariobarzanes according to his commission and commaundement given by the Senate: moreover, both there and elsewhere he tooke as excellent good order as could be devised, in reducing of thinges to quietnes, without warres. Furthermore, finding that the Cilicians were growen somewhat stowt and unruly, by the overthrowe the Romanes had of the Parthians, and by reason of the rising and rebellion in Syria: he brought them unto reason by gentle perswasions, and never received giftes that were sent him, no not from Kinges and Princes. Furthermore, he did disburden the provinces of the feastes and banckets they were wont to make other governors before him. On the other side also, he woulde ever have the company of good and learned men at his table, and would use them well, without curiositie and excesse. He had never porter to his gate, nor was seene by any man in his bed · for he would alwayes rise at the breake of daye, and would walke or stande before his dore. He would curteously receive all them that came to salute and visite him. Further they report of him, that he never caused man to be beaten with roddes, nor to teare his owne garments. In his anger he never reviled any man, nether did dispightfully set fine upon any mans heade. Finding many thinges also belonging to the common wealth, which private men had stollen and

LIVES OF THE NOBLE

CICERO imbecelled to their owne use: he restored them agayne unto the cities, whereby they grewe very riche and wealthie: and yet did he save their honor and credit that had taken them away, and did them no other hurte, but onely constrayned them to restore that which was the common wealthes He made a litle warre also, and drave away the theeves that kept about

Mons Amanus. the Mountayne Amanus, for the which exployte his souldiers

Cicero called
Imperator.

called him Imperator, to saye, chiefe Captaine. About that tyme there was an Orator called Cæcilius, who wrote unto him from Rome, to praye him to sende him some Leoperds, or Panthers out of Cilicia, bicause he woulde shewe the people some pastyme with them. Cicero boasting of his doinges, wrote to him agayne, that there were no more Leoperds in Cilicia, but that they were all fledde into Caria for anger, that seeing all thinges quiet in Cilicia, they had leasure now to hunte them. So when he returned towardes Rome, from the charge of his government, he came by Rhodes· and stayed a fewe dayes at Athens, with great delight, to remember how pleasauntly he lived there before, at what time he studied there. Thither came to him the chiefest learned men of the citie, and his frendes also, with whom he was acquainted at his first being there. In fine, having received all the honorable enterteinment in Græce that could be: he returned unto Rome, where at his arrivall he found great factions kindled, the which men saw plainly would growe in the ende to civill warre. Thereuppon the Senate having decreed that he should enter in triumphe into the citie. he aunswered, that he would rather (all parties agreed) follow

Cicero seeketh to pacifie the quarrell betwext Pompey and Cæsar.

Cæsars coche in triumphe. So he travelled verie earnestly betwene Pompey and Cæsar, eftsoones wryting unto Cæsar, and also speaking unto Pompey that was present, seeking all the meanes he coulde, to take up the quarrell and mishking betwext them two. But it was so impossible a matter, that there was no speeche of agreement woulde take place. So Pompey hearing that Cæsar was not faire from Rome, he durst no lenger abide in Rome, but fled with divers of the greatest men in Rome. Cicero would not followe him when he fled, and therefore men thought he would take parte with Cæsar: but this is certaine, that he was in a marvelous

GRECIANS AND ROMANES

perplexitie, and could not easely detei mine what way to take. Whereuppon he wiote in his Epistells: What way should I take? Pompey hath the juster and honester cause of warre, but Cæsar can better execute, and provide for him selfe and his frendes with better safetie so that I have meanes enowe to flie, but none to whome I might repaire. In all this sturre, there was one of Cæsars frendes called Trebatius, which wrote a letter unto Cicero, and told him that Cæsar wished him in any case to come to him, and to run with him the hope and fortune he undertooke but if he excused him selfe by his age, that then he should get him into Græce, and there to be quiet from them both. Cicero marveling that Cæsar wrote not to him him selfe, aunswered in anger, that he would doe nothing unworthie of his actes all the dayes of his life thitherto · and to this effect he wrote in his letters. Now Cæsar being gone into Spayne, Cicero imbarked immediatly to go to Pompey. So when he came unto him, every man was very glad of his comming, but Cato. Howbeit Cato secretly reproved him for comming unto Pompey, saying: that for him selfe he had bene without all honestie at that time to have forsaken that parte, the which he had alwayes taken and followed from the beginning of his first practise in the common wealth: but for him on thother side, that it had bene better for the safetie of his contrie, and chiefly for all his frendes, that he had bene a newter to both, and so to have taken thinges as they had fallen out · and that he had no maner of reason nor instant cause to make him to become Cæsars enemie, and by comming thither to put him selfe into so great perill. These perswasions of Cato overthrewe all Ciceroes purpose and determination, besides that Pompey him selfe did not employe him in any matter of service or importance But hereof him selfe was more in fault then Pompey, bicause he confessed openly that he did repent him he was come thither. Furthermore, he scorned and disdained all Pompeys preparacions and counsells, the which in deede made him to be had in gealousie and suspicion. Also he would ever be fleering and gybing at those that tooke Pompeys parte, though he had no list him selfe to be merie.

5 : YY 353

He would also goe up and downe the campe very sad and heavy, but yet he woulde ever have one geast or other to make men laugh, although they had as litle lust to be merie as he: and surely, it shall doe no hurte to call some of them to minde in this place. Domitius being verie desirous to preferre a gentleman to have charge of men, to recommende him, he sayd he was an honest, wise, and sober man. Whereto Cicero presently answered: Why doest thou not kepe him then to bring up thy children? An other time when they commended Theophanes Lesbian, (that was maister of all the artificers of the campe) bicause he had notablie comforted the Rhodians when they had received a greate losse of their navy. See, sayd Cicero, what a goodly thing it is to have a Græcian, master of artificers in the campe! When both battells came to joyne together, and that Cæsar had in manner all the advauntage, and kept them as good as besieged. Lentulus told him on a time, that he heard say all Cæsars frendes were madde, and melancholy men. Why, quoth Cicero to him againe. doest thou say that they doe envie Cæsar? An other called Martius, comming lately out of Italie, sayd, that there ranne a rumor in Rome, that Pompey was besieged. What, quoth Cicero to him againe and diddest thou take shippe to come and see him thy selfe, bicause thou mightest beleve it, when thou haddest seene it? Pompey being overthrowen, one Nonius sayed there was yet good hope left, bicause they had taken seven Eagles within Pompeys campe. Thy perswasion were not ill, quoth Cicero, so we were to fight but with pyes or dawes. Labienus reposed all his trust in certaine Oracles, that Pompey of necessitie must have the upper hand. Yea sayd Cicero, but for all this goodly stratageame of warre, we have not longe since lost our whole campe. After the battell of Pharsalia, where Cicero was not by reason of his sickenesse: Pompey being fled, and Cato at that time at Dyrrachium, where he had gathered a great number of men of warre, and had also prepared a great navie: he prayed Cicero to take charge of all this army, as it perteyned unto him, having bene Consul. Cicero did not only refuse it, but also tolde them he would meddle no more with this warre But this was enough to

Cato gave place to Cicero, and offered him the charge of the navy at Dyrrachium

354

have made him bene slaine for the younger Pompey and his frendes called him traitor, and drewe their swordes upon him to kill him, which they had done, had not Cato stepped betwene them and him, and yet had he muche a doe to save him, and to convey him safely out of the campe. When Cicero came to Brundusium, he stayed there a certaine time for Cæsars comming, who came but slowly, by reason of his troubles he had in Asia, as also in Ægypt. Howbeit newes being brought at length that Cæsar was arrived at Tarentum, and that he came by lande unto Brundusium: Cicero departed thence to goe meete him, not mistrusting that Cæsar woulde not pardon him, but rather being ashamed to come to his enemie being a conqueror, before such a number of men as he had about him. Yet he was not forced to doe or speake any thing unseemely to his calling. For Cæsar seeing him comming towardes him farre before the rest that came with him he lighted from his horse and imbraced him, and walked a great way a foote with him, stil talking with him only, and ever after he did him great honor and made much of him. Insomuche as Cicero having written a booke in praise of Cato Cæsar on the other side wrote an other, and praised the eloquence and life of Cicero, matching it with the life of Pericles, and Theramenes. Ciceroes booke was intituled *Cato*, and Cæsars booke called *Anticato*, as much to say, as against Cato. They say further, that Quintus Ligarius being accused to have bene in the field against Cæsar, Cicero tooke upon him to defend his cause. and that Cæsar sayd unto his frendes about him, What hurte is it for us to heare Cicero speake, whome we have not heard of long time? For otherwise Ligarius (in my opinion) standeth already a condemned man, for I know him to be a vile man, and mine enemie. But when Cicero had begonne his Oration, he moved Cæsar marvelously, he had so sweete a grace, and suche force in his words that it is reported Cæsar chaunged divers colours, and shewed plainly by his countenance, that there was a marvelous alteracion in all the partes of him. For, in thend when the Orator came to touche the battell of Pharsalia, then was Cæsar so troubled, that his bodie shooke withall, and besides, certaine bookes

The force of Ciceroes eloquence, how it altered Cæsar.

355

he had, fell out of his handes, and he was driven against his will to set Ligarius at libertie. Afterwardes, when the common wealth of Rome came to be a kingdom, Cicero leaving to practise any more in the state, he gave him selfe to reade Philosophie to the young men that came to heare him : by whose accesse unto him (bicause they were the chiefest of the nobilitie in Rome) he came againe to beare as great sway and authoritie in Rome, as ever he had done before. His studie and endevour was, to wryte matters of Philosophie dialogue wise, and to translate out of Græke into Latin, taking paynes to bring all the Græke wordes, which are proper unto logicke and naturall causes, unto Latin. For he was the first man by report that gave Latin names unto these Græke words, which are proper unto Philosophers, as, Φαντασία, he termed, *Visio.* Κατάθεσις *Assensus.* Εποχὴ, *Assensus cohibitio.* Κατάληψις, *Comprehensio.* Τὸ ἄτομον, *Corpus individuum.* Τὸ ἄμερες *Corpus simplex.* Τὸ κενον *Vacuum,* and many other suche like wordes. But though he were not the first, yet was it he that most did devise and use them, and turned some of them by translation, others into proper termes : so that at length they came to be well taken, knowen, and understanded of everie man. And of his readinesse in wryting of verses, he would use them many times for his recreation : for it is reported, that whensoever he tooke in hand to make any, he would dispatch five hundred of them in a night. Nowe, all that time of his recreacion and pleasure, he woulde commonly be at some of his houses in the contrie, which he had neere unto Thusculum, from whence he would wryte unto his frends, that he led Laertes life : either spoken merily as his maner was, or else pricked forward with ambition, desiring to returne againe to be a practiser in the common wealth, being wearie with the present time and state thereof. Howsoever it was, he came oftentimes to Rome, onely to see Cæsar to keepe him his frend, and would ever be the first man to confirme any honors decreed unto him, and was alwayes studious to utter some newe matter to praise him and his doinges. As that was he sayd touching the statues of Pompey, the which

being overthrowen, Cæsar commaunded them to be set up
againe, and so they were For Cicero sayd, that by that
curtesie in setting up of Pompeys statues againe, he did
establishe his owne. So, Cicero being determined to wryte
all the Romane historie, and to mingle with them many of
the Græcians doings, adding thereunto all the fables and
devises which they doe write and reporte: he was hindered
of his purpose against his will, by many open and private
troubles that came upon him at once: whereof notwithstanding he him selfe was cause of the most of them. For
first of all, he did put away his wife Terentia, bicause she
had made but small accompt of him in all the warres so
that he departed from Rome having no necessarie thing with
him to enterteine him out of his contrie, and yet when he
came backe againe into Italie, she never shewed any sparke of
love or good will towardes him. For she never came to Brundusium to him, where he remeyned a long time and worse then
that, his daughter having the hart to take so long a jorney in
hand to goe to him, she neither gave her company to conduct
her, nor money or other furniture convenient for her, but so
handled the matter, that Cicero at his returne to Rome
founde bare walles in his house and nothing in it, and yet
greatly brought in det besides. And these were the honestest
causes alleaged for their divorse. But besides that Terentia
denyed all these, Cicero him selfe gave her a good occasion
to cleere her selfe, bicause he shortly after maried a young
maiden, being fallen in fancie with her (as Terentia sayd)
for her beawtie: or, as Tyro his servaunt wrote, for her
riches, to thende that with her goods he might pay his dets.
For she was very rich, and Cicero also was appointed her
gardian, she being left sole heire. Now, bicause he ought
a marvelous summe of money, his parents and frends did
counsell him to mary this young maiden, notwithstanding
he was too olde for her, bicause that with her goodes he
might satisfie his creditors. But Antonius speaking of this
mariage of Cicero, in his aunswers and Orations he made
against the Philippians: he doth reprove him for that he
put away his wife, with whome he was growen olde, being
merie with him by the way for that he had bene an idle

Cicero did put
away his wife
Terentia

Cicero maried
a young
maiden.

357

man, and never went from the smoke of his chimney, nor had bene abroade in the warres in any service of his contrie or common wealth. Shortly after that he had maried his second wife, his daughter dyed in labor of child, in Lentulus house, whose seconde wife she was, being before maried unto Piso, who was her first husband. So the Philosophers and learned men came of all sides to comfort him: but he tooke her death so sorowfully, that he put away his second wife, bicause he thought she did rejoyce at the death of his daughter. And thus muche touching the state and troubles

of his house. Nowe touching the conspiracie against Cæsar, he was not made privie to it, although he was one of Brutus greatest frendes, and that it grieved him to see thinges in that state they were brought unto, and albeit also he wished for the time past, as much as any other man did. But in deede the conspirators were affrayed of his nature, that lacked hardinesse: and of his age, the which oftentimes maketh the stowtest and most hardiest natures, faint harted and cowardly. Notwithstanding, the conspiracie being executed by Brutus and Cassius, Cæsars frendes being gathered together, everie man was afrayed that the citie woulde againe fall into civill warres. And Antonius also, who was Consul at that time, did assemble the Senate, and made some speache and mocion then to draw things againe unto quietnes. But Cicero having used divers perswasions fit for the time, in the end he moved the Senate to decree (following the example of the Athenians) a generall oblivion of thinges done against Cæsar, and to assigne unto Brutus and Cassius some governmentes of provinces. Howbeit nothing was concluded: for the people of them selves were sorie, when they sawe Cæsars bodie brought through the market place. And when Antonius also did shew them his gowne all bebloodied, cut, and thrust through with swordes: then they were like madde men for anger, and sought up and downe the market place if they coulde meete with any of them that had slaine him: and taking fire brandes in their handes, they ranne to their houses to set them a fire. But the conspirators having prevented this daunger, saved them selves: and fearing that if they taried at Rome, they should have many such alaroms,

they forsooke the citie. Then Antonius began to looke
aloft, and became fearefull to all men, as though he ment to
make him selfe king but yet most of all unto Cicero, above
all others. For Antonius perceiving that Cicero began
againe to increase in credit and authoritie, and knowing that
he was Brutus very frend: he did mislike to see him come
neere him, and besides, there was at that time some gealousie
betwext them, for the diversitie and difference of their
manners and disposicions. Cicero being affrayed of this,
was first of all in minde to go with Dolabella, to his province
of Syria, as one of his Lieutenaunts. But they that were
appointed to be Consuls the next yeare following after Antonius, two noble citizens, and Ciceroes great frends, Hircius,
and Pansa. they intreated him not to forsake them, undertaking that they would plucke downe this over great power
of Antonius, so he would remaine with them. But Cicero,
neither beleving nor altogether mistrusting them, forsooke
Dolabella, and promised Hircius and Pansa, that he would
spend the sommer at Athens, and that he would returne
againe to Rome so soone as they were entred into their
Consulship. With this determination Cicero tooke sea alone,
to goe into Græce. But as it chaunceth oftentimes, there
was some let that kept him he could not saile, and newes
came to him daily from Rome, as the manner is, that
Antonius was wonderfully chaunged, and that nowe he did
nothing any more without the authoritie and consent of the
Senate, and that there lacked no thing but his person, to
make all things well. Then Cicero condemning his dastardly
feare, returned foorthwith to Rome, not being deceived in
his first hope. For there came suche a number of people
out to meete him, that he coulde doe nothing all day long,
but take them by the handes, and imbrace them: who to
honor him, came to meete him at the gate of the citie, as
also by the way to bring him to his house The next morning Antonius assembled the Senate, and called for Cicero by
name. Cicero refused to goe, and kept his bedde, fayning
that he was werie with his jorney and paines he had taken
the day before: but in deede, the cause why he went not,
was, for feare and suspicion of an ambushe that was layed

for him by the way, if he had gone, as he was informed by
one of his verie good frends.   Antonius was marvelously
offended that they did wrongfully accuse him, for laying of
any ambush for him.   and therefore sent souldiers to his
house, and commaunded them to bring him by force, or else

to sette his house a fire.   After that time, Cicero and he
were always at jaire, but yet coldly enough, one of them
taking heede of an other : untill that the young Cæsar
returning from the citie of Apollonia, came as lawfull heire
unto Iulius Cæsar Dictator, and had contention with Antonius for the summe of two thowsande five hundred Myriades,
the which Antonius kept in his handes of his fathers goodes.

Thereuppon, Philip who had maried the mother of this
young Cæsar, and Marcellus, who had also maried his sister,
went with young Cæsar unto Cicero, and there agreed
together, that Cicero should helpe young Cæsar with the
favour of his authoritie, and eloquence, as well towardes the
Senate, as also to the people·   and that Cæsar in recompence of his good will should stande by Cicero, with his
money and souldiers.   For this young Cæsar, had many of
his fathers old souldiers about him, that had served under
him.   Now there was an other cause that made Cicero glad
to imbrace the friendshippe of this young Cæsar, and that

Ciceroes
dreame of
Octavius, the
adopted sonne
of Iulius
Cæsar.

was this.   Whilest Pompey and Iulius Cæsar were alive, and
in good case : Cicero dreamed one night that the Senators
sonnes were called into the Capitol, bicause Iupiter had
appointed to shew them him, that one day should come to
be Lord and king of Rome, and that the Romanes being
desirous to see who it should be, ranne all unto the temple :
and that all the children likewise were waiting there in
their goodly garded gownes of purple, untill that sodainly
the dores of the temple were open, and then that al the
children rose one after an other, and went and passed
by the image of Iupiter, who looked upon them all, and
sent them discontented, saving this young Cæsar, unto
whom he put foorth his hand as he passed by, and sayd :
My Lordes of Rome, this childe is he that shall end all your
civill warres, when he commeth to be Lord of Rome.   Some
say, that Cicero had this vision in his dreame, and that he

caried in good memory the looke of this child, howbeit that he knew him not: and that the next morning he went of purpose into the fielde of Mars, where these young boyes did exercise them selves, who, when he came thither, had broken up from playing, and were going home, and that amongest them he first saw him whom he had dreamed of, and knew him verie well, and musing at him the more, asked him whose sonne he was. The boy aunswered, that he was the sonne of one Octavius, (a man otherwise of no great calling) and of Accia, the sister of Iulius Cæsar · who having no childe, made him his heire by his last will and testament, and left him all his landes and goodes. After that time, it is reported, that Cicero was verie glad to speake to him when he met with him, and that the boy also liked Ciceroes frendshippe, and making of him: for by good happe the boy was borne the same yeare that Cicero was Consul. And these be the reasons alleaged, why Cicero did favor this young Cæsar. But in truth, first of all the great malice he bare unto Antonius, and secondly his nature that was ambitious of honor, were (in my opinion) the chiefest causes why he became young Cæsars frend: knowing that the force and power of his souldiers, would greatly strengthen his authority and countenance in manedging the affaires of the state, besides that the young man coulde flatter him so well, that he called him father. But Brutus being offended with him for it, in his Epistells he wrote unto Atticus, he sharply reproveth Cicero, saying, that for feare of Antonius he flattered this young Cæsar: whereby it appeared, he did not so much seeke for the libertie of Rome, as he did procure him selfe a loving and gentle maister. This notwithstanding, Brutus brought with him Ciceroes sonne that studied Philosophie at Athens, and gave him charge of men under him, and imployed him in great affaires, wherein he shewed him selfe verie forward, and valliant. Now Ciceroes authoritie and power grew againe to be so great in Rome, as ever it was before. For he did what he thought good, and so vexed Antonius, that he drave him out of the citie, and sent the two Consuls Hircius and Pansa against him, to fight with him: and caused the Senate also to decree, that

Octavius, and Accia · the parents of Octavius Cæsar.

Octavius Cæsar was borne in the yere of Ciceroes Consulship.

Ciceroes great power at Rome.

young Cæsar should have sergeaunts to carie roddes and axes before him, and all other furniture for a Prætor, as a man that fighteth for his contry. After that Antonius had lost the battell, and that both the Consuls were slaine, both the armies came unto Cæsar. The Senate then being affraied of this young man, that had so great good fortune, they practised by honors and gifts to call the armies from him, which he had about him, and so to minish the greatnes of his power: saying, that their contric now stoode in no neede of force, nor feare of defence, sith her enemie Antonius was fled and gone. Cæsar fearing this, sent men secretly unto Cicero, to pray him to procure that they two together might be chosen Consuls, and that when they should be in office, he should doe and appoint what he thought good, having the young man at his commaundement, who desired no more but the honor only of the name. Cæsar him selfe confessed afterwardes, that being affrayed he should have bene utterly cast away, to have bene left alone: he finely served his turne by Ciceroes ambition, having perswaded him to require the Consulship, through the helpe and assistance that he would geve him. But there was Cicero finely colted, as old as he was, by a young man, when he was contented to sue for the Consulship in his behalfe, and to make the Senate agreable to it: wherefore his frendes presently reproved him for it, and shortly after he perceived he had undone him selfe, and together also lost the libertie of his contrie. For this young man Octavius Cæsar being growen to be verie great by his meanes and procurement: when he saw that he had the Consulshippe upon him, he forsooke Cicero, and agreed with Antonius and Lepidus. Then joyning his armie with theirs, he devided the Empire of Rome with them, as if it had bene lands left in common betwene them: and besides that, there was a bill made of two hundred men and upwards, whom they had appointed to be slaine. But the greatest difficultie and difference that fell out betwene them, was about the outlawing of Cicero. For Antonius woulde hearken to no peace betwene them, unlesse Cicero were slaine first of all: Lepidus was also in the same mind with Antonius: but Cæsar was against them

Octavius
Cæsar forsaketh Cicero.

Note the
fickelnes of
youth.

The meeting of the
Triumviri:
Antonius,
Lepidus,
Octavius
Cæsar.

362

both. Their meeting was by the citie of Bolonia, where
they continued three dayes together, they three only secretly
consulting in a place environned about with a litle river.
Some say that Cæsar stuck hard with Cicero the two first
dayes, but at the third, that he yeelded and forsooke him.
The exchaunge they agreed upon betwene them, was this.
Cæsar forsooke Cicero· Lepidus, his owne brother Paulus. Cicero ap-
and Antonius, Lucius Cæsar, his uncle by the mothers side. pointed to
Such place tooke wrath in them, as they regarded no kinred be slaine.
nor blood, and to speake more properly, they shewed that
no brute or savage beast is so cruell as man, if with his
licentiousnes he have liberty to execute his will. While
these matters were a brewing, Cicero was at a house of his
in the contrie, by the city of Thusculum, having at home
with him also his brother Quintus Cicero. Newes being
brought them thither of these proscriptions or outlawries,
appointing men to be slaine: they determined to goe to
Astyra, a place by the sea side where Cicero had an other
house, there to take sea, and from thence to goe into Macedon unto Brutus. For there ran a rumor that Brutus
was verie strong, and had a great power. So, they caused
them selves to be conveyed thither in two litters, both of
them being so weake with sorow and griefe, that they could
not otherwise have gone their wayes. As they were on their
waye, both their litters going as neere to ech other as they
could, they bewailed their miserable estate. but Quintus
chiefly, who tooke it most grievously. For, remembring
that he tooke no money with him when he came from his
house, and that Cicero his brother also had verie litle for
him selfe· he thought it best that Cicero shoulde holde on
his jorney, whilest he him selfe made an arrant home to
fetche suche thinges as he lacked, and so to make hast
againe to overtake his brother. They both thought it best
so, and then tenderly imbracing one an other, the teares
falling from their eyes, they tooke leave of ech other. Within
few dayes after, Quintus Cicero being betrayed by his owne
servaunts, unto them that made search for him: he was
cruelly slaine, and his sonne with him. But Marcus Tullius Quintus
Cicero being caried unto Astyra, and there finding a shippe Cicero slaine.

readie, imbarked immediatly, and sayled alongest the coast unto mount Circe, having a good gale of winde. There the mariners determining forthwith to make sayle againe, he came a shore, either for feare of the sea, or for that he had some hope that Cæsar had not altogether forsaken him : and therewithall returning towardes Rome by lande, he had gone about a hundred furlong thence. But then being at a straight howe to resolve, and sodainly chaunging his minde: he woulde needes be caried backe againe to the sea, where he continued all night marvelous sorowfull, and full of thoughts. For one while he was in minde to goe secretly unto Octavius Cæsars house, and to kill him selfe by the hearth of his chimney, to make the furies of hell to revenge his blood : but being affraied to be intercepted by the way, and cruelly handled, he turned from that determination. Then falling into other unadvised determinations, being perplexed as he was, he put him selfe againe into his servauntes handes, to be conveyed by sea to an other place called * Capites. There he had a very proper pleasaunt sommer house, where the North winds, called Etesiæ, doe geve a trimme fresh ayer in the sommer season. In that place also there is a litle temple dedicated unto Apollo, not farre from the sea side. From thence there came a great shole of crowes, making a marvelous noyse, that came flying towardes Ciceroes shippe, which rowed upon the shore side. This shole of crowes came and lighted upon the yard of their saile, some crying, and some pecking the cords with their bills : so that every man judged straight, that this was a signe of ill lucke at hand. Cicero notwithstanding this, came a shore, and went into his house, and layed him downe to see if he coulde sleepe. But the most parte of these crowes came and lighted upon the chamber windowe where he lay, making a wonderfull great noyse : and some of them got unto Ciceroes bedde where he lay, the clothes being cast over his head, and they never left him, till by litle and litle they had with their bills pluckt of the clothes that covered his face. His men seeing that, and saying to them selves that they were too vile beasts, if they would tarie to see their maister slaine before their eyes, considering that brute

beasts had care to save his life, seeing him so unworthily
intreated, and that they should not doe the best they coulde
to save his life: partely by intreatie, and partely by force,
they put him againe into his litter to carie him to the sea.
But in the meane time came the murderers appointed to
kill him, Herennius a Centurion, and Popilius Læna, Tribune
of the souldiers (to wit, Colonell of a thowsande men, whose
cause Cicero had once pleaded before the Iudges, when he
was accused for the murther of his owne father) having
souldiers attending upon them. So Ciceroes gate being
shut, they entred the house by force, and missing him, they
asked them of the house what was become of him. They
aunswered, they could not tell. Howbeit there was a young
boy in the house called Philologus, a slave infranchised by
Quintus Cicero, whom Tullius Cicero had brought up in the
Latin tongue, and had taught him the liberall sciences: he
told this Herennius, that his servauntes caried him in a
litter towards the sea, through darke narrowe lanes, shadowed
with wodde on either side. Popilius the Colonell taking
some souldiers with him, ranne about on the outside of the
lanes to take him at his comming out of them, and Herennius on thother side entred the lanes. Cicero hearing him
comming, commaunded his men to set downe his litter, and
taking his beard in his left hande, as his manner was, he
stowtly looked the murderers in the faces, his heade and
beard being all white, and his face leane and wrinckled, for
the extreame sorowes he had taken· divers of them that
were by, helde their handes before their eyes, whilest Herennius did cruelly murder him. So Cicero being three score
and foure yeares of age, thrust his necke out of the litter,
and had his head cut of by Antonius commaundement, and
his hands also, which wrote the Orations (called the Philippians) against him. For so did Cicero call the Orations he
wrote against him, for the malice he bare him: and do yet
continue the same name untill this present time. When
these poore dismembred members were brought to Rome,
Antonius by chaunce was busily occupied at that time about
the election of certaine officers: who when he heard of them
and saw them, he cried out alowde that now all his out-

lawries and proscriptions were executed: and thereuppon commaunded his head and his hands should straight be set up over the pulpit for Orations, in the place called Rostra. This was a fearefull and horrible sight unto the Romanes, who thought they saw not Ciceroes face, but an image of Antonius life and disposicion: who among so many wicked deedes as he committed, yet he did one act only that had some shew of goodnes, which was this. He delivered Philologus into the handes of Pomponia, the wife of Quintus Cicero: and when she had him, besides other cruell tormentes she made him abide, she compelled him to cut his owne flesh of by litle morsells, and to broyle them, and then to eate them. Some historiographers doe thus reporte it. But Tyro who was a slave infranchised by Cicero, made no mencion of the treason of this Philologus. Howbeit I understoode that Cæsar Augustus, long time after that, went one day to see one of his Nephewes, who had a booke in his hande of Ciceroes: and he fearing least his Uncle woulde be angrie to finde that booke in his handes, thought to hide it under his gowne. Cæsar saw it, and tooke it from him, and red the most parte of it standing, and then delivered it to the young boy, and sayd unto him: He was a wise man in deede, my childe, and loved his contrie well. After he had slaine Antonius, being Consul: he made Ciceroes sonne his colleague and fellow Consul with him, in whose time the Senate ordeyned, that the images of Antonius should be throwen downe, and deprived his memory of all other honors: adding further unto his decree, that from thence foorth none of the house and familie of the Antony should ever after beare the christen name of Marcus. So, Gods justice made the extreame revenge and punishment of Antonius, to fal into the house of Cicero.

GRECIANS AND ROMANES

THE COMPARISON OF
CICERO AND DEMOSTHENES

HIS is as muche as we coulde gather by our knowledge touching the notable actes and deedes worthie of memorie, wrytten of Cicero and Demosthenes. Furthermore, leaving the comparison a side of the difference of their eloquence in their Orations: me thinkes I may say thus muche of them. That Demosthenes did whollie _{Demosthenes} imploy all his wit and learning (naturall or artificiall) unto eloquence. the arte of Rethoricke, and that in force, and vertue of eloquence, he did excell all the Orators in his time: and for gravetie and magnificent style, all those also that only wryte for shewe or ostentacion: and for sharpnesse and arte, all the Sophisters and Maisters of Rethoricke. And that Cicero Ciceroes rare was a man generallie learned in all sciences, and that had and divers studied divers bookes, as appeareth plainely by the sundrie doctrines. bookes of Philosophie of his owne making, written after the manner of the Academicke Philosophers. Furthermore, they may see in his Orations he wrote in certeine causes to serve him when he pleaded: that he sought occasions in his by-talke to shewe men that he was excellently well learned. Furthermore, by their phrases a man may discerne some sparke of their manners and condicions. For Demosthenes Demosthenes phrase hath no maner of finenesse, geastes, nor grace in it, and Ciceroes but is altogether grave and harshe, and smelleth not of the maners. lampe, as Pytheas sayd when he mocked him: but sheweth a great drinker of water, extreame paines, and therewith also a sharpe and sower nature. But Cicero oftentimes fell from pleasaunt tawntes, unto plaine scurrilitie: and turning all his pleadinges of matters of importaunce, to sporte and laughter, having a grace in it, many times he did forget the comlynesse that became a man of his calling. As in his

367

Oration for Cælius, where he sayeth, It is no marvell if in so greate aboundance of wealth and finenesse he give him selfe a litle to take his pleasure : and that it was a folly not to use pleasures lawefull, and tollerable, sith the famousest Philosophers that ever were, did place the chiefe felicitie of man, to be in pleasure. And it is reported also, that Marcus Cato having accused Muræna, Cicero being Consul, defended his cause, and in his Oration pleasauntly girded all the sect of the Stoicke Philosophers for Catoes sake, for the straunge opinions they holde, which they call Paradoxes : insomuch as he made all the people and Iudges also fall a laughing a good. And Cato him selfe also smiling a litle, sayd unto them that sate by him : What a laughing and mocking Consul have we, my Lordes? but letting that passe, it seemeth that Cicero was of a pleasaunt and merie nature ; for his face shewed ever greate life and mirth in it. Whereas in Demosthenes countenaunce on thother side, they might discerne a marvelous diligence and care, and a pensive man, never weary with paine : insomuch that his enemies, (as he reporteth him selfe) called him a perverse and froward man.

Demosthenes
modest in
praising of
him selfe :
Cicero too
full of osten-
tacion.

Furthermore, in their writings is discerned, that the one speaketh modestly in his owne praise, so as no man can justly be offended with him : and yet not alwayes, but when necessitie enforceth him for some matter of great importaunce, but otherwise verie discreete and modest to speake of him selfe. Cicero in contrarie maner, using too often repeticion of one selfe thing in all his Orations, shewed an extreame ambition of glorie, when incessantly he cried out:

Let speare and shield geve place to gowne,
And geve the tung the laurell Crowne.

Yea furthermore, he did not onely praise his owne actes and deedes, but the Orations also which he had wrytten or pleaded : as if he shoulde have contended against Isocrates, or Anaximenes, a maister that taught Rethoricke, and not to goe about to reforme the people of Rome :

Which were both fierce and stowt in armes,
And fit to worke their enemies harmes.

For, as it is requisite for a Governour of a common wealth to seeke authoritie by his eloquence: so, to covet the praise of his owne glorious tongue, or as it were to begge it, that sheweth a base minde. And therefore in this poynt we must confesse that Demosthenes is farre graver, and of a nobler minde: who declared him selfe, that all his eloquence came onely but by practise, the which also required the favor of his auditorie: and further, he thought them fooles and madde men (as in deede they be no lesse) that therefore woulde make any boast of them selves. In this they were both alike, that both of them had great credit and authoritie in their Orations to the people, and for obtayning that they would propound: insomuche as Captaines, and they that had armies in their handes, stoode in neede of their eloquence. As Chares, Diopithes, and Leosthenes, they all were holpen of Demosthenes: and Pompey, and Octavius Cæsar the young man, of Cicero: as Cæsar him selfe confesseth in his *Commentaries* he wrote unto Agrippa, and Mæcenas. But nothing sheweth a mans nature and condicion more, (as it is reported, and so is it true) then when one is in authoritie: for that bewrayeth his humor, and the affections of his minde, and layeth open also all his secret vices in him. Demosthenes coulde never deliver any suche proofe of him selfe, bicause he never bare any office, nor was called forward. For he was not Generall of the armie, which he him selfe had prepared against king Philippe. Cicero on thother side being sent Treasorer into Sicile, and Proconsul into Cilicia and Cappadocia, in such a time as covetousnes raigned most (insomuch that the Captaines and Governors whom they sent to governe their provinces, thinking it villanie and dastardlinesse to robbe, did violently take thinges by force, at what time also to take bribes was reckoned no shame, but to handle it discreetly, he was the better thought of, and beloved for it) he shewed plainely that he regarded not money, and gave foorth many proofes of his curtesie and goodnes. Furthermore, Cicero being created Consul by name, but Dictator in deede, having absolute power and authoritie over all thinges to suppresse the rebellion and conspirators of Catiline: he proved Platoes

DEMOS-
THENES
AND
CICERO

Demosthenes and Ciceroes cunning in their Orations in the common wealth.

Authoritie sheweth mens vertues and vices.

Ciceroes abstinence from money.

5 : AAA

DEMOS-
THENES
AND
CICERO
Demosthenes
a money
taker.

prophecie true, which was: That the cities are safe from daunger, when the chiefe Magistrates and Governors (by some good divine fortune) doe governe with wisedom and justice. Demosthenes was reproved for his corruption, and selling of his eloquence: bicause secretly he wrote one Oration for Phormio, and an other in the selfe same matter for Apollodorus, they being both adversaries. Further, he was defamed also for receiving money of the king of Persia, and therewithall condemned for the money which he had taken of Harpalus. And though some peradventure woulde object, that the reporters thereof (which are many) doe lye: yet they can not possibly deny this, that Demosthenes had no power to refraine from looking of the presentes which divers kinges did offer him, praying him to accept them in good parte for their sakes: neither was that the part of a man that did take usurie by trafficke on the sea, the extreamest yet of all other. In contrarie maner (as we have sayd before) it is certeine that Cicero being Treasorer, refused the gifts which the Sicilians offered him, there: and the presentes also which the king of the Cappadocians offred him whilest he was Proconsul in Cilicia, and those especially which his frendes pressed upon him to take of them, being a great summe of money, when he went as a banished man out of Rome.

Furthermore, the banishment of the one was infamous to him, bicause by judgement he was banished as a theefe. The banishment of the other was for as honorable an acte as ever he did, being banished for ridding his contrie of wicked men. And therefore of Demosthenes, there was no speeche after he was gone: but for Cicero, all the Senate chaunged their apparell into blacke, and determined that they would passe no decree by their authoritie, before Ciceroes banishment was revoked by the people. In deede Cicero idlely passed his time of banishment, and did nothing all the while he was in Macedon: and one of the chiefest acts that Demosthenes did, in all the time that he delt in the affaires of the common wealth, was in his banishment. For he went unto every city, and did assist the Ambassadors of the Græcians, and refused the Ambassadors of the Macedonians. In the which he shewed him selfe a better citizen, then either

GRECIANS AND ROMANES

Themistocles, or Alcibiades, in their like fortune and exile. So when he was called home, and returned, he fell againe to his old trade which he practised before, and was ever against Antipater, and the Macedonians. Where Lælius in open Senate sharply tooke up Cicero, for that he sate still and sayd nothing, when that Octavius Cæsar the young man made peticion against the law, that he might sue for the Consulshippe, and being so young, that he had never a heare on his face. And Brutus selfe also doth greatly reprove Cicero in his letters, for that he had maintained and nourished, a more grievous and greater tyrannie, then that which they had put downe. And last of all, me thinketh the death of Cicero most pitiefull, to see an olde man caried up and downe, (with tender love of his servauntes) seeking all the waies that might be to flie death, which did not long prevent his naturall course: and in the ende, olde as he was, to see his head so pitiefully cut of. Whereas Demosthenes, though he yeelded a litle, intreating him that came to take him: yet for that he had prepared the poyson long before, that he had kept it long, and also used it as he did, he can not but be marvelously commended for it. For sith the god Neptune denyed him the benefit of his sanctuarie, he betooke him to a greater, and that was death: whereby he saved him selfe out of the souldiers handes of the tyran, and also scorned the bloody crueltie of Antipater.

THE LIFE OF DEMETRIUS

How sences and artes doe agree and differ.

HO first likened arts to our sences, semeth to have respected especially that one property of them both, in receiving objects of contrary quality: for, in the use and end of their operacion, there is great difference. The senses receive indifferently, without discretion and judgement, white and blacke, sweete and sower, soft and hard: for their office is only to admit their severall objects, and to carie and referre the judgement thereof to the common sence. But artes being the perfection of reason, receive and allow those things onely which make for their operacion, regarding and eschuing the contraries. Thone chiefly, and for use: thother by the way, and with intent to avoyde them. So Phisicke dealeth with diseases, Musicke with discordes, to thend to remove them, and worke their contraries: and the great Ladies of all other artes, Temperaunce, justice, and wisdom, doe not only consider honestie, uprightnes, and profit: but examine withall, the nature and effectes of lewdnes, corruption, and damage. And innocencie, which vaunteth her want of experience in undue practises: men call simplicitie, and ignoraunce of thinges, that be necessarie and good to be knowen. And therefore the auncient Lacedæmonians in their solemne feastes forced their Ilotes the bondmen, to overcharge them selves with wine: and suche they shewed them unto their youth, by the apparant beastlines of dronken men, to worke in them an abhorring of so lothesome vice. Wherin, although I can not much praise them for humanity or wisedom, that corrupt and spoile one man, by example of him, to correct and reclaime an other: yet (as I hope) it shall not be reprehended in me, if amongest the rest I put in one or two paier of suche, as living in great place and accompt, have increased their fame with infamy. Which in truth, I doe not, to

The maner of the Spartans to make their slaves dronke.

372

please and draw on the reader with variety of report: but as
Ismenias the Theban Musitian shewed his schollers, both
those that strake a cleane stroke, with, Do so, and such as
bungled it, with, Do not so: and Antigenidas thought men
should like better, and with greater desire contend for skill,
if they heard and discerned untunable notes: so thinke I, The cause of
we shall be the forwarder in reading and following the good, describing
if we know the lives, and see the deformity of the wicked. the lives of
This treaty conteineth the lives of Demetrius, surnamed the wicked.
the Fortgainer, and M. Antony the Triumvir, and great
examples to confirme the saying of Plato: That from great Plato: of
minds, both great vertues and great vices do procede. They vertue and
were both given over to women and wine, both valliant and vice.
liberal, both sumptuous and high minded, fortune served
them both alike, not only in the course of their lives, in
attempting great matters, somtimes with good, somtimes
with ill successe, in getting and losing things of great con-
sequence, overthrowing both when they feared not, restoring
both when they hoped not. But also in their ende there
was no great difference, thone brought to his death by his
mortal enemies, and the others fortune not much unlike.
But now to our historie. Antigonus had two sonnes by his Demetrius
wife Stratonicè, the daughter of Corræus: the one of them parentage.
he named Demetrius, and the other Philip, after his fathers
name. Thus farre the most wryters doe agree: howbeit
some holde opinion, that Demetrius was not the sonne of
Antigonus, but his Nephewe. But bicause his father dyed
leaving him a childe, and that his mother was straight
maried againe unto Antigonus: thereuppon came the reporte
that he was Antigonus sonne. Howsoever it was, Philip, The death of
that was not much younger then Demetrius, dyed. Now for Philip the
Demetrius, though he was a verie bigge man, he was nothing younger
so high as his father, but yet so passing and wonderfull brother of
fayer, that no painter could possibly draw his picture and Demetrius.
counterfeat to his likenes. For they saw a sweete counten- Demetrius
ance, mixed with a kinde of gravetie in his face, a feare beawtie.
with curtesie, and an incomparable Princely majestie accompanied with a lively spirit and youth, and his wit and
manners were such, that they were both fearefull, and

pleasaunt unto men that frequented him. For as he was most pleasaunt in company having leasure, and most geven to banketing, pleasaunt life, and more wantonly geven to follow any lust and pleasure, than any king that ever was: yet was he alwayes very carefull and diligent in dispatching matters of importance. And therefore he marvelously commended, and also endevoured to follow Dionysius, (as much to say, as Bacchus) above all the other goddes, as he that had bene a wise and valliant Captaine in waire, and that in peace invented and used all the pleasure that might be. He marvelously loved and reverenced his father, and it seemeth that the dutiefulnes he shewed unto his mother, was more to discharge the due obedience and dutie of a sonne, than otherwise to enterteine his father, for feare of his power, or hope to be his heire. And for proofe hereof we read, that

one day as he came home from hunting, he went unto his father Antigonus, geving audience to certaine Ambassadors, and after he had done his duetie to him, and kissed him: he sate downe by him even as he came from hunting, having his dartes in his hande, which he caried out a hunting with him. Then Antigonus calling the Ambassadors alowde as they went their way, having received their aunswere: My Lords, sayd he, you shall carie home this reporte of my sonne and me, be witnesses I pray you, how we live one with an other. As meaning to shewe thereby, that the agreement betwext the father and the sonne together, is a great safetie to the affaires of a king, as also a manifest proofe of

his greatnes so gealous is a king to have a companion, besides the hate and mistrust it should breede. So that the greatest Prince and most auncientest of all the successors of Alexander, boasted that he stoode not in feare of his sonne, but did suffer him to sitte by him, having a dart in his hand So was this house onely of all other the Macedonian

The sport of
the East
kinges, was
to kill their
owne chil-
dren, wives,
and mothers. kinges, least defiled with suche villanie, many successions after: and to confesse a troth, in all Antigonus rase there was not one, but Philip onely, that slue his owne sonne. But we have many examples of divers other houses of kinges, that have put their sonnes, wives, and mothers to death. and for their brethren, it was an ordinarie thing with them

374

to kill them, and never sticke at it. For like as Geometri- DEMETRIUS
cians would have men graunt them certaine proposicions
which they suppose without proofe: even so was this holden
for a generall rule, to kill their brethren, for the safetie of
their estate. But further, to shewe you more plainly that Demetrius
Demetrius was of a noble and curteous nature, and that he curtesie.
dearely loved his frendes: we may alleage this example.
Mithridates, the sonne of Ariobarzanes, was his familiar
frend and companion (for they were both in maner of an
age) and he commonly followed Antigonus courte, and never
practised any villanie or treason to him, neither was he
thought such a man: yet Antigonus did somewhat suspect
him, bicause of a dreame he had. He thought that being Antigonus
in a goodly great fielde, he sowed of these scrapinges of gold, dreame.
and that of that seede, first of all came up goodly wheate
which had cares of gold: howbeit that shortly after returning that way againe, he found nothing but the straw, and
the eares of the wheate cut of, and that he being angrie
and verie sorie for it, some tolde him that Mithridates
had cut of these golden eares of wheate, and had caried
them with him into the realme of Pont. Antigonus being
marvelosly troubled with this dreame, after he had made
his sonne sweare unto him that he would make no man
alive privy to that he would tell him: he told him all his
dreame what he had dreamed, and therewith that he was
determined to put this young man Mithridates to death.
Demetrius was marvelous sory for it, and therefore the
next morning, this young noble Prince going as he was
wont to passe the time away with Mithridates, he durst
not by word of mouth utter that he knew, bicause of his
othe: howbeit, taking him aside from his other familliers,
when they were both together by them selves, he wrote on
the ground with the end of his dart, Mithridates loking on
him: Flie Mithridates. Mithridates found straight what Demetrius
he ment, and fled the very same night into Cappadocia: saveth Mithri-
and shortly after it was his destinie to fulfill Antigonus dates life.
dreame. For he conquered many goodly contries, and it Mithridates
was he onely that established the house of the kingdom of king of Pont.
Pont, the which the Romanes afterwardes overthrewe, about

the eight succession. By these examples we may easily conjecture the good nature and curtesie of Demetrius. For like as the elementes (according to Empedocles opinion) are ever

*Bicause he sayd, that love and discord were ever the efficient causes of generation and corruption of all thinges.
at * strife together, but specially those that are nearest eache to other: even so, though all the successors of Alexander were at continuall warres together, yet was it soonest kindled, and most cruell betwene them which bordered nearest unto eche other, and that by being neare neighbours, had alwaies occasion of brawle together, as fell out at that time betwene

Enmitie betwixt Antigonus and Ptolomy.
Antigonus and Ptolomy. This Antigonus lay most commonly in the contry of Phrygia: who having intelligence that Ptolomy was gone into Cyprus, and that he overranne all Syria, winning by force, or faier meanes, all the townes and cities subject unto them: he sent his sonne Demetrius

Demetrius, generall to Antigonus, against Ptolomy.
thether, beeing at that time but two and twenty yeares of age, and it was the first time that ever he tooke charge as generall to his father, in matters of great importance. But he being a young man, and that had no skill of warres, fighting a battell with an olde souldier (trained up in the discipline of warres under Alexander the great, and that through him, and in his name, had fought many great battels) was soone

Demetrius overthrowen in battaile, by Ptolomy.
overthrowen, and his armie put to flight, by the citie of Gaza. At which overthrow were slayne five thowsand men, and almost eight thowsand taken and besides, Demetrius lost his tents and pavilions, his gold and silver, and to be short,

The bountifulnes of Ptolomy the Conqueror, unto Demetrius conquered.
all his whole cariage. But Ptolomy sent him all his thinges againe, and his friends also that were taken after the battell, with great curteous wordes: that he would not fight with them for all thinges together, but onely for honor, and Empire. Demetrius receiving them at his handes, besought the gods that he might not long live a debter unto Ptolomy for this great curtesie, but that he might quickly requite it with the like againe. Now Demetrius tooke not this overthrow like a young man, though it was his first souldierfare: but like an olde and wise Captaine, that had abidden many overthrowes, he used great diligence to gather men againe, to make new armors, and to keepe the cities and contries in his hands under obedience, and did traine and exercise his souldiers in armes, whome he had gathered togither. Anti-

gonus having newes of the overthrowe of his sonne Demetrius, DEMETRIUS
said no more, but that Ptolomy had overcomen beardles men:
and that afterwardes he should fight with bearded men. But
now, bicause he would not discorage his sonne altogether,
who craved leave once againe to fight a battell with Ptolomy:
he graunted him. So, shortly after came Cilles, Ptolomyes
generall, with a great puysant armie, to drive him altogether
out of Syria. For they made no great accompt of Demetrius,
bicause he had bene once overthrowen before. Howbeit Demetrius
Demetrius stale apon him, gave him charge on the sodaine, victorie of
and made him so affraid, that he tooke both the campe, and Ptolomy.
the generall, with seven thowsand prisoners besides, and
wanne a marvelous treasure of money: which made him
a glad man, not so much for the gaine he should have by
it, as for the oportunitie he had thereby to come out of
Ptolomyes det, nothing regarding the treasure nor the honor
he had gotten by this victorie, but onely the benefit of his
requitall of Ptolomyes curtesie towardes him. But yet he
did nothing of his owne head, before he had written to his
father: and then receiving full graunt and commission from
him to dispose of all things as he thought good, he sent
backe Cilles unto Ptolomy, and al his other friends besides, Demetrius
with great and rich gifts which he bountifully bestowed thankefulnes
on them. This misfortune and overthrow did utterly put unto Ptolomy.
Ptolomy out of all Syria, and brought Antigonus also from
the citie of Celænes, for the exceeding joy he had of this
victorie, as also for the great desire he had to see his sonne.
After that, he sent Demetrius into Arabia, against a people Demetrius
called the Nabathæians, to conquer them: but there he was invaded
in great daunger and distresse in the deserts for lacke of Arabia.
water, howbeit he never shewed any signe that he was
affraid. Thereby he so astonied the barbarous people, that
he had leysure enough to retyre with safetie, and with a
great booty of a thowsand camells, which he brought away
with him. About that time Seleucus, (whome Antigonus
had driven from Babylon) returning thither againe, he came
and conquered it without other ayde then of him selfe: and
went with a great armie against the people and nations confining upon the Indians, and the provinces adjoyning unto

5 : BBB 377

mount Caucasus, to conquer them. Thereuppon Demetrius hoping to find Mesopotamia without any gard or defence, sodainly passed over the river of Euphrates, and came unlooked for unto Babylon, and there distressed the garrison of Seleucus, that kept one of the castells or citadells of the citie, being two of them: and then putting in seven thowsand souldiers to keepe them, he commaunded the rest of his men to get what they could, and to bringe it away with them. After that, he marched towards the sea to returne home, leaving thereby the Realme and kingdom of Seleucus in better state and safetie, then it was when he invaded it. For it appeared that he had taken all the contry from Seleucus, leaving him nothing in it, by spoiling and forraging all that was there. At his returne home, newes were brought him that Ptolomy lay at the seege of the citie of Halycarnassus: whereuppon he drew thither with speede to make him raise the seege, and thereby saved the city from him. Now, bicause by this exployte they wanne great fame, both of them, (Antigonus and Demetrius) fell into a marvelous desire to set all Græce at libertie, the which Ptolomy

Antigonus
and Deme-
trius do goe
about to set
Græce at
libertie.
and Cassander kept in servitude and bondage. Never king tooke in hande a more honorable nor juster warre and enterprise, then that was. For, what power or riches he could gather together, in oppressing of the barbarous people: he bestowed it all in restoring the Græcians to their libertie, and onely to winne fame and honor by it. So, they being in consultacion what way to take, to bring their purpose and desire to passe, and having taken order to begin first at Athens: one of Antigonus chiefest friends about him, told him that he should take the citie, and place a good garrison there for them selves, if they could once winne it: for, said he, it will be a good bridge to passe further into all Græce. Antigonus would not harken to that, but said, that the love and good will of men was a surer bridge, and that the citie of Athens was as a beacon to all the land, the which would immediatly make his doings shine through the world, as a cresset light, upon the toppe of a kepe or watche tower. Thus Demetrius hoysed sayle, having five thowsand silver talents, and a fleete of two hundred and fiftie sayle, and

GRECIANS AND ROMANES

sailed towardes the citie of Athens: in the which Demetrius Phaleiian was governor in the behalfe of Cassander, and kept a great strong garrison there within the haven and castell of Munichea. He had an excellent good winde to further his jorney, so that with his good foresight and speede he made, he arrived in the haven of Piræa, the five and twenty day of the moneth Thargelion, (now called Maye) before any man knew of his comming. Now when this fleete was within a kenning of the citie, and lesse, that they might easily see them from thence: every man prepared him selfe to receive them, taking them to be Ptolomyes shippes. But in fine, the Captaines and governors understanding too late who they were, did what they could to helpe them selves: but they were all in hurly burly, as men compelled to fight out of order, to keepe their enemies from land-ing, and to repulse them, comming so sodainly upon them. Demetrius having found the barre of the haven open, launched in presently. Then being comen to the view of them all, and standing upon the hatches of his galley, he made signes with his hand that he prayed silence. The tumult being pacified, he proclaymed alowd by one of his Heraulds, that his father had sent him in happy hower to deliver the Athenians from all their garrisons, and to restore them againe to their auncient libertie and freedom, to enjoye their lawes and auncient government of their forefathers. After the proclamacion made, all the common people straight threwe downe their weapons and targets at their feete, to clappe their handes with great showtes of joy: praying him to land, and calling him alowde their Savior, and benefactor. Now for them that were with Demetrius Phalerian, they all thought good to let the stronger in, although he per-formed not that he promised, and also sent Ambassadors unto him to treate of peace. Demetrius received them very curteously, and sent with them for pledge, one of the dearest friends his father had, Aristodemus Milesian. Furthermore, he was not careles of the health and safety of Demetrius Phalerian, who, by reason of the chaunge and alteracion of the government of the common wealth at Athens, stoode more in feare of the people of Athens, than of his enemies.

379

DEMETRIUS
Demetrius
Antigonus,
honoreth
Demetrius
Phalerius.

Therefore Demetrius regarding the fame and vertue of the man, caused him to be conveyed (according to his desire) unto Thebes, with good and sufficient safe conduct. And for Demetrius him selfe, although he was very desirous to see the citie, he saide he would not come into it, before he had first restored it unto her auncient libertie and freedom, and also driven away the garrison thence: and thereuppon he cast trenches round about the castell of Munychia. In the meane season bicause he would not be idle, he hoysed sayle, and coasted towards the citie of Megara, within the which Cassander also kept a strong garrison. Demetrius busily following these matters, was advertised that Crate-sipolis, surnamed Polyperchon, (who had bene Alexanders wife) a Lady of passing fame and beauty, and lay at that time in the citie of Patras, would be glad to see him: he leaving his armie within the territorie of the Megarians, tooke his jorney presently unto her, with a few of his lightest armed men, and yet he stale from them, and made his tent to be set up a good way from them, bicause this Ladie

might not be seene when she came unto him. Some of his enemies having present intelligence thereof, came and set upon him before he knew it. Demetrius was so scared, that he had no further leysure, but to cast an ill favored cloke about him, the first that came to hand, and disguising him selfe to flie for life, and escaped very hardly, that he was not shamefully taken of his enemies for his incontinencie. But though they missed him, they tooke his tent, and all his

Demetrius
winneth
the city of
Megara, and
restoreth it to
her libertie.

money in it. After that, the citie of Megara was taken and won from Cassanders men, where Demetrius souldiers would have sacked all · howbeit the Athenians made humble inter-cession for them, that they might not be spoyled. Deme-trius thereuppon, after he had driven out Cassanders garrison, he restored it againe to her former libertie. In doing that, he called to mind the Philosopher Stilpo, a famous

man in Megara, though he lived a quiet and contemplative life. He sent for him, and asked him if any of his men had

taken any thing of his. Stilpo aunswered him, they had not: For, quoth he, I sawe no man that tooke my learning from me. This notwithstanding, all the slaves of the citie were in manner caried away. Another time, Demetrius making much of him, as he was going his way saide unto him : Well, Stilpo, I leave you your citie free. It is true, O king, quoth he, for thou hast left us never a slave. Shortly after, he returned againe unto Athens, and layde seege to the castell of Munichia, the which he tooke, and drave out the garrison, and afterwards rased it to the ground. After that, through the intreatie and earnest desire of the Athenians, who prayed him to come and refresh him selfe in their citie : he made his entry into it, and caused all the people to assemble, and then restored unto them their auncient lawes and libertie of their contry, promising them besides, that he would procure his father to sende them a hundred and fiftye thowsand busshells of wheate, and as much woode and tymber as should serve to make them a hundred and fiftie gallies. Thus, the Athenians through Demetrius meanes, recovered the Democratia again, (to wit, their populer government) fifteene yeares after they had lost it, and lived all the time betwene their losse and restitucion from the warre called Lamiacus warre, and the battell that was fought by the citie of Cranon, in the state of Oligarchia, to wit, under the government of a fewe governors in sight, but in truth a Monarchie or kingdome, bicause they were under the government of one man Demetrius Phalerian, that had absolute authoritie over them. But by this meanes they made their savior and preserver of their contry, Demetrius (who seemed to have obteined such honor and glory through his goodnes and liberalitie) hateful and odious to all men, for the overgreat and unmeasurable honors which they gave him. For first of all, they called Antigonus and Demetrius kings, who before that time had alwayes refused the name, and the which, (among all other princely honors and prerogatives graunted) they that had devided betwene them the Empire of Philip and Alexander, durst never once presume to chalenge, nor to take uppon them. So unto them only they gave the style and names of the goddes saviors, and tooke away their yearely Maior, whome they called Eponymos, bicause they did shew the yeares of olde time, by the names of them that had bene Maiors.

DEMETRIUS Furthermore, in stead thereof they ordeyned in the counsell of the citie, that there should yearely be chosen one by voyces of the people, whom they should name the Priest of their Saviors, whose name they should write and subscribe in all publike graunts and covenants, to shewe the yeare: and besides all this, that they should cause their pictures to be drawen in the veyle or holy banner, in the which were set out the images of their goddes, the patrones and protectors of their citie. And furthermore they did consecrate the place, where Demetrius first came out of his coche, and there did set up an aulter, and called it Demetrius aulter comming out of his coche: and unto their tribes they added two other, the Antigonides and the Demetriades. Their great counsell at large which they created yearely of five hundred men, was then first of all brought into sixe hundred, bicause every tribe must needes furnishe of them selves, fifty coun-

The boldnes of Stratocles Athenian.
sellers. *But yet the straungest acte, and most new found invention of flattery, was that of Stratocles,* (being the common flatterer and people pleaser) who put forth this decree, by the which it was ordeined: that those whome the common wealth should send unto Antigonus and Demetrius, should in stead of Ambassadors be called Theori, as much to say, as ministers of the sacrifices. For so were they called, whome they sent to Delphes to Apollo Pytheas, or unto Elide, to Iupiter Olympias, at the common and solemne feasts of all Græce, to doe the ordinary sacrifices and oblations for the health and preservation of the cities. This Stratocles in all things els was a desperate man, and one that had alwayes led a wicked and dissolute life: and for his shameles boldnes, he seemed wholy to follow the steppes or Cleons foole hardines, and olde insolencie, which (when he lived) he shewed unto the people. He openly kept a harlot in his house called Phylacion. One day she having bought for his supper, beastes heades and neckes commonly eaten,

Stratocles cruell saying.
he sayd unto her: Why, how now? thou hast bought me acates which we tosse like balls, that have to doe in the common wealth. Another time when the armie of the Athenians was overthrowen by sea, by the Ile of Amorgos: he would needes prevent the newes of this overthrowe, and

came through the streete of Ceranicus, crowned with garlands DEMETRIUS
of flowers, as if the Athenians had wonne the battell: and
was also the author of a decree, whereby they did sacrifice
unto the goddes, to give them thankes for the victorie: and
meate was given amongest every tribe, in token of common
joy. But shortly after the Messengers arrived, which brought
report of the shipwracke and overthrowe. The people were
in an uprore withal, and sent for Stratocles in a marvelous
rage. But he with a face of brasse came unto them, and
arrogantly defended the peoples ill will, and angrily told
them: Well, and what hurt have I done you, if I have made
you mery these two dayes? Such was Stratocles impudencie
and rashnes. But, as the Poet Aristophanes sayth:

> But whotter matters were that time in hand,
> Than fire that wasteth both by sea and land.

For there was another that passed Stratocles in knaverie.
Who procured a decree, that as often as Demetrius came
into the citie of Athens, he should be received with all
ceremonies and like solemnitie, as they use in the feasts of
Ceres and Bacchus: and further that they should give unto
him that did excell all the rest in sumptuousnes and riches,
at such time as Demetrius made his entry into the citie, so
much money out of the common treasure, as should serve to
make an image or other offring, which should be consecrated
to the temples in memorie of his liberalitie. And last of The moneth of
all, they chaunged the name of the moneth Munichion (to Munychion
wit the moneth of Ianuary) and called it Demetrion: and altered, and
the last day of the moneth which they called before the called Deme-
new and old moone, they then called it the Demetriade: trion, for the
and the feastes of Bacchus also called then Dionysia, they honor of
presently named Demetria. But the goddes by divers signes Demetrius
and tokens shewed plainly, that they were offended with name.
these chaunges and alteracions. For the holy banner in the Wonders.
which (according to the order set downe) they had paynted
the images of Antigonus, and Demetrius, with the pictures
of Iupiter and Minerva: as they caried it a procession
through the streete Ceranicus, it was torne a sonder in the
middest by a tempest of winde. And furthermore, about

383

LIVES OF THE NOBLE

DEMETRIUS
Hemlocke,
the usuall
erbe, with the
juyce whereof
they poysoned
offenders at
Athens.

the aulters which were set up in the honor of Demetrius and Antigonus, there grew a great deale of hemlocke, the which otherwise was unpossible to growe there. On the feast day also of Bacchus, they were compelled to leave the pompe or procession for that daye, it was such an extreame hard frost out of all season: and besides, there fell such a myll dewe and great frost upon it, that not onely their vines and olives were killed with it, but also the most part of the wheate blades which were newly sprong up. And therefore the

Philippides
the Poet.

Poet Philippides (an enemie of the aforesayd Stratocles) in one of his comedies writeth certaine verses against him to this effect:

The partie for whose wickednes the veyle was rent in twayne,
Which with the honor due to God did worship men most vayne,
Is he for whom our budding vines were blasted with the frost.
Those thinges and not our comedies have us so deerly cost.

This Philippides was very well beloved of king Lysimachus, insomuch that for his sake the king had done many pleasures to the common wealth of Athens. For he loved him so dearly, that as often as he saw him, or met with him at the beginning of any warre, or matter of great importance: he was of opinion that he brought him good lucke. For in deed he did not so much esteeme him for the excellencie of his arte, but he was much more to be beloved and esteemed, for his vertuous and honest condicions. He was no trouble-som man, nether was he infected with the finenesse of court, as he shewed one day when the king made much of him, and giving him good countenance said unto him: What wilt

Philippides
notable
aunswer unto
king Lysima-
chus, not de-
siring to heare
his secrets.

thou have me give thee of my things Philippides? Even what it shall please thee, O king, so it be none of thy secrets. Thus much we thought good to speake of him in bytalke, bicause an honest player of comedies, should matche with a shameles and impudent Orator of the people. But yet there was another Democlides, of the village of Sphettus, that dreamed out a more straunger kind of honor, touching the consecration of their targets, which they dedicated to the temple of Apollo in Delphes, that is to say, that they should goe and aske the oracle of Demetrius. But I wil shew you
384

the very effect and forme of the law as it was set downe.
In good hower : the people ordeyne that he should be chosen
one of the Citizens of Athens, which shall goe unto our
savior : and after that he hath done due sacrifice unto him,
he shal aske Demetrius our savior, after what sort the people
shall with greatest holines and devotion, without delay,
make consecration of their holiest gifts and offerings : and
according to the oracle it shall please him to give them, the
people shal duely execute it.   Thus, laying upon Demetrius
al these foolish mockeries, who besides was no great wise
man, they made him a very foole.   Demetrius being at *Demetrius*
that time at leisure in Athens, he married a widow called *maried unto*
Eurydice, which came of that noble and auncient house of *Eurydicé, at*
Miltiades, and had bene married before unto one Opheltas *Athens.*
Prince of the Cyrenians, and that after his death returned
againe to Athens.   The Athenians were very glad of this
marriage, and thought it the greatest honor that came to
their citie, supposing he had done it for their sakes.   Howbeit he was soone wonne to be married, for he had many *Demetrius*
wives, but amongest them all, he loved Phila best, and gave *had many*
her most honor and preheminence above them all : partly *wives to-*
for the respect of her father Antipater, and partly also for *gether.*
that she had bene first maried unto Craterus, whome the *Phila . Deme-*
Macedonians loved best when he lived, and most lamented *trius wife,*
after his death, above all the other successors of Alexander. *Antipaters*
His father I suppose made him to marry her by force, *Daughter,*
although in deede her yeares was not meete for him : for *and Craterus*
he was marvelous young, and she very olde.   And when *widow.*
Demetrius seemed not to be contented withall, his father
rowned him softly in the eare with this saying ·

> Refuze no woman nere so old,
> Whoze mariage bringeth store of gold.

Wherein he alluded cunningly to these verses of Euripides :

> Refuze not to become a thrall,
> Where lucre may insewe withall.

But so much did Demetrius honor his wife Phila, and all
his other wives he married, that he was not ashamed to

keepe a number of Curtisans, and other mens wives besides: so that he onely of all other kings in his time, was most detected with this vice of lecherie. While these things passed on in this sort, he was commaunded by his father, to fight with Ptolomy for the Realme of Cyprus. So there was no remedie but he must needes obey him, although otherwise he was very sory to leave the warre he had begonne, to set the Græcians at libertie, the which had bene farre more honorable and famous. Howbeit, before he departed from Athens, he sent unto Cleonides Ptolomyes generall, that kept the cities of Corinthe and Sicyone, to offer him money if he would sette those cities at libertie. But Cleonides would not be delt withall that way. Thereuppon Demetrius straight way tooke sea, and sayled with all his armie towards Cyprus, where at his first comming he overcame Menelaus Ptolomyes brother. But shortly after, Ptolomy went thither in person with a great armie both by sea and land, and there passed betwixt them fierce threatnings and prowde words to eche other. For Ptolomy sent to Demetrius to bid him to depart if he were wise, before all his armie came together: which would tread him under their feete, and marche upon his bellie, if he taried their comming. Demetrius on the other side sent him word, that he would doe him this favor to let him escape, if he would sweare and promise unto him to withdrawe his garrisons which he had in the cities of Corinthe, and Sycione. So the

Battell by sea
in the Ile
of Cyprus,
betwixt
Demetrius
Antigonus,
and Ptolomy. expectacion of this battell made these two Princes not onely very pensive to fight one with the other, but also all the other Lords, Princes, and kings: bicause the successe thereof was uncertaine, which of them two should prevaile. But every man judged this, that which of them obteyned the victorie, he should not only be Lord of the Realme of Cyprus and Syria, but therewith also of greater power then all the rest. Ptolomy in person with fiftie sayle beganne to rowe against his enemie Demetrius, and commaunded his brother Menelaus that when he sawe them fast grappled in fight together, he should launche out of the haven of Salamina, and give charge upon the rereward of Demetrius shippes, to breake their order, with the three score gallies

he had in charge. Demetrius on the other side prepared DEMETRIUS
tenne gallies against these three score, thinking them enowe
to choke up the haven mouth being but narrowe, so that
none of the gallies that were within could come out: and
furthermore, he dispersed his armie by land upon the fore-
land poynts which reache into the sea, and went him selfe
into the maine sea with nyne score gallies, and gave such a
fierce charge upon Ptolomy, that he valliantly made him flie. Demetrius
Who when he sawe his armie broken, fled as speedily as he victorie of
could with eight gallies onely: for all the rest were either Ptolomy.
broken or suncke in fight, and those eight onely escaped,
besides three score and tenne which were taken, and all their
souldiers in them. And as for his cariage, his traine, his
friends, his officers, and houshold servaunts, his wives, his
gold and silver, his armor, engines of batterie, and all such
other warlike furniture and munition as was conveyed abourd
his carects and great shippes riding at anker: of all these
things nothing escaped Demetrius hands, but all was brought
into his campe. Among those spoyles also was taken that Lamia, the
famous Curtisan Lamia, who at the first had her name onely, famous Cur-
for her passing playing upon the flute: but after she fell to tisan, taken
Curtisan trade, her countenance and credit increased the trius, upon
more. So that even then when her beautie through yeares the defeating
fell to decaye, and that she found Demetrius much younger of Ptolomy.
then her selfe. yet she so wanne him with her sweete conversation and good grace, that he onely liked her, and all the
other women liked him. After this victorie by sea, Menelaus made no more resistance, but yeelded up Salamina and Salamina
his shippes unto Demetrius, and put into his handes also yelded up to
twelve hundred horsemen, and twelve thowsand footemen Demetrius.
well armed. This so famous and triumphant victorie was
yet much more beautified, by Demetrius great bountie and
goodnes which he shewed in giving his enemies slaine in
battell honorable funeralls, setting the prisoners at liberty
without ransom paying, and giving moreover twelve hundred
complet armors unto the Athenians. After this, Demetrius Aristodemus
sent Aristodemus Milesian unto his father Antigonus, to a notorious
tell him by word of mouth the newes of this victorie. Antigonus
Aristodemus was the greatest flatterer in all Antigonus Court.

DEMETRIUS Court, who devised then, as it seemeth to me, to adde unto this exployte the greatest flatterie possible. For when he had taken land after he was come out of the Ile of Cyprus, he would in no wise have the shippe he came in to come neare the shoare, but commaunded them to ride at anker, and no man so hardy to leave the shippe: but he him self got into a litle boate, and went unto Antigonus, who all this while was in marvelous feare and perplexitie for the successe of this battell, as men may easily judge they are, which hope after so great incertainties. Now when worde was brought him that Aristodemus was comming to him all alone, then was he worse troubled than afore, insomuch that he could scant keepe within dores him selfe, but sent his servaunts and friends one after another to meete Aristodemus, to aske him what newes, and to bring him worde presently againe how the world went. But not one of them could get any thing out of him, for he went on still fayer and softly with a sad countenance, and very demurely, speaking never a worde. Wherefore Antigonus hart being cold in his belly, he could stay no lenger, but would him selfe goe and meete with Aristodemus at the gate, who had a marvelous preasse of people following on him, besides those of the Court which ranne out to heare his aunswer. At length when he came neare unto Antigonus, holding out his right hand unto him, he cryed out alowd, God save thee, O king Antigonus: we have overcome king Ptolomy in battell by sea, and have wonne the Realme of Cyprus, with sixteene thowsand and eyght hundred prisoners. Then aunswered Antigonus, And God save thee to: truely Aristodemus thou hast kept us in a trawnse a good while, but to punishe thee for the payne thou hast put us to, thou shalt the later receive the reward

The first time Antigonus and Deme- trius were called kinges.

of thy good newes. Then was the first time that the people with a lowde voice called Antigonus and Demetrius kings. Now for Antigonus, his friendes and familliers did at that present instant put on the royall band or diadeame uppon his heade: But for Demetrius, his father sent it unto him, and by his letters called him king. They also that were in Ægypt with Ptolomy, understanding that, did also call and salute him by the name of king: bicause it shoulde not

388

seeme that for one overthrowe received, their hartes were deade. Thus this ambition by jelousie and emulation, went from man to man to all Alexanders successours. For Lysimachus then also beganne to weare the diadeame, and likewise Seleucus, as often as he spake with the Græcians: for before that tyme, he delt in matters with the barbarous people as a king. But Cassander, though others wrote them selves kinges, he onely subscribed after his wonted manner. Now this was not onely an increase of a newe name, or chaunging of appaiell, but it was such an honor, as it lyft up their hartes, and made them stand upon them selves: and besides it so framed their manner of life and conversation with men, that they grewe more prowd and stately, then ever they were before: like unto common players of tragedies, who apparelling them selves to playe their partes upon the stage, doe chaunge their gate, their countenaunce, their voyce, their manner of sitting at the table, and their talke also. So that afterwards they grew more ciuell in commaunding their subjects, when they had once taken away the viser and dissimulation of their absolute power, which before made them farre more lowly and gentle in many matters unto them. And all this came through one vile flatterer, that brought such a wonderfull chaunge in the worlde. Antigonus therefore puffed up with the glory of the victorie of his sonne Demetrius, for the conquest of Cyprus: he determined forthwith to set upon Ptolomy. Him selfe led the armie by land, having his sonne Demetrius still rowing by the shore side with a great fleete of shippes. But one of his familliers called Medius, being asleepe had a vision one night that told him, what should be the ende and successe of this jorney. He thought he sawe Antigonus ronne with all his armie who should have the upper hande, and that at the first he ranne with great force and swiftnes. but that afterwardes his strength and breath fayled him so much, that when he should retuine, he had scant any poulse or breath, and with much adoe retyred agayne. And even so it chaunced unto him. For Antigonus by land, was eftsoones in gieat daunger: and Demetrius also by sea was often in hazard to leave the coast, and by storme and

Note the force of flattery by Aristodemus Milesian.

Antigonus and Demetrius jorney against Ptolomy.

Medius dreame.

DEMETRIUS weather to be cast into places, where was nether haven, creekes, nor harbarough for his shippes. And at length, having lost a great number of his shippes, he was driven to returne without any attempt given. Nowe Antigonus was at that tyme litle lesse then foure score yeare olde, but yet his fatte and corpulent bodie was more cumbersom to him then his yeares: therefore beeing growen unmeete for warres, he used his sonne in his place. Who for that he was fortunate, as also skilfull through the experience he had gotten, did wisely governe the waightiest matters. His father besides did not passe for his youthfull partes, lavishe expences, and common dronkennes he gave him selfe unto. For in tyme of peace, he was given over to all those vices: but in tyme of warre, he was as sober and continent, as any man so borne by nature. And therefore it is reported, that Lamia beeing manifestly knowen to be Mystresse over him, one daye when he was come from hunting, he came (as his manner was) to kisse his father: and that Antigonus

Antigonus mirth with his sonne Demetrius.

smyling upon him sayde, What, howe now Sonne, doest thou thinke thou art kissing of Lamia? Another tyme Demetrius was many dayes together drinking and ryoting, and sawe not his father: and then to excuse him selfe unto him, he tolde him he had gotten a rewme that made him keepe his chamber, that he could not come to him. So I heard sayde Antigonus: but was it of Thasos or Chios, that rewme? he spake it, bicause that in either of those two Ilands, there were excellent good wines. Another tyme Demetrius sent his father worde that he was not well. Thereuppon Antigonus went to see him, and comming thither, he mette a fayer younge boye at his doore. So he went uppe to his chamber, and sitting downe by his bedds side, he tooke him by the hande to feele his poulse. Demetrius tolde him that his fever had left him but a litle before. I knowe it well, sayde Antigonus: for I mette the younge boye even at the doore as I came in. So Antigonus did gently beare with his sonnes

A strauoge custom of the Scythians in their dron-kennes.

faultes, in respecte of his many other vertues he had. The voyce goeth that the Scythians, when they are disposed to drinke dronke together, doe divers tymes twange the strynges of their bowes, as though that woulde serve to keepe the

390

strength of their courage and hardines, which otherwise the
pleasauntnes of the wine woulde take from them. But
Demetrius gave him selfe to one thinge at one selfe tyme.
Sometyme to take his pleasure, sometyme to deale in matters
of waight, and in all extreamitie he ever used but one of
them, and woulde never myngle the one with the other:
and yet this notwithstanding he was no lesse politike and
circumspect to prepare all manner of munition for warres.
For as he was a wise Captaine to leade an armie, so was he
also very carefull to provide all thinges meete for their furniture, and woulde rather have too muche, then too litle. But
above all, he exceeded in sumptuous building of shippes, and
framing of all sortes of engines of batterie, and specially
for the delight he tooke to invent and devise them. For
he had an excellent naturall witte to devise suche workes,
as are made by witte and hande, and did not bestowe his
witte and invention in handie craftes, in trifeling toyes and
bables: as many other kinges that have given them selves
to playe on flutes, others to paynte and drawe, and others
also to Turners crafte. As Æropus kinge of Macedon, who
delighted to make fine tables, and pretye lampes. And
Attalus, surnamed Philometor (to saye, as lover of his
mother) that woulde plante and sette Phisicall herbes, as
Helleborum, Lingewort, or Beares foote: Hyoscynamum,
Henbane, Cicuta, Hemlocke, Aconitum, Libardbaine or
Woolfebaine, and Dorycinum: for the which we have no
Englishe worde: all these would he set him selfe with his
owne handes in the gardeins of his pallaice, and also gather
them in tyme of the yeare, to knowe the vertue and power of
them. As Arsaces, the kinges of Parthia, that boasted they
coulde them selves make their arrowe heades, and sharpen
them. But the artificers workes which Demetrius practised,
shewed that they came from a king. For his manner of
workemanshippe had a certen greatnes in it, the which even
with the sutteltie and finenes of his workes, shewed the
trymme handeling of the workeman: so that they appeared
not onely worthye the understanding and riches of a king,
but also the forging and making by the handes of a great
king. For his friendes did not onely wonder at their greatnes,

DEMETRIUS

Demetrius a skilfull Captaine, and an excellent Shipwright.

Sondry delights of Princes.

Demetrius wonderfull workes.

391

but his very enemies also were delighted with the beautie of them. And this is more true, then meete to be spoken: the enemies could but marvell when they sawe his gallies rowing alongest the coaste, with fifteene or sixteene bankes of ores: and his engines of batterie which they called Elepolis (to saye, engines to take cities) were a spectacle of great admiration unto those whome he beseeged, as the events following did throughly witnesse. For Lysimachus who of all other kings did malice Demetrius most, comming to raise the seege from the citie of Soli in Cilicia, the which Demetrius beseeged: he sent unto him to pray him to let him see his engines of batterie, and his gallies rowing uppon the sea. Demetrius graunting him, Lysimachus returned with

wonderfull admiration. The Rhodians also having long time defended his seege, at the last made peace with him, and prayed him to leave some one of his engines with them, for a perpetuall testimonie and remembrance both of his power, and also of their corage and valliantnes. The cause why Demetrius made warre with the Rhodians, was, bicause they were confederats with king Ptolomy: he brought against

their walles the greatest engine he had, the foote whereof was like a tyle, more long then broade, and at the base on either side it was eyght and fortie cubits longe, and three score and sixe highe, rising still narrow even to the very top: so that the upper partes were narrower then the nether, and within it were many pretty roomes and places conveied for souldiers. The forepart of it was open towards the enemie, and every roome or partition had windowes, out of the which they bestowed all kind of shot, bicause they were full of armed men, fighting with all sortes of weapons. But nowe, bicause it was so well framed and counterpealed, that it gave no way, nor reeld of ether side, which way soever they removed it, but that it stoode fast and upright upon her foundacion, making a terrible noyse

and sownde: that made the worke as wonderfull to behold, as it was a marvelous pleasure for men to see it. In this warre were brought unto Demetrius two notable armors weying fortie pownd a peece, and made by one Zoilus an armorer: who to shewe the hardnes and goodnes of the temper, suffered them to be proved and shot at at six score paces, with the engines of their batterie: and albeit the armors were shot at, and hit, yet were they never pearsed, and but onely a litle race or skretch seene, as it were of a bodkin or penknife, and had no more hurte. Demetrius alwayes ware one of them in these warres, and Alcimus Albanian the other, the strongest and valliantest man he had in all his hoast, and that onely caried a complete armour weying sixe score pownde, where all other souldiers ware none above three score. This Alcimus was slayne at Rhodes valliantly fighting by the Theater. In this seege the Rhodians did valliantly defende them selves, that Demetrius could doe no acte worthy memorie. This notwithstanding, although he sawe he could not prevaile, but lose his tyme, yet was he the more obstinately bent against them, to be even with them: bicause they had taken a shippe of his, in the which his wife Phila had sent unto him certaine hangings of tapestrie, linnen, apparell, and letters, and bicause they had sent them all unto Ptolomy, assoone as they had taken them. But therein they did not follow the honest curtesie of the Athenians: who having intercepted certaine currers of king Philips that made warre against them, they opened all the letters they caried, and red them, saving onely his wife Olympiaes letters she sent him, the which they sent unto king Philip sealed, as they were when they received them. Nowe though this part did much greve and offend him, yet he could not finde in his hart to serve them in that sorte, when he might have done it not longe after. For by chaunce at that tyme, Protogenes an excellent paynter, borne in the city of Caunus, did paynt them the draught of the citie of Ialysus. Demetrius found this table in a house in the suburbes of the citie, being almost ended. The Rhodians thereuppon sending a Herauld unto him, to beseeche him to spare the defacing of so goodly a work: he returned them aunswer, that he would rather suffer his fathers images to be burnt, then so excellent and passing a worke as that to be loste, and brought to nothing. For it is reported, that Protogenes was seven yeares drawing of the same: and it is also sayde, that Apelles him selfe when he sawe it did

DEMETRIUS
Protogenes
table of the
citie of Ialy-
sus, greatly
commended
by Apelles
him selfe.

Demetrius
concludeth
peace with
the Rhodians.

Demetrius
victories in
Græce.

so wonder at it, that his speeche fayled him, and he stoode
muet a longe tyme, and at last sayde: Surely there is a
wonderfull peece of worke, and of great labor, yet they want
those graces and ornaments whereby those that I paynt doe
reache unto heaven.   This table afterwardes being brought
to Rome, and hanged up with others, was in the ende burnt
by fire.   Nowe as the Rhodians were desirous to be rid of
this warre, and that Demetrius also was willing to take any
honest occasion to doe it: the Ambassadors of the Athenians
came happely to serve both their desires, who made peace
betweene them with these condicions: that the Rhodians
shoulde be confederats with Antigonus and Demetrius,
against all men, but Ptolomy onely.   The Athenians sent
for Demetrius, upon Cassanders comming to laye seege to
their citie.   Whereuppon Demetrius immediatly hoysed
sayle towards Athens, with three hundred and thirty gallies,
and a great number of men of warre besides: so that he did
not only drive Cassander out of the province of Attica, but
followed him even to the straight of Thermopyles, and there
overthrew him in set battell, and received the citie of Hera-
clea, which willingly yelded unto him, and six thowsand
Macedonians that came unto him to take his part.   So in his
returne backe, he set all the Græcians at libertie on this side
the straight: he made league with the Bœotians, and tooke
the citie of Cenchrees, and the castells of Phyle and Pan-
actos, in the fronters and confines of Attica, in the which
Cassander had left garrisons to keepe the contry in subjection: and after he had driven them out of the contry,
he rendred the forts againe unto the Athenians.   Therefore
though it seemed the Athenians had before bestowed to
their uttermost power all kinds of honors that could be
offered him, every man striving for life to preferre the same:
yet they found out new devises to flatter and please him.
For they ordeyned that the place behind the temple of
Minerva, called Parthenon (as who would say, the temple of
the virgin) should be prepared for his house to lye in: and
they sayd, that the goddesse Minerva did lodge him with
her.   But to say truely, he was too unchast a ghest, to thinke
that a mayden goddesse would be content he shoulde lye with

her. And yet his father Antigonus perceiving that they
had lodged his sonne Philip on a time in a house, where
there were three younge women, he sayde nothing to Philip
him selfe, but before him he sent for the harbinger, and
sayde unto him : Wilt thou not remove my sonne out of
this straight lodging, and provide him of a better? And
Demetrius, that should have reverenced the goddesse Minerva, though, for no other respect, but bicause he called her
his eldest sister, (for so he woulde she shoulde be called) he
defiled all the castell where was the temple of these holy
virgines, with horrible and abominable insolencies, both
towards younge boyes of honest houses, as also unto younge
women of the citie. So that this place seemed to be most
pure and holy, at such time as he laye with his common
Curtisans, Chrysis, Lamia, Demo, and Anticyra. It shall
not be greatly for the honor of the citie of Athens, to tell
perticularly all the abhominable partes he committed there.
But Democles vertue and honestie deserveth worthye and
condigne remembrance. This Democles was a younge boye
that had no heare on his face, of whose beautie Demetrius
being informed by the surname he had, as commonly called
through the citie, Democles the fayer : he sought divers
waies to intise him, both by fayer meanes, large promisses
and giftes, and also with threates besides. But when he
saw no man could bringe him to the bent of his bowe, and
that the younge boye in the ende seeing him so importunate
upon him, came no more to the common places of exercise
where other children used to recreate them selves, and that
to avoide the common stooves, he went to wash him selfe
in another secret stoove : Demetrius watching his time and
hower of going thither, followed him, and got in to him
being alone. The boy seing him selfe alone and that he
could not resist Demetrius, tooke of the cover of the ketle
or chawdron where the water was boyling, and leaping into
it, drowned him selfe. Truely he was unworthy of so lamentable an ende, but yet he shewed a noble hart, worthy of his
beautie and contry. But he did not as another called Clæe-
netus, the sonne of Cleomedon, who brought letters from
Demetrius directed to the people, whereby, through Deme-

DEMETRIUS trius intercession and request, his fathers fine of fifty talents in the which he was condemned (and for nonpayment remained prisoner) was clerely remitted and forgiven. But by this acte, he not onely shamed and dishonored him self, but also troubled all the citie. For the people thereuppon released Cleomedon of his fine, but therewith they made a decree that no Citizen should thenceforth bring any moe letters from Demetrius. But afterwards, understanding that Demetrius was marvelously offended with this decree : they did not onely revoke their first decree, but they did also put some of them to death, which were the procurers and authors of the decree, and others also they banished. And further they made a lawe, that the people of Athens should account all religious to the gods, and just unto men, whatsoever it pleased Demetrius to order and appoynt. At that time there was one of the chiefest men of the citie, that saide Stratocles was a mad man to preferre such matters. In deede, quoth Demochares surnamed Laconian, he were a mad man if he were otherwise : and he spake it, bicause this Stratocles had many great pleasures at Demetrius hands for this flatterie. Howbeit Demochares being accused and condemned upon these wordes, he was banished Athens. See after what sorte the Athenians used them selves, who seemed to be delivered from the garrison they had before, and to be restored unto their former libertie and freedom. From

Demetrius jorney into Peloponnesus. thence Demetrius went into Peloponnesus, and never an enemie of his durst tary his comming, but all fled before him, and left him their castels and townes. Thus Demetrius wan unto him selfe all the contry called Acte, and all Archadia, saving the citie of Mantinea : and for the summe

Demetrius maried Deidamia, king Pyrrhus sister : and chaunged the name of the citie of Sicyone, and called it Demetriade. of an hundred talents given amongest them, he delivered the cities of Argos, Sicyone, and of Corinthe, from the garrisons that laye amongest them. About that tyme fell out the great feast of Iuno in Argos, called Heræa. Therefore Demetrius, to honor this feaste with the Græcians, married Deidamia (the Daughter of Æacides, king of the Molossians, and sister of Pyrrhus) and perswaded the Sicyonians to leave their citie, and to come and builde in an other goodly place neare unto it, where they now doe dwell : and so with the

396

place and situacion, he chaunged also the name of the citie. DEMETRIUS
For in steade of Sicyone, he made it to be called Demetriade. Then at a generall assembly of the states of Græce,
which was kept in the straight of Peloponnesus, called
Isthmos: Demetrius was chosen Lieuetenant generall of all Demetrius
the Græcians, as Philip and Alexander, (both kings of chosen gene-
Macedon) had bene before him, unto whom he did not only Græce.
compare him selfe, but thought him selfe greater then they,
bicause fortune smiled on him, and for that he had so good
successe in all his affayres. Whereas Alexander did never
take away the title and name of king, from any other kings:
nether did ever call him selfe king of kings, although he had
given unto divers of them the name and power of a king.
And in contrary manner also, Demetrius laughed them to
scorne which called any other Princes, kings, but his father
and him selfe. Moreover he tooke great pleasure to heare Demetrius
his flatterers, who being at banketts called for wine to pride.
drinke to king Demetrius, and then to Seleucus maister of
the Elephants, to Ptolomy Admiral, to Lysimachus keeper
of the treasure, and to Agathocles Sicilian, governor of the
Iles. All the kings, but Lysimachus, laughed at these toyes
when they were reported to them: but Lysimachus was very
angry, and thought great skorne that Demetrius should
reckon him a gelding, for that it was an old custom commonly to give an Euenuke the charge of keeping the treasure. So Lysimachus of all other Princes did beare him
most malice, and bicause he would finely tawnt him for that
he ever kept Lamia his Curtisan with him: Until this present time, said he, I never saw harlot play in a tragedy
before. Demetrius aunswered him againe, that his harlot
was chaster, then Penelope his wife. So Demetrius departing for that time out of Peloponnesus, tooke his jorney
towards Athens, and wrote before to the Athenians, that
when he came thither he would be received into the fraternitie of the holy mysteries, and that he ment they should
shew him at one selfe time, all that was to be seene, even
from the least to the highest seciets of their ceremonies,
called Epoptices, bicause they made the brethren of the
fraternitie see them long time after that they had bene first

DEMETRIUS received into the lesser ceremonies: the which was not lawfull then, neither was ever heard of before. For these smaller misteries in olde time were celebrated in the month of November, and the greater in the month of August: and beside it was not lawfull to celebrate or use these ceremonies within the space of a yeare one of thother. When these letters were openly red, no man durst speake against them, but Pythodorus the Priest, who caried the torche lighted when they shewed these misteries. Howbeit his words prevailed not, for by the devise of Stratocles it was enacted at an assembly of the citie, that the month of March in the which they were at that time, should be called and reputed November. And so, as they could best helpe it by their ordinaunces of the citie, they did receive Demetrius into the fraternitie of the misteries: and afterwards againe, this selfe month of March which they had translated into November, became sodainly August: and in the self same yeare was celebrated the other ceremonie of these great misteries, whereby Demetrius was admitted to see the most straightest and secretest ceremonies. Therefore Philippides the Poet inveying against the sacriledge, and impietie of religion prophaned by Stratocles, made these verses of him:

Philippides verses against Stratocles the boaster.

> Into one mooneth his comming hither
> Hath thrust up all the yeare togither.

And afterwards bicause Stratocles was the procurer that Demetrius was lodged in the temple of Minerva within the castell:

> Of chaste Minervaze holy Church he makes a filthie stewes,
> And in that Virgins very sight his harlots doth abuse.

But yet of all the insolent parts done at that time in Athens, (although many were committed) none of all the rest greved the Athenians more, then this did: that Demetrius commaunded them they should presently furnish him with two hundred and fifty talents. The taxation of this payment was very harde unto them, both for the shortnes of the time appoynted them, as also for the impossibilitie of abating any part of it. When he had seene all this masse

of money laid on a heape before him, he commaunded it
should be given to Lamia, and among his other Curtisans,
to buy them sope. The shame the Athenians received by
this gift, greved them more, than the losse of their money:
and the words he spake to the great contempt of them
and their citie, did more trouble them, then the payment
they made. Some say notwithstanding, that Demetrius did
not alone use the Athenians thus shamefully, but the Thessalians also in the same manner. But passing this over:
Lamia of her selfe, and through her owne countenance, did
get a great summe of money together of divers persons for
one supper she made unto Demetrius, the preparation
whereof was of such exceeding charge, that Lycæus borne in
the Ile of Samos, did set downe the order thereof in writing.
And therefore a certain Poet no lesse pleasantly, then truely,
called this Lamia, Elepolis: to wete, an engine to take
cities. And Demochares also borne in the citie of Soli,
called Demetrius a fable, bicause he had Lamia ever with
him: as in the fables which olde women tell litle children,
there is ever lightly a Lamia, as much to say, as a witche,
or sorceresse. So that the great credit and authoritie this
Lamia had, and the love which Demetrius bare her: did
not onely cause his wives suspect and envy him, but made
him hated also of all his friends and familliers. And therfore certen gentlemen whom Demetrius sent in ambassade
unto king Lysimachus, he talking famillierly with them, and
passing the time away, shewed them great wounds of the
clawes of a lyon upon his armes and legges, telling them
also how he was forced to fight with the lyon, when through
king Alexanders fury he was shut up in his denne with him:
they smiling to heare him, told him that the king their
maister had also certeine markes and bytings on his necke,
of a vile beast called Lamia. And to say truely, it was a
wonderfull thing, that marrying (as he did) his wife Phila so
much against his will, bicause she was too olde for him:
how he was so ravished with Lamia, and did so constantly
love her so long together, considering that she was also very
old, and past the best. Therefore Demo, surnamed Mania,
(as much to say, the mad woman) pleasantly aunswered

DEMETRIUS

Demetrius
prodigall gift
of 250 talents
to his Curti-
sans to buy
them sope.

Lamia made
Demetrius a
supper of her
owne cost.

Lamia
Elepolis.

399

Demetrius, asking her one night when Lamia had plaied on the flute all supper time, what she thought of Lamia? An old woman, O king, quoth she. Another time when frute was served in, after the bord was taken up: Doe you see said Demetrius, how many pretty fine knackes Lamia sendeth me? My mother, aunswered Demo againe, will send you moe then these, if you please to lye with her. It is reported of this Lamia, that she overthrew Bocchoris judgement in

a matter. In Ægypt there was a young man that had a marvelous fancie unto a famous Curtisan, called Thonis: who did aske him suche a great summe of money to lye with her, that it was unpossible for him to give it her. At length, this amorous youth beeing so deepe in love with her, dreamed one night he laye with her, and enjoyed her: so that for the pleasure he tooke by his conceyt and imagination, when he awaked, his earnest love was satisfied. This Curtisan whome he had cast fancie to, hearing of his dreame, did put him in sute before the Iudges, to be payed her hyer for the pleasure the younge man had taken of her by imagination. Bocchoris hearing the summe of her complaynt, commaunded the younge man to bringe before him in some vessell, at a daye appoynted, as muche money as she did aske him to lye with her. Then he badde him tosse it too and froe in his hande before the Curtisan, that she shoulde but onely have the shadowe and sight of it: For, quoth he, imagination and opinion, is but a shadowe of truth. Lamia

sayde this was no equall judgement: For, sayth she, the shadowe onely, or the sight of the money, did not satisfie the covetousnes of the Curtisan, as the younge mans lust was quenched by his dreame. Thus enough spoken of Lamia. But now, the misfortunes and jeasts of him we presently write of: they do transport our historie, as from a comycall into a tragicall theater, that is to saye, from pleasaunt and light matter, into lamentable and bytter teares. For all the Princes and Kinges conspyred generally

agaynst Antigonus, and joyned all their force and armies together. Therefore Demetrius departed forthwith out of Græce, and came to joyne with his father, whose courage he founde more lively and better given to this warre, then his yeares required: besides that Demetrius comming made him the bolder, and did lifte uppe his harte the more. And yet it seemes to me, that if Antigonus woulde but have yeelded uppe a fewe trifling thinges, and that he coulde or woulde have brydeled his over immoderate covetous desire to raigne: he had bothe kept for him selfe all the tyme of his life, and also lefte after his deathe unto his sonne, the supreamest dignitie and power, above all the other Kinges and successors of Alexander. But he was so cruell, and rashe of nature, and as insolent and brave in his doinges, as in his wordes: that thereby he stirred uppe, and brought uppon him as his enemies, many great and mighty Princes. For even at that present time he said, that he would as easely disperse and scatter a sunder that conspiracie against him, as chowghes or other litle birdes comming to pecke up the corne newly sowen, are easely scared awaye with a stone, or making any litle noyse. So he caried to the field with him, above three score and tenne thowsand footemen, tenne thowsand horsemen, and three score and fifteene Elephantes. His enemies had three score and foure thowsande footemen, and five hundred horsemen more then he, with foure hundred Elephants, and six score cartes of warre. When the two armies were one neere unto the other, me thinkes he had some imaginacion in his head that chaunged his hope, but not his corage. For in all other battells and conflictes, having commonly used to looke bigge of the matter, to have a lowde high voyce, and to use brave wordes, and some-time also even in the chiefest of all the battell to geve some pleasant mocke or other, shewing a certaine trust he had in him selfe, and a contempt of his enemie: then they sawe him oftentimes alone, and verie pensive, without ever a word to any man. One day he called all his armie together, and presented his sonne unto the souldiers, recommending him unto them, as his heire and successor, and talked with him alone in his tent. Whereat men marvelled the more, bicause that he never used before to imparte to any man the secrets of his counsell and determination, no not to his owne sonne, but did all things of him selfe: and then commaunded that thing openly to be done, which he had secretly purposed.

For proofe hereof it is said, Demetrius being but a young man, asked him on a time when the campe should remove: and that Antigonus in anger aunswered him, Art thou affrayed thou shalt not heare the sownd of the trompet? Furthermore, there fell out many ill signes and tokens that killed their harts. For Demetrius dreamed that Alexander the great appeared armed unto him at all peeces, and that he asked him what word or signall of battell they were determined to geve at the day of the battell. He aunswered, that they were determined to geve, Iupiter, and Victorie. Then said Alexander, I will goe to thine enemies that shall receive me. And afterwardes, at the very day of the overthrow, when all their armie were set in battell ray: Antigonus comming out of his tent, had such a great fall, that he fell flat on his face on the ground, and hurte him selfe verie sorely. So when he was taken up, then lifting up his handes to heaven, he made his prayers unto the goddes, that it would please them to graunt him victorie, or sodaine death without great paine, before he shoulde see him selfe vanquished, and his armie overthrowen. When both battells came to joyne, and that they fought hand to hand: Demetrius that had the most parte of the horsemen with him, went and gave charge upon Antiochus the sonne of Seleucus, and fought it out so valliantly on his side, that he overthrewe his enemies, and put them to flight. But too fondly following the chase of them that fledde, and out of time: he marred all, and was the occasion of the losse of his victorie. For when he returned from the chase, he could not joyne againe with their footemen, bicause the Elephants were betwene both. Then Seleucus perceiving Antigonus battell was naked of horsemen, he did not presently set upon them, but turned at one side as though he woulde environ them behinde, and made them affrayed: yet making head as he would charge them, only to geve them leasure to come on their side, as they did. For the most parte of Antigonus hoast did forsake him, and yeelded unto his enemies: and the rest of them fled every man. And when a great trowpe of men together went with great furie to geve charge on that side where Antigonus was: one of them that were

Demetrius dreame and signes.

Demetrius upon the first onset, made Antiochus the sonne of Seleucus, flie.

Overrashly chasing the enemies, he lost his victorie, and was overcome.

about him, sayd unto him : Your grace had neede take heede,
for these men come to charge us.   He aunswered againe:
But how should they know me ?   And if they did, my sonne
Demetrius will come and helpe me   This was his last hope,
and still he looked everie way if he could see his sonne
comming towards him : untill at length he was slaine with The death of
arrowes, darts, and pikes   For of all his freindes and king Anti-
souldiers there taried not one man by his bodie, but Thorax gonus.
of the citie of Larissa in Thessalie.   Now the battell having
suche successe as you have heard, the Kings and Princes
that had won so glorious a victorie, as if they had cut
a great bodie in sundrie peeces : they devided Antigonus
kingdome among them, and everie man had his part of all
the provinces and contries which Antigonus kept, adding
that unto their other dominions which they possessed affore.
Nowe Demetrius flying with all possible speede that might Demetrius
be, with five thowsand footemen and foure thowsand horse- flight.
men, he got to the citie of Ephesus· where everie man
mistrusted, that being needie of money as he was, he would
not spare the temple of Diana in Ephesus, but would rifle
all the gold and silver in it.   And in contrarie maner also,
Demetrius being affrayed of his souldiers, least they would
spoyle it against his will . he sodainly departed thence, and
sayled towardes Græce, putting his greatest confidence and
affiance in the Athenians, bicause he had left his wife Deidamia at Athens, with shippes and some money, supposing
he could goe no whether with better safety in his adversitie, then to Athens, of whose good wills he thought him
selfe assured.   Wherefore when Ambassadors of the Athenians came unto him, and found him not farre from the Iles
Cyclades, as he sailed with great speede towardes Attica, and
that they had declared unto him, he should forbeare to come
unto their citie, bicause the people had made an ordinance
to suffer no moe kings to come into Athens, and that they
had sent Deidamia his wife honorablie accompanied unto the
citie of Megara . then was Demetrius for verie anger and The unfaith-
passion of minde, cleane out of countenaunce, although untill fulnes of the
that time he had paciently borne his adversitie, and his hart towards
had never failed him.   But this nipped him to the harte, Demetrius.

when he sawe that (contrarie to expectacion) the Athenians had deceived and failed him in his greatest neede, and that in his adversitie he found their former frendshippe counterfeate, and altogether dissembled. Whereby most plainly appeareth, that the most uncerteine and deceiveable profe of peoples good wills and cities towardes Kings and Princes, are the immesurable and extreame honors they doe unto them. For sith it is so, that the trueth and certainty of honor proceedeth from the good will of those that give it: the feare which the common people commonly stand in of the power of kings, is sufficient cause for them to mistrust that the people doe it not with good will and from their harts, considering that for feare they doe the selfe same things, which they will also doe for love. Therefore grave and wise Princes should not passe so much for the images and statues they set up for them, or the tables or divine honors they doe decree unto them: as to regard their owne workes and deedes, and weying them truely, so to beleve and receive their honors for true, or otherwise to reject and mistrust them, as things done by compulsion. For commonly it is that which maketh the people to hate kings the more, when they doe accept these immesurable and extreame honors done unto them, but those sortes chiefly hate them most, that against their wills are forced to doe them those honors. Demetrius seeing then how injuriously the Athenians had used him, and at that time not knowing how to be revenged of them: he modestly sent unto them only to make his complaints, and to demaund his shippes, among the which was that galley of sixteene banckes of owers. The which when he had received, he hoysed saile immediatly towards the straight of Peloponnesus, and there found all things to goe against him. For in every place where he had left any garrison, the Captaines that had the charge of them, either yeelded them up, or else revolted, and kept them against him. Therfore leaving Pyrrhus his Lieutenaunt in Græce, he tooke sea againe, and sailed towards Cherronesus, and there with the mischieves he did, and with the spoiles he got in king Lysimachus land, he payed his men, and enriched his army, the which began againe to increase, and to be

Overgreat honors are signes of unconstant frendship.

dreadfull to his enemies. But now for Lysimachus, the other kings made no great accompt of him, neither did they sturre to geve him aide, bicause he was nothing inferior unto Demetrius: and for that he was of greater power and possessions then them selves, they therefore were the more affrayed of him. Shortly after, Seleucus sent unto Demetrius, to require his daughter Stratonice in mariage, notwithstanding that he had a sonne alreadie called Antiochus, by his wife Apama a Persian. Howbeit he thought that his affaires and greatnes of his estate and kingdom, was able enough to maintaine many successors after him. And furthermore, he considered with him selfe that he should have neede of Demetrius allyance, bicause he saw Lysimachus him selfe matche with one of Ptolomyes daughters, and his sonne Agathocles with his other daughter. Demetrius seeing this good fortune offered him beyond all hope, presently tooke his daughter with him, and sailed with all his shippes directly towards Syria. In the which voyage he was constrained of necessitie to lande sometimes, and specially in Cilicia, the which Plistarchus the brother of Cassander kept at that time, being geven him by the other kings for his parte and porcion of the spoyle of Antigonus, after he was overthrowen. This Plistarchus thinking that Demetrius landed not to refresh him selfe, but to forrage and spoyle: bicause he woulde complaine of Seleucus for the allyance he made with their common enemie, without the consent and privitie of all the other Kings and Princes confederats, he went purposely unto his brother Cassander. Demetrius having intelligence thereof, sodainly invaded the land, and spoyled as farre as the citie of Cyndes, and caried away (which he had leavied) twelve hundred talentes, which he found yet left of his fathers treasure: and then with all the speede he could possible he returned to his shippes, and hoysed sayle. Shortly after, his wife Phila also came unto him. So Seleucus received them all neere unto the citie of Orossus, and there their meeting was Princely, without sorow or suspicion one of the other. First of all Seleucus did feast Demetrius in his tent, in the middest of his campe. and afterwards Demetrius feasted him againe in his galley, with thirteene bankes of owers. Thus

405

they passed many dayes together, feasting and rejoycing eche with other, being unarmed, and having no souldiers to waite upon them. untill at length Seleucus with his wife Stratonice departed, and tooke his way with great pompe towardes the citie of Antioche.   Nowe for Demetrius, he kept the province of Cilicia, and sent his wife Phila unto her brother Cassander, to aunswere the complaints and accusacions of Plistarchus against him   In the meane time

Deidamia his wife departed out of Græce to come unto him · who after she had remained with him a few dayes, dyed of a sickenesse   Afterwardes Demetrius comming againe in favor with Ptolomy, by Seleucus his sonne in lawes meanes.

he maried his daughter Ptolemæide.   Hitherunto Seleucus used Demetrius verie curteously: but afterwards he prayed him to deliver him Cilicia againe, for a summe of money that he offered him: but Demetrius plainly denyed him. Then did Seleucus shew a cruell and tyrannicall covetousnesse for in anger, and with fierce threats and countenaunce

he asked him the cities of Tyr, and Sidon.   But therein me thinkes he lacked honestie and civility: as though he that had under his obedience and subjection all that which lay betwext the Indians, and the sea of Syria, was in suche neede and povertie: that for two cities onely, he shoulde drive his father in law from him, who had susteined so hard and bitter chaunge.   But thereby he rightly confirmed

Platoes saying. that he that will be riche in deede, must endevor him selfe not to increase his riches, but rather to diminish his covetousnes.   For he shall never be but a begger, and needie, whose covetous desire hath no ende. This notwithstanding, Demetrius yeelded not for feare, but provided to replenish the cities with good garrisons to keepe them against him. saying, that though he had bene overcome ten thowsande times more in battell, yet it should never sincke into his head that he shoulde be contented, and thinke him selfe happie to buy Seleucus allyance so deere On thother side, being advertised that one Lachares having spied oportunitie when the Athenians were in civill warres one against the other, and that he had overcomen them, and did tyrannically usurpe the government: he then perswaded

him selfe that he might easely winne it againe, if he came
thither upon the sodaine. Thereuppon he crossed the seas
with a great fleete of shippes, without any daunger: but he
had such a great storme and tempest upon the coast of
Attica, that he lost the most parte of his shippes, and a
great number of his men besides. But for him selfe he scaped,
and began to make a litle warre with the Athenians. Yet
perceiving that he did no good there, but lost his time: he
sent some of his men to gather a number of shippes againe
together, and he him selfe in the meane time went into
Peloponnesus, to laye siege to the citie of Messena, where
his person was in greate daunger. For fighting hard by the
wall, he had such a blowe with a dart, that it hit him full
in the mouth, and ranne through his cheeke. Notwithstanding this, after he was healed of that wound, he brought
into his subjection againe, certaine townes that had rebelled
against him. After that, he returned againe into Attica,
and tooke the cities of Eleusin, and of Rhamnus: and then
spoyled all the contrie, and tooke a shippe straight with
corne, and hong up the marchaunt that ought it, and the
maister of the shippe that brought it. Thereby to terrifie
all other marchauntes, that they shoulde be affrayed to bring
any more corne thither, and so to famish the citie, by keeping them from all thinges necessarie for their sustenaunce:
and so it happened. For a bushell of salt was sold at
Athens for fortie silver Drachmas, and the bushell of wheate
for three hundred Drachmas. In this extreame necessitie,
the Athenians had but a short joy for the hundred and
fiftie gallies they sawe neere unto Ægina, the which Ptolomy
sent to aide them. For when the souldiers that were in them
sawe that they brought unto Demetrius a great number of
shippes out of Peloponnesus, out of Cyprus, and divers other
partes, which amounted in the whole to the number of three
hundred saile: they weyed their anckers, and fled presently.
Then Lachares forsooke the city, and secretly saved him
selfe. Nowe the Athenians, who before had commaunded
uppon paine of death, that no man should make any motion
to the counsell, to treate of any peace with Demetrius: they
did then upon Lachares flying, presently open the gates next

unto Demetrius campe, and sent Ambassadours unto him, not looking for any grace or peace, but bicause necessitie drave them to it. During this so hard and straight siege, there fell out many wonderfull and straunge things: but among others, this one is of speciall note. It is reported that the father and the sonne sitting in their house, voide of all hope of life: there fell a dead ratte before them from the toppe of the house, and that the father and sonne fought who should have it to eate. Moreover, that at the selfe same

A rare devise of Epicurus, at the straight siege of Athens, to kepe his schollers alive with beanes.

siege the Philosopher Epicurus maintained him selfe and his schollers, by geving them a proporcion of beanes everie day, by the which they lived. Thus the citie of Athens being brought unto this extremitie, Demetrius made his entrie into it, and gave commaundement to all the citizens, that they shoulde assemble everie man within the Theater: where he made them to be compassed in with armed souldiers, and then placed all his gard armed about the stage. Afterwards he came downe him selfe into the Theater, through high galleries and entries by the which the common players used to come to play their partes in tragedies, insomuche as the Athenians were then worse affrayed then before: howbeit Demetrius presently pacified their feare, as soone as he be-ganne to speake unto them. For he did not facion his

Demetrius clemency unto the Athenians.

Oration with a hastie angrie voyce, neither did he use any sharpe or bitter wordes: but onely after he had curteously told them their faults and discurtesie towards him, he sayd he forgave them, and that he would be their frende againe: and furthermore, he caused tenne millions of bushells of wheate to be geven unto them, and stablished such Gover-nors there, as the people misliked not of. Then Democles the Orator, seeing that the people gave out great showtes of joy in the praise of Demetrius, and that the Orators dayly contended in the pulpit for Orations, who should exceede other in preferring newe honors for Demetrius: he caused an order to be made, that the havens of Piræus and Munychia should be put into Demetrius handes, to use at his pleasure. This being stablished by voyces of the people, Demetrius of his owne private authoritie did place a greate garrison within the forte called Musæum, bicause the people should

408

rebell no more against him, nor divert him from his other
enterprises. Thus when he had taken Athens, he went to
set upon the Lacedæmonians. But Archidamus king of
Lacedæmon, came against him with a puisant armie, whom
he discomfited in battell, and put to flight, by the citie of
Mantinea. After that he invaded Laconia with all his
armie, and made an inrode to the citie of Sparta, where
he once againe overthrew the Lacedæmonians in set battell,
tooke five hundred of them prisoners, and slue two hundred:
insomuch that every man thought he might even then goe
to Sparta without any daunger to take it, the which had
never yet bene taken affore by any. But there was never
king that had so often and sodaine chaunges of fortune
as Demetrius, nor that in other affaires was ever so often
litle, and then great: so sodainly downe, and up againe:
so weake, and straight so strong. And therefore it is reported, that in his great adversities when fortune turned
so contrarie against him, he was wont to crie out uppon
fortune, that which Æschylus speaketh in a place·

> Thou seemst to have begotten me, of purpose for to showe
> Thy force in lifting of me up, me downe againe to throw.

Nowe againe when his affaires prospered so well, and that
he was likely to recover a great force and kingdome· newes
were brought him, first that Lysimachus had taken all his
townes from him, which he helde in Asia: and on the other
side, that Ptolomy had won from him all the realme of
Cyprus, the citie of Salamina onely excepted, in the which
he kept his mother and children very straightly besieged.
This notwithstanding, fortune played with him, as the
wicked woman Archilochus speaketh of, who,

> Did in the one hand water show,
> And in the other fire bestow.

For taking him away, and (as it were) the citie of Sparta
also out of his handes by these dreadfull newes, even when
he was certaine to have won it: she presently offered him
hopes of other great and new thinges, by this occasion following After the death of Cassander, Philip who was the

5 : FFF

DEMETRIUS eldest of all his other sonnes, and left his heire and successor in the kingdome of Macedon: he reigned no long time over the Macedonians, but deceased soone after his father was dead. The two other brethren also fell at great variance, and warres together: so that the one called Antipater, slue his owne mother Thessalonica: and the other being Alexander, called in to aide him Demetrius, and Pyrrhus, the one out of the realme of Epirus, and the other out of Peloponnesus. Pyrrhus came first before Demetrius, and kept a great parte of Macedon for recompence of his paines, comming to aide him at his desire: so that he became a dreadful neighbour unto Alexander him selfe, that had sent for him into his contrie. Furthermore, when he was advertised that Demetrius did presently upon the receite of his letters, set forward with all his armie to come to aide him: the young Prince Alexander, was twise as muche more amazed and affrayed, for the great estate and estimacion of Demetrius. So he went to him notwithstanding, and received him at a place called Deion, and there imbraced and welcomed him. But immediatly after, he told him that his affaires were nowe in so good state, that praised be the goddes he should not now neede his presence to aide him. After these words the one began to mistrust the other. So it chaunced one day, that as Demetrius went to Alexanders lodging where the feast was prepared: there came one to him to tell him of an ambush that was layed for him, and how they had determined to kill him when he should thinke to be merie at the banket. But Demetrius was nothing abashed at the newes, and only went a litle softlier, not making such hast as he did before, and in the meane time sent to commaunde his Captaines to arme their men, and to have them in readines: and willed his gentlemen and all the rest of his officers that were about him, (which were a greater number by many than those of Alexanders side) every man of them to go in with him into the hall, and to tarie there till he rose from the table. By this meanes the men whome Alexander had appointed to assault him, they durst not, being affrayed of the great traine he had brought with him. Furthermore, Demetrius faining that he was not well at ease at that time

410

Side notes: Great dissention and strife for the realme of Macedon, after the death of Cassander. Antipater and Alexander, the sonnes of Cassander.

Demetrius invadeth Macedon.

Wyles betwext Alexander and Demetrius.

to make merie, he went immediatly out of the hall, and the
next morning determined to depart, making him beleve
that he had certaine newes brought him of great importaunce: and prayed Alexander to pardon him, that he could
no lenger keepe him companie, for that he was driven of
necessitie to depart from him, and that an other time they
woulde meete together, with better leasure and libertie.
Alexander was veric glad to see that Demetrius went his
way out of Macedon not offended, but of his owne good
will: whereuppon he brought him into Thessaly, and when
they were come to the citie of Larissa, they began againe to
feast one an other, to intrappe eche other: the which offered
Demetrius occasion to have Alexander in his hand, as he
would wish him selfe.   For Alexander of purpose would not
have his gard about him, fearing least thereby he should
teach Demetrius also to stand upon his gard.   Thus Alexander turned his practise for an other, upon him selfe: for
he was determined not to suffer Demetrius to scape his
handes, if he once againe came within daunger.   So Alexander being bidden to supper to Demetrius, he came accordingly.   Demetrius rising from the borde in the middest of
supper, Alexander rose also, being affiayed of that straunge
manner, and followed him foote by foote to the verie dore.
Then Demetrius sayd but to his warders at the gate, Kill
him that followeth me.   With those wordes he went out of
the dores, and Alexander that followed him was slaine in the
place, and certaine of his gentlemen with him which came
to rescue him: of the which, one of them as they killed him
sayd, that Demetrius had prevented them but one day.   All
that night, (as it is no other likely) was full of uprore and
tumult   Howbeit, the next morning the Macedonians being
marvelously troubled and affrayed of Demetrius great power,
when they saw that no man came to assaile them, but that
Demetrius in contraiie maner sent unto them to tell them
that he would speake with them, and deliver them reason
for that he had done: then they all began to be bolde againe,
and willingly gave him audience.   Nowe Demetrius needed
not to use many woides, nor to make any long Orations, to
win them unto him for, bicause they hated Antipater as a

*Demetrius
killeth Alex-
ander the
sonne of
Cassander.*

LIVES OF THE NOBLE

DEMETRIUS

Demetrius proclaimed king of Macedon.

horrible manqueller and murderer of his mother, and bicause they had no better man to preferre, they easely chose Demetrius king of Macedon, and thereuppon brought him backe into Macedon, to take possession of the kingdom. This chaunge was not misliked of the other Macedonians that remained at home in their contrie, for that they yet remembred the traiterous and wicked fact of Cassander, against Alexander the great: for which cause they utterly hated and detested all his issue and posteritie. And furthermore, if there were any sparke of remembrance in their harts, of the bounty and goodnes of their grandfather Antipater: Demetrius received the frute and benefit, for his wife Philaes sake, by whom he had a sonne that should succeede him in the kingdom, and was a proper youth, in campe with his father. Demetrius having this great good happe and fortune comen unto him, he received newes also that Ptolomy had not onely raised his siege from the citie of Salamina, where he kept his mother and children straightly besieged: but further, that he had done them great honor, and bestowed great giftes upon them. On the other side also he was advertised, that his daughter Stratonice, who had before

Antiochus, the sonne of Seleucus maried his mother in law, Stratonice, with his fathers good will.

bene maried unto Seleucus, was now maried againe unto Antiochus, the sonne of the sayd Seleucus, and how that she was crowned Queene of all the barbarous nations inhabiting in the high provinces of Asia: and that came to passe in this maner. It chaunced that this young Prince Antiochus (as love overcommeth all men) became in love with his mother in law Stratonice, who alreadie had a sonne by Seleucus his father. She being young, and passing fayer, he was so ravished with her, that though he proved all the wayes possible to maister his furie and passion that way: yet he was still the weaker. So that in the end, condemning him selfe to death bicause he found his desire abhominable, his passion incurable, and his reason utterly overcome: he resolved to kill him selfe by litle and litle, with abstinence from meate and drinke, and made no other reckoning to

Erasistratus Phisitian to Seleucus.

remedie his griefe, faining to have some secret inward disease in his body. Yet could he not so finely cloke it, but that Erasistratus the Phisitian easely found his griefe, that love,

412

not sicknes, was his infirmitie: howbeit it was hard for him
to imagine with whom he was in love. Erasistratus being
earnestly bent to finde out the partie he loved, he sate by
this young Prince all day long in his chamber, and when
any fayer young boy or wife came to see him, he earnestly
looked Antiochus in the face, and carefully observed all the
partes of the bodie, and outward movings, which do commonly bewray the secret passions and affections of the mind.
So having marked him divers times, that when others came
to see him, whatsoever they were, he still remeined in one the Phisitians
selfe state, and that when Stratonice his mother in lawe came care, to finde
alone or in companie of her husband Seleucus to visite him, Prince Antio-
he commonly perceived those signes in him, which Sappho chus love.
wryteth to be in lovers (to wit, that his words and speech Sappho
did faile him, his colour became red, his eyes still rowled to describeth
and fro, and then a sodaine swet would take him, his pulse the signes
would beate fast and rise high, and in the end, that after the and tokens
force and power of his hart had failed him, and shewed all lover.
these signes, he became like a man in an extasie and traunse,
and white as a kearcher) he then gathering a true conjecture by these so manifest signes and declaracions, that it
was only Stratonice whom this young Prince fansied, and the
which he forced him selfe to keepe secret to the death:
thought that to bewray it to the king it would offend him
muche, but yet trusting to his great affection and fatherly
love he bare to his sonne, he ventred one day to tell him,
that his sonnes sicknesse was no other but love, and withall,
that his love was impossible to be enjoyed, and therefore
that he must of necessitie dye, for it was incurable. Seleucus
was cold at the harte to heare these newes: so he asked him,
What, is he incurable? Yea, Sir, aunswered the Phisitian,
bicause he is in love with my wife. Then replied Seleucus
againe, Alas Erasistratus, I have alwayes loved thee as one of
my dearest frendes, and wouldest thou not now doe me this
pleasure, to lette my sonne marry thy wife, sith thou knowest
it well that I have no moe sonnes but he, and that I see he
is but cast away, if thou helpe me not? But your grace would
not doe it your selfe, sayd Erasistratus: if he were in love
with Stratonice. O, sayd Seleucus to him againe, that it were

DEMETRIUS the will of the gods, some god or man could turne his love that way: for mine owne parte, I would not only leave him the thing he loved, but I would geve my kingdom also to save his life. Then Erasistratus seeing that the king spake these words from his hart, and with abundance of teares: he tooke him by the right hand, and told him plainly, Your grace needeth not Erasistratus helpe in this. For being father, husbande, and king, your selfe also may onely Seleucus love unto his sonne Antiochus. be the Phisitian, to cure your sonnes disease. When Seleucus heard that, he called an assemblie of the people, and declared before them all that he was determined to crown his sonne Antiochus king of the high provinces of Asia, and Stratonice Queene, to marry them together: and that he was perswaded that his sonne, (who had alwayes shewed him selfe obedient to his fathers will) would not disobey him in this mariage. And as for Stratonice, if she misliked this mariage, and would not consent unto it bicause it was no common matter: then he prayed that his frendes would perswade her she should thinke all good and comely that should please the king, and withall that concerned the general benefit of the realme and common wealth. Hereuppon Antiochus and Stratonice were married together. But now to returne againe to the history of Demetrius. Demetrius came by the kingdom of Macedon and Thessalie, by this meanes as you have heard, and did moreover possesse the best parte of Peloponnesus, and on this side the straight, the cities of Megara, and Athens. Furthermore he led his armie against the Bœotians, who were at the first willing to make peace with him. But after that Cleonymus king of Sparta was come into the city of Thebes with his army, the Bœotians encouraged by the faire wordes and allurement of one Pisis, borne in the citie of Thespis, who at that time bare all the sway and chiefe authoritie amongst them: they gave up their treaty of peace they had begon with Demetrius and determined to make warre. Therupon Demetrius went to besiege the citie of Thebes, The citie of Thebes yeelded unto Demetrius. and layed his engines of battery unto it: insomuch as Cleonymus for feare, stale secretly out of the citie. Thereuppon the Thebans being also affrayed, yeelded them selves unto Demetrius mercie: who putting great garrisons into

DEMETRIUS

Hieronymus
the historio-
grapher,
Demetrius
Lieutenaunt

the cities, and having leavied a great summe of money of
the province, left them Hieronymus the historiographer, his
Lieutenant and Governor there. So it appeared that he
used them very curteously, and did them many pleasures,
and specially unto Pisis. For when he had taken him
prisoner, he did him no hurt, but received him very curteously, and used him well: and furthermore, he made him
Polemarchus, (to wit, campe maister) in the city of Thespis.
Shortly after these things were thus brought to passe, king
Lysimachus by chaunce was taken by an other barbarous
Prince called Dromichetes. Thereupon, Demetrius, to take
such a noble occasion offred him, went with a great army to
invade the contry of Thracia, supposing he should find no
man to withstande him, but that he might conquer it at his
pleasure. Howbeit, so soone as Demetrius backe was turned,
the Bœotians revolted againe from him, and therwithall
newes was brought him, that Lysimachus was delivered out
of prison. Then he returned backe with all speede, marvelously offended with the Bœotians, whom he found already
discomfited in battell, by his sonne Antigonus, and went
againe to lay siege to the citie of Thebes, being the chiefe
city of al that province of Bœotia. But at that present
time, Pyrrhus came and forraged all Thessaly, and entred
even to the straight of Thermopyles. Therefore Demetrius
was constrained to leave his sonne to continewe the siege
at Thebes, whilest he him selfe went against Pyrrhus, who
sodainly returned againe into his realme. So Demetrius
left ten thowsand footemen, and a thowsand horsemen in
Thessaly to defend the contry, and returned with the rest of
his army to win Thebes. Thereupon he brought his great
engine of batterie called Elepolis, against the wall, as you
have heard before, the which was thrust forward by litle and
litle, with great labor, by reason of the weight and heavines
of it: so that it could scant be driven forward two furlongs
in two months. But the Bœotians and the Thebans did
valliantly defend them selves: and Demetrius of a malicious
minde and desire of revenge, (more oftner then needefull, or
to any purpose) compelled his men to go to the assault, and
to hazard them selves: so that there were daily a great

415

number of them slaine. Antigonus his sonne perceiving it: Alas, said he, why doe we thus suffer our men to be slaine and cast away to no purpose? Wherefore Demetrius angrily aunswered him againe: What needest thou to care? Is there any *corne to be distributed to those that are dead? But notwithstanding, bicause men should not thinke he still ment to put others in daunger, and durst not venter him selfe: he fought with them, till at length he was shot through the necke with a sharpe arrow head, that was shot at him from the wall. Wherewithall he fell very sicke, but yet raised not his siege, nor removed his campe, but tooke the citie of Thebes againe by assault: the which being not long before againe replenished with people, was in ten yeares space twise won and taken. Now he put the Thebans in a marvelous feare, by his cruell threats he gave them at his comming into Thebes: so that they looked to have received the extreamest punishment the vanquished could have, through the just wrath and anger of the conqueror. Howbeit after Demetrius had put thirtene of them to death, and banished some: he pardoned all the rest. About that time fell out the celebration of the feast called Pythia, in the honour of Apollo: and bicause the Ætolians kept all the high wayes to bring them unto the city of Delphes in the which of olde time they did use to celebrate those sports aforesaid: he caused them to be kept and solemnised at Athens as in a place where this god in reason should be best honored and reverenced, bicause he was patrone of the citie, and for that the Athenians maintained that he was their progenitor. From thence he returned into Macedon, and knowing that it was against his nature to live idelly, and in peace, and seing on the other side also that the Macedonians did him more service, and were more obedient to him in warres, and that in time of peace they grew seditious, full of vanity and quarrell: he went to make warre with the Ætolians, and after he had spoiled and destroyed their contry, he left Pantauchus his Lieutenant there, with a great part of his army. Demetrius him selfe went in the meane time with the rest of his army against Pyrrhus: and Pyrrhus also against him, but they missed of meeting ech

*Corne monethly distributed to the souldiers, as their wages.

Demetrius jorney against Pyrrhus.

416

with other. Whereupon Demetrius passed further unto DEMETRIUS the realme of Epirus, the which he spoiled and forraged. Pyrrhus on the other side went on so farre that he met with Pantauchus, Demetrius Lieutenant, with whom he fought a battell, and came to the sword with him: so that he did both hurt him, and was also hurt by him. But in the end Pyrrhus had the upper hand, he put Pantauchus to flight, and slue a great number of his men, and tooke five thowsand prisoners: the which was the chief overthrow of Demetrius. For Pyrrhus wan not the Macedonians ill will so much for the mischieves and hurts he had done unto them, as he got him selfe great fame and renowne with them, bicause him selfe alone had with his owne hands done all the noble exployts of warre in that jorney: for the which, he was afterwardes had in great estimacion among the Macedonians. Nowe many of them began to say, that he was the only king of all others, in whom the lively image of the hardines and valliantnes of Alexander the great was to be seene: and that all the rest, (but specially Demetrius) did but counterfeate his gravetie and Princely countenaunce, like players upon a stage that would counterfeate his countenaunce and gesture And to say truly, there was much finenes and curiosity Demetrius about Demetrius, to make him a playing stocke in common insolencie. playes. For some say, that he did not only weare a great hat with his diadeame upon his head, and was apparelled in purple gownes imbrodered with gold: but also that he did use to weare certaine wollen shooes on his feete died in purple colour, not woven, but facioned together like a felt, and gilt upon it. And furthermore, he had long before Demetrius caused a cloke to be made of a marvelous rich and sumptuous cloke drawen peece of worke. For upon it was drawen the figure of the with the figure
of the world, world, with starres and circles of heaven, the which was not and starres. throughly finished by the chaunge of his fortune. So, there was never king of Macedon after him that durst weare it· albeit there were many prowde and arrogant kings that succeded him. Now the Macedonians were not onely sory, and offended to see suche things, as they were not wont to be acquainted withall: but they much more misliked this curious maner of life, and specially bicause he was ill to come to, and worse to be spoken with. For he gave no audience, or if he did, he was very rough, and would sharply take them up that had to do with him. As, he kept the Ambassadors of the Athenians two yeres, and would geve them no answere: and yet made as though he loved them better, then any other people of Græce. Another time also he was offended, bicause the Lacedæmonians had sent but one man only Ambassador unto him, taking it that they had done it in despite of him.

And so did the Ambassador of the Lacedæmonians answere him very gallantly, after the Laconian maner. For when Demetrius asked him, How chaunceth it that the Lacedæmonians do send but one man unto me? No more but one, said he, O king, unto one. On a time he came abroad more plainly and popularlike, then he was wont to do: whereby he put the people in good hope that they might the easelier speake with him, and that he would more curteously heare their complaints. Thereupon many came, and put up their humble supplicacions and bills of peticion unto him. He received them, and put them up in the lappe of his cloke. The poore suters were glad of that, and waited upon him at his heeles, hoping they should quickely be dispatched: but when he was upon the bridge of the

river of Axius, he opened his cloke, and cast them all into the river. This went to the harts of the Macedonians, who then thought they were no more governed by a king, but oppressed by a tyran: and it grieved them so much more, bicause they did yet remember (either for that they had seene them selves, or otherwise heard their forefathers say)

howe curteous king Philip was in all such matters, and howe that one day as he passed through the streete, a poore old woman pluckt him by the gowne, and eftsoones humbly besought him to heare her, but he aunswered her he was

not then at leasure. Whereuppon the poore woman plainly cried out to him, Leave then to be king. This word so nettled him, and he tooke such a conceit of it, that he returned presently to his pallace, and setting all other

matters a part, did nothing else many dayes but gave him selfe to heare all sutes, and began with this poore olde woman. For truly nothing becommeth a Prince better, then

418

to minister justice: for Mars (as Timotheus saith) signifieth
force, and is a tyran: but justice and law, according to
Pindarus, is Queene of all the world. Moreover, the wise
Poet Homer saith not that Princes and Kings have received
the custody of engines, and of munition, neither also strong
and mighty ships of Iupiter, to kepe them to destroy townes
withall: but with them to maintaine law and justice. And
therefore he calleth not the cruell and bloody king, but the
just and merciful Prince, Iupiters frend and scholler. And
Demetrius boasted that he had a name and title contrarie
unto Iupiter, whom they called Polieus, or Poliouchos, signifying protector and preserver of cities: and that he was
called Poliorcetes, a Fortgainer. Thus the ill was taken for Demetrius
the good, and vice preferred for vertue: bicause he could called a Fort-
not discerne the truth from falsehod, which turned his injus- gainer.
tice to glory, and iniquity to honor. But now to returne
where we left: Demetrius fell into a great and daungerous
sickenes in the citie of Pella, during which time he almost
lost all Macedon, by a sodaine invasion Pyrrhus made, who
in maner rode it all over, and came as farre as the city of
Edessa. Howbeit so sone as he recovered health again, he
easely drave him out, and afterwards made peace with him,
bicause he would not fighting with him (whom he should
have daily at his dores stil skirmishing somtime here, somtime there) lose the oportunity, and weaken him selfe to
bring that to passe which he had determined. For he had
no small matters in his head, but thought to recover all the
realmes his father had: and besides, the preparacion he
made was no lesse sufficient, then the purpose of such an
imagination required. For he had leavied and assembled an Demetrius
army of a hundred thowsand footemen, lacking but two armie and
thowsand: and unto them he had also well neere twelve preparacion
thowsand horsemen, and had besides gotten above five hun- for the re-
dred shippes together, which were built part in the haven covering of
of Piræus, part at Corinth, part in the city of Chalcis, and his realme
part about Pella. He him selfe in person went through againe.
their workehouses, and shewed the artificers how they should
make them, and did help to devise them: so that every
man wondred not onely at his infinite preparacion, but at

DEMETRIUS the greatnes and sumptuousnes of his works. For at that
time there was no man living that ever saw a gally of
fifteene or sixteene banks of owers. But this is true, that
afterwardes Ptolomy, surnamed Philopator, built a gally of
forty bankes of owers, the which was two hundred foure
score cubits long, and from the keele in height to the top
of the poope, eight and forty cubits: and to looke to the
tackle and guide her, required foure hundred mariners, and
foure thowsand water men to row her, and besides all that
she could yet cary above the hatches, wel nere three thowsand fighting men. Howbeit this gally never served to
other purpose but for show, and was like to a house that
never sturred: and it was never removed out of the place
where it was built but with marvelous a do, and great
daunger, more to make men wonder at it, then for any
service or commodity it could be imployed unto. But now,
the beawty of Demetrius shippes did nothing hinder their
swiftnes and goodnes for fight, neither did the hugenes of
their building take away the use of them, but their swift-
nesse and nimblenes deserved more commendacion, then
their sumptuousnes and statelines. Thus as this great power
and preparacion was in hand, being such as never king before
(since the time of Alexander the great) had assembled a
greater to invade Asia: these three kings, Ptolomy, Seleucus, and Lysimachus, did all joyne together against him.
And afterwardes also, they sent Ambassadors unto Pyrrhus
in the name of them all, to draw him to their side, alluring
him to come into Macedon, perswading him not to repose
any trust in the peace Demetrius had made with him, to
make accompt of it as a good and sure peace: for, they said
that Demetrius did not give him pledge that he would never
make warre with him, but rather first tooke oportunity him
self to make warre with whom he thought good. Pyrrhus
considering so much, and finding their words true: there
rose a sharpe and cruell warre on every side against Demetrius, who tracted time, and stayed yet to begin. For at
one selfe time, Ptolomy with a great fleete of shippes came
downe into Græce, and made all Græce revolt from him:
and Lysimachus also on Thraciaes side, and Pyrrhus upon

Three kings
Seleucus,
Ptolomy, and
Lysimachus
conspired
against
Demetrius.

the borders of Epirus, confining with the realme of Macedon, DEMETRIUS
they entred with a great army, and spoiled and sacked all as
they went. Thereupon Demetrius leaving his sonne Antigonus in Græce, he returned with all possible speede into
Macedon, to goe first against Lysimachus. But as he was
preparing to go against him, newes were brought him that
Pyrrhus had already taken the citie of Berrhœa. This newes
being blowen abroad amongest the Macedonians, all Demetrius doings were turned topsie turvey. For all his campe
was straight full of teares and complaints, and his men
began openly to shew their anger against him, speaking all
the ill they could of him : so that they would tary no lenger,
but every one prayed leave to depart, pretending to looke
to their busines at home, but in truth to go and yeeld them
selves unto Lysimachus. Wherefore Demetrius thought it
best for him to get him as farre from Lysimachus as he could,
and to bend all his army against Pyrrhus : bicause the other
was their contry man, and familiarly knowen among the most
of them, for that they had served together under Alexander
the great, and that as he thought, the Macedonians would
not preferre Pyrrhus a straunger, before him. But there
his judgement failed him. For as soone as Pyrrhus had
pitched his campe hard by him, the Macedonians that had
ever loved valliantnes, and had of ancient time esteemed
him worthier to be king, that was the best souldier and
valliantest in the field, and furthermore had heard the report
of his great clemency and curtesy he had shewed to the
prisoners he had taken : they having had good will of long
time sought but good occasion to forsake Demetrius, and to Demetrius
yeeld them selves unto Pyrrhus, or to any other prince armie for-
whatsoever he were. Then they secretly began to steale saketh him,
away one after an other, by smal companies at the first : but and goeth to
afterwards there rose such a general tumult against him Pyrrhus.
throughout all the campe, that some of them were so desperat
to go into his tent to bid him flie, and save himselfe, bicause
the Macedonians were too weary with fighting for his curiosity. And yet Demetrius found these words more gentle,
and modest, in respect of the vile and cruel words which
others gave him. So he went into his tent, and cast a black

DEMETRIUS cloke about his face, in stead of his rich and stately cloke he was wont to weare: not like unto a king, but like a common player when the play is done, and then secretly stale away. When this was knowen in the campe, many of his souldiers ran to his tent to rifle it, and every man tooke such hold of it to have his part, that they tare it in peces, and drew their swords to fight for it. But Pyrrhus comming in the middest of the tumult, pacified this sturre, and presently without blow given, wan al Demetrius campe: and afterwards he devided the realme of Macedon with Lysimachus, in the which Demetrius had quietly raigned the space of seven yeres. Now Demetrius being thus miserably overthrowen, and turned out of all his realme: he fled unto the city of Cassandria. There he found his wife Phila, who tooke it marvelous heavily, and could not abide to see him againe a private man, driven out of his kingdom, and the most miserable king that ever was of all other. Wherefore intending no more to follow vaine hope, and detesting the fortune of her husband: she being more constant in calamity then in prosperity, killed her selfe with poison she tooke.

Phila, Demetrius wife poysoneth her selfe.

Demetrius went from thence into Græce, purposing to gather together the rest of his shipwracks: and there assembled all his Captaines and frends that he had. So it seemeth to me, the comparison Menelaus maketh of his fortune, in one of the tragedies of Sophocles, in these verses:

My state doth turne continually about on fortunes wheele,
Whose double dealing divers times inforst I am to feele:
Resembling right the moone whose face abideth at no stay
Two nights together, but doth chaunge in shape from day to day:
At first she riseth small with hornes. And as in age she growes,
With fuller cheekes and brighter light a greater face she showes.
And when she commeth to the full, and shineth faire and bright,
Among the goodly glistring starres the goodlyest in the night:
She fades and falles away againe, and runnes a counterpace,
Untill she have forgone the light and figure of her face.

Demetrius straunge fortune.

The comparison might I say much better be applied unto Demetrius fortune, to his rising and falling, and to his overthrowe and reliefe againe. For when every man thought his force and power utterly overthrowen, then began he to

rise againe by repaire of souldiers, which by litle and litle
came unto him, and straight revived him with good hope.
This was the first time that he was ever seene meanely
apparelled, like a private man up and downe the contry,
without some shewe or tokens of a king. And there was
one that seeing him in this estate at Thebes, pleasauntly
applied these verses of Euripides unto him :

Of god immortall, now becomne a mortall wight :
Ismēnus bankes and Dirces streames he haunteth in our sight.

Now when he beganne to have some hope againe, and was
(as it were) entred into the great high way of kinges, and
had gotten souldiers about him, which made a bodie and
shew of royall power : he restored the Thebans their libertie
and government againe. But the Athenians once more
revolted from him, and did revoke the dignitie and Priesthoode of Diphilus, who had bene that yeare created Priest
of the saviours, in steade of the Governour, which they
called in old time Eponymos, as we have told you before :
and made a lawe, that from thencefoorth the auncient and
common Governors of their citie should be restored againe
to their auncient manner : and they sent also into Macedon
unto king Pyrrhus, rather to terrifie Demetrius (whome they
sawe beginne to rise againe) then for any hope they had he
woulde come and helpe them. Howebeit Demetrius came
against them with great furie, and did straightly besiege the
citie of Athens. Then the Athenians sent Crates the Philo- Crates the
Philosopher
delivereth
Athens from
Demetrius
siege.
sopher to him, a man of great estimacion and authoritie,
who so handled him, partely by intreatie, and partely also
through his wise perswasions and counsells he gave him for
his profit : that Demetrius presently raised the siege. Wherfore, after he had gathered together so many shippes as were
left him, and had imbarked twelve thowsande footemen, and
a small number of horsemen : he presently tooke sea, and
sailed towards Asia, meaning to take the provinces of Caria
and Lydia from Lysimachus, and to make them to rebell
against him. There Eurydice, sister to his wife Phila,
received him by the citie of Miletum, having with her one
of Ptolomyes daughters and hers, called Ptolemæide, the

DEMETRIUS

Demetrius
marieth
Ptolemæide.

which had bene affore affianced to him by Seleucus meanes. So he maried Ptolemæide there, with the good will and consent of her mother Eurydice. After his mariage he presently went into the field againe, and did set forwardes to winne some cities, whereof many willingly received him, and others he tooke by force. Amongst them he tooke the city of Sardis, whether came divers Captaines unto him of king Lysimachus, who yeelded them selves, and brought him a greate number of men, and muche money besides. But Demetrius receiving advertisement that Agathocles, Lysimachus sonne, followed him with a great armie: he went thence into Phrygia, making account, and also hoping, that if he coulde winne Armenia, he might easely make Media rebell, and then that he woulde see if he coulde conquer the high provinces of Asia, where he might have many places of refuge, if fortune turned against him. Agathocles followed him verie neere, and yet skirmishing divers times with him,

Demetrius
troubles in
Asia.

Demetrius alway had the better: howebeit Agathocles did cut of his vittells from him everie waye and kept him at suche a straight, that his men durst no more stray from the campe to forrage: wherefore, they susteyned greate want of vittells, and then beganne his men to be affrayed, and to mistrust that he would make them followe him into Armenia and Media. The famine dayly increased more and more in his armie, and it chaunced besides, that missing his waye, and failing to gage the forde well as he passed over the river of Lycus, the furie and force of the river caried his men downe the streame, and drowned a greate number of them: and yet notwithstandinge these greate troubles, they mocked him besides. For one wrote at the entrie and comming in to his tent, the first verse of the tragedie of *Œdipus Colonian*, wrytten by Sophocles, chaunging onely some word:

Thou impe of old and blind Antigonus,
To what a point hast thou now caried us?

Plague, by
ill meate.

But in the end, the plague began also in the middest of this famine, (a common thing, and almost a matter of necessitie, it should so be) bicause that men being driven to neede and necessitie, doe frame them selves to eate all that

comes to hande: whereupon he was driven to bring backe
those few men that remained, having lost of all sortes (good
and bad) not so fewe as eight thowsand fully told. When
he came into the province of Tarsus, he commaunded his
men in no case to meddle with any thing, bicause the contrie
was subject unto king Seleucus, whom he would in no wise
displease. But when he sawe it was impossible to stay his Demetrius
men being now brought to such extremitie and neede, and famine.
that Agathocles had bard up the straights and passages of
mount Taurus against him: he wrote a letter unto Seleucus,
first declaring his miserable state and hard fortune, and then
presenting his humble petition and request unto him, praying him to take pitie upon his frend, whom spitefull fortune
had throwen into such miserie and calamitie, that coulde not
but move his greatest enemies to have compassion of him.
These letters somewhat softened Seleucus hart, insomuche
that he wrote to his Governors and Lieutenauntes of those
partes, to furnish Demetrius person with all thinges needefull for a Princes house, and vittells sufficient to maintaine
his men. But one Patrocles, a grave wise man accounted, Patrocles
and Seleucus faithfull frend also, came to tell him, that the stirreth up
charge to entertaine Demetrius souldiers, was not the greatest Seleucus
fault he made therin, and most to be accompted of· but against
that he did not wisely looke into his affaires, to suffer Deme- Demetrius.
trius to remaine in his contry, considering that he had alway
bene a more fierce and venturous Prince then any other, to
enterprise any matters of great importaunce, and nowe he was
brought to such dispaire and extremitie, that he had framed
his men which were but ranke cowardes (contrarie to their
nature) to be most desperat and hardie in greatest daungers.
Seleucus being moved with these perswasions, presently tooke
his jorney into Cilicia with a great armie. Demetrius being
astonied with this sodaine chaunge, and dreading so great
an armie, got him to the strongest places of mount Taurus.
Then he sent unto Seleucus, first of all to pray him to suffer
him to conquer certaine barbarous people thereaboutes, who
lived according to their owne lawes, and never had king: to
thend that he might yet there with safetie end the rest of
his life and exile, staying at length in some place where he

DEMETRIUS might be safe. Secondly if that liked him not, then that it woulde yet please him to vittell his men for the winter time onely, in the same place where they were, and not to be so hard harted unto him as to drive him thence, lacking all needefull thinges, and so to put him into the mouth of his most cruell and mortall enemies. But Seleucus mistrusting his demaundes, sent unto him that he shoulde winter if he thought good, two monethes, but no more, in the contrie of Cataonia, so he gave him the chiefest of his frendes for ostages: howbeit in the meane time he stopped up all the wayes and passages going from thence into Syria. Demetrius nowe seeing him selfe kept in of all sides, like a beast to be taken in the toyle: he was driven to trust to his owne strength. Thereuppon he overranne the contry thereaboutes, and as often as it was his chaunce to have any skirmish or conflict with Seleucus, he had ever the better of him: and sometime also when they drave the armed cartes with sithes against him, he overcame them, and put the rest to flight. Then he drave them away that kept the toppe of the mountaines, and had barred the passages to kepe him that he should not goe into Syria, and so kept them him selfe. In fine, finding his mens hartes lift up againe, and pretily encoraged: his hart also grewe so bigge, that he determined to fight a battell with Seleucus, and to set all at sixe and seven. So that Seleucus was at a straight with him selfe, and wist not what to doe. For he had returned backe the ayde which Lysimachus sent unto him, bicause he was affrayed of him, and mistrusted him. On thother side also he durst not fight with Demetrius alone, being affrayed to venter him selfe with a desperate man: and also mistrusting muche his unconstant fortune, the which having brought him to great extremitie, raised him up againe to great prosperitie. But in the meane space Demetrius fell into a great sickenesse, the which brought his bodie very weake and low, and had almost utterly overthrowen his affaires. For his souldiers, some of them yeelded them selves to his enemies, and others stale away without leave, and went where they listed. Afterwardes when he had hardly recovered his health, and within forty dayes space was pretily growen to strength againe: with those few

Desperate men are not to be fought with.

426

souldiers that remained with him, he seemed to his enemies,
that he would goe and invade Cilicia. But then sodainly
in the night without sownding any trumpet, he removed
his campe, and went another way: and having passed over
mount Amanus, he spoyled all the contry under it, as farre
as the region of Cyrrestica. But Seleucus followed him,
and camped hard by him. Thereuppon Demetrius sodainly
armed his men, and went out by night to assault Seleucus,
and to take him sleping when he mistrusted nothing. So that
Seleucus knew nothing of his stealing on him but late enough,
until that certaine traitors of Demetrius campe that fled
before, went quickly to advertise him finding him asleepe,
and brought him newes of the daunger he was in. Then
Seleucus in a mase and feare withall, got up, and sownded
the alarom: and as he was putting on his hose and making
him ready he cryed out, (speaking to his friends and familliers
about him) We have now a cruell and daungerous beast to
deale with. Demetrius on the other side perceiving by the
great sturre and noyse he heard in the enemies campe, that
his enterprise was discovered: he retyred againe with speede,
and the next morning by breake of day, Seleucus went and
offred him battell. Demetrius prepared him selfe to joyne
with him, and having given one of his faithfull friendes the
leading of one of the wings of his armie, him selfe led the
other, and overthrew some of his enemies on his side. But
Seleucus in the middest of the battell lighted from his horse,
and taking his helmet from his head, he tooke a target on
his arme, and went to the first ranckes of his armie, to
make him selfe knowen unto Demetrius men: perswading
them to yeeld them selves unto him, and to acknowledge
in the end, that he had so long time deferred to give them
battell, rather to save them, then to spare Demetrius. Demetrius souldiers hearing him say so, they did him humble
reverence, and acknowledging him for their king, they all
yeelded unto him. Demetrius having sundry times before
proved so many chaunges and overthrowes of fortune, thinking yet to scape this last also, and to passe it over: he fled
unto the gates Amanides, which are certaine straights of
the mount Amanus. There he founde certaine litle thicke

DEMETRIUS groves, where he determined to stay all night with certaine gentlemen of his house, and a fewe other of his houshold servaunts and officers which had followed him: meaning, if he could possible, to take his way towards the citie of Caunus, to goe to that sea coast, hoping to heare of his shippes there. But when it was tolde him he had no vittells nor provision left onely to serve him that day: he began then to devise some other way. At length, one of his famillier friends Sosigenes came unto him, that had foure hundred peeces of golde about him in his girdell. So hoping that with the same money he might flie to the sea, they tooke their way by night directly, to the toppe of the mountaine. But when they perceived that the enemies kept watch there, and that there were great store of fires hard by them: they then dispaired to passe any further, least they should be seene. So they returned to the selfe same place from whence they came, not all of them, for some of them fled: neither had they that remayned also any life in them as before. So, one among the rest tooke upon him, to say, that there was no other way to scape, but to put Demetrius into Seleucus hands. Demetrius therewithall drew out his sword, and would have slaine him selfe: but his friends about him would not suffer him, but perswaded him to yeld him selfe

Demetrius yeldeth him selfe unto Seleucus.

unto Seleucus. Thereuppon he sent unto Seleucus, to tell him that he yelded him selfe unto him. Seleucus was so joyfull of the newes, that he sayd it was not Demetrius good fortune that saved him, but his owne: who besides many other happy good turnes she had done him, gave him yet so honorable occasion and good happe, as to make the world to knowe his clemencie and curtesie. Thereuppon immediatly he called for his officers of houshold, and commaunded them to set up his richest pavilion, and to prepare all thinges meete to receive him honorably. There was one Appolonides a gentleman in Seleucus Court, who sometime had bene very famillier with Demetrius: him Seleucus sent immediatly unto Demetrius, to will him to be of good chere, and not to be affrayd to come to the king his Maister, for he should find him his very good friend. So soone as the kings pleasure was knowen, a few of his Courtiers went at

428

the first to meete him: but afterwards, every man strived DEMETRIUS
who should goe meete him first, bicause they were all in
hope that he should presently be much made of, and growe
in credit with Seleucus. But hereby they turned Seleucus
pitie into envie, and gave occasion also to Demetrius enemies
and spitefull men, to turne the kings bowntifull good nature
from him. For they put into his head many doubts and
daungers, saying, that certainly so soone as the souldiers
sawe him, there would grow great sturre and chaunge in
their campe. And therefore, shortly after that Apollonides
was come unto Demetrius, being glad to bringe him these
good newes, and as others also followed him one after another,
bringing him some good words from Seleucus, and that Demetrius him self after so great an overthrow (although that
before he thought it a shamefull part of him to have yeelded
his body into his enemies hands) chaunged his mind at that
time, and began then to grow bold, and to have good hope to
recover his state againe   behold, there came one of Seleucus
Captaines called Pausanias, accompanied with a thowsand
footemen and horsemen in all, who compassed in Demetrius
with them, and made the rest depart that were come unto
him before, having charge given him not to bring him to
the Court, but to convey him into Cherronesus of Syria, Demetrius
whether he was brought, and ever after had a strong garrison kept as
about him to keepe him. But otherwise, Seleucus sent him prisoner in
Syria by
Officers, money, and all things els meete for a Princes house: Seleucus
and his ordinary fare was so delicate, that he could wishe for
no more than he had. And furthermore, he had places of
libertie and pleasure appointed him, both to ride his horse
in, and also pleasaunt walkes, and goodly arbors to walke or
sit in, and fine parkes full of beasts where he might hunt:
moreover, the king suffered his owne houshold servaunts
that followed him when he fled, to remaine with him if
they would. And furthermore, there daily came some one
or other unto him from Seleucus, to comfort him, and to
put him in hope, that so soone as Antiochus and Stratonice
were come, they would make some good agreement and peace
betwene them. Demetrius remaining in this estate, wrote
unto his sonne Antigonus, and to his friends and Lieue-

tenants which he had at Corinthe, and Athens, that they should give no credit to any letters written in his name, though his seale were to them · but that they should keepe the townes they had in charge for his sonne Antigonus, and all the rest of his forces, as if he him selfe were dead.

The naturall love of Antigonus, to his father Demetrius. When Antigonus heard the pitifull captivitie of his father, he marvelous greevously tooke his hard fortune, wearing blackes for sorrow, and wrote unto all the other kings, but unto Seleucus specially, beseeching him to take him as a pledge for his father, and that he was ready to yeld up al that he kept, to have his fathers libertie. The like request did many cities make unto him, and in manner all Princes, but Lysimachus: who promised Seleucus a great summe of money to put Demetrius to death. But Seleucus, who of long time had no great fancie to Lysimachus, but rather utterly despised him · did then thinke him the more cruell and barbarous, for this vile and wicked request he made unto him. Wherefore he still delayed time, bicause he would have Demetrius delivered by his sonne Antiochus and Stratonices meanes, for that Demetrius should be bownd to them for his deliverie, and for ever should acknowledge it to them. Now for Demetrius, as he from the beginning

Demetrius turned his captivitie into pleasure. paciently tooke his hard fortune, so did he daily more and more forget the miserie he was in. For first of al, he gave him selfe to riding and hunting, as farre as the place gave him libertie. Then by litle and litle he grew to be very grosse, and to give over such pastimes, and therewithall he fell into dronkennes and dyeing: so that in that sort he passed away the most part of his time, as it should seeme, either to avoid the grevous thoughts of his hard fortune, which came into his mind when he was sober : or els under culler of dronkennes and eating, to shadow the thoughts he had : or els finding in him selfe that it was that manner of life he had long desired, and that through his vaine ambition and follie till that time he could never attayne unto, greatly turmoyling and troubling him selfe and others, supposing to find in warres, by sea and land, the felicitie and delight which he had found in ease and idlenes, when he nether thought of it, nor loked for it. For what better

430

ende can evill and unadvised kings and Princes looke for, of all their troubles, daungers, and warres? who in deede deceive them selves greatly, not onely for that they followe their pleasure and delights as their chiefest felicitie, in steede of vertue and honest life: but also, bicause that in truth they can not be mery, and take their pleasure as they would. So, Demetrius after he had bene shut up in Cherronesus three yeares together, by ease, grossenes, and dronkennes, fell sicke of a disease whereof he dyed, when he was foure and fiftye yeare old. Therefore was Seleucus greatly blamed, and he him selfe also did much repent him that he so suspected him as he did, and that he followed not Dromichetes curtesie, a barbarous man borne in Thracia, who had so royally and curteously intreated Lysimachus, whom he had taken prisoner in the warres. But yet there was some tragicall pompe in the order of his funerall. For his sonne Antigonus understanding that they brought him the ashes of his bodie, he tooke sea with all his shippes, and went to meete them, to receive them in the Iles: and when he had received them, he set up the funerall pot of golde (in the which were his embers) uppon the poope of his Admirall galley. So, all the cities and townes whereby they passed, or harbered, some of them did put garlands of flowers about the pot, others also sent a number of men thether in mourning apparell, to accompany and honor the convoye, to the very solemnitie of his funeralls. In this sort sayled all the whole fleete towards the citie of Corinthe, the pot being plainely seene farre of, standing on the toppe of the Admirall galley: all the place about it being hanged about with purple, and over it, the diademe or royall band, and about it also were goodly younge men armed, which were as Pensioners to Demetrius. Furthermore, Xenophantus the famousest Musition in that time, being set hard by it, played a sweete and lamentable songe on the flute, wherewithall the ores keeping stroke and measure, the sownd did meete with a gallant grace, as in a convoye where the mourners doe knocke their breastes, at the foote of every verse. But that which most made the people of Corinthe to weepe and lament, which ranne to the peere, and all

GRECIANS AND ROMANES

alongest the shore side to see it· was Antigonus, whom they sawe all beblubbored with teares, apparrelled as a mourner in blackes Nowe, after they had brought a wonderfull number of gailands and nosegayes, and cast them uppon the funerall pot, and had solemnized all the honors possible for the funeralls at Corinthe : Antigonus caried away the pot to burye it in the citie of Demetriade, the which bare the name of Demetrius that was deade, and was a newe citie, that had bene replenished with people, and built of litle townes which are about Iolcos.   Demetrius left two children by his fist wife Phila, to wete, Antigonus, and Stratonice and two other sonnes, both of them named Demetrius, the one surnamed the leane, of a woman of Illyria, and the other king of the Cyrenians, of his wife Ptolemæide : and another by Deidamia called Alexander, who lived in Ægypt.   And it is reported also, that he had another sonne called Corrhæbus, by his wife Eurydice, and that his posteritie raigned by succession from the father to the sonne, until the time of Perseus. who was the last king of Macedon, whome the Romanes overcame by Paulus Æmylius, and wanne all the Realme of Macedon unto the Empire of Rome. Now that the Macedonian hath played his part, give the Romane also leave to come uppon the stage.

Demetrius
posteritie.

Perseus king
of Macedon,
(the last king
of Macedon)
came of the
posteritie of
Demetrius.

EDINBURGH

T. & A. CONSTABLE

Printers to Her Majesty

1896

CPSIA information can be obtained at www.ICGtesting.com
Printed in the USA
LVOW110757010513

331766LV00003B/250/P